Oi Sean e Sochi !

Hope you will enjoy these nice stories.

Love

Uncle Tim and Aunt Vivi

Dec, 2015

S0-CDG-549

Make God First

ERIC B. HARE

This book is published in collaboration
with the Youth Department as an enrichment of
the Morning Watch devotional plan.

REVIEW AND HERALD PUBLISHING ASSOCIATION
Washington, DC 20039-0555
Hagerstown, MD 21740

Copyright © 1964, 1986, by Review and Herald Publishing Association

Book design and cover art by Richard Steadham

Printed in U.S.A.

ISBN 0-8280-0354-8

Publisher's Note

One of the most beloved storytellers among Adventist young people was Eric B. Hare. Mention his name, and thousands of Adventists, young and old, will instantly recall "Clever Queen," "The Haunted Pagoda," "Mee Mee," "Dr. Rabbit," "Silver and the Snake"—all stories from the author's mission days in Burma. And each story had a moral, which was not lost on the hearers.

Eric B. Hare was born in Australia in 1894. He and his wife, Agnes, spent some twenty years as missionaries in Burma. Following a few years of service in California, he was called to the Sabbath School Department of the General Conference. He retired officially from that post in 1962, but over a period of fourteen years of "retirement," he met nearly eight hundred appointments! He passed to his rest in 1982.

During 1965, many juniors could sit at Elder Hare's knee, as it were, and learn lessons about the Bible and the Christian life through his Morning Watch book, *Make God First*. Now a new generation of juniors has come on the scene. In order that they, too, might benefit from the inspiration of Elder Hare's teaching, *Make God First* is being republished. His ministry to youth goes on.

In using this daily devotional book, it is suggested that each day you first read the entire Bible selection noted at the top left corner of that day's reading. This will give you the setting for the memory verse and the devotional thought.

"In the beginning God created the heaven and the earth." Genesis 1:1.

I'm so glad that the Bible begins with God. "In the beginning God . . ." We are at the beginning of a new year. Before us lies an unknown path. We want this to be the happiest year of our life, and it can be if we will put God in "the beginning" of each day of the year. In *Messages to Young People,* page 38, we read, "Those who in everything make God first and last and best are the happiest people in the world." We can make God first by picking up His precious Book and reading a portion of it each day. Again in *Messages to Young People*, page 246, we read: "God's holy, educating Spirit is in His word. A light, a new and precious light, shines forth from every page. Truth is there revealed, and words and sentences are made bright and appropriate for the occasion, as the voice of God speaking to the soul." For this coming year we need God, and we need His light.

In our church paper, the *Review and Herald*, Elder Ernest Lloyd told a story of a lone traveler who was going along a foot trail over a hillside one stormy night. He carried a lantern in his hand to help him keep on the path, but it was so cold that at last he put the lantern under his heavy coat. This kept him warm, but in the darkness, without knowing it, he lost the way. Suddenly a gust of wind blew open his coat, and as the light shone out, he was horrified to see that he was almost on the brink of a deep stone quarry. A few more steps without the light surely would have taken him to his death. He quickly found his way back to the trail, and you may be sure he kept the light outside after that and followed it every step of the way. Job made God first in his life, and God led him safely through sorrow, disaster, and sickness. Then He gave him "twice as much as he had before" (Job 42:10). Daniel made God first in his life, and God made him "fairer and fatter in flesh" and "ten times better" in wisdom than the other wise men, and He led him safely through temptation and the lions' den. You can easily believe that Daniel was one of the happiest people in all of Babylon. God wants to lead you this year and make you one of the happiest people in the world. Won't you make God first, the reading of His Word first, and prayer first, every day of this year?

7

"I will put enmity between thee and the woman, and between thy seed and her seed; it shall bruise thy head, and thou shalt bruise his heel." Genesis 3:15.

This is the first promise in the Bible. For four thousand years it brought hope to the hearts of tired and discouraged men and women. Did you know that there are more than three thousand promises in the Bible? Elder J. N. Loughborough was one of our beloved Advent pioneers. He read the Old Testament through sixty-nine times and the New Testament seventy-one times. His dear old Bible is kept in the Church Ministries Department at the General Conference. If ever you visit there, ask to see it, and on one of the flyleaves you will see a list of the promises in the Bible. It is evidently his own counting, and it says:

Old Testament promises for the present, 2,253; for the future, 791. Total Old Testament promises, 3,044. New Testament promises for the present, 274; for the future, 253. Total New Testament promises, 529. Total promises in all the Bible, 3,573.

This first promise, which we have selected for our Morning Watch text, gave hope to Adam and Eve in the hour of their great discouragement when they realized that their sin had brought death and a curse into the world. They memorized it and told it to their children and to their grandchildren. Then they, in turn, memorized it and told it to *their* children and grandchildren, and so on down to Moses. Moses wrote it down, and it became part of the Bible for everyone. It gave hope to all who heard it or read it, right on down to devout old Simeon who took Baby Jesus in his arms and said, "Mine eyes have seen thy salvation." But it does not end there. There is hope in that promise for you and for me, that through Christ we can overcome the devil and his temptations and bruise his head today and every day.

Solomon declared, "There hath not failed one word of all his good promise, which he promised by the hand of Moses his servant" (1 Kings 8:56). And Peter says these "exceeding great and precious promises" "are given unto us" (2 Peter 1:4).

As you read through the Bible Year, keep your eyes open for the many precious promises. Underline them and treasure them. They were written for you.

"Noah was a just man and perfect in his generations, and Noah walked with God." Genesis 6:9.

What a wonderful feeling of security there is in walking with God! As Noah built the ark and preached for 120 years he kept his thoughts on God and talked to Him as a companion. That is the way Noah walked with God. He was mocked and he was abused, but God saved him and his family when millions upon millions of wicked people were destroyed.

The three Hebrews walked with God in the same simple way—praying, reading the Scriptures, daily deciding to do nothing that God would not approve. The angry king threw them into the fire, but God went with them into the fire, and not a hair of their heads was even singed.

Have you heard of Desmond T. Doss? He was only a humble medic in World War II, but he walked with God too. He put God first every day of his life, by prayer and reading his Bible. At first the soldiers made fun of him and his Bible reading, and often called him a sissy and threw their boots at him. But when it came to danger, they soon changed their tune. There came the memorable battle of the precipice, when the United States armed forces were landing on Okinawa. There were 155 men who waited for Doss to say a prayer before they scaled the cliff on rope nets. After a few days only fifty-five came back down.

Doss was the last man. He dragged the wounded, man after man, to the cliff and lowered them by a rope. "Come on down, Doss!" shouted the captain. "You'll only get yourself killed." But Doss replied, "Just give me a little more time. I can't leave these wounded men up here to die." And alone he lowered seventy-five men. At last he himself was badly wounded, but he came home alive and was greatly honored, for President Truman personally presented to him the Congressional Medal of Honor—the highest award a grateful nation can bestow on a hero.

It pays to make God first. It pays to take God with you everywhere you go. It pays to keep away from places where God or the angels wouldn't go. Won't you decide to walk with God this year?

"I do set my bow in the cloud, and it shall be for a token of a covenant between me and the earth." Genesis 9:13.

It was after the most awful storm and destruction that Noah and his family saw their first rainbow. What a comfort it must have been to them to know that the rainbow was the sign of God's promise that the waters should no more become a flood to destroy all flesh. Only God could make a rainbow and only God can comfort in a time of fear and sorrow.

Often we see a second rainbow just beneath the primary rainbow. But, strange enough, though the *red* is on the outside of the arc of the primary rainbow, in the second rainbow the *violet* is on the outside of the arc! Only God would think of that. Bright moonlight can also form a rainbow. Have you ever seen a rainbow at night? I have.

It was years ago when our little school among the devil worshipers of Burma was struggling for existence. It seemed impossible for the gospel to break down the fear and the superstition of the jungle people. I had gone down the river to Moulmein for supplies. Most of the day it had rained, but when the steamer reached the end of its journey that night, a full moon was playing hide and seek with the clouds. I was standing on the deck with a government officer watching the logs and rubbish floating down the angry river when all of a sudden, there it was—a night rainbow! The officer beside me trembled. "It looks like a bad sign to me," he said. "I've never seen a rainbow at night before."

I replied, "It looks like a good sign to me. It reminds me of God's promises. I'm sure that in spite of floods, storms, fear, and superstition, all will be well someday." And sure enough, soon our mission work was well established.

Are there clouds of trouble or sorrow all around you today? Look for a rainbow and remember God's promises.

In *Messages to Young People,* pages 109 and 110, we read: "Satan seeks to draw our minds away from the mighty Helper. . . . When Satan thrusts his threatenings upon you, turn from them, and comfort your soul with the promises of God. The cloud may be dark in itself, but when filled with the light of heaven, it turns to the brightness of gold; for the glory of God rests upon it."

"And there he builded an altar unto the Lord, and called upon the name of the Lord." Genesis 12:8.

It was Abraham's custom to call upon the name of the Lord *wherever* he was. We can rejoice to know that God hears our prayers *wherever we* are. Elisha went into the house, shut the door, and prayed. Daniel opened the window and prayed. Peter went up to the housetop; Hannah went to the Temple; and Nehemiah breathed a quick prayer while he was before the king. Jonah prayed in the belly of a great fish, and Ba Twe prayed his first prayer at the top of a tall dead tree.

Ba Twe was a heathen boy who came to our mission school in Burma. During his first year he came to Sabbath school and to prayer meeting every week; but he would never take part. "Oh, no! I'm a heathen. God wouldn't listen to me," he said. Then during the summer vacation one day, while minding his father's buffaloes, he lay down beside them while they were resting in the shade, and went to sleep; and when he woke up they were gone. "Oh, what will I do?" he said. "The buffaloes will wander into someone's garden and spoil it, and I'll get into plenty of trouble!" He ran down to the river and looked all around, but they were not there. He ran out to the rice fields, but they were not there. Just then he saw a tall dead tree. "I'll climb that tree and look all around," he said.

From the top of the tree he saw other buffaloes with other boys driving them home, but his buffaloes were nowhere to be seen. "Oh, what will I do?" he cried.

And the little voice in his heart said, "Pray, pray, pray!"

"But God wouldn't listen to me," he argued. "I'm not a Christian."

But the little voice kept saying, "Pray, pray, pray!"

So he prayed, "O God, please, God, help me find my buffaloes." He was too frightened to say "for Jesus' sake. Amen." He almost expected God to strike him with thunder and lightning. He hurried down the tree as though to get away from God as quickly as possible. But as he jumped from the lowest limb, there were his buffaloes!

"He heard me!" said Ba Twe in amazement. "Before I was a Christian He heard me!" And right there, at that moment, Ba Twe gave his heart to Jesus.

Remember, *wherever* you are today, God is always near enough to hear your prayer.

11

"Let there be no strife, I pray thee, between me and thee . . . ; for we be brethren." Genesis 13:8.

On this day, January 6, several large churches celebrate the visit of the Wise Men to Baby Jesus in Bethlehem. Of course, no one can be certain of the very day on which that visit occurred, but one thing is certain—Jesus came to bring peace to the world. Without Him there always will be strife and quarreling. It was the hope of the promised Saviour that made Abraham so humble and kind that he let Lot choose first, thus avoiding a quarrel.

The manager of the large plantation on which Elder Stahl had established the Metrano Mission became very angry and wrote a letter to General Cooper, the president of the corporation in Lima, demanding that the mission be closed. When Elder Stahl heard that General Cooper was coming to investigate, he rode down the trail to meet him. "I'm so glad I can have this opportunity of talking to you about the mission," said Brother Stahl.

"I don't want to talk to you," retorted the general.

Brother Stahl tried again. "The Indians used to be savages; now they are leading new, clean lives."

"I told you I don't want to hear anything about the mission" was all he would say, so Elder Stahl bowed and went away. That night he was impressed to go over to the plantation headquarters. When he arrived he found the general suffering from a head wound resulting from falling off his horse soon after he had refused to let Elder Stahl talk to him.

Elder Stahl treated the wound, and when the general was comfortable, he was glad to talk about the mission. Soon the hard feelings melted away, and the mission remained on the plantation. It was Jesus in Elder Stahl's heart that brought peace. "The warfare against self is the greatest battle that was ever fought," we read in *Steps to Christ*, page 43. When we humble ourselves and let Jesus come into our heart, strife and quarreling vanish.

It takes two to make a quarrel. Our Burma Karens say, "You can't clap hands with one hand," and it's true. If *you* decide to be humble and kind, there will be no strife.

Won't you decide to follow this path to happiness and peace?

"Blessed be the most high God. . . . And he gave him tithes of all." Genesis 14:20.

As we read this account it does not sound as if this was the first time Abraham had paid tithe. Later, as we read of the tithing laws given to the children of Israel, the reformation in tithe paying at the time of Nehemiah, the blessings pronounced upon tithing by Malachi, and the affirmation given to it by Jesus, we can only conclude that this is one of God's paths to happiness that He has always planned for His children. In every country of the world people are bearing witness to the happiness and blessings that come to the tithepayer.

Away across the sea in Barotseland, Africa, lived a dear old man named Shwebele. He and his kind old wife were the only Seventh-day Adventists in the village. One year at harvesttime they were both sick with malaria and unable to harvest their kaffir corn.

The village people were all busy harvesting their fields and beating drums and cans to keep the birds from devouring the grain. They dared not stop the noise from early morning to dark lest clouds of birds descend upon the fields and devour their grain.

Shwebele's friends wagged their heads and sadly said, "There is no hope for Shwebele's field. There is no one to reap and no one to beat the drum. The birds will eat up everything."

But Shwebele prayed. "O God, please take care of my fields. You promised to rebuke the devourer. I claim that promise, for I have paid a faithful tithe." And the birds did not settle in Shwebele's fields! The birds did not eat up his grain!

"He must have some magic medicine," said one.

"Yes, seven-day man's medicine from the mission," they agreed.

"Tell us," said the astonished village people, "what kind of medicine you have used on your field, that the birds dare not settle on your corn." And Shwebele told them about his loving God and his angel watcher.

"Is that it!" they said. "We can't see the angel, but the birds can!" When the neighbors' harvesting was finished they all kindly reaped Shwebele's field for him.

God wants you to follow this path to happiness. He wants *you* to prove Him so He can pour *you* out a blessing.

"And he believed in the Lord; and he counted it to him for righteousness."
Genesis 15:6.

This is the first time in the record of Abraham's experiences that we read the words "and he believed." God called him out of Ur, and he *went forth*. God called him into Canaan and promised to make him a great nation, and he *departed*. After Lot chose to live in the plain of Jordan, God renewed the promise to Abraham, and he *came* and *dwelt* in Hebron. After Abraham rescued Lot from his enemies, God renewed the promise again, and said that Abraham's children would be as the stars of heaven in number. Then we read that Abraham *believed.*

Is it hard for you to believe God and have faith that He exists? If so, it may be because you never have seen God. Most likely you never have seen the President of the United States or the Queen of England, yet you believe they are real people.

One evening a man went down into the basement of his house to get something. On his way back, at the foot of the stairs, he turned the light out. Just then he noticed his little 3-year-old daughter standing at the top of the stairs. The father, looking toward the lighted room, could see his little girl, but the little girl, looking down into the dark basement, couldn't see anything. "Daddy, where are you?" she said.

"Down here, sweetheart," he replied. "Jump. I'll catch you."

"But I can't see you, Daddy," she replied.

"But I can see you," said Daddy. "Come on and jump. I'll catch you." And she did jump—right into her own father's loving arms.

Why could the little girl believe and have faith that her daddy would catch her? She had learned to obey her daddy and she loved him. That's the way it was with Abraham; he obeyed, and believing came easily. This is another pathway to happiness. Ellen G. White has said it in these beautiful words: "All your happiness, peace, joy, and success in this life are dependent upon genuine, trusting faith in God. This faith will prompt true obedience to the commandments of God. Your knowledge and faith in God is the strongest restraint from every evil practice, and the motive to all good."—*Messages to Young People,* p. 410. Won't you love, obey, and believe your heavenly Father today and every day?

"Shall not the Judge of all the earth do right?" Genesis 18:25.

In our Scripture texts today we have read of Abraham communing with God, the judge of all the earth, about saving the city of Sodom.

"All the way up the steep road leading to eternal life are well-springs of joy to refresh the weary. Those who walk in wisdom's ways are, even in tribulation, exceeding joyful; for He whom their soul loveth walks, invisible, beside them."—*Messages to Young People*, p. 150.

In order for the children of God to be the happiest people in the world, God gave to them the privilege of communing with Him along the way. As there can be no happy physical life without continual breathing, so there can be no happy spiritual life without continual praying.

Abraham discovered this secret, and he *prayed* and *kept on* praying. The more he prayed the bolder he became in prayer. You may be sure that Satan will try to stop you from praying. He may ridicule you, try to make you too busy, try to discourage you by saying it's no use to pray any more. That is when you need to pray more than ever. In Psalm 37:5, after saying, "Commit thy way unto the Lord," David says, *"Rest* in the Lord, and *wait* patiently for him."

Some time ago I read of a woman who had attended a symphony concert in a large opera house in one of our great cities. When she returned home she discovered that she had lost a very valuable diamond brooch. Frantically she telephoned the manager of the opera house and asked whether such a pin had been found. The man asked her the number of the seat where she had been sitting and then told her to *hold the line* while he went to look. He found the pin, but when he got back to the telephone, the woman had hung up. He waited, hoping she would call again—but she didn't. He even advertised that he had found her treasure, but he never heard from her again. How happy she might have been if she had only *held the line,* or if she had *called again.*

You will need God very much as you walk through this year. Determine that you will *hold the line open* between you and God every day.

15

"Up, get you out of this place; for the Lord will destroy this city." Genesis
19:14.

Sodom was a beautiful city in the plain that "was well watered . . . ,
even as the garden of the Lord" (Genesis 13:10). But there must have
been saloons, dance halls, and gambling dens, for their sin was very
grievous, and God decided to destroy the city with fire. How fortunate it
was for Lot and his family that he heeded the message "Up, get you out of
this place." How sad that his sons-in-law paid no heed to the warning
message.

To us comes the same kind of message today. "Come out of her, my
people" (Revelation 18:4). "Wherefore come out from among them, and
be ye separate, saith the Lord" (2 Corinthians 6:17). "The true Christian
will not desire to enter any place of amusement or engage in any
diversion upon which he cannot ask the blessing of God. . . . No
Christian would wish to meet death in such a place. No one would wish
to be found there when Christ shall come." *Messages to Young People,* p.
398.

How I wish that every time you are tempted to go to some place of
worldly amusement you could hear the angels shout, "Up, get you out of
this place."

December 30, 1903, the Iroquois Theater in Chicago burned down,
and 602 people were burned or trampled to death.

January 4, 1908, a theater in Boyertown, Pennsylvania, burned, and
170 people died.

November 28, 1942, the Coconut Grove nightclub in Boston caught
fire, and 491 people perished and 170 others were injured.

July 6, 1944, the tent of the Ringling Brothers and Barnum and
Bailey Circus, in Hartford, Connecticut, caught fire, and 168 were killed
and some 200 injured.

The true Christian "will not be found at the theater, the billiard hall,
or the bowling saloon. He will not unite with the gay waltzers, or indulge
in any other bewitching pleasure that will banish Christ from the mind."
Messages to Young People, p. 398.

If you are ever tempted to go to places where Christ and the angels
will not go, stop and listen! You will hear the still small voice saying,
"Up, get you out of this place." Then make God first by keeping out of
places of sinful pleasure, and you will be happy.

"God hath made me to laugh." Genesis 21:6.

Those whom God makes to laugh are the happiest people in the world. We can't begin to imagine how happy Sarah was at this time. God had promised her and Abraham a son, but God had waited and waited, and Abraham and Sarah had grown older and older. Then when it looked *humanly* impossible, God fulfilled His promise—and Isaac was born. Do you know what the name *Isaac* means? It means "laughter"!

Let us always remember that with God *nothing* is impossible.

A young woman in the Southern States longed to go to school, but she had no money. She waited four years, but still there was no money. Then she walked 150 miles to one of our boarding schools, but the matron said, "I'm sorry; all our student-aid fund is used up. I'm afraid you'll have to go home and try again next year."

But the young woman said, "I believe God wants me to be in school this year, for He opened the way for me to come even though I did have to walk."

"All right, then," said the matron. "Go upstairs, find an empty room, and pray that some money will come in the morning mail." Several hours went by. The morning mail came. In that mail was a check to help support one more student. The matron asked one of the teachers to go upstairs and find the girl and tell her the good news. The teacher went upstairs and found her—still on her knees, praying for God to send the money. It had seemed impossible to the matron, but there is nothing impossible with God.

"The power of God, combined with human effort, has wrought out a glorious victory for us. Shall we not appreciate this? All the riches of heaven were given to us in Jesus. . . . God has resources of power of which we as yet know nothing, and from these He will supply us in our time of need."—*Messages to Young People*, p. 106.

Do you have a dream for your life that seems to be impossible? Something you hardly would dare tell to anybody? Something that everybody knows *you* couldn't do, or that couldn't happen to you? Keep holding on to God. He will make *you* to laugh someday. There is nothing impossible with Him!

"Weeping may endure for a night, but joy cometh in the morning." Psalm 30:5.

All her grown-up life Sarah had been with Abraham, a stranger in a strange land. She was about 65 years old when they were called out of Haran and the promise of the "seed" was given. For twenty-five years she had hoped for a son, and then she sadly gave up hoping. But the promised son came when Sarah was 90! And for thirty-seven years she was gloriously happy. She died happy in the assurance that God's promises would be fulfilled. However, it was a sad time for Abraham and Isaac when Sarah died. They mourned as they laid her away in the cave of Machpelah. This is the first grave mentioned in the Bible, and later Abraham, Isaac, Rebekah, Leah, and Jacob were all buried there. Today a Mohammedan mosque has been built over the traditional spot.

To all of us there come seasons of sorrow when we weep for loved ones who have died. But, thank God, we are able to comfort one another with the words "The dead in Christ shall rise first: then we which are alive and remain shall be caught up together with them in the clouds, to meet the Lord in the air: and so shall we ever be with the Lord" (1 Thessalonians 4:16, 17). What a grand and glorious day that will be—when God will wipe away all tears from our eyes!

I think of my old schoolmates Norman and Alma Wiles, missionaries to the Big Nambus tribe in the New Hebrides Islands. Norman was sick. There was a threatened tribal war on their island. Norman got out of bed and succeeded in bringing peace. He then returned to his bed but later died of blackwater fever. Alone, Alma dug a shallow grave. Alone, she buried her dead companion. Alone, she mourned. But God had seen those tears! In His plan, tears are like seeds, which in His own time will grow up and blossom with joy and gladness. And God not only comforted Alma with the hope of a glorious resurrection but He watered the gospel seed in the hearts of the people; and today there are thousands of Sabbath school members in the New Hebrides Islands.

Are you mourning today for a loved one who has passed away? Take comfort. "Joy cometh in the morning."

"The Lord, before whom I walk, will send his angel with thee, and prosper thy way." Genesis 24:40.

The story of how the angel went all the way with Eliezer, five hundred miles from Beersheba to the city of Nahor in Mesopotamia, and how "it came to pass" exactly as he prayed, "before he had done speaking," is one of the loveliest stories in the Bible.

It will keep us happy if we remember that day by day God has commissioned a guardian angel to be with each one of us also.

For several years Pastor Norman Ferris was our missionary on Pitcairn Island. One day he was repairing the engine in a launch the islanders had purchased. It was necessary to take the engine all to pieces, but he and his helpers could not get the flywheel off the main shaft. It had rusted on, and no amount of tapping, pulling, coaxing, or the free use of rust removers would do any good. After three days two of the workmen gave up and said, "We're going fishing." The island men shook their heads, saying, "It's no good; tip it into the sea."

Then Pastor Ferris closed his eyes and prayed: "Dear Lord, I have come to the end of my ability. My unseen companion and watchman, who has been with me and helped me so often in the past, is so much stronger than I am. Just let him take over if this experience will bring honor to Your name." Before he could say Amen there was a noise and a bang—and the flywheel lay in the bottom of the boat!

"What's the matter?" shouted his friend Mr. Anderson, who was not far away.

"We've just had a miracle!" replied Mr. Ferris. And before many days the engine was in operating condition and the launch was running perfectly.

"When you rise in the morning, do you feel your helplessness, and your need of strength from God? and do you humbly, heartily make known your wants to your heavenly Father? If so, angels mark your prayers, and . . . when you are in danger of unconsciously doing wrong . . . , your guardian angel will be by your side, prompting you to a better course, choosing your words for you, and influencing your actions."— *Messages to Young People*, p. 90.

19

"Lying lips are abomination to the Lord: but they that deal truly are his delight." Proverbs 12:22.

Lying produces some of the greatest unhappiness juniors can ever know. The Bible tells us that Satan "abode not in the truth, because there is no truth in him. When he speaketh a lie, he speaketh of his own: for he is a liar, and the father of it" (John 8:44). Satan told the first recorded lie, "Ye shall not surely die." Cain told the next. When God asked him where his brother Abel was, he said, "I know not" (Genesis 4:9). Sarah told a lie when she said, "I laughed not" (chapter 18:15).

In today's scripture Jacob told lies to his poor old blind father, Isaac. It was not just one little lie, for it was supported by a host of lies; even his mother lied. Jacob told lies not only with his *lips* but also with his *actions* and with his *clothing.*

Satan is going to try to tempt *you* too to tell lies in one way or another. Ellen G. Morrison told a story in the *Guide* some time ago that is typical of the way Satan tempts all juniors:

Don came rushing into the house after school, and as he slammed the door behind him with great vigor, he heard a splintering crash. A picture on the wall near the door had fallen to the floor and broken to pieces. No one was home. So Don decided to leave it there, and make it look as if it had fallen down by itself.

Mother came home an hour later, and seeing the broken picture, she said, "Don, did you hit that picture when you came in this afternoon?"

"No, Mother, I didn't," he said. "I didn't even touch it." It was almost the truth, but (good for Don) he just couldn't feel right about it. It took a little courage, but at last he said, "Mother, it's my fault anyway. I slammed the door so hard that it fell down. I'm so sorry." He felt so good after telling the real truth that he decided even little white lies would be "out" for him, always.

Fortunately, God has made provision for liars to confess their sins, and Jacob, Joseph's brothers, David, and Peter did confess; and they found their way to happiness again. If you have ever told lies, won't you repent too? If you really love the truth, keep in the company of those who have "dealt truly" and are the "delight" of the Lord.

"Behold, I am with thee, and will keep thee in all places whither thou goest, and will bring thee again into this land; for I will not leave thee, until I have done that which I have spoken to thee of." Genesis 28:15.

Poor Jacob had made a serious mistake. He had told lies and deceived, and he must have thought as he fled from his home that he was a failure. But he repented and confessed his sins and then, wonder of wonders, God in a dream showed him a ladder that reached from heaven down to earth. And the voice of God assured him that there was still hope, that he was not cast off, God was still with him, and it was possible for him to live a successful life pleasing to God.

If we have true faith and courage, failure can be a step toward success.

Elias Howe wrestled with his sewing machine idea for years. Model after model he built and broke, until at last, in 1845, he sewed a suit of clothes for himself on his own machine.

Alexander Graham Bell had to try over and over again, until in the 1870s he produced the telephone.

Thomas A. Edison must have failed a thousand times before he succeeded in giving the world the electric lamp in 1879.

So if you have ever failed and made mistakes, don't give up. Make things right and take another step up the ladder toward heaven.

"God has given the youth a ladder to climb, a ladder that reaches from earth to heaven. Above this ladder is God, and on every round fall the bright beams of His glory. He is watching those who are climbing, ready, when the grasp relaxes and the steps falter, to send help. Yes, tell it in words full of cheer, that no one who perseveringly climbs the ladder will fail of gaining an entrance into the heavenly city."—*Messages to Young People*, p. 95.

Peter describes the steps on this ladder when he says, "Add to your faith virtue; and to virtue knowledge; and to knowledge temperance; and to temperance patience; and to patience godliness; and to godliness brotherly kindness; and to brotherly kindness charity" (2 Peter 1:5-7). And in commenting on these verses Sister White says, "Here is a course by which we may be assured that we shall never fall."—*Messages to Young People*, p. 116.

"And Jacob served seven years for Rachel; and they seemed unto him but a few days, for the love he had to her." Genesis 29:20.

'Tis love that makes us happy,
    'Tis love that smooths the way;
It helps us "mind," it makes us kind
    To others every day.
                                    —F. E. Belden

The first love we know in life is the love for our mother and father. After that comes love for brothers and sisters, then boy playmates if we are boys and girl playmates if we are girls. This continues until we are teenagers; then the boys begin to notice the girls and the girls begin to notice the boys. In college, young people begin to think of having their own home in the future, and it is natural for a young man to select one special girlfriend, and for a young woman to be especially interested in one special boyfriend. Then, usually when college days are over, comes the glad day when they get married and hope to live happily ever after. Each kind of love leaves its influence on the kind of love that follows it.

Now it is natural to have plenty of cuddling, hugging, and kissing between children and their parents, not so much between brothers and sisters, and none at all among playmates and young people. Then again it is natural for husband and wife to hug and kiss each other. But remember, "hands off" is the best advice anybody can give to boys and girls, young or old, until they are married.

It is natural for us to desire to *possess* and *own* things. This desire, when controlled and guided, makes us *work* and *save* and become thrifty. But uncontrolled, it makes some people *misers* and some people *robbers.*

So love is not a bad thing. It is the desire that, when controlled, brings us everything in life that is beautiful, lovely, pure, and fine.

But uncontrolled, it leads to sin and to disappointment, and instead of the happy years seeming as days, the days seem like weary years—and the unhappy people wish they were dead.

So play the game of love cleanly, according to the rules, and you'll be ready someday for the love that makes us happy, and that makes the years that go by seem like a few short days.

"I will not let thee go, except thou bless me." Genesis 32:26.

Jacob made his mistakes; he had his weak points; but he also had some very admirable traits of character, and *perseverance* was one of them. It took a lot of perseverance to work for his uncle, Laban. "I served thee fourteen years for thy two daughters, and six years for thy cattle," said Jacob to Laban, "and thou hast changed my wages ten times" (Genesis 31:41). Many another young man would have given up after one or two disappointments, but not Jacob; he kept on. He stuck at it, and succeeded.

When he recognized that he had been wrestling with the Lord all night, he again summoned all the perseverance he had, and said, "I will not let thee go, except thou bless me." And God did bless him.

Strangely enough, today is the birthday of another great man who had this trait of perseverance—Benjamin Franklin (1706-1790). This great man was the fifteenth child in a family of seventeen. His father was only a humble candlemaker in Boston, so there was not much money to clothe and feed the children. Little Ben went to school when he was 8, but had to leave school and go to work when he was 10. But Benjamin had brains; and Benjamin had perseverance. At 12 years of age he began to learn the printing trade. Every odd minute was used for study and research. He discovered a great deal about electricity, and he wrote and published *Poor Richard's Almanac* for twenty-five years. He was a signer of the Declaration of Independence, and for years he was deputy postmaster general of the Colonies. He put his whole heart and soul into everything he did, and once he said to his wife, "Debbie, I wish the good Lord had seen fit to make each day twice as long as it is."

"Nothing worth having is obtained without earnest, persevering effort. In business, only those who have a will to do see successful results. Without earnest toil we cannot expect to obtain a knowledge of spiritual things. Those who obtain the jewels of truth must dig for them as a miner digs for the precious ore hidden in the earth. Those who work indifferently and halfheartedly will never succeed."—*Messages to Young People*, p. 259.

Say, how is *your perseverance?* What are you doing with *your time?* Do you put your heart and soul into your studies? Your piano practice?

"And Esau ran to meet him, and embraced him, and fell on his neck, and kissed him: and they wept." Genesis 33:4.

Repentance is another of God's ways to happiness. Jacob found this to be true. So also did Ta Wa and Mg Sein. Thara Chit Maung brought them to me for fighting during night study.

"Whatever started it, Ta Wa?" I asked.

"Well," he replied, "Mg Sein stood up and his shadow fell on my book. I had a pin in my hand, so I pricked him. Then he hit me on the head. Then I hit him. And—"

"And you're a church member! What an example for Mg Sein, who has just joined the baptismal class!"

"I know, Thara, I know. It's all my fault. I started it."

"Since you started it, Ta Wa, will you say you're sorry *first* and ask forgiveness *first?*"

"Yes, Thara, I will, I will."

Then I called in Mg Sein and asked Ta Wa to wait outside.

"Mg Sein," I began, "you've just joined the baptismal class and expect to overcome the devil and all of his temptations, and you couldn't even overcome a little pinprick?"

"I know, Thara, I know," he said. "I'm so ashamed. I started it."

"Then, Mg Sein, since you started it, will you say you are sorry *first?* And ask forgiveness *first?*" He agreed.

Then I called in Ta Wa and gave each the opportunity to say "I'm sorry" *first.*

I saw them swallow hard. I saw them open their mouths. But the words couldn't come. The perspiration stood out on their foreheads.

At last Ta Wa began, "I'm—"

"No—I'm sorry," interrupted Mg Sein. "I started it."

"But I started it first, please forgive me."

"No, you forgive me."

Their hearts were softened. They put their arms about each other's shoulders, and went back to night study, their hearts filled with joy.

"The sweetest joy comes to man through his sincere repentance toward God."—*Messages to Young People,* p. 108.

Are you really happy today? Maybe there's something of which you should repent!

"Put away the strange gods that are among you, and be clean, and change your garments." Genesis 35:2.

I suppose the strange gods that Jacob gathered up from his household, and buried under the oak that was by Shechem, were made of brass. But not all strange gods are made of brass. Anything that we put before God or allow to take the time of family worship, Sabbath school, church services, and Christian duty could be called an idol or a strange god.

"By idolatry he meant not only the worship of idols, but self-serving, love of ease, the gratification of appetite and passion."—*The Acts of the Apostles,* p. 317.

Do you have regular family worship? Are you faithful with your homework, your music practice, your chores? If not, why not? Is it because of TV? Radio programs? Trashy reading? Or is it just plain indifference, laziness (love of ease), and worldliness? What strange gods are these! Better gather them up and bury them somewhere.

Today is the birthday of a famous Scotchman—James Watt (1736-1819). When he was a little boy he was rather a dreamy, dull student, but when he was 13 he suddenly woke up and began to study in earnest. Soon he was attracting much attention by his ability in mathematics. He is generally given credit for inventing the steam engine, though actually a few crude, impractical steam engines had already been made. But James Watt made the steam engine practical, and to this day the unit of electric power bears his name—watt. So, when we talk of a seventy-five-watt lamp we are giving honor to a lad who put away indifference and laziness.

Daniel diligently overcame all temptation to carelessness in prayer. He allowed nothing to prevent his study, and he became a great prophet. David practiced and practiced with his slingshot, and practiced and practiced on his harp. And he became a great deliverer; and he played before the king.

The temptation to put pleasure before duty, to be lazy and indifferent, is the idol of which we must beware.

You can become great and successful in the eyes of God too. You have enough talents to make you happy and successful. But you must put away all the strange gods, and be clean.

"To have respect of persons is not good." Proverbs 28:21.

In our Scripture reading today we have seen the misery and sorrow caused by a father's favoritism and by some brothers' feelings of superiority.

Satan knows the misery and sorrow he can produce if he can only get people to "have respect of persons," and he tries his best to plant this seed in the heart of juniors. It may just happen that attending your school there is a child of foreign parentage, or a child from a poor home, or different in color from you. How eagerly Satan tries to make you act superior to them, so they will feel inferior to you!

Listen! Down in Macon, Georgia, there was born a little girl named Anna. Her mother was a slave who was sold to a man named Knight. Soon after this the slaves were freed, and Anna's family settled on a farm in Mississippi. Anna saw the white children of the district going to school, but they wouldn't let her go to school, because she was "colored." Anna was so hungry to learn that she helped the white girls with their work so they would teach her to read. But they "couldn't be bothered." So she secured an old Webster's speller and mastered every word in it. She subscribed to the *Signs of the Times* and read every word. She taught the other little unfortunate children. She was baptized. She went to one of our academies, but the other children and their parents made such a fuss that she had only one day in school there. One of our workers befriended her and sent her to Mt. Vernon Academy in Ohio, and although they tolerated her there, many of the students snubbed her and called her that "green girl from the south." But Anna Knight stayed on. Then she went to Battle Creek and took the nurse's course, and in 1901 she went to India as a missionary. She served the Lord there for eight years with great honor and distinction, and then served thirty-nine more years in the Adventist cause in North America. My guess is that many who shunned her once now wish they had been kind. I'd like to be there when Jesus says to Anna, "Well done, thou good and faithful servant," and watch their faces!

No favoritism or partiality to anyone, but kindness to all, is the pathway to happiness.

"How then can I do this great wickedness, and sin against God?" Genesis 39:9.

Two or three times during my lifetime I have heard of honorable men who have fallen into sin in a moment of great temptation to impurity. It has made me tremble, for I have wondered whether I could be stronger than they were if some big temptation came to me.

For years and years a great oak tree grew in Takoma Park. It was a thing of beauty. It gave cooling shade to passersby and provided food and playground for the chipmunks and squirrels of the vicinity. Then one day there was a terrible storm. The lightning flashed, the thunder roared, the rains came down, and the winds blew, and when Elder Wilcox, the *Review and Herald* editor, walked to work the next morning he found the great oak tree had fallen to the ground! He couldn't believe it! Impossible, he thought, that such a great strong tree should be overcome by a storm.

He stood looking on in shocked amazement. Others joined him. Then someone near the broken stump said, "Ah! No wonder! Come and see!"

They went to see, and they found that the heart of the tree was riddled with worms! Its heart was rotten! If that great tree had been able to keep the little worms out of its heart, it could have withstood the storm. It never would have fallen.

That is why men here and there fall into sin. Their thoughts are not pure; their hearts are not clean. They give in to little sins—secret sins that others cannot see—then, when the *great* temptation comes, down they go!

Joseph overcame the little temptations day by day. Joseph kept his thoughts pure and his heart clean. Then when the great temptation came he did not fall! What an inspiration he is to us!

Never underrate the importance of little things. It is by little things that the soul becomes Christlike or becomes evil.

So heads up! Shoulders back! No one need tremble and fear the day of great temptation. By the grace of God, overcome the little temptations day by day, and in the day of big temptations you *will* be an overcomer.

"And it came to pass the third day, which was Pharaoh's birthday, that he made a feast unto all his servants: and he lifted up the head of the chief butler. . . . And he restored the chief butler unto his butlership again." Genesis 40:20, 21.

This is the first mention of a birthday party in the Bible. Did you notice that *Pharaoh* made the feast, and *Pharaoh* bestowed the honors?

Maybe because the Wise Men brought gifts to Jesus it has become customary for others to give gifts and presents to a child when he reaches another birthday; but let us remember that when we grow up, *we* should bestow gifts on others on our birthdays.

February 12 is Abraham Lincoln's birthday; February 22 is George Washington's birthday, and many of us enjoy a holiday on this day.

April 21 is the birthday of England's Queen Elizabeth II. It is a public holiday, and many honors, favors, and promotions are given by her on that day.

The late Aga Khan, the spiritual leader of the Ismailis, was born August 10, and he celebrated that day by sitting on a scales while his followers matched his weight with diamonds and jewels, which he gave to build and support Mohammedan schools in many places.

What are you doing to bless others on your birthday? In 1919 the Sabbath School Department suggested that we Sabbath school members match the number of our years with a copper penny for each year to help send the gospel to all the world. The idea was a good one, but today many are matching their years with nickels or dimes or even dollars!

Why don't you?

"For life, health, food, and clothing, no less than for the hope of eternal life, we are indebted to the Giver of all mercies; and it is due to God to recognize His gifts, and to present our offerings of gratitude to our greatest benefactor. These birthday gifts are recognized of Heaven."—*Counsels on Sabbath School Work,* p. 143.

So let us grow up a little more. Let us think less of what we will *get* for our birthdays and more about how much we can *give* to bless others.

"It is not in me: God shall give Pharaoh an answer of peace." Genesis 41:16.

In Revelation 14:12 John gives us a picture of the people Jesus is going to take to heaven. "Here is the *patience* of the saints: here are they that keep the commandments of God, and the *faith* of Jesus." Notice that there are three outstanding characteristics of these redeemed ones. 1. They are patient; they have overcome pride; they have been humble and meek and long-suffering. 2. They keep the commandments; they have learned obedience and self-control. 3. They keep the faith of Jesus; they have overcome doubt, and have believed God and learned to trust Him in every trial.

Two days ago we read how Joseph met a great temptation to break the commandments. But he had learned how to be pure in thought and to hate wrongdoing. Next, although he was innocent, he was thrown into prison. How often he must have been tempted to doubt God and His love! But, no. He overcame doubt, and trusted God in the darkness.

Now in our Scripture reading today we see him tested on his feelings of pride and ambition. "I have heard say of *thee,*" said Pharaoh, "that *thou* canst understand a dream to interpret it." Oh, how easy it would have been for him to swell up with pride and say in his heart, "Of course, he surely means me!" But he didn't. Joseph had learned to keep the commandments; he had kept his faith; and now he easily humbled himself and overcame his pride, saying, "It is not in *me:* God shall give Pharaoh an answer of peace."

Wouldn't it be a happy world if everybody were humble and patient as Joseph was! How is your ego? Have you learned to overcome selfish pride and worldly ambition yet? As sure as you are worth anything, God will permit you to be tempted and tried, for "the trials of life are God's workmen, to remove the impurities and roughness from our characters. . . . Upon no useless material does the Master bestow such careful, thorough work. Only His precious stones are polished after the similitude of a palace."—*Messages to Young People,* p. 117.

And in God's tomorrow He must have a people whom He can trust with the glories of eternity.

"We are all one man's sons; we are true men." Genesis 42:11.

You can think into the words "We are true men" everything that makes a man "more precious than fine gold" (Isaiah 13:12). It is interesting to know that it was on this day, January 24, 1848, that James Wilson Marshall discovered gold at Sutter's Mill near Sacramento, California. It is only too bad that men in their greed for the golden metal have often forgotten to cultivate the gold of character. The good-for-nothing man and the man worth his weight in gold live in the same world. The difference lies in whether they develop character.

Many years ago two German boys who were brothers came to America. The elder brother, being an expert sauerkraut maker, went at once to Eldorado County, California, staked out a ranch, grew cabbages, and made sauerkraut. It was the best sauerkraut in the country, and the world made a path to his door to buy his kraut.

The younger boy apprenticed himself to a metallurgist for three years, and he soon became expert in assaying metals. After completing his course, he too went west, and stayed the first night there with his older brother. In the morning they went to look at the garden. With pride the elder brother pointed to the rows of the best cabbages one could ever wish to see. But the younger brother kept looking at the ground. Finally he picked up a handful of gravel from a little stream and examined it carefully.

"What are you doing?" asked his brother. "Here I show you the best cabbages in the world, and all you do is pick up a handful of dirt."

"Do you know what this is?" asked the younger brother, pointing to a piece of metal. "This is gold! You have been growing cabbages on a gold mine!" That ranch became one of the richest mines in the gold-rush days of 1849.

"A good character is a capital of more value than gold or silver. . . . And in that day when earthly possessions shall be swept away it will bring rich returns. Integrity, firmness, and perseverance are qualities that all should seek earnestly to cultivate."—*Messages to Young People,* p. 416.

"Be ye kind one to another, tenderhearted, forgiving one another."
Ephesians 4:32.

How beautiful it is to see how Joseph loved and respected his dear old father. Surrounded as he was with wealth and honor, his thoughts were of the one who had guided and cared for him, and he asked his brothers, "Is your father well?"

Few of us realize fully how much our fathers have done for us, how much they have worried over us, or how much they have loved us.

Dr. S. Parkes Cadman was one of America's well-known evangelists and authors. When he was a boy he lived in England and worked in a coal mine. One day he was given the job of driving a mule that hauled a car of coal through one of the long dark tunnels of the mine. On his track there was a very dangerous crossing. The track that crossed his track went up a steep incline, and once in a while a car full of coal broke loose and came thundering back to the crossing. Several boys had been killed by crashes at this spot.

As young Cadman approached this dangerous intersection on his very first trip he thought of all the terrible accidents he had heard about, and he was so afraid that cold perspiration broke out all over him. Suddenly his mule turned the last corner, and there, right at the crossing, he saw a light! He was so glad that big happy tears welled up in his eyes and ran down his cheeks. Nearer and nearer he came to the light. A man was holding a lantern in his hands. It looked like—it was—it was his father! His father was a coal miner; he remembered how he had felt the first time he drove a mule through a dark tunnel, and now he was there to hold a light for his boy as he made his first trip!

Dr. Cadman often told that story of his father's care and love, and he always said, "That was the most beautiful light I have ever seen in all my life, and my dirty, coal-smeared father standing there with a grin on his face and the light in his hand was the handsomest man I have ever seen."

I am sure that your father has often held a light for you also at the dangerous places in your life. Thank God for good fathers.

"For how shall I go up to my father, and the lad be not with me?" Genesis 44:34.

When Judah asked his father's permission to take Benjamin to Egypt the second time they went to buy corn, he went security for him; he gave his word of honor that he would bring Benjamin back or bear the blame forever. Now that Joseph was testing his brothers to see whether they were still jealous, Judah begged to be allowed to become a servant in the place of Benjamin, in whose sack the governor's cup had been found, and he said, "How can I go up to my father, and the lad be not with me?" In other words, he said, "How can I break my promise? I must keep my word."

Maybe Judah had some unlovely traits of character, but dependability and reliability—the keeping of one's word of honor—is one of the most beautiful and most valuable.

In the year A.D. 79, Pompeii, one of the most beautiful cities in Italy, was destroyed by the volcano Vesuvius. Many people were buried by tons of ashes that fell on them while they were trying to escape; others were smothered to death in deep underground basements where they had fled for safety. But there was one who did not try to escape; he did not flee for safety. He was the Roman soldier who was stationed at the city gate. He remained at his post of duty and perished in his proper place. There he had been stationed by his captain. There, while the heavens poured fiery hot ashes upon him and lava streamed about him, he stood with his hands grasping his weapons. And there, more than sixteen hundred years later, he was discovered, still at his post.

This immortal story has become a symbol of this beautiful thing called reliability or dependability.

It is not likely you ever will be called upon to perish at your post of duty, but keep your word of honor to all people at all times.

"Strength of character consists of two things, the power of will, and power of self-control. . . . The real greatness and nobility of the man is measured by his power to subdue his feelings, not by the power of his feelings to subdue him. The strongest man is he, who, while sensitive to abuse, will yet restrain passion and forgive his enemies."—*Messages to Young People,* p. 412.

"See that ye fall not out by the way." Genesis 45:24.

The worst way to fall is to fall *out,* because it is hard to say you're sorry and make friends again. Joseph had given his brothers the secret of how not to fall out, and also of its cure. Joseph had forgiven his brothers, and he wanted them to keep a forgiving spirit always in their hearts. There is a story told in the book *Growing in Wisdom,* by Idalee Vonk, about a grown-up family of five brothers and sisters, Philip, Roger, Louis, Gertrude, and Ellen.

When their old father died, Philip ran off with all the inheritance money. He didn't even say Goodbye. For years they didn't hear from him, and they decided that he must have used up all the money.

Then one Christmas they each received a Christmas card from Philip! There was no address given, so they could not reply, but they said to one another, "He must be getting hard up. He wants to make friends again. He'll be asking us for help soon." You can only imagine how they felt after all Philip had done, but at last Ellen said, "If he is in trouble, I'll help him all I can; after all, he's our brother."

"I will too," agreed Roger, Gertrude, and Louis, and they started an account in the bank for Philip.

Five more years went by. Five times Christmas cards came from Philip, but never an address, and then one night someone knocked on Louis' door. It was Philip!

Louis began to explain, "If you are in need, we have started an account——"

"No! No!" said Philip. "I've come back to ask your forgiveness. How could I ever have wronged you all so much? But one night when all the money was gone I went into a church to get out of the cold. Afterward, all I could remember was one word, 'Repent! Repent!' But I couldn't sleep, and that night I decided I would pay back every penny that I had stolen. It has taken a long time to save the money, but here it is," and he took out his wallet and gave each of them their share of the full amount. Can you imagine the happiness it brought to them all? Can you imagine who was the happiest?

Keep your heart soft and tender, and full of a forgiving spirit; and you need never worry about falling *out* with anybody.

"Fear not to go down into Egypt; . . . I will go down with thee into Egypt; and I will also surely bring thee up again." Genesis 46:3, 4.

How comforting it was for Jacob to know that God was going with him into Egypt. He knew he would be safe with God, no matter what happened.

This assurance has comforted God's servants all through the ages.

When Ellen Gould Harmon was only 17 years old, God called her to a very special place in His service. God gave her a vision of the Advent people traveling the straight and narrow path to heaven. In a second vision the angel said: "Make known to others what I have revealed to you." But Ellen was exceedingly troubled, she had poor health, and she suffered so much that it looked as if she had only a short time to live. It seemed impossible for her to do the work the angel gave her. She was afraid she might become proud if she spoke as God's servant. Then came the promise. The angel told her that the hand of God would be stretched out to save her, and if she delivered the message faithfully and endured to the end, she would eat of the fruit of the tree of life and drink of the water of life.

Ellen grasped the promise, and she was faithful. She later became Ellen G. White, and lived to deliver God's messages for seventy-one years. She wrote more than eighty books, and traveled in many countries all over the world. She could not have done it without God and His protection. In 1854 she and her husband were to take the train from Jackson, Michigan, to Wisconsin. They felt a strange anxiety about the journey and prayed for God's protection. When the train came in they got aboard a forward car, but it seemed to be full; so they passed back into the next car and there found seats.

The train had gone only three miles when there was an awful crash. The engine was derailed. The front car was raised nearly on end, and the car they had first tried to find seats in was badly broken, but the car in which they were sitting was unfastened from the wrecked cars as though an angel had separated them from the wreck. How comforting it was for them to know that God was with them.

If time lasts, you might be called into God's service. Never be afraid to go. You are always safe for eternity when you go with God.

"Honour thy father and thy mother." Exodus 20:12.

What a beautiful example Joseph has given us of honoring our fathers and our mothers. Today Christians everywhere make careful plans to care for their aged, sick, or invalid parents. They bring them into their homes where they can enjoy the companionship of their children and grandchildren, and when they need extra help, they care for them in a nursing home. Take a pencil and figure out how much money it has cost your dear parents for your food, clothing, and tuition alone from the time you were born till you will be on your own at 18, and you will find the total comes to many thousands of dollars, and this does not begin to include the thousands of hours they have given to your care in cooking your meals, washing your clothes, and looking after you when you were sick. What a privilege it is, therefore, for Christian people to return some of this love and care when their parents are old.

Queenie was just a little 8-year-old Solomon Islands girl. It was during World War II. Her father was away at work in the mountains. The enemy had landed on her island and had passed the word around that they were going to burn the Adventist village where Queenie lived, because they were helping the Allies. In their fear and excitement everybody picked up a bundle of food or clothing and fled to the mountains—everybody but Queenie, her baby brother only a few hours old, and her dear, sick mother. Queenie was only 8 years old, but she wouldn't run away to save her life and leave her mother and little brother, not she! She got a little bundle of food and put it on her back, wrapped up the little baby and held him in one arm, then pulled and coaxed her mother to try to walk just a little bit. The mother was so weak; she went so slowly; she had to rest so often; but Queenie kept pulling and coaxing. Soon after dark they saw the flames from their burning village, but Queenie kept going, carrying the little baby and pulling and coaxing her mother, till by midnight they reached safety and all was well. What a noble example Queenie has given us all! I met Queenie when I visited our Kambubu College a few years ago. I was so proud of her.

Make up your mind now that you too will honor your dear parents and care for them when the need arises.

"The sceptre shall not depart from Judah . . . until Shiloh come." Genesis
49:10.

In spite of the fact that some of the kings of Judah and Israel were bad
men, we must always remember that both the good and the bad ruled
with the permission of God. And even among the rulers of the nations,
Daniel tells us that "the most High ruleth in the kingdom of men, and
giveth it to whomsoever he will."

Today is the birthday of Franklin D. Roosevelt, president of the
United States of America for more than twelve years (1933-1945),
longer than any other American president. He was born in 1882. He was
a member of the New York Senate (1913-1919) and practiced law in
New York City (1919-1927). Sad to say, in 1921 he was struck with
polio, and for a while it looked as if that would be the end of his career.
His friends were anxious; his enemies clapped their hands. They thought
he couldn't make it, but he wouldn't give up. To the surprise of the whole
world he made a heroic comeback. In 1928 and again in 1930 he was
elected governor of New York, and from 1933 to 1945 he was four times
elected president of the United States.

Although he was very busy with the duties that come to a president,
he found time to launch a caring successful project to help others.
Having suffered so much from polio himself, his heart went out to all the
other victims of this awful disease, and in 1938 he established the
National Foundation for Infantile Paralysis to help treat and rehabilitate
children who have been affected with this strange disease. In connection
with this he sponsored the famous March of Dimes for two weeks just
before his birthday, to raise funds for this project. In 1962 the March of
Dimes raised approximately $24,835,000 and gave assistance to some
twenty-two thousand polio patients. Thousands of polio patients
learned to walk, and lived to thank this courageous president for the
helpful birthday idea he had.

It is our duty to pray for the powers that are ordained of God, and to
be subject to them. Let us do our duty faithfully and cheerfully until Jesus
comes as King of kings. "For there is no power but of God: the powers
that be are ordained of God. . . . Render therefore to all their dues . . . ;
honour to whom honour" (Romans 13:1-7).

"Forgive, I pray thee now, the trespass of thy brethren." Genesis 50:17.

The most joyful moments Joseph's brothers ever had were when they knew they were forgiven for their terrible behavior toward him.

Now that their father, Jacob, was dead, they wanted the assurance of Joseph's forgiveness once more.

But it isn't easy to ask to be forgiven. Ellen G. White says: "The warfare against self is the greatest battle that was ever fought. The yielding of self, surrendering all to the will of God, requires a struggle; but the soul must submit to God before it can be renewed in holiness."— *Steps to Christ,* p. 43.

Years ago a little old, sincere Christian woman was walking quietly down a street in New York City, carrying a basket of apples, when along came a mischievous young sailor. He rudely pushed against her and upset her basket, then stood by and laughed as she picked them up again. Meekly the little old lady picked up the apples without saying a word. Then with a look of pity and kindness, she said to the laughing sailor, "God forgive you, son, as I do." Those quiet words did something to that boy. He stopped his laughing, and then the battle was on. The still small voice inside of him said, "You ought to be ashamed of yourself." His bad heart replied, "I was only having fun." The still small voice said, "You ought to say you're sorry—go on." His face went red. "Go on; go on!" His voice choked up, but at last the words came. "Forgive me, and God bless you, kind mother. I'll never do the like again," and he put some money into her hand. How many were happy? *Both* went away so happy.

Of course, it isn't easy to ask forgiveness, and it isn't easy to give forgiveness. You can depend on Satan making it as hard as he possibly can. But it is God's way to happiness. And the measure with which we forgive is the measure with which God forgives us.

A little blind boy was asked one day what forgiveness is, and he said, "It is the perfume that flowers breathe out when they are trampled upon." That's the kind of forgiveness Joseph gave to his brothers.

Make sure you give out this perfume of forgiveness.

"Take this child . . . and nurse it for me, and I will give thee thy wages."
Exodus 2:9.

Who gave Jochebed her wages for nursing Baby Moses? No doubt the princess gave her money, but that was not all the wages she received. God gave her better wages than money, for she had the satisfaction of seeing Moses grow up, turn his back on the pleasures of Egypt, and become under God the mighty deliverer of His people.

I hope that many of you juniors will grow up and choose to be teachers, because the wages that God pays teachers are the best in all the world.

Once upon a time two sisters were asked to teach a class of children in Sabbath school. "I can't teach," said the first sister, "and anyway, I'm too busy. I have just decided to embroider a lovely centerpiece for my table." So she didn't teach.

The second sister said, "I cannot teach either, but I think I ought to try, and I'll do my best." And so she did.

At night they sat at the table. One sister had a beautiful piece of linen with a pattern marked on it, already with a few inches of colored thread showing on it. The other sister had a headache and was making notes from a book on teaching. A week went by. The pattern on the centerpiece was taking shape, and the first sister smiled with satisfaction. The second sister was struggling through a book on storytelling.

Several weeks went by. The table center was finished and put on the living room table, and the visitors ohed and ahed as they saw it. The following Sabbath a little boy went home, thrilled and excited. "Mother, those people in the Bible are real! You ought to hear my Sabbath school teacher tell about them."

Several years went by. The centerpiece was faded and worn. "I can't stand the sight of it one more day," said the first sister as she stuffed it into the ragbag. The following Sabbath the other sister had the joy of seeing a junior boy baptized—born into the kingdom of God. Oh, what wages!

There is no satisfaction so great as the joy of leading a soul to Christ.

What are you going to be when you grow up?

"I will be with thy mouth, and teach thee what thou shalt say." Exodus *4:12.*

It is easy to understand how God could tell Moses what to say. Moses was a grown-up man and well educated. But our pioneer storybooks and our papers have many stories in them that show how God can fulfill this promise to juniors and even to younger children.

There are the stories of the young people, and even of a little 5-year-old girl in Sweden who preached "The hour of his judgment is come." And there is another story I like to tell of a little girl who went to camp meeting in Buckston, Maine, when she was just 6 years old. Her greatest treasure was a little pink umbrella that she carried around with her all the time, and even took to bed with her. When she heard the ministers pleading with the people to give up everything and get ready for Jesus, she began to fear that she loved her pink umbrella too much, and thought she should give it up for Jesus, too. But how could she do it? She hugged it tightly in her arms, looked at it lovingly, and then burst into tears and said, "Dear Jesus, I want to love You and go to heaven too. Take away my sins. I give myself to You, umbrella and all." Her mother threw her arms around her little girl as she said, "Oh, Mother, I'm so happy. Jesus loves me, and I love Him better than any pink umbrella or anything."

Of course, the preacher explained that since she wouldn't let the umbrella take her love from Jesus, she might keep it, and the little one was happy. But she had no idea how much encouragement her few words and tears brought to the people in the big tent that day, and to one girl there, 17 years old, who received a great blessing from this little one's words. This teenager was Ellen Harmon! Do you know who she was and who she became afterwards?

You remember, Jesus said to His disciples, "When they deliver you up, take no thought how or what ye shall speak: for it shall be given you in that same hour what ye shall speak. For it is not ye that speak, but the Spirit of your Father which speaketh in you" (Matthew 10:19, 20). And this promise is for all, old and young, who will keep close to Him.

God wants to teach *you* what to say too. Won't you keep close to Him and let Him do it?

"I will bring you out from under the burdens of the Egyptians, . . . and I will redeem you with a stretched out arm." Exodus 6:6.

Ever since the days of the martyr Abel, the people of God have had periods of persecution and bad treatment from those who are enemies of God. God has permitted these trials to come so that His people could learn to pray and trust in Him.

The children of Israel suffered a great deal at the hands of the Egyptians, "but the more they afflicted them, the more they multiplied and grew" (Exodus 1:12). The same was true in the days of the early Christian church. They were persecuted and scattered abroad, but "the hand of the Lord was upon them: and a great number believed, and turned unto the Lord" (Acts 11:21). The same is true in many places today. In a certain country, which better not be named, in the year 1956 nine Seventh-day Adventists were killed, forty-nine were beaten and wounded, eighty-nine laymen were imprisoned, 108 workers and colporteurs were imprisoned, and 234 believers had to flee from their homes to the mountains and the rocks. Two of those who were killed were junior boys who were known in their community as "singing Sabatistas." They loved the Lord and were soon to be baptized. They were caught by their enemies, tied back to back, and then ordered to sing. "Sing, you heretics, sing!" The mob shouted angrily; and our juniors sang. And when their songs were finished they were kicked and beaten, then stabbed to death.

We are sure that those dear boys will be given special honor and white robes, with Stephen and John the Baptist, someday. But listen; before this trouble we had only two thousand Adventists in that country, but now the membership is up to nearly 100,000!

"While the Lord has not promised His people exemption from trials, He has promised that which is far better. He has said, 'As thy days, so shall thy strength be.' . . . If you are called to go through the fiery furnace for His sake, Jesus will be by your side even as He was with the faithful three in Babylon."— *Thoughts From the Mount of Blessing,* p. 30.

Sometimes I think we have things too easy, and our lives are too soft. But our turn at persecution will come someday. Let us learn now how to trust in the Lord, so that we will be faithful.

"To day if ye will hear his voice, harden not your heart." Psalm 95:7, 8.

Many people have misunderstood the third verse of our Scripture reading today, where it says, "I will harden Pharaoh's heart," and have thought that Pharaoh was not to blame for refusing to let God's people go. But in chapter 8, verse 15, we read: "When Pharaoh saw that there was respite, he hardened his heart." And that is the correct meaning, for God has given everybody the privilege of choosing, and each person can make his heart like *wax* or like *clay.* Put *wax* in the sunshine, and it becomes soft; put *clay,* and it becomes hard.

Elder W. A. Spicer used to tell a story about a barrelmaker in Brussels who said he didn't believe there was a God and who never read the Bible or went to church. However, an Adventist evangelist came to this town, and this man's wife and little 3-year-old daughter went to the meetings. "Don't you ever go there again," said the man angrily, when he found out they were going. "If you do, I will kill you." But his wife softly replied, "Husband, I love God, and as long as I live I will go to worship Him." And she went again. When she came home the husband was furious. He knocked her down, dragged her over to his chopping block, lifted his sharp ax and shouted, "Now I'm going to chop your head off." "You could easily do it," said his wife softly. "You are stronger than I am, but you'd never get another woman to love you and cook for you and look after your little girl for you the way I do." Suddenly he felt ashamed and threw the ax down; but he was too angry to speak to her for a long time.

She kept on going to the meetings and was baptized. Then one Sabbath morning the little girl climbed on her father's knee, put her arms around his neck, and said, "Daddy, please come to Sabbath school with me and Mommy. Don't you know Jesus is coming soon to take us to heaven?" Tears came to the father's eyes and with a choking voice he said, "Do you really want me to come?" "Of course," she answered, giving him a big kiss. "What would Mommy and I do without you in heaven?" He went to Sabbath school; he kept on going; at last he was baptized and became a deacon in the church. You see, *he himself* had hardened his heart. He *chose* to resist the Spirit of God; then later he *chose* to believe and respond to the Spirit.

See to it, juniors, that *you* harden not your heart.

"And Moses . . . intreated the Lord. And the Lord did according to the word of Moses." Exodus 8:30, 31.

God gave Moses special training to prepare him to be the leader of His people and to deliver them from the hand of Pharaoh. Today is the birthday of William Miller, another man whom God trained and used to establish the Second Advent message in America. He was born in 1782 and lived most of his life in Low Hampton, New York. He was the oldest of sixteen brothers, so there was little time for school. But his mother taught him to read, and he loved to sit by the fireplace at night and read the Bible, the psalmbook, the prayer book, and history books. After he was married his companions influenced him to read books that denied Christ and ridiculed the Bible, so although he believed in God, he was not a Christian. For two years he was a soldier in the War of 1812, and what he saw there made him wonder whether there really would be a judgment. Now, Mr. Miller's grandfather was a good old Baptist minister, and soon a little company of Baptists was raised up and a little church was built near his house. Just to please his mother, William used to go to church on Sunday. When there was no preacher, one of the deacons would read a sermon, but because he couldn't read very well they asked William to read instead. So Mr. Miller read sermons to the people—sermons that he did not believe. Before long he was converted and began to study his Bible earnestly. He found the prophecies in Daniel about the judgment and the cleansing of the sanctuary, and he believed they meant that Jesus was coming in 1844.

Then one day the still small voice spoke to him, "Go and tell it to the world." And he did. And because of his preaching, many began to study and to understand the true meaning of the cleansing of the sanctuary. Soon they found what the Bible says about the true Sabbath, and that is how the Seventh-day Adventist message began.

"There is no limit to the usefulness of one who, by putting self aside, makes room for the working of the Holy Spirit upon his heart, and lives a life wholly consecrated to God. If men will endure the necessary discipline, without complaining or fainting by the way, God will teach them hour by hour, and day by day."—*The Desire of Ages*, pp. 250, 251.

"For this cause have I raised thee up, for to shew in thee my power; and that my name may be declared throughout all the earth." Exodus 9:16.

Pharaoh hardened his heart, and all the world has heard the story. But if Pharaoh had softened his heart, and obeyed God, and allowed the children of Israel to go in the first place, the mercy and greatness of God would have been told around the world just as much and maybe more.

A few years ago I was visiting our Sabbath schools in the land of the Pharaohs. At one place I met a strong, muscular young man with a handshake like a grip of iron. "Who is that young man?" I asked the worker—Brother Fikry. "His name is Adlai Botross," he said. "When I first came here and hired this hall in which to hold meetings, he was the worst man in town. He used to be a prize fighter, and when he got drunk he was the terror of the town. Of course, we had some enemies in this place, and they promised Adlai some money and some whisky if he would disturb the meetings. He was glad for the chance. So at the very first meeting, there he was, sitting under the light switch, ready to turn out the lights and shout. Then the others were to come in and beat me up. But the singing touched his heart, and he listened all the way through.

" 'What's the matter with you?' said our enemies to him after the meeting. 'Here we promise you money and whiskey, and you just sit.'

" 'Oh, I forgot all about it,' said Adlai. 'That man is a good preacher; but I'll do it tomorrow night.'

"The next night he came again, and again sat quietly all through.

" 'What's the matter with you?' asked our enemies again after the meeting.

" 'Listen,' said Adlai, 'I don't intend to disturb that man tonight or any night. He is preaching the truth, and you know it. I'm going to come to every meeting, and if any of you want to disturb that preacher, you'll have to disturb me first.'

"He did come to every meeting. Our enemies were too afraid of him to try disturbing the preacher any more, and Adlai Botross was the first to be baptized."

God sees in every one of us something worthwhile—something He needs. Won't you let Him show His power in you?

43

"We will go with our young and with our old, with our sons and with our daughters . . . ; for we must hold a feast unto the Lord." Exodus 10:9.

God has always had a place for junior boys and girls, and even tiny tots, in His great plan of salvation. God wants boys and girls in family worship, in Sabbath school, in church, and in heaven. When God called His people out of Egypt He wasn't willing that even one junior be left behind. We are on our way from this wicked old earth to heaven, and if you could hear the hearts of your parents talking, they would be saying, "With our young and our old, with our sons and our daughters, will we go, for we must be together in heaven." God has put these longings in the hearts of parents, for that is part of His plan.

Have you ever read *Pilgrim's Progress?* You know, the first part of that book tells how a man named Christian struggled through this world and into the kingdom of heaven. Then the second part tells how his wife, Christiana, and the children struggled through this world to the kingdom of heaven also. Well, one day a grandmother finished reading this book to her 5-year-old grandson Johnny. As she closed the book, Johnny looked into her face and said, "Grandma, in all the book, which person did you like the best?" Grandma thought quickly, then replied, "I think I liked Christian the best."

"You did?" asked Johnny, a little surprised.

"Yes," replied Grandma. "Didn't you?"

"No," said Johnny, "I didn't."

"Well, which one did you like the best?" asked Grandma.

"I liked Christiana the best, I did," said Johnny.

"And why did you like Christiana the best?" asked Grandma.

"Because Christiana took the children with her. That's why," said Johnny.

"I think you're right," agreed Grandma thoughtfully.

I know that your parents' greatest hope is to take *you* with them into the kingdom of heaven. See that you make it as easy for them as is possible. Come willingly to family worship; go willingly to Sabbath school; and sit willingly with them when they go to church to worship the Lord.

"When I see the blood, I will pass over you, and the plague shall not be upon you to destroy you, when I smite the land of Egypt." Exodus 12:13.

There is a story that I love to tell. It is about a little firstborn son in a Hebrew home on that first Passover night. The lamb had been slain. Jared, the faithful servant, had been told to sprinkle the blood upon the doorposts. The lamb had been roasted and eaten with bitter herbs, and now while the older members of the family all waited the fateful midnight hour, the little son was told to sleep. He tried and tried to go to sleep, but he couldn't. "Father, I've named the patriarchs and all the animals that Noah took into the ark, but still I cannot sleep. Father, are you sure the blood is on the doorposts?"

"Yes, yes, my firstborn," said the father soothingly. "I gave the word. You have nothing to fear. The angel will see the sign and pass over you."

He tried again, but he could not sleep. "Oh, Father," he cried, "I seem to see the angel pausing sadly at our door. What if the blood has been removed or if Jared forgot!"

"Rest, rest, little one," said the father. "Jared is faithful, and even if some hungry dog licked the blood from the side posts, the blood would still be on the top, and the angel would see it. Sleep, sleep, my little one."

The night wore on; sleep came at last, but with it a frightful dream. "Father, oh, Father," he cried out, "my heart is filled with fear of coming danger. Take me, please, take me to the door and let me see the blood."

The father lit a torch, tenderly lifted his little son in his arms, and took him to the door. But the blood had not been sprinkled! It was still in the bowl. Trembling, the father took the hyssop and he himself applied the blood in eager haste. A sigh of relief escaped the little boy's lips, and he was asleep before he was put on his bed again. And when the great cry arose and the children of Israel went out of Egypt, he didn't even wake up. His father carried him in his arms, still sleeping peacefully.

Have you been baptized? Are you careful to take part in the ordinance of humility and of the Lord's Supper each quarter? This is one way we apply the blood of Jesus to the doorposts of our heart. Jesus has shed His blood for us—but *we* must apply it.

"Fear ye not, stand still, and see the salvation of the Lord. . . . And the Lord said unto Moses, . . . Speak unto the children of Israel, that they go forward." Exodus 14:13-15.

I can never forget how God enabled five of us missionaries to cross the Irrawaddy River with two motor cars when we were escaping from the war in Burma. There were no boats running across the river any more, and it looked impossible to get to the other side of that wide river. At last we hired two large country boats and tied them together, but we could not find any big, long planks to place across the boats on which to put the cars. There was a sawmill in the town of Myingyan, three miles away. But it was locked up. The owner and the workmen had fled into the country, and no one knew where they were. We were stuck. I heard the boatmen laughing at our trouble.

"They will have to leave their cars and go across the river in canoes!" said one.

"I'm going to have a wheel!" "I'm going to have a suitcase!" said others.

Sick and weary, I turned to God in prayer: "O God, it is not as hard to get only five of us across the river as it was to get the children of Israel across the Red Sea." But no answer came. I prayed again and again; midnight came, but no answer. One o'clock, two, three, four o'clock, and then the answer came: The still small voice seemed to say in my heart, "Go to the sawmill in the town. Go now!" I woke up the boatman and said, "My God has just told me to go now to the sawmill."

"All right," he said, "I'll go with you." We got a bullock wagon and went into the town, and we found the gates of the sawmill open! The son of the mill owner had come for some important papers and had just opened the gates as we arrived. He sold us four big long planks, and we loaded them onto the cart and drove out of the gate. The mill owner's son came out after us, closed the gate, and went back to his father's hiding place.

The old boatman and I walked in silence for a while behind the planks my God had provided for us, then he touched my hand and said, "Your God did talk to you, didn't He?"

God did talk to me that night, but what if I had not obeyed?

"If thou wilt diligently hearken to the voice of the Lord thy God . . . I will put none of these diseases upon thee, which I have brought upon the Egyptians: for I am the Lord that healeth thee." Exodus 15:26.

Our great God is still changing bitter experiences into sweet ones. It was January 18, 1958, in the middle of winter, in New York City. Elder and Mrs. W. A. Fagal and their son had gone to bed. The daughter was attending a program, and the mother was reading in bed till she would return. Suddenly Mrs. Fagal smelled smoke, and jumping out of bed, she found there was a fire in the basement. She rushed next door and telephoned, and soon the firemen came and put the fire out. It had damaged only the basement, but the firemen said, "You must not sleep in the house tonight. The smell of smoke is not good." The neighbors were kind and took them in. Early in the morning they heard the fire trucks coming past, and looking out, they found their house was on fire again! This time the upstairs was burning.

"Never mind the clothes and the furniture," said Mrs. Fagal to the firemen who were trying to save some of their belongings. "Only try to get the letters on the desk. They are the Faith for Today letters. Some have checks in them, some have lessons, and some have application cards in them. Please try to get them." Soon one of the firemen came out with the brief case. Some of the letters were in it, but others were on the desk. "I couldn't get anything else," said the fireman.

Still Mrs. Fagal kept praying, "Dear Lord, please keep the letters safe. Don't let them burn up. The people need this truth. Please, Lord." In a few hours there was nothing left but a heap of ashes. It was so cold that in the gutters and on the street the water from the fire hoses had become sheets of ice. Even the water at the bottom of the ashes was solid ice. Later on the Fagals poked around in the ashes, looking to see whether there was anything not burned. They dug down through the ashes till they came to the ice at the bottom, and there, frozen in the ice, were the Faith for Today letters that had been washed off the desk by the water from the firemen's hose!

The ice was melted off; the letters were dried; and although they were smudgy, they were still readable and the checks still cashable.

When some great disappointment comes to you, remember that God can change the bitter into sweet.

"Neither murmur ye, as some of them also murmured, and were destroyed of the destroyer." 1 Corinthians 10:10.

God had delivered His chosen people. But before He could bring them into the Promised Land it was necessary for Him to prove them, to see whether they would obey His commands. He tested them at the bitter waters of Marah; they failed and murmured. He tested them with a fifteen-day journey through the wilderness; they failed and murmured. Again and again they failed and murmured, and the murmurers never did get into the Promised Land.

Today is the birthday of the world's greatest inventor, Thomas Alva Edison. He was born in Milan, Ohio, in 1847. One of his outstanding qualities was that he never acknowledged failure or defeat; he never quit. He is credited with making 1,100 inventions in sixty years. After completing ten thousand experiments with a project in his electrical laboratory, some friends told him not to be discouraged about his failures. But Edison replied, "I have not failed. I've found ten thousand ways that won't work!" He has given the world the well-known saying "Success is 1 percent inspiration and 99 percent perspiration."

When he was 9 years old his mother bought him a chemistry book. Young Tom proved every experiment to make sure it worked. He had one hundred bottles marked "poison" to keep others from touching them. When he was 12 years old he got a job selling newspapers, candy, and peanuts on a train.

Between his trips through the train, he kept on experimenting in the baggage car, till one day there was an explosion and he set the car on fire. At 16 years of age he got a job as a telegrapher. He had to report train activities every hour to Toronto, in Canada. Soon he invented a device that would do the reporting automatically. In 1877 he invented the phonograph, in 1879 the incandescent electric lamp, and in 1887 his motion picture machine, called the kinetoscope. He was called the Wizard of Menlo Park.

Yet in his greatness he was humble. "I can *invent*," he said, "but I cannot *create*." God has given you talents also. You may make some mistakes; you may encounter some failures; but never murmur and never quit.

"When thou art converted, strengthen thy brethren." Luke 22:32.

I love to think of Aaron and Hur "staying," or holding up, or strengthening, the hands of Moses as he prayed for Israel to be victorious over the Amalekites. It is so easy to criticize our brethren, our teachers, and our workers, but Aaron and Hur left us a beautiful example of being kind and helpful. You know that today is the birthday of Abraham Lincoln. He was born in a log cabin in Kentucky, on February 12, 1809. Maybe more than any other President of the United States he is loved for his kindness and helpfulness to all. Many books have been written of how this great man has lifted, strengthened, and supported his fellowmen, but here is a paragraph from one of my favorite books, a paragraph on how God made Abraham Lincoln:

"He took a little babe and called to his side, His favorite angel, the angel of sorrow. Stooping, he whispered, 'O Sorrow, thou well-beloved teacher, take thou this child of mine and make him great. Take him to yonder cabin in the wilderness; make his home a poor man's home; plant his narrow path thick with thorns; cut his little feet with sharp rocks as he climbs the hill of difficulty. Make each footprint red with his own life blood; load his little back with burdens; give him days of toil and nights of study and sleeplessness. Wrest from his arms whatever he loves, make his heart, through sorrow, as sensitive to the sigh of a slave as a thread of silk in a window is sensitive to the slightest wind that blows; and when you have digged lines of pain in his cheek and made his face more marred than the face of any man of his time, bring him back to me, and with him I will free four million slaves."—E. V. Odle, *Quest and Conquest.*

What a man was Lincoln. He was called names, criticized, and made fun of. But when his personal papers were opened and classified, there was not found *one unkind word* about anyone in all of his letters.

"Kind words, looks of sympathy, expressions of appreciation, would be to many a struggling and lonely one as the cup of cold water to a thirsty soul. A word of sympathy, an act of kindness, would lift burdens that rest heavily upon weary shoulders."—*Thoughts From the Mount of Blessing,* p. 23.

God expects you to be kind, and to strengthen the weak.

"In the multitude of counsellors there is safety." Proverbs 11:14.

In our story today Moses has given us a splendid example of taking advice. If there is one thing we all need, it is to realize that we do not know everything yet. We can always learn from others; and it pays to take advice. Solomon said that in the multitude of counselors there is safety. In his delightful little book *University of Hard Knocks,* Ralph Parlette tells a pathetic little story about himself that illustrates the point excellently.

Little Ralph was 3 years old, and he thought he knew everything about what was good for him. One day he sat at the table in his high chair and there on the table before him, within reaching distance, was the coffeepot. At once he knew that was just what he wanted. He needed that coffeepot in his business. He reached out for it, but his mother, sitting right beside him, said, "No, don't touch that coffeepot!" The idea! That mother of his was always spoiling his fun and meddling in his business. He did want that coffeepot. And the longer he thought about it, the more determined he was to have it—and the more angry he became with his unsympathetic mother. Always giving advice! What did she know about it anyway? He decided emphatically not to take her advice, and while Mother was looking elsewhere, he reached out and got the coffeepot. He also got about a quart of the hottest coffee a boy ever spilled over himself. He felt the pain for weeks afterward. They put apple butter all over him, and coal oil and egg white and starch and anything else the neighbors could think of that might help. [Today we know that cold water is the best emergency treatment for hot-water burns.]

As time went by, little Ralph learned that his mother really did know more than he did, and that if he did not take her advice a hot coffeepot might spill on him.

Paul tells us that in the last days perilous times shall come and men will be lovers of their own selves, boasters, disobedient to parents, unthankful, unholy, despisers of those that are good. (See 2 Timothy 3:1-3.) This is the Bible way of saying that people of the world rebel against taking advice, and that's why so many get into *hot water.*

Learn to take advice from your parents and teachers. You may miss many a spilled quart of boiling-hot coffee if you do.

"If ye will obey my voice indeed, and keep my covenant, then ye shall be a peculiar treasure unto me above all people." Exodus 19:5.

Obedience must be very important, because so much is said about it in the Bible.

Disobedience results in death, but obedience is rewarded with life.

I found this happy-ending story in the Washington *Star*, February 20, 1961: Seven-year-old Harry Stage went from his home in Phoenix, Arizona, with his father to a farm about twenty-five miles away. While his father was talking to Mr. Faubion, the ranch owner, Harry was playing near a little platform. Soon he climbed onto the platform, and there on the ground at one side of it he saw a piece of plywood. Without thinking, he jumped down onto it. It was the cover to an irrigation well sixteen inches wide and 250 feet deep, with water at the bottom of it! As Harry jumped on it, it gave way, and down went Harry feet first. Down, down, down till he hit the water. Most of the plywood went with him, and no doubt this slowed his fall a little. When he hit the water he was able to push against the sides of the well with his hands and keep himself from going under. "Daddy, get me out of here," he shouted.

"Don't worry, son, and don't be scared," replied his father calmly. "We'll get you out. Just push against the sides of the pipe so you don't sink."

"OK, Daddy," Harry shouted back, "I will."

Mr. Faubion drove seven miles to a neighbor's ranch and got many cowboy lariats. He tied them together and they made a rope 300 feet long. The father put a strong loop on the end of it and let it carefully down the well. "I've got it, Daddy," called Harry. "I can hold on while you pull me up."

"No, no, son," said his father. "Put that loop over your head and under your arms." "OK, Daddy," called back Harry, "I'll try." He tried and he did it, and soon he called out, "OK, I'm ready, Daddy." And soon Harry was out and in an ambulance. He had two broken legs, but was very much alive.

"You're the bravest and luckiest boy in Arizona," said Mr. Faubion.

Then his father added proudly, "He was always an obedient boy."

Are you always obedient? It really pays.

"If ye love me, keep my commandments." John 14:15.

In Exodus 20 are written down the ten commandments of God, which have been the great rules of life for all men and women, boys and girls, ever since there were people on the earth. Some people say the commandments are too hard to keep, so they don't try. But listen to what Ellen G. White says: "The church of God is made up of vessels large and small. The Lord does not ask for anything unreasonable. He does not expect the smaller vessels to hold the contents of the larger ones. . . . Do your best, and God will accept your efforts."—*Messages to Young People,* p. 96.

One day when my son Leonard was just a little 4-year-old, he came walking into my office. "Daddy, Daddy! I love you," he said.

"You do?" I asked kindly.

"Yes, Daddy, I love you. You made me a toy car, didn't you, Daddy?"

"Yes, son," I replied. "I do lots of things for you because I love you too, don't I? But you don't do very much for me, do you?"

"But, Daddy, I want to. Tell me what to do and I'll do it."

I thought quickly, then said, "Son, I'll tell you what to do. See that big green box in the other room? I need it right here by my desk. Will you bring it in for me?"

"Yes, Daddy, I'll bring it," he said, and off he went. He caught hold of the handle and pulled and grunted, but he couldn't move it. I knew he couldn't do it. But then he called, "Daddy, come and help me." I smiled as I went over and took the other handle, and together we pulled that big box into my office just where I wanted it.

"I did it, Daddy. Didn't I, Daddy? I did it," he said triumphantly. And I took him on my knee and hugged him tight.

"Of course you did it, son," I whispered. And from my little boy I leaned how we could keep the commandments of God.

I want you to notice that Lenny didn't try to carry the box because he *had to,* but because he *wanted to.* In doing his best to carry the box, he showed that he really did love me.

Do you really love God for all He has done for you? Then you can easily find a way to keep His commandments. He will help you as I helped Leonard.

"All the words which the Lord hath said will we do." Exodus 24:3.

A very solemn promise is called a vow. God does not force anyone to make a vow, but if a vow is made, He does require that it be fulfilled. Men who do not fulfill a vow are called traitors, betrayers, deserters, or deceivers, and they are despised by everyone.

On the battlefield of Saratoga in New York State stands a fine monument to commemorate the winning of the great battle. In the base of the tall shaft there are four little niches that were designed to hold the marble likenesses of the heads of the four American generals who fought in this battle. The marble heads of Generals Schuyler, Morgan, and Gates are there, but the fourth niche is empty and will always remain so. It was designed for General Benedict Arnold, who became a traitor to his country before it was finished.

Arnold took the oath of loyalty at the age of fifteen and became a soldier, but before long he deserted. He ran a bookstore and drugstore for a while, but became tired of that and returned to the army. He served gallantly in several encounters against the British and was made a brigadier general. A year later he became a major general. He was put in command of the forces at Philadelphia in 1778, but soon got into trouble and was court-martialed. Two years later he was sent to take command of the American forces at West Point. But he had kept his anger for the superior officers who had reprimanded him. In July, 1780, Arnold entered into negotiations to betray the fort to the British for $30,000. The plot was foiled because the British agent was caught. Arnold escaped to the British lines, and was given a commission in the British Army, but he was despised and scorned even by the British. He died alone and friendless in a little upstairs room in London, June 14, 1801. It is said that the doctor who was attending him at the time of his death asked, "Is there anything else you need?"

"Yes," replied Arnold feebly, "I need a friend."

In *Messages to Young People,* on page 138, we read: "Those who stand under the bloodstained banner of Prince Immanuel should be faithful soldiers in Christ's army. . . . They cannot be soldiers of Christ, and engage with the confederacy of Satan, and help on his side, for then they would be enemies of Christ."

"Thou shalt not make unto thee any graven image . . . : thou shalt not bow down thyself to them, nor serve them." Exodus 20:4, 5.

We can't help feeling a little disgusted with the children of Israel for falling into the sin of idol worship so soon after seeing their mavelous deliverance by the mighty, living God. But listen, graven images are not all golden calves. What about the idols of self, popularity, money, and fashion? Were *you* ever tempted to bow down to *them* and serve *them?* In her priceless book *Let's Talk It Over,* Lora E. Clement tells a story about two sisters, Ruth and Janet, who took a vacation in Miami once upon a time. They had been working hard in college and decided that they would not spoil their fun by telling anyone they were Seventh-day Adventists. They took a room at the Breakers Hotel; nearby was a movie theater. Since nobody knew them in the town, they decided to go watch just one movie. But it so happened that some other nice young people who also stayed at the Breakers Hotel saw them there and invited them to a beach party the next day. Ruth and Janet both played guitars, and the young people had a good time.

"Let's have a game of cards," said one of the young men.

"Oh, yes, let's," said some of the others.

Ruth looked at Janet and whispered, "Just once won't hurt us." So they played cards. And the next day they danced "just once."

Then on Friday afternoon one of the young men said, "I've hired a launch to take you all for an outing and a beach picnic tonight."

"And you'll bring your guitars, girls, won't you?" asked Mrs. Marshall, the young man's mother.

But that evening Ruth and Janet talked things over.

"I wish we hadn't tried to cover up our religion."

"I wish we had never gone to that first movie."

"Why can't one of us get a sick headache?"

"Oh, yes; or go home on the midnight train and be yellow! I've had enough of this. I'm going straight to Mrs. Marshall and tell her we are Seventh-day Adventists even if we did make some mistakes." And she did; and Mrs. Marshall understood perfectly and admired them all the more for their courage and their convictions.

Just be sure that *you* don't bow down to some golden calf someday and worship it.

"I will . . . be gracious to whom I will be gracious, and will shew mercy on whom I will shew mercy." Exodus 33:19.

Israel had sinned against the Lord so terribly that they deserved to be consumed. But in response to Moses' pleading, God extended His gracious mercy toward all who would repent. Remember, there are always hope and happiness ahead for the one who is really sorry for his sins and who repents.

Once upon a time, according to an oft-told story, two brothers moved out to California and started a sheep ranch. They were dishonest young men, and after being suspected for some time, they were caught actually stealing their neighbors' sheep. In those days in the "wild and woolly" West it was just too much trouble to have the men arrested, taken to court, and put in jail, so the neighbors took the law into their own hands and with a red-hot branding iron they branded both men on the forehead—S.T. for "sheep thief"—then let them go. One of the brothers was so utterly ashamed that he moved away, built a tiny cabin high up in the hills, and, afraid that the story would follow him, became a hermit and kept away from people as much as he could. The other brother said, "I can't run away from it. I'll stay right here and make things right." And he did. He gave back the sheep that he had stolen, lived an honest life, and in time was looked up to as one of the leading citizens of the community. One day one of the neighbor boys was helping him shear some sheep, and when he took his hat off to wipe the perspiration from his brow the boy was surprised to see scars on his forehead that looked like S.T. That night he said to his father, "Did you ever see those scars on that man's forehead? What does S.T. stand for?" The father didn't want to tell his boy of the man's sin and punishment of so long ago, so he thought for a moment and then said, "Let me see; don't we have S-T Matthew and S-T Mark and S-T Luke and S-T John in the Bible?"

"Well, Dad," replied the boy, "that could be it, for if there ever was a saint around here, it is he!"

I hope you never fall; but if you do, get right back up, receive God's gracious mercy, and become an "S-T."

"Six days thou shalt work, but on the seventh day thou shalt rest." Exodus 34:21.

The first lesson Israel had to learn was to obey. That's why God gave them the Ten Commandments. Obedience to those commandments would make them different from all other people in the world. And the commandment that would make them most different would be the keeping of the seventh-day Sabbath.

Very early in my ministry in Burma I set out one day with an evangelist to visit one of our church members. We knew his name—Aung Baw—and we knew he lived in the Doyin district; we also knew that he was cross-eyed and that when he was young he had been a prizefighter. But we did not know in which of the thirty or more villages in that district he lived. We hired a bullock wagon and went to the nearest village in the Doyin district and asked the headman if he could direct us to Aung Baw, who used to be a prizefighter and was cross-eyed.

"Aung Baw—Aung Baw?" said the headman. "Used to be a prizefighter, and you say he's cross-eyed? No, I'm sorry. I've never heard of him; but try the next village."

We tried the next village and the next, with always the same result. At last I became desperate.

"Somebody must know him," I said. "He belongs to our mission and he keeps the seventh-day—"

"Oh, you mean that seventh-day man," blurted out one of the seven headmen we had asked. "Why, yes! Everybody knows him, but we didn't know his name and we didn't know he had been a prizefighter. But we all know he keeps the Sabbath. He's different. Look! see that mountain with the little pagoda on top of it? Well, straight down at the bottom of that mountain you'll find that seventh-day man."

And sure enough, within an hour we had found Brother Aung Baw. We could have looked for a cross-eyed prizefighter for days, and might never have found him.

Someday the angels are going to be looking for people to take to heaven. If you love Jesus and are keeping the Sabbath, they will have no trouble finding *you.*

"Take ye from among you an offering unto the Lord: whosoever is of a willing heart, let him bring it, . . . gold, and silver, and brass." Exodus 35:5.

When the hearts of the children of Israel were right with God they loved to bring offerings to help along the Lord's work. And it has always been the same. We had only two organized Sabbath schools 110 years ago. Twenty-six years later we had 177 Sabbath schools, with 5,851 members. Then the Advent people began to bring their offerings, at first for their Sabbath school supplies. After eight more years they began to bring offerings for the Lord's work in the mission fields. In twenty-five more years they had brought in one million dollars for missions! And there were more than four thousand Sabbath schools, with nearly 103,000 members. By the end of 1984, members had brought in $628 million for the Lord's work, and there were more than 50,000 Sabbath schools and more than 5,340,000 members. In 1984 the Sabbath school offering totaled more than $30,212,000, or an average of nearly one dollar every second! That is the way God blesses when His people bring a willing offering.

In Puerto Rico there lived a little widow woman who had quite a large family. Everyone called her Mother Borrilla. One day she went to Sabbath school, and when she heard the appeal for an offering she felt that she ought to give $2. Now, $2 was just about all she had, but she loved the Lord and she knew He would give her strength to wash clothes and earn some more. So she willingly gave her $2 for an offering. Soon after going home she went out into the backyard, and what do you think? Two mina birds flew overhead, and each one had a $1 bill in its beak! They must have found them somewhere and thought they would make a nice lining for their nest. But a mysterious thing happened. They opened their beaks, and the two $1 bills floated right down to Mother Borrilla's feet. She knew God would bless her for her willing sacrifice in some way or another, but she hardly expected a miracle like this.

Do you bring a willing, loving offering to the Lord every Sabbath? And does God bless you for it?

"Ye shall keep my sabbaths, and reverence my sanctuary: I am the Lord."
Leviticus 19:30.

When the tabernacle was finished, it was filled with the glory of the Lord. Every time the priest entered the tabernacle, and every time the children of Israel came near it, they were quiet and reverent, because they could see the cloud and almost feel the presence of God. When *you* go to church do *you* feel God's presence there? An astronomer once said, "I have swept the heavens with my telescope and nowhere have I found God." But there was another astronomer by the name of Kepler, who, after discovering the planetary motions, said, "God, these are *Thy* thoughts I am thinking after Thee." What made the difference? Just going to church won't make you a Christian any more than going to a garage makes you a mechanic. It is your being quiet and reverent in church that enables you to find the glory of God there, and once you have found God, He can do anything He wants to with you.

Once upon a time, when our first missionaries were going to India, a little baby boy was born in Seattle, Washington. His father was not an Adventist, but his mother was, and she took her baby boy to Sabbath school and to church soon after he was born. She taught him to sit quietly in church, and when he was big enough she taught him that church is God's house. Every Sabbath he looked forward to putting on his Sabbath clothes so he could go to God's house. When he grew bigger he heard the Word of God read and preached there; he heard about the missionaries who were doing God's work all over the world. And when he was twelve he said, "Mother, God needs more than nickels and quarters; I think He needs me for a missionary too." He was baptized, and when he was old enough he went to Walla Walla College. After he was graduated he went to the Philippine Islands as a missionary and was there for nineteen years. Then the Lord's work organized in South America needed a president, so he served there for ten years. In 1954 our denomination needed a new General Conference President, and Reuben R. Figuhr was ready for the responsibility.

Don't just go to church. Go to see the glory of God and to feel His presence, and let God have His way with *you*.

"And Moses said unto Hobab, . . . Come thou with us, and we will do thee good. . . . And thou mayest be to us instead of eyes." Numbers 10:29-31.

Hobab, the brother-in-law of Moses, had an outstanding talent. He knew the country through which the children of Israel were to pass very well, and he was needed. He was reluctant to accept the responsibility of a guide. But he did, for later we read of his inheritance being with the children of Judah. Today is the birthday of another man with an outstanding talent who also was needed for a great responsibility—George Washington. He was born in 1732. As a boy he was quiet and shy, but as a soldier and a leader of soldiers he showed great wisdom and skill. He took the side of the British against the French in the dispute over the Ohio Valley. Later he took the part of the Americans against the British in their struggle for independence. He was elected as the first president of the United States in 1789, and was elected again "against his will" in 1793. The people would have gladly elected him the third time, but he refused. Of him it is said that he was "first in war, first in peace, and first in the hearts of his countrymen."

There are many stories told of his boyhood, but here is the one that I like the best. When he was 14 years old he wanted to join the Navy. His father was dead and his Navy idea broke his mother's heart. But he teased and coaxed until she unwillingly gave her consent. Then he packed his things in a trunk and put it on board the warship he was to join. However, at the last minute his mother couldn't go through with it, and she withdrew her consent. No doubt, young George was disappointed. He might even have felt angry, I don't know, but he was obedient and went back to school. He had skill in mathematics and specialized in surveying, and his first job was as a surveyor for Lord Fairfax. Then he became a public surveyor for the colony of Virginia. Yes, George Washington had a special talent that his country needed. When he died, December 14, 1799, at the age of 67, he was mourned by the whole world as one of the great men of his time.

You have some special talent. God needs you. Let obedience to your mother anchor you in your days of preparation, and you will be ready when responsibility calls you.

"Is the Lord's hand waxed short? thou shalt see now whether my word shall come to pass unto thee or not." Numbers 11:23.

We feel sorry that the children of Israel grumbled and murmured about the manna God provided for them in the wilderness. Nobody but a mighty God with a mighty hand could have supplied the tons of manna necessary to feed that great multitude every day. And God had to punish them for their grumbling and murmuring. Remember that, the next time you are tempted to grumble about having to eat spinach or turnips or squash or anything else you do not particularly like. Also remember that we have the same mighty God with the same mighty hand today, and when we are in need He can provide us food as easily as He provided food for the Israelites.

Once upon a time there lived on the Isle of Wight a sea captain by the name of Sargent. He was the first Seventh-day Adventist on the island. His wife and twelve children dreaded the many long days he was away sailing the seven seas. Once Captain Sargent was delayed because of a terrible storm. At home Mrs. Sargent used up the last shilling and saw the last food in the pantry disappear, and still the captain did not come home. What could they do? There was only one thing left to do—they prayed. "Give us this day our daily bread" was their prayer.

While they were praying the woman from the next house knocked on the door. "You know," she said, "I am one of the servants at the king's summer palace on the island here. He was supposed to arrive yesterday, and we had prepared a lot of food for him and his company. But he did not come. We hate to waste the food. Would you mind accepting this basketful? And if you will let the children come with me, there is lots more." So they had food from the king's table until their father came home. One of those twelve children, Alfred, was one of our missionaries in Burma for many years. He loved to tell that story.

During the time of trouble you may wonder sometimes where your food is coming from. Remember, God has promised, "Bread shall be given him; his waters *shall be* sure" (Isaiah 33:16). "When the poor and needy seek water, and there is none . . . , I the God of Israel will not forsake them. I will open rivers in high places, and fountains in the midst of the valleys" (chapter 41:17, 18).

"Jealousy is cruel as the grave: the coals thereof are coals of fire, which hath a most vehement flame." Song of Solomon 8:6.

It is so hard for some people to glory in the success of others. God has placed within each heart the desire to succeed, and without this desire we would be a sorry lot. It is a wonderful thing to be an *honest* winner, but it is also a wonderful thing to be an honest loser. Covetousness, jealousy, envy, revenge, and hate all belong to the same family, and if we are not careful they will lead us to belittle our classmates, our teachers, and even our leaders. Covetousness and jealousy have been at the root of all the wars and all the killings in the world.

History is full of examples of people who have rebelled against their leaders, exactly as did Aaron and Miriam.

Southern radicals did not like President Lincoln. One of the reasons was that he was against slavery. And one week after he was elected, eleven Southern states formed their own government and rebelled against the Union. They bombarded Fort Sumter, in the harbor at Charleston, South Carolina, April 12, 1861, and that started the Civil War, often called the War of the Rebellion. In January, 1863, Lincoln issued his Emancipation Proclamation, which set free 4 million slaves.

The South hated him all the more, and fought on for two more years. Finally, the war was over, on April 9, 1865, and all the slaves were freed. But in that war about 204,000 soldiers were killed on the battlefields and some 414,000 died of disease. Thus, about 618,000 soldiers lost their lives, compared with some 405,000 United States servicemen who perished in World War II. But it was hard for the spirit of rebellion to die out of some people's hearts, and only six days after peace was proclaimed, John Wilkes Booth, a Confederate supporter, with his heart burning for revenge, shot President Lincoln on April 15, 1865.

I like the spirit of people who say, the day after a president is elected, "Yesterday I was against him; today I am for him. He is my president and I am proud of what he is and what he stands for." And when a new president is elected I love to see the outgoing president congratulate him. That is the spirit we all need. See to it that *you* are an honest winner and an honest loser.

"Let us go up at once, and possess it; for we are well able to overcome it."
Numbers 13:30.

What was it that made Joshua and Caleb different from the other eight spies. It was faith. They all saw the goodly land flowing with milk and honey. But eight of them mainly saw the giants. Joshua and Caleb saw a mighty God driving out the wicked nations before them.

One of the greatest men I have ever known was Captain G. F. Jones, although he was actually only five feet four inches tall. He was born in 1864, became a certified sea captain when only twenty-six years old, and accepted the Seventh-day Adventist message a few years later after picking up a page from a *Present Truth* paper on the deck of his ship. In 1902 he became a missionary to the Pacific Islands, and in 1921 he was asked to spend a little time in New Guinea to help those who had been faithfully sowing the seeds of truth there for thirteen years. The situation seemed hopeless, but as he prayed about it, God impressed his heart with the words of Judges 18:9 and 10: "Arise, that we may go up against them: for we have seen the land, and, behold, it is very good: and are ye still? be not slothful to go, and to enter to possess the land. . . . For God hath given it into your hands." Captain Jones took this for a command to go into the interior. He went to see the British commissioner in Port Moresby to obtain permission to go over the mountain.

"You're too small," said the commissioner. "Why, those savages in the interior would eat you."

Drawing himself to the utmost of his five-foot-four-inch height, he replied, "Mr. Commissioner, I may be only a very little man, but I am plenty big enough for God to save New Guinea with if He wants to."

What can you do with a man like that? Nobody could stop him! Up over the mountains he went, and soon the younger men were following along with schools and churches. And that's where those wonderful carriers came from who made a whole contingent of American soldiers keep at least one Sabbath by putting down their bundles as the sun set Friday night and saying, "Sun he go down. God's day he come. We stop." Captain Jones belonged to the tribe of Caleb. It's a good tribe to belong to. Do you belong to it?

"Children, obey your parents in the Lord." Ephesians 6:1.

How hard it was for the children of Israel to learn to obey God! Caleb and Joshua did their best to tell them to go up and possess the land as God had told them to do. But they would not; and they even wanted to stone Caleb and Joshua!

Then the Lord said, "All right, you must wander around in the wilderness for forty years till all the grumblers have died."

"Oh, no," they said, "we are so close now; we will go up after all."

"You'd better not go," said Moses. "God won't go with you now."

"We'll go anyway," they said.

So they went, and the Amalekites smote them.

Josephine Cunnington Edwards tells a story about an African boy named Watford whose father was one of our schoolteachers in Nyasaland. "You cannot go swimming in the river, my son!" said his mother. "There are crocodiles in it. Only last year two boys were eaten."

Watford scowled. In the distance he could hear the happy shouts of other children swimming. "Mother and Father don't want me to have any fun," he whined. Then while Mother wasn't looking he darted off to the river. "I'll just look on," he said to himself.

But on the way he met another boy. "Didn't your father tell you not to go swimming?" he asked.

"Yes."

"Well, mine did too, but I'm just going to slip in and out—just to cool off."

"I am too. There are no crocodiles there. Our fathers just don't want us to have any fun, that's all." They pulled off their clothes and slipped into the water.

But the other lad didn't slip out again. There *was* a crocodile there; the boy let out a horrible scream and disappeared. Watford and everybody else jumped out in an awful hurry and scrambled up the riverbank to safety. But he will never forget the fleeting glimpse of the horror-filled face and clutching hands of the boy who helped him to disobey.

When God and your parents tell you to obey, you had better do it and save yourself a lot of sadness.

"Even to morrow the Lord will shew who are his, and who is holy; and will cause him to come near unto him." Numbers 16:5.

It is easy to tell who are the workers God has chosen to be leaders. Like Moses and Aaron, they are humble and reluctant to accept the responsibility. It is also easy to tell which workers choose themselves. Like Korah, Dathan, and Abiram, they are proud and ambitious, and they "lift up" themselves above the congregation. Sister White says in *Messages to Young People,* "Each has his place in the eternal plan of heaven. Each is to work in cooperation with Christ for the salvation of souls. Not more surely is the place prepared for us in the heavenly mansions than is the special place designated on earth where we are to work for God."—Page 219.

The history of the Advent message is full of accounts of humble young people who have found their special place in the service of God. James White was only 21 years old when he began to preach, and he won a thousand people to the truth in six weeks. Ellen Harmon was only 17 when she humbly became a mouthpiece for God. Uriah Smith was 21, J. N. Loughborough was 20, and S. N. Haskell was 19 when they each began to preach.

Another of the pioneers—Luther Warren—was only a boy of 14 when his heart burned within him to do something for God. But he didn't go to the conference president and say, "Are you the only one who can lead out in this work? Let me have a turn now." Oh, no. Luther humbly began to influence his companions for Christ. One day he was walking down the road with Harry Fenner, 17 years old, and they were talking about what they could do to further the Advent cause. "Harry, let's go over the fence and pray about it," said Luther. So they climbed over the rail fence, found a quiet place among the bushes, and prayed. Soon they had a little band of boys praying with them, and doing helpful work for the sick and needy.

Do you wonder that when Luther Warren had graduated God chose him to be a preacher and a leader? He sought ways to do God's work, and in 1894 he organized the first MV Sunshine Band, which idea in a few more years had spread around the world.

God has a special place for *you* too. Keep humble, and He will lead you to it.

"And it shall come to pass, that the man's rod, whom I shall choose, shall blossom." Numbers 17:5.

God worked a miracle to show to Israel that Aaron and his family had been chosen among the tribe of Levi for the priesthood. And there was no mistaking it, Aaron's rod not only blossomed but also yielded almonds. When God calls *you* to higher responsibility He will make it very plain, even if He has to work a miracle, that all may know He has chosen you. About the middle of the eighteenth century, David Brainerd heard about a savage tribe of Indians living in the New Jersey forests. He felt called of God to go and preach Christ to them. The more he prayed about it, the more burdened he became, and feeling sure that God was indeed calling him, he made his plans and took his journey through the wilderness until he found himself near their village. Here he camped awhile to rest, and to pray that angels would attend him on this dangerous undertaking. When he at last reached their wigwams, he was astonished to find the whole village out to meet him, as though he were a long-looked-for friend. He had expected to find hostile enemies, but led by their chief they welcomed him and reverenced him as if he were a prophet. He stayed with them and preached, and raised up a Christian church of seventy or eighty members. It was years later that he found out the secret of their early friendship. Their scouts had discovered him as he journeyed toward them and had decided to kill him when he retired in his tent. Peering between the folds of the canvas, they found him kneeling in prayer. And as they watched they saw a rattlesnake crawl over his feet, pause beside him a moment, then glide out of the tent on the opposite side. The scouts hurried back to their village and told with great excitement that a man under the protection of the Great Spirit was coming to them. Even the savage Indians knew that Brainerd's "rod had blossomed." Keep close to God. You need never be in doubt. God can make *your* rod blossom and bear almonds too.

"The spirit of covetousness, of seeking for the highest position and the highest wage, is rife in the world. The old-time spirit of self-denial and self-sacrifice is too seldom met with. But this is the only spirit that can actuate a true follower of Jesus."—*Messages to Young People,* p. 303.

"He shall dwell on high: his place of defence shall be the munitions of rocks: bread shall be given him; his waters shall be sure." Isaiah 33:16.

Five of us missionaries were fleeing from the war in Burma in March, 1942. We were in a group of about two hundred evacuees. One afternoon as we came down the hillside to the camp, the captain shouted out, "There's only water enough here for eighty people. Drink only half a cup of water each, and no face washing and no tooth brushing." It made us feel more thirsty than ever, but when we got to camp the good people formed lines by the five-gallon cans of chlorinated water, each waiting patiently to get a drink. But when the selfish ones came, they pushed and shoved and snatched water from others, and soon the water was all gone. "There's a spring coming out of a rock not far away," someone shouted. So over to the spring we all went, but the line was too long. I decided to wait until after the evening soup and campfire worship. At this time there were only six men standing in line, so I took my place at the end of the line and waited with our three waterpots.

"Push up to the spring," said the first man to leave. "You're a white man. They are only coolies."

"Not tonight," I replied. "I'll wait my turn like a Christian."

Then the five men in front of me began to jabber. "Ta-ta-ta-ta-ta-ta-ta," said the man in front of me as he wriggled his fingers up and down, and I knew he had recognized me as the man who had played the trumpet at campfire. It felt wonderful to be recognized as a Christian at nighttime in no-man's-land. Just then the next man moved away, and we all took one step nearer to the spring. The next thing I knew, this man had filled my waterpots from his can of water. Then pointing to *my* heart, he lisped in broken English, "You Clistian." Then pointing to *his* heart, he lisped, "Me Clistian."

I tried to talk to him in English, in Hindustani, in Burmese, in Karen; but it was no use. So I just threw my arm over his shoulder and patted his back, and he threw his arm over my shoulder and patted my back, and together we said over and over, "You Clistian; me Clistian." God's wonderful "Clistian" water—the sweetest I ever drank.

Someday you'll need water. Keep close to God; He has promised that your *water* shall be sure.

"Make thee a fiery serpent, and set it upon a pole: and . . . every one that is bitten, when he looketh upon it, shall live." Numbers 21:8.

There was no healing power in the bronze figure of the fiery serpent on that pole. The power was with God, and it required an act of faith and obedience on the part of the sufferers to receive that healing power. Israel already had been taught a severe lesson about worshiping graven images, and this time they did not worship the image of the serpent. But they did preserve it, and a later generation did worship it and burn incense before it, and King Hezekiah destroyed it. It is interesting to see how some of the Bible stories have been changed and carried over into the legends of other nations. The Greeks and Romans worshiped the sun, and called the god of light, who drove the chariot of the sun, Apollo. They said Apollo had a son called Aesculapius, who was taught the art of medicine and became so skilled that he could restore life to the dead. In art Aesculapius is represented as a strong, earnest youth bearing a knotted staff around which a serpent is entwined. The staff is called a caduceus.

Have you ever seen a caduceus anywhere? If you look at the insignia of the United States Medical Corps, there you will find it—a staff with two serpents entwining it and surmounted by wings. If you ever become a medical doctor, the caduceus will be on your insignia also. But remember, there is no charm in that caduceus. It has no power to protect you or to heal. It is only used as a symbol of healing. Your protection, as well as all healing power, is still in the hands of God. Keep your eyes *on* Him and your faith *in* Him.

Through His servant, God has given us much instruction, which, if we will only *look upon it* and heed it, will mean life to us. "Health is a blessing of which few appreciate the value; yet upon it the efficiency of our mental and physical powers largely depends. . . . By allowing ourselves to form wrong habits, by keeping late hours, by gratifying appetite at the expense of health, we lay the foundation for feebleness." "Without health, no one can . . . fulfill his obligations to himself, to his fellow-beings, or to his Creator. Therefore the health should be as carefully guarded as the character."—*Messages to Young People,* pp. 235, 232.

"Then the Lord opened the eyes of Balaam, and he saw the angel of the Lord standing in the way." Numbers 22:31.

When Balaam's eyes were opened he not only saw the angel but also realized that the Lord had opened the mouth of a dumb animal, and he had actually seen it and heard it speak.

Today is the birthday of another man whose eyes were opened, and who under the blessing of God was able to make *wire* talk. Alexander Graham Bell was born in Scotland in 1847. It was time for the third angel's message to go to all the world. It was time for knowledge to be increased. Bell's father was a teacher of speech in Edinburgh University and had specialized in the technique of lip movements, so that students could be taught to speak correctly. With his system of "visible speech" he also succeeded in teaching people who had been born deaf to speak. Young Alexander was intensely interested in his father's work, and he carried on some experiments of his own at home. By manipulating the lower jaw of his pet dog, he actually succeeded in teaching it the sounds "Ow-ah-oo, ga-ma-ma," which he interpreted to mean "How are you, Grandmamma?" His friends were delighted with his demonstrations.

By the time he was 17 he was teaching in a small academy. He soon went to London to attend the university there. While there he experimented in teaching deaf-born children, and he was successful. Soon after this the family moved to Canada, and before long he was teaching in a school for deaf mutes in Boston. He was so successful that he won a professorship in Boston University. By 1844 the telegraph had been invented, and with a friend, Thomas Watson, he began his experiments in carrying the human voice over a wire. Many people laughed at him, but he kept at it and at it, until on March 10, 1876, Watson heard Bell calling clearly over the wire, "Watson, come here; I want you." And today there are 151,000,000 telephones in the United States.

One little peep into the telephone exchange room at the General Conference office would show you how much this invention is helping to do the work of God speedily. If *you* keep close to God, He can open your eyes and cause *you* to speak for Him too.

"Surely there is no enchantment against Jacob, neither is there any divination against Israel: . . . it shall be said of Jacob and of Israel, What hath God wrought!" Numbers 23:23.

As the message of the third angel has been taken to country after country around the world, Satan has stirred up many Balaks to try to curse God's work. Religious leaders, devil doctors, bandits, apostates—all have tried, but the work of God goes on.

Our first mission among the Quechua Indians was established by Pedro Kalbermatter and his brave wife. The people wanted our missionaries and had already built a house for them, but the landowners and the religious leaders did not want them. They knew that missions meant education and gospel light, and they wanted to keep the people in darkness and ignorance. So they told Pedro to get out of the country by a certain date and threatened his life if he did not.

Pedro stayed on, and one morning while he was working on a schoolhouse he saw a mob of angry white men riding toward him. His first thought was to protect himself with his rifle, but he thought, No! Jesus wouldn't do that, so he quickly buried his gun, and then committing himself to God, he went out to meet them. Cursing and threatening, they ordered him to go away. He answered kindly that the Lord had brought him there and he would stay till the Lord should send him away. They tried to ride him down, but not a horse would ride over him or even strike him with its hoofs.

At last, baffled and still cursing, the mob rode away, and Pedro Kalbermatter and his brave wife stayed. Today we have 337 churches and about 152,000 church members in the Inca Union Mission! And although our enemies laughed when the early Sabbathkeepers began to proclaim the third angel's message, and prophesied it would soon come to nought, today there are 5,340,000 Sabbath school members in all the world. With Balaam we say, "What hath God wrought!"

Someday enemies may try to bewitch or curse *you.* Never fear. The words of Balaam are still true: "He hath blessed: and I cannot reverse it."

Make God first and you will find that "they that be with us are more than they that be with them" (2 Kings 6:16). And you can say, "If God be for us, who can be against us?" (Romans 8:31).

"There shall come a Star out of Jacob, and a Sceptre shall rise out of Israel." Numbers 24:17.

Balaam's prophecy of the Star that would rise out of Jacob was remembered down through the ages for fourteen hundred years. Then King Jesus was born, and a host of shining angels praised God and took up their abode over Bethlehem. Then the Wise Men in the East saw the glory of this distant company of angels as a great and glorious star. They followed it and found Jesus. All the stars are the handiwork of God, and if we will but take time to look at them, and think of their greatness, their brightness, and their dependability, they will help us find our way out of the darkness of discouragement and despair and into the light of the presence of God.

In China there is an old legend of two surveyors who were crossing a trackless desert. They had a rough map they had made from information other travelers had given them. There was a tree marked on it here and there, and it showed the dry bed of a little stream and a hill or two.

But one night a terrible storm arose. They hid in a cave while the lightning flashed, the thunder roared, and the rain pelted down. When morning came the landmarks had all been swept away, and they realized that they were lost. Their map was useless. All day long they tried to figure out some way to safety, but there seemed no way out. They were desperate. Night came again, but with the night there came the stars. "We're saved! We're saved!" cried one of the men. "The stars are still there." The stars were still there, and the men took their direction from the stars and found their way back home again.

David spoke truly when he said, "The heavens declare the glory of God; and the firmament sheweth his handywork. Day unto day uttereth speech, and night unto night sheweth knowledge. There is no speech nor language, where their voice is not heard. Their line is gone out through all the earth, and their words to the end of the world" (Psalm 19:1-4).

If *you* ever get lost in discouragement or despair, look up at the stars and find your way back to God.

"The name of the Lord is a strong tower: the righteous runneth into it, and is safe." Proverbs 18:10.

Did you ever hear our Seventh-day Adventist schools and colleges called cities of refuge for Seventh-day Adventist boys and girls? Well, they certainly are. In this great battle of life the devil is seeking the life of every one of us, and thousands of our workers can bear testimony to the truth that our schools and our colleges have saved them from certain destruction in the world.

Once upon a time there was a boy named Dick. He was the youngest son in a family of six. His mother died when he was only 9 years old, but his big sister Lottie took charge. Lottie was a Seventh-day Adventist, so Dick and his brother went to Sabbath school and church with her, and after a few years Dick was baptized. But Dick went to public school, then high school. He was very popular, and the school clubs, parties, and dances got a hold on him. He played football, and it became an idol to him. He played on Sabbath in spite of the pleadings of his father and his sister. And it looked as if the world just about had him, when one Sabbath while he was playing in the last test game of the season he broke his leg and was carried from the ball field to the hospital. Then he had time to think. Lottie's last words to him before the game, "I'll be praying for you," came to him again and again.

His leg got better, but there was a change in him. One thing after another happened to remind him of God. Then one day he found his Bible in his suitcase. He took it up and read "My son, give me thine heart." He went to an Adventist youth meeting, reconsecrated himself to God, and finally went to Walla Walla College. At last he was safe. No more Sabbathbreaking, no more dances, no more football; instead, an intense burden to become a missionary to the Indians in Peru possessed him. And you can read the whole entrancing story in Richard A. Hayden's book *From Football Field to Mission Field.* Had it not been for our Adventist city of refuge in Walla Walla, the cause of God would have been robbed of a valuable missionary. Make sure *you* go to your Adventist church school, then to your Adventist academy, and then to your Adventist college—and you too will be safe.

"As an eagle stirreth up her nest, [and] fluttereth over her young . . . : so the Lord alone did lead him." Deuteronomy 32:11, 12.

The eagle has become a symbol of courage, swiftness, and strength. When the United States became a nation the bald eagle was selected as its emblem.

A little more than 120 years ago an Indian traded a bald eagle to a farmer for a bushel of corn. The eagle became a great pet and when the farmer joined the Army and went to take part in the Civil War, the eagle went too. The farmer soldier was in the Eighth Wisconsin Regiment, and the eagle became the regiment's mascot. They called it Old Baldy. When the regiment was moved up to the front lines during the battle of Atlanta, Old Baldy went with them, and as you can imagine, when the guns were booming and the bullets were flying, it was very encouraging to the soldiers to see Old Baldy flying around above them and to hear him screaming defiantly.

One day Old Baldy was nowhere to be seen, and when the eagle regiment went into battle, the men were discouraged and blue. If Old Baldy had deserted them, it must mean bad luck. As the first shots were fired, however, with a scream and a screech Old Baldy came zooming down from the sky. A great cheer went up, their weariness and their troubles were forgotten, and the eagle regiment rushed on to win the battle. When at last Old Baldy died, he was stuffed, and placed in the Wisconsin capitol.

Sometimes an eagle finds itself in a dark valley, surrounded with storm and clouds, but it won't stay there. With its mighty wings it darts upward, pierces the clouds, and is once more in the clear sunshine above.

The darkness and the tempest are now below it, and the eagle rejoices to be in its own beloved nest. It took a great deal of effort and faith to go through the darkness, but what a satisfying reward was gained!

So we may be surrounded by difficulties, discouragement, and darkness; but we need not stay there. With a will and a prayer, on the wings of faith, we can rise into the sunlight of the presence of God.

"The eternal God is thy refuge, and underneath are the everlasting arms."
Deuteronomy 33:27.

Moses was the man of God who led and counseled and blessed the children of Israel. We are the spiritual children of Israel, and the man of God who led and counseled and blessed the early Adventists was James White.

James was the fifth child in a family of nine, and as a child he was not very strong. But by the time he was 16 his health began to improve. He made rapid strides in his schoolwork, and at 19 years of age he was teaching school. The family were all members of the Christian church, and when they heard William Miller, Joshua Himes, and T. M. Preble preach about the second coming of Christ, one by one they believed. Young James was a dynamic leader, and he felt impelled to preach, but who would support him? There was no Adventist Church yet, and he couldn't expect his Christian church to support him, and he had no funds of his own. Still, he felt he must go. So one day his father said, "Well, James, if you must go, I'll give you the use of a horse for the winter. And may the God of our fathers support and bless you." Then a neighbor said, "I have a saddle and some straps you can make a bridle of. You may have them for your horse." So, taking his prophetic chart and his books, and buttoning them under his heavy winter coat, off he went.

One night he was preaching in a schoolhouse and a group of rough men, urged on by some angry Universalists, began to disturb the meeting with catcalls, howls, and snowballs. It was impossible for James's voice to be heard. But he would not stop. He closed his Bible, and lifting up his voice, cried, "Repent and call on God for mercy and pardon." The noise quieted down, and a hundred people rose for prayer that night. But the mob was not through yet. They gathered around outside the entrance, but just then a man of "noble countenance" came up to James White, and taking him by the arm, led him through the mob. He turned to thank the man as soon as they were free, but the man was not there! Who was the man? Can you guess? That's what Moses meant when he said, "The eternal God is thy refuge." Someday you may need help. Remember that His everlasting arms are around *you* too.

"And there arose not a prophet since in Israel like unto Moses, whom the Lord knew face to face." Deuteronomy 34:10.

Let me tell you some more about James White, who was the "Moses" of the early Adventists. The year 1844 came. In the summer of that year James met a lovely young woman who was nearly 17 years old and whose name was Ellen Harmon. October 22 came, the day on which the early Adventists thought Jesus would come the second time. The disappointment was terrible, but God brought comfort to the believers through Ellen. He gave light to the brethren about the true meaning of the cleansing of the sanctuary. He brought the Sabbath truth to the little Adventist group in Washington, New Hampshire. One by one, some of the Adventists accepted the Sabbath. One by one they were disfellowshipped from the other churches, or they left of their own desire. James and Ellen were married in 1846, and the third angel's message was on its way. It was a small group. The people were poor, but they had a Moses in James White and they had a prophetess in Ellen.

Soon the publishing work was begun and in 1863 the General Conference was organized and the name *Seventh-day Adventist* chosen. The next year James White was elected the second General Conference president, and he held this office during three separate periods for more than ten years. During this time Sabbath schools were organized and the tithing system was adopted. By 1880 James White had seen the Seventh-day Adventist believers grow in number from a mere handful to more than fifteen thousand church members. The following year he was stricken with a malignant form of malaria, and on August 6, 1881, he passed away.

"Is Jesus precious to you?" Ellen whispered to James, when she saw death was near.

"Yes, oh, yes," he answered faintly.

"Have you no desire to live?"

"No," he replied weakly.

"Jesus loves you. The everlasting arms are beneath you."

"Yes, yes," he said. And so another Moses passed to his rest.

Pray that God will give you confidence in the leaders of this great cause and keep you always loyal to them.

"Be strong and of a good courage; be not afraid . . . : for the Lord thy God is with thee whithersoever thou goest." Joshua 1:9.

Strong faith and courage were always prominent in the life of Joshua, the second pioneer leader in Israel. Strong faith and courage have always been prominent in the lives of the pioneers of the Advent Movement. Perhaps one of the most courageous was J. N. Loughborough. He was only a boy of 12 in 1844, at the time of the Disappointment. But he was on fire with love for the Lord. When he was 17 years old he began to preach. They called him the boy preacher, and his genial, youthful, dependable nature, with the blessing of God, brought him success. When he was 20 years old he attended some meetings held by J. N. Andrews, and soon accepted the Sabbath truth. He kept on preaching, but at that time we had no organization and no pay; every man with a message had to preach at his own expense, relying on the gratitude and generosity of his hearers.

But it was not easy, and four years later, in addition to preaching on Sabbath and Sunday, John had to work in the hay fields and do harvesting to make ends meet. "This is too much," said Mrs. Loughborough. "We can't live any longer in this way." And in a moment of discouragement John said, "Mary, let us go to Waukon. I'll make a living at carpentry, and as I can, I will preach the message." They went to Waukon, Iowa, but not for long. A few weeks later James and Ellen White came to visit them, and their courage revived. They came back to the work and stayed with it through thick and thin.

At the General Conference in 1868 an earnest appeal was made for workers to be sent to build up the little company in San Francisco. Go to California? Why, in those days going to California was like going to the farthest parts of the earth. But J. N. Loughborough and D. T. Bourdeau volunteered to go. It took them twenty-four days to go by boat to Panama, then by train across the isthmus to the Pacific coast, and by boat again to San Francisco; but they had come to a new land and were filled with faith and courage.

Sometimes into your life will come days when things go wrong and disappointments threaten to discourage you. Think then of the examples of these pioneers and be strong and of good courage.

*"We have heard how the Lord dried up the water of the Red sea for you.
. . . The Lord your God, he is God in heaven above, and in earth beneath."*
Joshua 2:10, 11.

The Lord has many ways of letting the people "hear" in advance
about His power, and about the coming of His messengers. The day after
Elders Loughborough and Bourdeau arrived in San Francisco a stranger
from Petaluma, a town about fifty miles to the north, called on them. He
was a member of an independent church and he said, "We saw a news
item in a newspaper saying that two men with a tent were sailing for
California, intending to hold evangelistic meetings, and we prayed that
if these men were the Lord's servants, they would have a prosperous
journey. Then one of our number dreamed that he saw two men kindling
fires to light up the surrounding country, but the ministers in Petaluma
tried to put the fires out by throwing brush and turf on them; but the fires
flamed higher and higher, till at last one of them said, 'It is no use; leave
them alone. The more we try to put out the fires the better they burn.'
They sent me to San Francisco to see if I could find them, and to see if
they would hold some meetings in Petaluma. And I have found you. Will
you come?"

The elders saw in all this the leading of their mighty God, and in less
than a month they opened meetings in the tent in Petaluma.

The ministers in that town began their opposition, just as the dream
had shown, but nothing could put the fires out. After raising up a church
in Petaluma they went to Windsor, then Piner, then Santa Rosa, then
Healdsburg, and soon there were churches in these five towns. There was
opposition in each place till at last the ministers got together and said,
"Let the Adventists alone. The more we oppose them the more their
doctrine spreads."

Several years later, in December, 1884, Elder Loughborough was
back in California again, holding some revival meetings in the little
church in Ferndale. Among those who were baptized at that time was a
young woman named Henrietta Johnson. And a few years later she
became my mother!

Learn to trust this great God, and let Him go before you and select
your school, your place of abode, and your work for Him.

"Sanctify yourselves: for to morrow the Lord will do wonders among you." Joshua 3:5.

The next day after Joshua said these words, all the Israelites passed over the Jordan River on dry ground. It was a miracle, and thereby everybody who heard about it knew that the living God was among His people.

The same living God still works miracles for His servants. It was November, 1856. Elder and Mrs. White were visiting the churches in Illinois, holding meetings and strengthening and encouraging the brethren, when a definite burden came to Sister White that a company in Iowa, two hundred miles away, needed help. It was good sleighing weather, and Brother Hart and Brother Everts prepared to take the Whites to this place in a two-horse sleigh. Then it rained for twenty-four hours. "We must give up the journey," said Brother White; but Sister White said, "We shall go."

"Yes," replied Brother White, "if the Lord works a miracle."

The next day it turned colder and began to snow. At 5:00 p.m. they began their journey and got as far as Green Vale. It snowed for days. They were snowbound for a week. Then they started again and got to a hotel a few miles from the great Mississippi River. The river was frozen over, but again it began to rain. There was danger that the rain would melt the ice so it would not be possible for the horses to draw the sleigh over it.

"Can we cross the river?" they asked everyone they met.

"No." "It's risky." "I'd never try it." "Some have already broken through the ice." "You can't make it." These answers stunned them.

"We have come to the Red Sea," said Brother Hart. "Shall we cross?"

"Go forward, trusting in Israel's God," said Sister White.

And they went on. The sound of the horses' hoofs on the ice was fearful. But on they went. Men gathered on the opposite bank to watch them. They prayed and kept going, and at last they reached the Iowa riverbank! The God who had parted the waters of the Jordan River for the ancient Israelites had frozen the waters of this much greater river to let these servants pass safely over.

The living God is your God. Sanctify yourself every day. Who can tell? Maybe tomorrow *you* will need a miracle.

"When your children shall ask their fathers in time to come, saying, What mean these stones? Then ye shall let your children know, saying, Israel came over this Jordan on dry land." Joshua 4:21, 22.

I'm so glad we have memorials that remind us of God's mighty works. I would love to have seen that stone memorial in Gilgal that reminded everybody about the way God brought His people into the land of Canaan. We have a memorial in Washington, New Hampshire, that reminds us of the way God brought into being His remnant church. It is a little white church in the valley not far from Millen Pond. In 1844 it was one of the Christian churches. One Sunday the district elder, Frederick Wheeler, who was a Methodist Adventist, was conducting the communion service. In the congregation that morning was a visitor, Mrs. Rachel Oakes Preston, the mother of their schoolteacher. In his sermon Elder Wheeler said, "All who confess communion with Christ in such a service as this should be ready to obey God and keep His commandments in all things."

He noticed that the visitor was quite agitated, and after the service he went to visit her in her daughter's home. "I came near getting up in the meeting and saying something," she said.

"What did you have in mind to say?" asked Brother Wheeler kindly.

"I wanted to tell you that you had better set that communion table back and put the cloth over it until *you* begin to keep the commandments of God," said Mrs. Preston. Then he remembered that this good woman was a Seventh Day Baptist who believed that Christians should keep Saturday for Sunday. They talked and visited together, and not many weeks later Elder Wheeler kept his first Sabbath. This was in March, 1844. Several of the members of that little church joined him, and that was the first group of Sabbathkeeping Adventists. That little church still stands. It is only a memorial now, but one of the greatest thrills I have ever had was to knock on the door of the Farnsworth home one day and get the key and go into the little white church. I stood in the pulpit where Frederick Wheeler spoke those words. Then I told my children the story I have just told you.

Keep your eyes open for memorials that will remind you of the certainty of the Advent message.

"By faith the walls of Jericho fell down, after they were compassed about seven days." Hebrews 11:30.

God is still able to make walls fall down flat if He can find the right kind of faith in the hearts of His servants. Missionary L. B. Halliwell told a wonderful story many years ago about one of our colporteurs, Brother Andre, who made his headquarters in Fortaleza, in northeast Brazil. One day a man from a distant town bought a copy of *Bible Readings.* On his way back home he read and studied, and by the time he arrived he was keeping the seventh-day Sabbath. He began at once to tell his friends, and soon a little group was keeping the Sabbath with him. Some months later a minister from another church in this distant town happened to meet Brother Andre while he was in Fortaleza on business.

"Quite a group of people are keeping your Sabbath in our town," he said. "You'd better go up there and preach to them."

Brother Andre started off at once on the long trip. At last he came to a village twenty-five miles from the place. He began to inquire around for a mule that he could hire to make this last part of the journey. Soon a policeman appeared and took him to the mayor.

"What are you going to do out there?" asked the mayor.

"I'm going to visit my friends and preach to them," answered Brother Andre.

"No, you're not!" said the mayor. "You can visit them all you want, but it is against the law to preach, and if you try to preach, I'll have the police arrest you and put you in the brand-new jail there."

"Then you had better arrest me now and put me in jail now," said Brother Andre, "for I am going there and I am going to preach."

"But we can't arrest you before you break the law," said the mayor.

"Well, I'm going," said Brother Andre. And he did go.

But while he was preaching and while the policeman was getting ready to arrest him, the Lord sent a great storm and a great wind, and it blew upon that brand-new jail—and its walls fell down flat! Brother Andre kept on preaching, and a few months later, when Mr. Halliwell and some other workers went up to baptize the group, the brand-new jail was still in ruins.

Remember that there is nothing too hard for the living God to do for you if *you* have the right kind of faith.

"The love of money is the root of all evil." 1 Timothy 6:10.

The temptation to see, then covet, then take comes to everyone, rich and poor alike. When it came to Achan, he failed and bore the penalty. It came to a certain millionaire that Lora E. Clement tells about in her fine book *Managing Yourself.* This rich man failed to overcome the temptation also, and he went to jail for a long prison sentence. One day an old friend visited him and found him with needle and twine, sewing bags.

"Hello," said the friend, "I see you are sewing!"

"No," replied the rich man, "I'm reaping!"

Just so surely will everyone reap who covets and steals. But there are thousands of Seventh-day Adventist boys and girls who are so strictly honest that a temptation to covet and take has no appeal to them. One such young man was Bill. He went into a bank to cash a check for $20. The cashier counted out two fives and a ten. "That makes $20," he said.

Bill took the money in his hand and turned to go. But before leaving the bank he paused to check his money. There *were* two fives but there were also two tens. The two tens must have been stuck together! For the briefest second the temptation came to keep it. But Bill was just too honest. He went right back and very quietly explained it to the cashier and gave the extra $10 back.

Do you think he was foolish? Listen! A few months later the bank manager needed a chauffeur to drive his car. Bill was looking for work, and the cashier recommended Bill to the bank manager for the job.

"I'd trust that chap with a truckload of diamonds!" he said. "He's as honest as a spotlight! He's a Seventh-day Adventist."

Bill got the job, kept it for a while, then the bank manager made him his private stenographer! Not so foolish, was he?

"Never underrate the importance of little things. . . . It is by them that the soul is trained that it may grow into the likeness of Christ, or bear the likeness of evil. God helps us to cultivate habits of thought, word, look, and action that will testify to all about us that we have been with Jesus and learned of Him!"—*Messages to Young People,* p. 202.

"Fear not, neither be thou dismayed: . . . arise, go up to Ai. . . . For the Lord your God will deliver it into your hand." Joshua 8:1-7.

In the great Christian warfare against Satan and the·powers of darkness there have been many Ai's where it has been humanly impossible to establish a mission, and where only the Lord our God could deliver these places into our hands.

Take the island of Mussau, for instance. It was one of the bloodiest of all the islands in the Matthias group. No white man had ever landed on that island and lived. One day in 1931 Missionary Gilbert McLaren, with a group of Seventh-day Adventist young men from the Solomon Islands, anchored near one of the large villages on the island, hoping to go ashore and visit. In a very short time a dozen war canoes filled with angry, gesticulating warriors circled the mission launch *Veilomani I.* They shook their spears, beat their war clubs on the sides of their canoes, and shouted, "Go! Go! Go!" The more they shouted, the more menacing they became; and Missionary McLaren didn't know what to do. Even the Solomon Islands boys were afraid. Then God told the missionary what to do, and turning to his boys, McLaren said, "Sing!" And immediately their voices blended harmoniously in the beautiful song and words "Anywhere with Jesus I can safely go."

As they sang, the fierce warriors stopped their blood-curdling shouts and stopped banging their clubs against the sides of their canoes. The boys kept on singing. They sang every hymn they knew, then began all over again; and as the sun set, the war canoes silently paddled back to the village.

Early the next morning the chief himself came out. "Could you teach my people to sing like that?" he asked.

"Of course we could," said Missionary McLaren, "but it would take time. We would have to have a school. They would have to learn to read and write."

The chief nodded his head. "We want! We want!" he said.

In a few weeks the *Veilomani I* returned with two Solomon Islands missionaries, Salau and Oti, and before too long Mussau was a Christian island.

Is there an Ai in your life? Don't be discouraged. The Lord our God can give you the victory over it too. And He will.

"Choose you this day whom ye will serve; . . . but as for me and my house, we will serve the Lord." Joshua 24:15.

This beautiful invitation has helped many a young person to make a decision for Christ, and in turn it has been used by thousands of them to invite others to come to Christ. Today is the day set aside to honor the first missionary to Ireland—known to the world as Saint Patrick. He was born in southern Scotland and was taken prisoner by a band of Irish pirates in A.D. 411. He was only 16 years old at the time, and although his parents were Christians, he had not yet made his decision for Christ. He was set to herding his pagan master's swine and cattle on the hills of Antrim, and there in his loneliness he felt the need of God to help him forsake his sins. He gave his whole heart to God.

After six years of slavery he managed to escape and find his way back to his home in Scotland. As he studied to become a worker for God, he seemed to hear a voice from Ireland constantly calling, "We beseech thee, child of God, come and again walk with us." Early in his middle life he went back to Ireland and entered upon his lifework. He knew the language. He knew the needs of the people. He preached the Word and pleaded with souls to receive it. Many legends have been connected with Patrick's name. The Catholics claimed he was one of their bishops and made him a saint. But there is much evidence that shows he believed in the supreme word of God and had no allegiance to papal authority. He reduced the Irish language to writing and established schools; and there are definite indications that the early Irish church kept the seventh-day Sabbath. He lived to see Christianity triumph over the Irish pagan religion of druidism.

On the hill of Tara, where once the fires blazed on the druids' altars, there now stands a great statue of Patrick. It shows him with crook and miter, dressed like a Catholic bishop. But to us a far better memorial is the green hill of Slemish where as a slave boy Patrick first made his choice to serve God. He little realized what great results the blessing of God would bring because of that humble decision. In every land young people are making similar decisions.

Have you made your decision to serve God yet? If not, why not choose to do it this day?

"If the dew be on the fleece only . . . , then shall I know that thou wilt save Israel by mine hand, as thou hast said." Judges 6:37.

The Lord often has been pleased to give His servants signs so they might know that He is leading and guiding them. It was in November, 1846, about two years after the Great Disappointment, that the early Advent believers were called to a meeting in Topsham, Maine. Though they were good Adventists, James and Ellen White had not yet seen the importance of keeping the seventh-day Sabbath. They were at this meeting. So also was Captain Joseph Bates. He already had accepted the seventh-day Sabbath truth, but he was not so sure that Sister White was a messenger of God and that her visions were from God. You may be sure that Joseph Bates did his best to persuade the Whites of the Sabbath truth, and as he talked with them he often referred to the stars and other heavenly bodies, for as a sea captain he was a great lover of astronomy. Sister White, however, couldn't talk very well about the stars, "for," she confessed, "I have never looked into a book on astronomy." Nevertheless, one day during a meeting Mrs. White was taken off in vision and began describing the stars. Captain Bates was thrilled. "Now she is describing Jupiter," he said; "now Saturn and now the nebula in Orion, and she is telling more than the astronomers know," he exclaimed. That was all the sign he needed. From that time on he was a firm believer in the Lord's messenger. A few weeks after this experience Sister White had another vision. She saw the ark in the heavenly sanctuary; and in the ark were the Ten Commandments; and there was a halo of light around the fourth commandment. And that was all the sign she and Brother White needed. They began at once to keep the seventh-day Sabbath.

Thus it was that each helped the other, and the early remnant church was strengthened and blessed.

"The leader whom God chose to overthrow the Midianites, occupied no prominent position in Israel. He was not a ruler, a priest, or a Levite. He thought himself the least in his father's house. But God saw in him a man of courage and integrity. He was distrustful of himself, and willing to follow the guidance of the Lord."—*Patriarchs and Prophets,* p. 553.

Keep close to God. Maybe one day your "fleece" may be "wet."

"When I blow with a trumpet. . . , then blow ye the trumpets also on every side of all the camp, and say, The sword of the Lord, and of Gideon." Judges 7:18.

The blowing of trumpets is connected with victory for the cause of God on several occasions in the Bible story. In our modern story of missions the blowing of trumpets has brought success in a number of mission fields also. During the early years of our ministry among the Karens of Burma I used to take from ten to fifteen of my biggest schoolboys on a tour each summer vacation, to teach them how to preach. We carried a supply of simple medicines, a complete stereopticon outfit to show pictures on the life of Christ, and I always took my trumpet. In the summer of 1921 Brother L. W. Melendy, the Burma Union secretary, and Brother Harold Baird, my associate missionary, accompanied us on our tour and brought their trumpets; so we had three trumpets! One afternoon we came to the tumbledown village of Parkete. The boys took one look at it and said, "Nobody lives here anymore." Looking around, however, we found about a dozen people, so we got ready for our evening program. Half an hour before sunset the three trumpets began to play; half an hour before sunset the people began to come. They came from the village; they came from their nearby gardens and fields where they were camping. There came mothers and fathers, aunties and uncles, grandpas and grandmas, and lots of little children, till there were more than fifty at our meeting that night. "We know what did it," said the boys as they expressed their surprise at the good attendance. "It was the trumpets!" Then they added, "Wouldn't it be wonderful if every one of us had a trumpet!" And right then there was born in my heart a determination to have a brass band in the jungle someday.

The next year we went home to Australia on furlough, and I came back with twenty-three brass horns; and before long we were "blowing our trumpets" from village to village. It was a new day for our preaching. Now everybody came to our meetings; nothing could keep them away. For twenty years the brass band was used by God to overcome fear and superstition. Then, sad to say, it was totally destroyed during World War II. Do you blow a trumpet or play some other musical instrument? Do your very best; dedicate your talent to God; and He will use *you* to put Satan to flight too.

"The Spirit of the Lord came mightily upon him." Judges 14:6.

It was the Spirit of God coming mightily upon Samson who made him strong. What a pity Samson didn't always realize this and keep on walking with God in the path of obedience! The Spirit of God often has come upon His servants mightily and made them strong.

When Sister White was a young woman she weighed only eighty pounds, and she was not very strong physically. But when the Spirit of God came upon her and took her off in vision, she was phenomenally strong. Strong men have tried to move her hands or arms while she was in vision, but could not. One morning in 1845, before she was married and while she was still living with her father and mother in Portland, she was taken off in vision. She walked over to a bureau on which rested the Harmons' big family Bible that weighed 18 1/2 pounds. She picked it up and held it at arm's length in one hand for half an hour while walking around the room. All this time she was not breathing; yet when the vision was ended she felt no fatigue! Under ordinary circumstances she could hardly have lifted that big Bible with both hands.

If you ever visit the office of the Ellen G. White Publications in the General Conference office building you will be able to see that very Bible, and if you try to hold it at arm's length you will know that only the Spirit of God could have enabled her to do such a thing.

In writing to young people Sister White says: "God has made ample provision for His people; and if they rely upon His strength, they will never become the sport of circumstances. The strongest temptation cannot excuse sin. However great the pressure brought to bear upon the soul, transgression is our own act. It is not in the power of earth or hell to compel any one to do evil. Satan attacks us at our weak points, but we need not be overcome. However severe or unexpected the assault, God has provided help for us, and in His strength we may conquer."—*Messages to Young People*, p. 62.

We all need this kind of strength. Only the Spirit of God can give it to us. Let us always walk humbly with God in the path of obedience and be strong.

"And he wist not that the Lord was departed from him." Judges 16:20.

There was no excuse for Samson. He knew that worldly pleasures "destroy all relish for serious thought and for religious services" (*Messages to Young People,* p. 399). He knew there were worldly books and shows that "put God out of the mind, and separate the soul from the true Shepherd" (*ibid.*, p. 276). He knew that marriage with an unbeliever would give him a home "where the shadows are never lifted" (*ibid.*, p. 440) and that connecting with unbelievers would "grieve the Spirit of God and forfeit His protection" (*ibid.*, p. 441). Yes, he knew it all. His godly parents had told him many times, but the saddest thing about it all is that *he didn't know* "that the Lord was departed from him." He thought he was still all right and that everything was fine.

Some time ago, so the story goes, there was a lonely sheepherder on a lonely ranch in the Far West. His only comforts, above the barest necessities of life, were his old violin and a little radio, and in the evening when his work was done he would listen to the news, then tune up his violin, and play the tunes that made his heart happy. One evening he realized that there was something wrong. His pitch was too low and the tunes seemed dull, but what could he do? He had no tuning fork. Then he got an idea. He dropped a card to the radio station and said, "Will you please strike A during your evening broadcast? I'm far away from a piano, and the only comfort I have is my old fiddle. It's all out of tune, so will you please strike A so I can get it in tune again?"

The radioman granted the unusual request, and a few days later he received a letter of appreciation from the lonely man, saying, "Now I am in tune again."

Say! Is your life in tune with God? Are you sure? Have you been walking with dangerous companions in dangerous places? Send up a little prayer and ask God whether everything is really all right. He will surely let you know.

That is what David was doing when he prayed, "Create in me a clean heart, O God; and renew a right spirit within me" (Psalm 51:10). And I think that is why David was a man after God's own heart. (See 1 Samuel 13:14.)

"Intreat me not to leave thee, . . . for whither thou goest, I will go; and where thou lodgest, I will lodge: thy people shall be my people, and thy God my God." Ruth 1:16.

These beautiful words spoken by Ruth show that she had given her heart to God. All heaven rejoices when a sinner is born again. Some boys and girls are "born into this message." Some young people go to college and accept the truth there. Some attend evangelistic meetings, and give their hearts to God there.

Ruth, however, was not born into a family of believers. She did not go to an Adventist college or attend a series of evangelistic meetings. Her people were idolaters, but she had the privilege of living in a God-fearing home. Then God permitted sorrow to come to her, and in her sorrow she turned for comfort to the living God. She found what she needed and gave her heart to God. He still uses sorrow to turn people toward Him, and it often has been said, "God sometimes has to make a man lie on his back in order to make him look up."

There is a parable that tells of two godly old men who planted olive trees so that someday they could have olives to eat and have a supply of oil. As the first one planted his tree, he prayed: "Lord, it needs rain, that its tender roots may drink and swell. Please send gentle showers." And the Lord sent gentle showers. "Lord," he prayed again, "my tree needs warmth; please send sunshine." And the Lord sent sunshine. "Now send frost, Lord, to make its fibers tough." And, behold, the little tree stood sparkling with frost.

But one evening it died. The next day he went to see his friend and found *his* tree growing well.

"I prayed for rain and sun and frost," he said, "and my tree died."

Then his friend said, "I entrusted my tree to God. God made it, and He knows better than I what it needs. So I make no conditions, but simply pray, 'Lord, send what it needs. Storm or sunshine, wind, rain, or frost, as Thou knowest what is best'; and behold, it grows well!"

So whatever God permits to come into your life, easy experiences or hard ones, joy or sorrow, you can be sure that God is permitting it so you can grow up in favor with God and with man.

"Fear not; I will do to thee all that thou requirest: for all the city of my people doth know that thou art a virtuous woman." Ruth 3:11.

Boaz was a rich relative of Ruth's, and the story of his kindness to Ruth, and the way he redeemed the property of her deceased husband, and married her warms everybody's heart.

We have a rich relative, and elder brother, Jesus, who has redeemed us; and we have a heavenly Father who has promised to supply all our needs too.

In a clipping from one of our old periodicals I found a lovely story about a dear old Scotchman who was well acquainted with his heavenly Father. An evangelist had pitched a tent in a town some distance from where he lived, and he very much wanted to go and stay in that town while the meetings were being held, so he could attend every one of them. He started off, and on the way another Christian brother who was bound on the same errand caught up with him. When they were nearly there the Scotchman suggested that they pause for a moment behind the hedge for a short prayer. So they did, and the younger man was astonished to hear the old man say, "Lord, You know that I'm deaf and need a seat right up in the front, if You can let me have it, so I can hear Your Word. And, Lord, my toes are poking out of my shoes, and I am not much credit to You, so I wish You could get me a pair of new shoes. And, Lord, You know I have no silver, and I want to stay for all the meetings, so I want You to get me a place to stay."

When they got to the meetings the old man stood at the rear for a while, cupping his hand to his ear. But soon someone noticed him and gave him a seat right up front. After the meeting a woman whispered, "Are those the best shoes you have?"

"Yes," he said, "but I expect my Father to get me a new pair soon."

"Come with me," she said, "and I'll get you a new pair. Where are you staying?"

"I have no silver and I'm a stranger here, but my Father will find me a place to stay, for He knows I want to attend the meetings."

"Then you are welcome to stay at my house," she said.

And that night the dear old man thanked his Father in heaven for sending him the three things he had asked for.

Are you well acquainted with your heavenly Father?

"Go in peace: and the God of Israel grant thee thy petition that thou hast asked of him." Samuel 1:17.

God answered the earnest prayer of Hannah and gave her a baby boy. She called him Samuel, which means "asked of God." If you only knew how many earnest prayers have ascended for *you,* and how many times God has answered those earnest prayers, and healed your sicknesses and saved your life, and helped you overcome temptation, you would feel like calling yourself "Samuel" also.

A few years ago an Adventist soldier found himself in the U.S. Army in one of the European countries. He was a good Adventist young man, and had quite an ability in dealing with children. With the aid of a little chewing gum he managed to gather a small group of children together as he came off duty every afternoon. He told them Bible stories, and soon they were his friends.

One afternoon he missed one of his regular little visitors. He asked the others about him and learned that he was sick in bed. He went at once to visit him, but the little boy's mother said, "It's no use to see my son. He is unconscious, and the doctor says there's nothing anyone can do. He will soon die."

"I'm sorry to hear he is so ill," said the soldier. "You know he is one of my little friends. I tell the children stories every day. I wish you would let me go in and offer a prayer for him." Nobody could refuse such a request, so into the room went our soldier and fell on his knees and prayed. The mother felt so helpless that she could not stand being in the room; so she quietly went out. When she thought the prayer was finished she came back, but our soldier was still on his knees. She went away again, and came back again and again; but our soldier was still praying. When at last she found the soldier standing, he turned and said, "Your son will not die, but will recover."

Then the mother began to cry. "Who are you?" she asked. "What church do you go to?" Our soldier gave her the address of the nearby Seventh-day Adventist church. The next Sabbath she and her son were in church, and they kept on coming.

Are you really earnest when you pray? Our God still answers earnest prayers.

"But Samuel ministered before the Lord, being a child, girded with a linen ephod." 1 Samuel 2:18.

Many, many times in Bible days, and also in our modern days, children have ministered for God. In the *Review and Herald* of January 12, 1961, there was a beautiful story about a little blind girl who brought comfort to a sorrowing woman. They met on a transcontinental train going West when a kindhearted woman found a fellow passenger in the lounge weeping her heart away.

"Is there something I can do?" asked the lady. "Are you ill?"

"No, no, I'm not ill," replied the weeping woman, "but I have more trouble than I can bear. My husband died some years ago; my only son is in the Air Force in Europe; and my daughter in California is dying. I am hoping I can reach her before it is too late."

No wonder she wept as if her heart would break. Back to the coach went the would-be good Samaritan, and waking up the sleeping passengers one after another, she asked, "Is there a minister in this car? or a priest? or a rabbi?" But no one responded. Then in desperation she asked, "Well, isn't there someone who can pray? There's someone in the lounge who needs help badly."

Now among the passengers there was this little blind girl, maybe 10 or 12 years old, and when no one offered to help, she touched the arm of the woman and said, "Will I do? I know the Bible a little, and I can pray a little, too."

"Oh, yes, dear, you'll do," said the kind lady. "Come with me." And she led her into the lounge. The little girl felt for the hands of the weeping woman, then in a soft, tender voice began, "Our Father which art in heaven . . ." Then she repeated the twenty-third psalm and the Beatitudes, including "Blessed are they that mourn: for they shall be comforted." The sobbing stopped, and the heartbroken woman sat up.

"Thank you for bringing help," she said to the kind woman. "It helped such a lot." Then she turned to the little girl and patted her cheek. Suddenly she saw that she was blind. For a moment or two the words wouldn't come. Then she said, "Thank you, dear. You have not only brought me comfort but restored my faith."

Remember that God has a special place where *you* can minister for Him too.

"Speak, Lord; for thy servant heareth." 1 Samuel 3:9.

Samuel heard a voice speaking to him, but he didn't know it was God's voice until *after* he said, "Speak; for thy servant heareth." Do you know that God is speaking to every one of us? But too often we don't recognize the voice of God. In *Messages to Young People,* Sister White says: "God's holy, educating Spirit is in His word. A light, a new and precious light, shines forth from every page. Truth is there revealed, and words and sentences are made *bright* and *appropriate for the occasion,* as the voice of God speaking to the soul."—Page 246. (Italics supplied.) Just think! The voice of God is speaking to you as you read the Bible, as you study your Sabbath school lesson, as you read the Morning Watch. But does a sentence ever stand out as though it was written specially for you? I would like to recommend a little formula that has worked for me for many years, and I am sure it will work for you too. Here it is: As you take up your Bible to study your lesson or to read the Morning Watch, breathe this little prayer—"Speak, Lord; for thy servant heareth," and words and sentences will surely be made bright and appropriate for you.

During the battle of Rangoon in December, 1941, thousands of people were fleeing overland into India. No food stations had been prepared, no proper paths had been made, and hundreds of poor people died for lack of food and from the ravages of wild animals. We missionaries began to wonder whether we should flee also. Then one morning one of the missionaries reading the daily portion of the Bible Year read, " 'Ye shall not go out with haste, nor go by flight: for the Lord will go before you; and the God of Israel will be your reward' " (Isaiah 52:12).

As he read, the words were "made bright." We all knew it was the voice of God speaking to us. We obeyed. We stayed a little longer—till the paths were made and the food stations established, and we all got out safely.

Someday *you* will need to have God speak to you. Learn now to hear His voice by saying, "Speak, Lord; for thy servant heareth," as you read and study His Sacred Word.

"The wages of sin is death; but the gift of God is eternal life through Jesus Christ our Lord." Romans 6:23.

Hophni and Phinehas were bad boys. They were disobedient to their parents and to God. They were selfish; they desecrated the people's sacrifices, and the Bible says they were vile. The first time they sinned it most likely was only a little sin, but they did it again, and added sin to sin till at last they took the sacred ark of God into battle, with the result that the ark was taken by the enemy and they were both slain. That's just about what happens to everyone who plays with sin and does not forsake it.

In a *Youth's Instructor* some time ago Lora Clement told a story about a young woman she called Alice. Alice was brought up in a Christian home and went to church school and academy. Then she took a job so she could earn some money and go back to college in a year or two. Her work was in a large Christian office, but Alice fell in with a group of worldly friends who didn't care what the church taught or what anyone said. First it was the movies, then the theater occasionally, then the skating rink. There she met a wonderful young man. No, he was not a Christian, but he was so pleasant; he was such good company. To please him she used lipstick and painted her fingernails fiery red. Her employer spoke to her about it, but she became angry and found another job in a worldly office. Now and then she wondered whether she was slipping. What would her mother say if she knew? Her boyfriend teased her to try a cigarette one day. But "Oh, no! Never!" But he kept on urging until one day she tried a cigarette—just for once! Everybody did it, so what could be so bad about it? Then came the New Year's party, and the crowd decided to see the old year out in a nightclub. She remembered having a drink of liquor, but she remembered nothing else till she woke up in a hospital, the only survivor in an automobile wreck that snuffed out the lives of the other merrymakers. During the four months Alice spent in the hospital she had plenty of time to think, and fortunately, she made an about-face and turned over a new leaf.

It is not safe for anyone to play with sin. It really pays to walk in the path of obedience toward eternal life.

"I am the first, and I am the last; and beside me there is no God." Isaiah 44:6.

God worked miracle after miracle to prove that Dagon, the stone god, half man and half fish, which the Philistines worshiped, had no power to help them, and that He alone was God. God still works miracles to bless and help His people to prove that He alone is God. In one of the *Bedtime Stories* volumes is a lovely story about a miracle that God performed for the Brown family. Mrs. Brown had been sick, and all their money was used up. Mr. Brown had nothing in the bank, there was nothing in his pocket, and he still owed a big doctor bill. Things looked very blue for them all, and to make matters worse, Mrs. Brown needed to go to the doctor again. What could they do? They just had to see the doctor, bill or no bill. So Mr. Brown got his old Ford ready, bundled up Mrs. Brown, and after telling the Lord all about their embarrassing situation, they started off down the bumpy country road. They had gone only a few miles when the car stopped, and Mr. Brown couldn't start it again. He checked the gas and the oil and everything else he could think of, and everything looked OK. At last he got under the car to see whether there was something broken there. Sure enough, there was something on the road just under the engine. Had it dropped off the engine? He picked it up, but it wasn't metal; it wasn't rubber. It was paper! A roll of paper! Why, it looked like money! It was! It was a roll of bills! There was enough to pay the doctor bill and then some! What a miracle! But that wasn't all. Mr. Brown got in the car again and tried to start it, and off it went, just as though nothing had been the matter with it!

For a long time Mr. Brown could hardly believe it had happened.

"Mother," he said, "is the money real?"

"Yes, dear," she replied. "And God is real too."

"Then it's not a dream?"

"No indeed! You're very wide awake, and so am I."

Things like that don't just happen. No "dagon" or "baal" could ever do anything like that. Only the living God could stop a car right over a roll of money. And that living God is your God. Keep close to Him; you need Him every moment.

"And the kine took the straight way to the way of Beth-shemesh . . . , and turned not aside to the right hand or to the left." 1 Samuel 6:12.

Today we have read about another miracle the living God performed, this time with some dumb animals. Who ever heard of two cows going away from their calves and taking the right road to Bethshemesh? In the *Review and Herald* of March 12, 1959, Elder R. S. Watts tells of another miracle the living God performed with a dumb animal, this time with a water buffalo! A certain farmer had been planting rice all day in his paddy field on the island of Lubang in the Philippines. Just as he was ready to go home three water buffaloes came wandering into his paddy field. He tried to drive them away. Two of them left, but one refused to go. It turned right toward the farmer, opened its mouth, and spoke! "Prepare to meet God. He is coming soon. You must keep the Sabbath to be ready." After this the buffalo went away, and the farmer, astonished beyond description, ran back to his village and excitedly told his family and his neighbors about this strange experience with a talking buffalo!

Soon after this experience a relative of the farmer, Brother Faustino Tardeo, who was a Seventh-day Adventist, came to this village to spend his vacation, for this was his former home. He was soon giving Bible studies, and when they studied about the Sabbath, the farmer told again about this experience with the talking buffalo who told him he must keep the Sabbath to get ready for Christ's soon coming. It was such a striking coincidence that they believed God's hand was in it all, and the farmer and a number of his neighbors began to keep the Sabbath. And the president of the mission in that district, Elder P. C. Banaag, says that now there is quite a company of people there who are studying the truth. No wonder Isaiah says God's name is "Wonderful."

Paul declares that this wonderful God "hath chosen the foolish things of the world to confound the wise; and God hath chosen the weak things of the world to confound the things which are mighty; and base things of the world, and things which are despised, hath God chosen . . . to bring to nought things that are" (1 Corinthians 1:27, 28).

This God—*your* God—may do something wonderful for you or some of your friends someday to bring them into the truth.

"Come out from among them, and be ye separate, saith the Lord . . . ; and I will receive you, and will be a Father unto you, and ye shall be my sons and daughters." 2 Corinthians 6:17, 18.

Poor old children of Israel! They weren't satisfied to have God lead them and speak to them through His prophets. No! They were going to have a king at any price, "that we also may be like all the nations." They wanted to do what everyone else was doing! They wanted to be like the world! This is the strongest temptation that comes to any of us, and Satan makes it his business to try to make us believe that we cannot be happy unless we dress like the world, look like the world, talk like the world, sing like the world, and do everything like the world. If only you could be old before you were young! If only you could see *before* the temptation comes to you, the tears and broken hearts of those who have been deceived by old Satan, then you could easily believe that God never says, "Thou shalt not" to rob us of any pleasure. He never says, "Come out and be separate" to keep us from having a good time, but only to save us from sorrow, from tears, from shame, and from disappointment.

I was talking like this to the students in one of our large colleges a few years ago, and after one of the meetings a young woman put this little note into my hands:
"Dear Elder,

"I want you to know that I never found happiness until Jesus came into my life. Life in show business is most unhappy to those who are in it. I know this is true, for I've been in it since I was 4½ years old till I was 20. How fortunate I was to find God, and I am growing closer to Him all the time here at college. I love my Lord so much and I have put Him first, above all things. If anyone in the show business ever asks how happy one can be, think of me.

"Sincerely,
"Nonajane."

And if you could have seen her happy face you would have known she was telling the truth. If *you* want to be really happy, "Come out from among them, and be ye separate . . . ; and I . . . will be a Father unto you, and ye shall be my sons and daughters," says the Lord.

"What doth the Lord require of thee, but to do justly, and to love mercy, and to walk humbly with thy God?" Micah 6:8.

The children of Israel were determined to have a king, so they could be like all the nations around them. So the Lord directed in choosing the best man they had. Saul was a choice young man, and goodly, but above all, he was humble. "Am I not a Benjamite of the smallest of the tribes of Israel? and my family the least of all the families of the tribe of Benjamin?" Humility is a trait of character that not only pleases God but also pleases our fellowmen. A number of years ago the young people from our college in England were out Ingathering. One young man called at a home where he expected to receive only the usual small donation. But he was a humble young man, and earnest. He loved the Lord and loved to help do the Lord's work, and it showed in his face. The woman in this house was well to do, and she was impressed. "Yes," she said, "I will be glad to help in a work like this. I will give you $500." The young man was almost speechless, but he managed to thank her, and went on showing her how much her donation would do. "I'll make it $1,000," she said. "That is a wonderful work." The young man kept on; the woman's interest still grew. "I'll make it $1,500," she said. Then looking the young man straight in the face, she added, "Wouldn't you like to be a missionary yourself?"

"Yes, indeed," he replied, "but I have not sufficient education yet."

"Then listen! If you will go to Africa as a missionary, I will pay your way through college and give your missionary society $3,500!" she said.

And the young man replied, "I certainly will be glad to do it." And she did; and he did; and Roy Warland was in Africa for years, and later was one of our conference Sabbath school secretaries in England, still the same lovable, humble man.

"Let this mind be in you, which was also in Christ Jesus," says Paul, "who, being in the form of God . . . made himself of no reputation, and took upon him the form of a servant, and was made in the likeness of men. . . . Wherefore God also hath highly exalted him and given him a name which is above every name" (Philippians 2:5-9).

What a pity Saul did not remain humble. And say, how do *you* rate for humility?

"And the Spirit of the Lord will come upon thee, and thou shalt . . . be turned into another man." 1 Samuel 10:6.

Saul is not the only young man who has been "turned into another man" by the Spirit of God. Let me give you the experience of Eugene Farnsworth. His father, William Farnsworth, was the first one in that little company of Adventists in Washington, New Hampshire, to take his stand for the seventh-day Sabbath. In 1855 Eugene was just a lad in his teens, and not too interested in religion. Elder J. N. Andrews had arrived at the Farnsworth home for a visit, and Eugene took a hoe and went out to work in the field, partly to avoid the preacher. But John Andrews was a lover of young people and knew what a power they could be for God when they were definitely on His side. So Elder Andrews got another hoe and went out to help Eugene in the field. "Well, Eugene," said the elder, "what are you going to make of yourself?"

"I intend to get an education first," said Eugene.

"Good! That will be the best thing you can do. And what then?"

"I think I shall study law."

"You might do worse," replied the elder. "And what then?"

"I intend to be the best lawyer in the state."

"And what then?"

"I hope to make a lot of money and may visit other countries."

"And what then?"

"I suppose I shall get married and have a nice home."

"And what then?" The questioning was becoming a little unpleasant.

"Oh, I suppose I shall grow old and die, like other men," said Eugene, a little embarrassed.

"And what then?" said the good elder as he fixed his eye on the young man and put his hand on his shoulder. "Eugene, what then?"

Eugene couldn't get away from that searching question. It followed him to bed, to work—everywhere—and in a meeting a little later on, when Elder and Mrs. White were also present, Elder Andrews whispered, "Eugene, isn't it time for you to make your decision now?" And he did, and the Spirit of God came upon him and turned him into one of our mighty pioneer preachers!

The Spirit of God wants to turn *you* into another person too. Won't you let Him?

"Turn not aside from following the Lord, but serve the Lord with all your heart." 1 Samuel 12:20.

Samuel was getting old, and although Israel had displeased the Lord by asking for a king, he pleaded with them not to turn aside from following the Lord. "Only fear the Lord," he begged (verse 24), "and serve him in truth with all your heart." The story of the Advent Movement is filled with the experiences of men and women who have served God with all their heart and have not turned aside in spite of trouble or hardship. In 1944 Mr. Soans, an expert welder, accepted the Sabbath truth during a series of meetings held by Pastor George Hamilton in the city of Bombay, India. Although he had worked at the largest electrical shop in the city for twenty years, he lost his job at once. Up and down the streets of Bombay he walked, looking for work. Up and down the streets Satan followed him, with his devilish insinuations: "Your God doesn't hear your prayers. He's going to let your wife and children starve." Two weeks went by. Mr. Soans was still looking for work. Then into the harbor came a ship filled with bales of cotton and ammunition. While the ship was being unloaded, one of the workmen dropped a cigarette into the hold where the bales of cotton were. By the time the fire was discovered it was impossible to put it out. "Our only hope is to sink the ship," said the officials, so four expert welders were called from the biggest electrical shop in Bombay to burn four holes under the waterline to sink the ship. On April 15, 1944, while they were working, the fire reached the ammunition, and the most awful explosion occurred, killing the four welders and hundreds of others. Mr. Soans was still looking for work! When he heard the explosion and pieced the story together he said, "I'm the happiest man in the world. If I hadn't lost my job because of the Sabbath, I would have been one of those welders who lost their lives." Soon after this Brother Soans opened his own welding shop, and the last I heard of him, he was making three times as much money as when on the job he lost.

It will pay you in every way to serve the Lord with all your heart too. Ellen G. White says, "Be faithful. Put heart into your work. . . . Those who learn to put thought into everything they undertake, however small the work may appear, will be of use in the world."—*Messages to Young People,* pp. 148, 149.

"To obey is better than sacrifice, and to hearken than the fat of rams."
1 Samuel 15:22.

How hard it was for Saul to learn to obey the voice of God! Just because he didn't know all the reasons why God had told him to destroy the Amalekites, he just pleased himself. We must all learn to obey, whether we understand the reason for the command or not. In a very early issue of the *Sabbath School Worker* I came across a story that illustrates this principle.

An Eastern king needed a faithful servant. Two men applied for the position. The king paid both men the day's wage in advance, then took them to a well and put a basket down beside it. "Now, men," he said, "try your best to fill this basket with water from the well. I'll be back this evening to see how you have gotten on." So saying, he went away; and the men began to work. It wasn't long before one man said, "What a silly business—trying to fill a basket with water!"

"But we have been paid our wages," said the other. "He knows why he told us to do it. That is not our business."

"Well, I'm not going to keep on doing such foolish work," said the first man, and throwing down his bucket, he went away. The other man worked on faithfully, drawing water and pouring it into the basket. And just before sunset the well was dry! Looking down into it, he saw something shining! He let down his bucket, moved it carefully this way and that, and drew up a beautiful diamond ring! "Ah, now I see why the king wanted us to pour water into the basket," he said. "If we had brought up the ring before the well was dry, it would have been found in the basket!" Just then the king came back. The man showed him the ring he had just drawn up. The king smiled and said, "It is yours. You have been faithful in a little thing; now I see I can trust you in great things. Henceforth you will stand at my right hand."

Life is just like that. Hundreds of people have been burned to death because they thought it was silly not to be able to smoke in bed. Poor foolish people!

You will be tempted to think that some commands your parents and teachers give you are foolish. But be wise! "To obey is better than sacrifice."

"The Lord seeth not as man seeth; for man looketh on the outward appearance, but the Lord looketh on the heart." 1 Samuel 16:7.

No doubt Eliab thought he was bigger and better and stronger than his smallest brother, David; and his father, Jesse, may have thought so too. Samuel certainly did, for when he saw Eliab he said to himself: "Surely the Lord's anointed is before him." But the Lord wasn't looking at the outward appearance; He was looking at the heart, and the Lord chose David—little David—the youngest of eight brothers. God's choices are often big surprises to grown-up men and women.

Once upon a time, away over in a little church in Scotland, there was a discouraged preacher. He had tried all one year to invite people to unite with the church, but the only one to take his stand and openly confess Jesus as his Saviour was a little lad. The church officers weren't happy, and one morning one of them went to the pastor and said, "There must be something wrong with your preaching, for only one person has taken his stand all year long, and he is *only a boy*." The poor preacher felt so discouraged, and after everybody had left the church, he stayed there, wondering why he had failed. He didn't notice the door open. The first thing he knew, the boy—the only one who had taken his stand that whole year—was standing beside him. The lad put his hand on the preacher's hand, and said, "Do you think that if I am willing to work hard I could become a preacher?"

"A preacher!" said the minister.

"Yes, and perhaps a missionary," said the boy. Tears came to the preacher's eyes as he said, "May God bless you, my boy. Yes, I think you *can* become a preacher."

That little lad was Robert Moffat, who became one of God's great missionaries to South Africa. God used him mightily in Africa, but not only there. Once when he was back in England he was telling of the land where he saw "in the morning sun the smoke of a thousand villages where no missionary has ever been," and David Livingstone responded to the call! But once Robert Moffat was only a boy.

Never mind *your* looks, whether you are tall or short, fat or thin. Keep your heart right, for "the Lord looketh on the heart."

"I come to thee in the name of the Lord of hosts. . . . This day will the Lord deliver thee into mine hand . . . ; that all the earth may know that there is a God in Israel." 1 Samuel 17:45, 46.

Did it ever occur to you that not all giants have two legs? Well, they don't! Anything beyond your strength or ability, anything that makes you call on God for help to overcome, is a giant. It might be a bad habit; it might be a hard job; it could be a tough problem in arithmetic! That's what Earl's father said one evening after they had studied about the ten spies who felt like grasshoppers before the giants in Canaan. It made Earl think as he sat down to do his homework, for he soon realized he had a tough problem. An hour later Howard called, "Hey, Earl, aren't you coming down to Timmy's?"

"Say, I almost forgot," Earl replied, "but I've got a tough problem that I'm stuck on."

"Aw, that old problem! I tried it once or twice too, and I couldn't do it. I'm sure no one will get it. Anyway, I heard Miss Andrews tell Professor Bowen that she was only giving us that problem to try our patience, and I'm sure not going to waste any more time on it." Just then Cousin Carol went through the room. She was staying in Earl's home, and she just seemed to be saying to herself in a sweet voice, "And there we saw the giants." Earl's face went red a little bit. Then he said, "Look, Howard, you may as well go on. Tell Timmy I cannot come. I'm going to lick that problem. I'm no grasshopper."

The next morning when they went to school, to their surprise they found Judge Dennison from Buffalo visiting the school he attended as a boy. He stayed and stayed, until time for math class. "Howard, come to the board and do the thirty-ninth problem," said Miss Andrews.

"Sorry, Miss Andrews. I couldn't do it," he said as his face went red. "I couldn't do it either," said the next boy and the next. Then it was Earl's turn. He went right up to the board and did it and explained it perfectly. The whole room, including the judge, applauded.

"Did anyone help you?" asked Miss Andrews.

"Yes, my cousin Carol! She said, 'And there we saw giants!' And I said to myself, 'I'm no grasshopper!' And I stuck at it till eleven o'clock and got it!" Then everybody applauded again.

Say, have *you* got giants? You can lick them with God's help.

"And Saul eyed David from that day and forward. . . . And Saul was afraid of David, because the Lord was with him, and was departed from Saul." 1 Samuel 18:9-12.

In the Scripture reading for today we have pictured one of the loveliest things in life—friendship—the friendship of David and Jonathan; and also one of the ugliest things we find in life—jealousy— Saul's jealousy of David. It is good for us all to examine our heart now and then to see whether there is anyone to whom we give a "cold shoulder" or anyone of whom we are envious, for jealousy is like having a poisonous viper fastened to the heart—to your heart—and honestly, there is nothing that a friend might do or say that makes him deserve to be put in "cold storage." Jealousy hurts. But it hurts the one who is jealous the most.

Some time ago I came across a little old fable about an eagle who was jealous of another eagle because it could fly swifter and higher than he could. The more he saw the rival eagle, the more jealous he felt, till he wished he could find some way to kill him. One day the jealous eagle saw a hunter and said to him, "I wish you would shoot that other eagle so I would never have to see him again."

"If I had some feathers to put into the end of my arrow," said the hunter, "I would try."

The jealous eagle gladly pulled some feathers out of his wing and gave them to the hunter. The hunter put the feathers into his arrow and shot; but the arrow didn't quite reach the rival eagle. The jealous eagle gave him some more feathers and said, "Try again." The hunter tried again, but missed. The jealous eagle gave him more feathers and more feathers, and the hunter shot again and again. At last the jealous eagle had lost so many feathers that he couldn't fly at all! Then the hunter turned around and killed him! And that was the end of the jealous eagle.

"Grief, anxiety, discontent, remorse, guilt, distrust, all tend to break down the life forces and to invite decay and death. . . . Courage, hope, faith, sympathy, love, promote health and prolong life."—*The Ministry of Healing*, p. 241.

So look out! Practice getting along with everybody and being kind to everybody. Rejoice with others when they win and succeed, and you will be loved and have many real friends.

"The Lord be between me and thee, and between my seed and thy seed for ever." 1 Samuel 20:42.

True friendship is a beautiful thing wherever you see it, and the unselfish friendship between Jonathan and David is the highest example of its kind in the Bible. When mourning the death of Jonathan, David said, "Very pleasant hast thou been unto me: thy love to me was wonderful, passing the love of women" (2 Samuel 1:26). Here is another friendship story I love to tell. Once upon a time there lived a very rich man in a very lovely palace in Blenheim, Oxfordshire, England. He had a Scottish gardener working for him. The rich man had a son and the gardener had a son; they were real friends. One day the two boys were swimming in a little lake in the rich man's garden when the rich boy got into difficulty and might have drowned had it not been for the quick, efficient aid the gardener's son gave him. Out of gratitude for saving his son's life, the rich man paid the expenses of the gardener's son through medical school at the London University. He became a very clever doctor and later shared in the discovery of the wonder-drug penicillin. You may know his name—Sir Alexander Fleming. The rich man's son also went through college, studied law, entered the army, went into politics, and became prime minister of Great Britain. You probably know his name too—Sir Winston Churchill. Now during the Second World War Sir Winston became sick with pneumonia. It was a critical illness and a very serious situation, for Britain greatly needed Churchill's leadership. So the greatest specialist in all the country was called to attend Sir Winston! Yes, you've guessed it. Sir Alexander Fleming was called, and again he saved the life of his boyhood friend. "This makes twice," said Sir Winston as he thanked Sir Alexander, "once when I was a boy and now when I am a man."

"The matter of choosing associates is one which students should learn to consider seriously. . . . It has been truly said, 'Show me your company, and I will show you your character.' The youth fail to realize how sensibly both their character and their reputation are affected by their choice of associates."—*Messages to Young People*, p. 411.

So live that your childhood friends will be your best and dearest lifelong friends.

"I will not put forth mine hand against my lord; for he is the Lord's anointed." 1 Samuel 24:10.

David has given us all a shining example in reverence and respect for our rulers and our elders and all who are ordained of God. How careful *we* should always be never to criticize them or do anything against them. You have all heard the story of how John Wilkes Booth "put forth his hand" against President Lincoln and shot him, but did you ever hear the story about John Wilkes Booth's brother Edwin, and what he unknowingly did to bring great happiness to President Lincoln? Well, as the story was told in the *Reader's Digest*, Edwin Booth, who was a famous American actor, had just finished his evening performance in New York one night during the Civil War. He crossed over on the ferry to Jersey City and hurried to the Pennsylvania Railway station to catch the train for Philadelphia. The train was already at the station when he got there, and just as he boarded the rear platform of one of the cars, the train started with a jolt that threw him off balance for a moment. That same jolt caused a well-dressed young man who was getting on behind him to lose his footing, and he fell between the train and the platform. Edwin Booth saw it happen, and immediately he held on to the handrail for all he was worth, reached down and grabbed the young man by the collar, and pulled him up onto the moving train. The young man was scared but not hurt. He recognized the actor and thanked him profusely. "That was a narrow one, Mr. Booth," he said. Edwin Booth smiled and went on. He did not even ask the name of the young man. In a few weeks, however, he received a letter from General Adam Badeau, military secretary to General Grant, thanking him for his heroic act and telling him the young man whose life he saved was Robert Todd Lincoln—the president's son! Booth kept that letter and later, when he heard that his brother had shot the president, it was the only consolation he had in those days of family shame.

"It is dangerous to utter a word of doubt, dangerous to question and criticize divine light. The habit of careless and irreverent criticism reacts upon the character."—*The Desire of Ages*, p. 323.

Won't you make up your mind to do all you possibly can to support your teachers, your church elders, and your rulers, and to bring them happiness?

*"So David took the spear and the cruse of water . . . ; and no man saw it
. . . : because a deep sleep from the Lord was fallen upon them."* 1 Samuel
26:12.

God delights in mercy, and He worked miracle after miracle to help
David when he showed mercy to the one who was trying to take his life.
Here is a story about another person who showed mercy, and a miracle
that happened to a young Union Army sentinel who was found asleep at
his post. William Scott was in Company K of the Third Vermont
Regiment during the Civil War. He was only 18 years old. One night he
volunteered to go on guard duty in the place of a sick comrade. All went
well that night. But the next day his own turn came to be on guard duty
that night. The next morning the relief guard found him asleep at his
post. He was court-martialed, found guilty, and condemned to be shot
within twenty-four hours. His comrades felt terrible. His captain said it
was his fault, that he should have known better than to let a soldier do
all-night guard duty two nights running. They appointed a committee
that went to L. E. Chittenden, a Vermont lawyer and a friend of
President Lincoln. "There must be some way to save him, Judge!" said
the captain. "He's a good boy. He's not to blame. If anyone is to be shot,
I am the one. I'm the guilty one. Won't you help us?" There was only one
who could help—President Lincoln; and to Lincoln they went. The
captain told the story. Lincoln understood. His heart was moved with
mercy. He thought of all the possible complications and said, "I'll have
to do it myself and I'll have to do it today." And down to the camp he
went.

He had a long talk with William Scott, and finally said, "William,
you are not going to be shot. I am going to send you back to your
regiment. But how are you going to pay my bill?" The lad hardly knew
what to answer. Then putting his hand on William's shoulder, the
president said, "William, if from this day you will do your duty, so that if
you suddenly came to the time to die you could look me in the face
and say, 'I have kept my promise; I have done my duty as a soldier,' then
my bill will be paid." What a beautiful thing is mercy! How do *you* rate?

"Vengeance is mine; I will repay, saith the Lord." Romans 12:19.

David had been anointed to be king before Saul began to persecute him. How easy it would have been for David to put Saul out of the way! Opportunity after opportunity presented itself, but David said, "I will not put forth my hand against the Lord's anointed"; and he patiently waited for God to work it out in His own way and in His own time. Remember that God can still do the "repaying" if only we will let Him. Elder A. V. Olson used to tell a story of the way God took a hand in affairs in one of the European countries in the early 1930s while he was president of the Southern European Division. In this country the Greek Orthodox Church was the state church, and Adventists were always persecuted. Only when the ruling cabinet was made up of men educated in Western countries did the Adventists enjoy a degree of freedom. Well, one time the king made the metropolitan of the state church the prime minister, and he called in a number of bishops and priests to make up his cabinet. Immediately they made a decree that on a certain date all Seventh-day Adventist churches and schools would be closed. The publishing house would be taken away and all ministers and colporteurs would be imprisoned. The Adventists would not be permitted to visit one another in their homes or on the streets. The men were determined to destroy our work. In vain our leaders went to see some of the cabinet members. They even went to the prime minister himself, but he said, "I have tried to destroy the Adventists for a long time. Now this is the time, and we are going to do it." Our workers sent word to the General Conference officers. They proclaimed a day of prayer and fasting and sent the word all around the world. And on that Sabbath day, which many of your grandparents will remember, all the Adventists everywhere with prayer and fasting pleaded with God to keep His work from being destroyed. God answered that prayer. Just a few nights before the decree was to be enforced, the prime minister went to bed and went to sleep—and *never* woke up! God had poured out His vengeance upon him and removed him from power. The new prime minister called a new cabinet, and the first thing they did was to rescind the decree to destroy the Adventists.

God has power. I wish we had more days of fasting and prayer for our workers in lands where liberties are restricted. Don't you?

"Love your enemies, bless them that curse you, do good to them that hate you, and pray for them which despitefully use you, and persecute you." Matthew 5:44.

Saul was dead at last, and David "mourned, and wept, and fasted until even." Only a person who loves God with all his heart and soul and strength could love an enemy like that. And there are many Seventh-day Adventists all over the world who have loved their enemies and done good to those who hated them. Elder A. V. Olson once told another story about one of our ministers in one of those countries of Southeast Europe who was persecuted, arrested, brought into court, and falsely accused by the priest in the village where he was working. The priest knew our minister was innocent, so did the Greek Catholic lawyer who prosecuted him, and so did the Greek Catholic judge; but they were determined to stop his work if possible, so he was sentenced to one year in prison. It was winter, and there were sixteen prisoners in the cell where he was sent. Each had a narrow bunk and one blanket. At first our brother was tempted to be discouraged, but soon he decided that God had some work for him to do there; so he did his best to be cheerful. Then one day two big policemen opened the door and put in one more prisoner, and who do you think it was? It was the Greek Catholic lawyer who had prosecuted our pastor. They recognized each other, and the lawyer was so ashamed that he went over to a corner and stayed there. Soon it came time to go to sleep. But the lawyer had no bunk and had no blanket. No one offered to share with him, so our brother went over and said, "Friend, you can't sit here all night. You'll get pneumonia. My bunk is small, but if we are real good friends, I think we can make it." The lawyer hesitated, but finally went over and shared the bunk with our brother.

"Are you ill?" asked our brother.

"Oh, no," was the reply. "I'm troubled and perplexed. There are sixteen men here who belong to my church, but not one of them offered me any help, only you, the man whom I prosecuted falsely."

"Jesus my Master has told us to love our enemies," said our pastor. After they got out of prison he was ever our pastor's friend.

There truly is Christian magic in loving our enemies and in doing good to those who hate us. *You* try it.

"When thou hearest the sound of a going in the tops of the mulberry trees, . . . then thou shalt bestir thyself: for then shall the Lord go out before thee." 2 Samuel 5:24.

Do you know what I think made the sound of "going" in the tops of the mulberry trees? I think it was the Spirit of God going before them like a mighty wind. You see, David depended on the Spirit of God for every victory, and that is something we must all learn to do. Listen to another chapter in Elder Olson's story about the minister who was imprisoned and who did good to the lawyer who had prosecuted him. The Holy Spirit turned *him* into a friend. But that's not all the Holy Spirit did. You can hardly believe it, but some time later two big policemen opened the prison door again and put in another prisoner. And who do you think this one was? It was the priest himself! And when the priest saw our pastor he was even more ashamed than the lawyer had been. He turned his back, and like the lawyer he went over into the corner and sat on the floor. When it came time to sleep, just as before, nobody offered to help the poor priest. So our brother went over and invited him to come and share his bunk and his blanket. At first the priest would not move or say a word, but our brother pulled him up and led him over to his bunk, and they lay down together. It was after midnight when our brother heard the priest sobbing.

"Are you sick?" he asked.

"No," replied the priest, "I'm not sick, but I'm troubled. Right here in this cell are sixteen men who belong to my church, and not one of them has offered me any help but you, the man I falsely accused. How could you do it?"

"It is because Jesus lives in my heart, and I try to do what Jesus would do," said our minister. The priest then asked for our brother's forgiveness and asked him to pray for him.

"If I ever get out of this place," said the priest, "remember that Adventists will always find a friend in this priest." And he was true to his word.

Who but the Spirit of God could change the heart of a wicked man like that! That's what I need; that's what you need. We all need to be filled with the Spirit of God always.

"If he commit iniquity, I will chasten him with the rod of men . . . . : but my mercy shall not depart away from him." 2 Samuel 7:14, 15.

God had to chasten David. God had to chasten Solomon. God has to chasten every one of us. But what a joyful thought—God's mercy does not depart from us! Let me tell you another chapter in Elder Olson's story about our minister who was falsely accused and put in prison. The last two mornings I have told you how the lawyer and the priest were each brought into the prison and how the Spirit of God, through the Christlike kindness of the minister, changed them into friends of the Seventh-day Adventists. Well, that's not the end of the story! Some time later the prison door opened, and the two policemen came in and said to our brother, "Take your few belongings and come." It was night. Where were they taking him? Home? To another prison? To the place of execution? He was soon to find out, for as they drove along, one of the policemen said, "I'm so sorry. We have learned to know you and respect you. You are a Christian, but now we are taking you to the worst prison in the country." And it was true. As soon as he was put in the new prison cell, the prisoners asked, "Why are you here?"

"For preaching the gospel," replied our brother kindly. "Why are you here?"

"I killed my wife," shouted one. "I killed my neighbor," shouted another. That was the kind of men they were. When the lights went out they began to scream and howl. The noise spread from cell to cell until it made our poor brother's blood run cold. Then the Spirit of God whispered in his heart, "Sing." So he lifted up his voice and sang.

"Sing again," they called when he finished; and he sang again.

"How can you sing such songs in a place like this?" they asked as they crowded around him.

"Because of my religion. I have Jesus in my heart," he replied.

"What does that mean?" they asked. And he told them.

"Does God still love us?" "Will God still have mercy on us?" "Won't you pray for us?" And our brother explained the love and mercy of God and prayed for those poor men, and by the time his year of imprisonment was up, seventeen of those criminals had given their hearts to God and had been baptized.

"For rebellion is as the sin of witchcraft, and stubbornness is as iniquity and idolatry." 1 Samuel 15:23.

We mustn't be surprised that rebellion and stubbornness are often the most common temptations that come to all of us. That's the way Satan got started. And he knows he can ruin and destroy anyone if only he can make him rebellious. God regards rebellion and stubbornness as very serious sins, and He longs to help us overcome them.

Once there was a junior lad whom we shall call Charles. He was rebellious and stubborn too. When his teacher corrected him he played truant from school for three days. Then his father and mother found out about what he had done. They were heartbroken, and wanted more than anything else to help him make things right. "Son," said his father, "you have not been square and honest with us. I have always said that I can trust my boy. But evidently I can't, for you have been living a lie for three whole days. I can't tell you how bad I feel about what you have done." Charles was ashamed and angry. He would rather have had a whipping than to see his father's sorrow like this. After talking things over with the boy and praying, the father said, "Son, you will be housebound for three days. We will make you a bed in the attic and we will bring your food and your books to you. You can study and make up your schoolwork. You will be there for three days and three nights to make up for the three days you were away from school." Charles moved into the attic. He had his books; he had his food; and he had time to think. Downstairs his father tried to read, but he couldn't. Mother tried to sew, but nothing went right. Nine o'clock came; ten o'clock. "Aren't you going to bed, Father?" asked Mother.

"Not just yet—I'm not sleepy," said Father.

"I think I'll wait a little longer too," said Mother. Eleven o'clock!

"I can't stand this another minute," said Father at last. "I'm going upstairs with Charles." Upstairs he went. Charles was wide awake. The father lay down beside him. He didn't need to talk. He just put his arm around his boy. Charles sobbed, "I'm sorry, Father," and put his arm around his father. They wept together for a little while, then they went peacefully to sleep. The second night and the third night Father went upstairs with Charles, and the rebellion was over.

Search your heart for the tiniest seed of rebellion and root it out.

"O my son Absalom, my son, my son Absalom! would God I had died for thee, O Absalom, my son, my son!" 2 Samuel 18:33.

Absalom was not only rebellious but he was wicked and quite deserving of the judgment of God that came upon him. But how his father loved him! In spite of his son's rebellion, his father would gladly have died in his place! That's the kind of love God has for us.

Several years ago Joe Hunt wrote a beautiful story in *The Youth's Instructor* about his father's love. Joe was just a little fellow when they lived on a farm, and more than anything else, Joe loved to drive the big team while his father filled the wagon with hay. It made him feel truly grown up. One day as he guided the team from one pile of hay to another he dropped one of the horses' reins, and as he tried to get it again, he lost his balance and fell onto the steel tongue of the wagon, right between the horses. The frightened animals lunged forward and dashed wildly across the field. For a while Joe held on to the tongue of the wagon. He heard his father shout "Whoa! whoa!" but the horses wouldn't stop. In a moment or two Joe figured out that if he dropped straight down to the ground, the wagon wheels wouldn't go over him. So he let go. There was a thud, an awful noise as the wagon went on overhead, but that was all. A moment more, and he sat up, spat the dirt out of his mouth, then got up and ran back to tell his father he was all right. He found his father hunched over, groaning with pain. He had jumped fearlessly between the wagon and the horses, trying to reach the reins and stop them, but the wagon had struck him with tremendous force, knocked him over, and two big wheels had passed over his body, almost crushing out his life. As Joe came near, the father looked up and with great effort said, "Are—you—all right—Joe?" Joe told him he was all right, and could say no more, for he realized his father had been hurt because he was trying to save him. Someone from the highway who saw the accident came and took the father to the hospital.

The next morning when Joe went to see him, there was a satisfied smile on his face. "How did you manage to escape, Joe?" he asked. Joe told him all about it. He smiled with satisfaction again, and in a few hours he died! Joe's father had given his life for him. Do you think Joe could have ever done anything that would have displeased his father?

Jesus gave *His* life for *you*.

"The Lord is my rock, and my fortress, and my deliverer . . . ; in him will I trust." 2 Samuel 22:2, 3.

In his battles with the enemies of Israel, David was always victorious because he trusted in the Lord. He found in God a rock and a fortress. In their battles against sin and self all through the ages the children of God have always been victorious when they made the Lord their rock and their fortress.

In 1937 it was my privilege to visit the Carlsbad Caverns in New Mexico, accompanied by my son Leonard. We walked down a winding trail that quickly became darker and deeper until we were 750 feet below the surface of the earth. We went through the King's Room and the Queen's Room and saw the many fantastic formations there; through Fairyland and the Cave of the Totem Pole. We went through the Big Room a mile and a half long and 348 feet high, and then into a room that had a huge stalagmite in the center of it. Our guide told us to be seated, and at once we noticed the name of the huge stalagmite—"Rock of Ages." There must have been five hundred people in our group, and as we sat down on the stone seats that had been carved out in rows, our guide said, "We are far away from the hustle and bustle and the noise of life. I want you to see how quiet it can be and how dark it can be down here 750 feet from the surface." With that he turned out the lights. How can I describe the darkness? It seemed that we could feel it! And the quietness? It was like the grave! For a few seconds we sat there wondering what would happen if the lights never came on again; then—far off in the distance—a quartet began to sing: "Rock of Ages, cleft for me, let me hide myself in Thee." It was the most beautiful singing I have ever heard! There was no need to fear; we had a living Rock. "Let the water and the blood, from Thy riven side which flowed, be of sin the double cure, cleanse me from its guilt and power." People were sobbing all around me. As the singing stopped I blew my nose and wiped my eyes as I breathed a little prayer of thankfulness that God was my rock and my fortress, and reconsecrated myself to His loving service.

Have you made Christ your rock of ages? Your fortress? Have you learned to put your trust in Him? Do it now, just for today; then do it every day.

"Unto him that loved us, . . . and hath made us kings and priests unto God and his Father; to him be glory and dominion for ever and ever." Revelation 1:5, 6.

Evidently David had once made a promise that his son Solomon would be king someday. So now Zadok the priest was commanded to anoint Solomon and proclaim him king. And all the people said, "God save king Solomon." Many times as Solomon grew up he must have said to himself, "Someday I'll be king," and that thought must often have helped him to do what was right.

In *Messages to Young People* we read: "Higher than the highest human thought can reach is God's ideal for His children."—Page 40. Think of it—if you can! God plans that we are to be kings and priests for Him! If we keep this thought in mind, how often we will say, What manner of persons ought we to be!

In the days of the French Revolution the people were sick and tired of the tyranny of their kings. So one day the mob surrounded the palace and dragged out Louis XVI and beheaded him. Again they went to the palace and dragged out Queen Marie Antoinette and beheaded her. Then they laid hands on Prince Louis, who would have been King Louis XVII someday. "To the guillotine! To the guillotine!" shouted the mob. "Make an end of royalty." But one man shouted, "Don't do that! That will only send him to heaven! I'll tell you what to do. Hand him over to Old Meg, the vilest woman in Paris. Let her clothe him in rags, feed him on filth, and teach him to lie and steal and swear. Let Old Meg curse his little soul and send him to hell!" The idea pleased the mob; so, according to some historians, Prince Louis was handed over to Old Meg. She clothed him in rags, fed him on garbage, and tried to teach him to lie and swear and steal. But it is said that every time Old Meg tried to teach him a new swear word, he would clench his little royal fists and stamp his little royal foot and say, "I will not say it! I will not say it! I was born to be a king and will not say it!"

What a boy! What a prince! And what a lovely example! For God has planned that you shall be a king unto God someday. Keep the thought always in mind, and when you are tempted to do evil, clench your fists and stamp your feet and say, "I will not! I was born to be a king, and I will not do it!"

"Give therefore thy servant an understanding heart . . . that I may discern between good and bad." 1 Kings 3:9.

Today is a good day for everyone to pray for an understanding heart that will help to "discern between good and bad"—a good day to resurrect one's faith in God if it has died. In the *Reader's Digest* for September, 1950, Dr. A. J. Cronin tells the story of how his faith in God was resurrected after being dead for many years. After graduating from the University of Glasgow, in Scotland, he went to practice medicine in a mining community in South Wales. At first he felt somewhat superior to the deeply religious Welsh people, and almost pitied their simple faith and reliance on God. But as he lived among them, and saw them live and worship and suffer and die, he realized that they had something that all his university knowledge had not given him. Then one day there was a terrible explosion in one of the mines, and fourteen miners were entombed. For five days the men remained buried in the mine. For five days the village prayed while the rescuers worked day and night to open up the caved-in tunnel. Then, on the fifth day, as the men got near the victims of the accident they heard them singing! It was the good old hymn "O God, Our Help in Ages Past." They had no food, no water, no light, but they had faith; and they had chosen to keep their faith alive by singing. Dr. Cronin was there to look after those who might be injured. But they came out unharmed! And as they came up to the surface the great crowd of more than a thousand people joined in singing "O God, Our Help in Ages Past." Dr. Cronin was never the same again. His dead faith came to life and has remained alive ever since.

Say, how is your faith? Today is a good day for you to take it out, and shine it up, and keep it alive. Remember: "The natural man is not subject to the law of God; neither, indeed, of himself, can he be. But by faith he who has been renewed lives day by day the life of Christ. Day by day he shows that he realizes that he is God's property. . . . He has bought us, and He desires us to remember that our physical, mental, and moral powers belong to Him."— *Messages to Young People*, pp. 68, 69.

"I dwell in the high and holy place, with him also that is of a contrite and humble spirit." Isaiah 57:15.

In 1791 there was born in New York City a man by the name of John Howard Payne. He became quite a famous actor, not only in America but also in England and in France. From 1842 to 1845 and again from 1851 to 1852 he was the United States consul in the country of Tunis, North Africa. He died at his post in 1852 and was buried there in Tunis; but thirty years later, in 1882, his body was exhumed, brought back to America, and buried among America's famous dead in the cemetery at Dumbarton Oaks, near the heart of the capital city. On the day of his burial in Washington, D.C., Congress and the Supreme Court adjourned in honor of the occasion, and the president, the vice president, and the members of the Cabinet led the funeral procession down Pennsylvania Avenue. Can you imagine why they paid him all this honor? Was it because he was a famous actor? Oh, no! Was it because he was an honorable U.S. consul? Oh, no! You couldn't guess. It was because he was the author of that beautiful, much-loved song "Home, Sweet Home!" At his graveside a choir of a thousand voices sang:

" 'Mid pleasures and palaces though we may roam,
Be it ever so humble, there's no place like home!
A charm from the skies seems to hallow us there,
Which, seek through the world, is ne'er met with
    elsewhere."

Every language on earth has a word for "house," but only the languages of Christian peoples have a word for "home." Home is a house where people live who love God and love one another. Solomon purposed to "build an house unto the name of the Lord," and no doubt God was pleased to bless that house with His presence. But Isaiah tells us that God will dwell "with him also that is of a contrite and humble spirit." What a lovely thought! We can make our hearts beautiful homes in which God will be pleased to dwell!

Is *your* heart contrite? Do you acknowledge your mistakes and quickly say you are sorry? And are *you* humble? If you are, you will know the joy of the presence of God.

"Know ye not that ye are the temple of God, and that the Spirit of God dwelleth in you? If any man defile the temple of God, him shall God destroy." 1 Corinthians 3:16, 17.

Solomon built a house for God, but there were certain conditions God's people had to meet in order for Him to dwell among them. They had to keep God's commandments (1 Kings 6:12, 13). Even so with our body temples there are conditions we must meet if we would have God live in us by His Spirit. We must keep our bodies clean and pure, and stay away from everything that might defile them. Tobacco is one of the things that defiles and destroys body temples. According to an interesting book, *Our Banquet,* by Mr. St. John, tobacco was first seen by European men in November, 1492, when two sailors with Columbus went ashore on the island later named Cuba and declared they "saw naked savages twist large leaves together and smoke like devils." When the weed was introduced into England it was not popular. King James wrote a "Counterblast" against it, and made import duties so high that only the rich could afford it. In Russia at first the use of tobacco was prohibited. A severe whipping was given for the first offense, the nose was cut off for the second offense, and death was the punishment for the third offense. Although the government does not mete out punishment these days for smoking, nobody can deny the fact that tobacco metes out its own punishment. Most authorities agree that smoking is one of the chief causes of lung cancer. Tobacco steals prizes from athletes and high marks from students. Tobacco taints the breath, discolors the teeth, and is the greatest single cause of fire in the United States today (*Reader's Digest,* September, 1950, p. 108). Some time ago on a cigar shop counter in San Francisco there stood a brass monkey with a cigarette constantly lighted in its mouth. The machinery inside kept it puffing day after day. One day, however, the brass monkey wouldn't work—it just wouldn't smoke! The mechanic took it apart and found the wheels all gummed up with the nicotine and tar! If tobacco will do that to a brass monkey, what will it do to you?

You need God. You need God to dwell within your body temple. Tobacco defiles. Keep away from it.

"Better is the end of a thing than the beginning thereof." Ecclesiastes 7:8.

It took Solomon thirteen years to build his house, and when it was finished it was beautiful. That is the way it ought to be done. If you started school at 6 years of age, do you know what you ought to be doing about thirteen years after that? You should be graduating from high school or beginning your college work. Would you achieve the best scholastic standing at the end of your course if you were a smoker or if you were a nonsmoker? Which would leave the most money in your pocket, smoking or not smoking? One smoker in Springfield, Massachusetts, estimated that cigarettes had cost him $7,000 in his lifetime. Charles Boles, a former chief petty officer of the Navy, gave up smoking and put his tobacco money into a jar day by day. He found at the end of a year that he had enough to pay the taxes on his home! Allan Schoberlein, of Aurora, Illinois, quit smoking at the age of 26 and began to save his tobacco money—40 cents a day. In thirty-two years, with interest, he had $8,000 in his savings account. He planned to retire when he was 70 and he would then have $12,000 saved because he didn't spend it on tobacco! That is a good ending, isn't it?

One time some newspaper reporters interviewed Giovanni Martinelli, the great singer, and while being introduced they offered him a pipe, a cigar, and some cigarettes.

"No, no, no," he said. "Excuse me; smoke makes my throat sore."

"But," said one of the men, "I read in a cigarette ad that you said, 'These cigarettes never make my throat sore.'"

"Yes, yes, of course I said that; and it is true. They never do," said Martinelli; then he smiled and added, "because I never smoke them. I have never smoked anything in my life." Cigarettes don't make my throat sore either! I hope they will never make your throat sore.

Plan now to have a good ending when you finish high school—and a still better ending when you retire!

"When thy people Israel be smitten down before the enemy, because they have sinned against thee, and shall turn again to thee, and confess thy name, and pray, and make supplication unto thee in this house: then hear thou in heaven, and forgive the sin of thy people Israel." 1 Kings 8:33.

At last the Temple was dedicated. The people had promised to obey the commandments of God so they could be assured of His presence with them. Yet Solomon realized there was always a danger that the people would be tempted and would sin. So he prayed earnestly that when the people would confess their sins, God would hear and forgive. No matter who we are, no matter how long our body temples have been given to God, temptation to defile those bodies in one form or another is sure to come. Thousands of young people have become tobacco, liquor, or drug addicts because some evil person tempted them to try it "just once" when they were juniors!

One day Abraham Lincoln was riding in a stagecoach with a Kentucky colonel.

"Will you have a drink of whiskey with me?" asked the colonel as he pulled out a bottle.

"No, thank you, Colonel," said Lincoln. "I never drink whiskey."

"Then, Mr. Lincoln, will you have a cigar? I have some of Kentucky's finest cigars with me," urged the colonel.

"Well, now, Colonel," he replied, "seeing you are so kind and generous, maybe I should have a smoke with you. But before I do, let me tell you a little story. When I was about 9 years old my mother called me to her bedside and said, 'Abe, I'm very, very sick, and the doctor says I'm not going to get well. Before I die I want you to promise me that you will never use whiskey or tobacco as long as you live.' Colonel, I promised my mother I never would, and up to this hour I never have. I have kept that promise. Now would you advise me to break that promise and smoke with you?"

The colonel put his hand on Lincoln's shoulder and said, "No, Mr. Lincoln, I wouldn't do it for the world. And I would give $1,000 today if I had made my mother a promise like that and kept it as you have."

That was a good promise to make. Why don't *you* make a promise like that to your mother *right now!*

"It was a true report that I heard. . . . Howbeit I believed not the words, until I came, and mine eyes had seen it: and, behold, the half was not told me." 1 Kings 10:6, 7.

We are not told who gave the queen of Sheba the first report about the wisdom and glory of Solomon. No doubt she asked every traveler she saw about it, and everyone told her a little more, but when she came and saw for herself—behold, the *half* had not been told. This has been the experience of many of our overseas workers who have had the privilege of attending a General Conference session in America for the first time. Take Pastor Kalee Paw, for example, who was Burma's delegate to the Cleveland General Conference in 1958. From his fascinating book *Jungle Flower*, let me quote a few sentences. "[On our way to the General Conference] we walked through Jerusalem, Bethlehem, Jericho, and Bethany in the footsteps of Jesus. . . . We paused in the Garden of Gethsemane and breathed a prayer of reconsecration. Suddenly the Bible story became real and living. There was the Mount of Olives. There was Calvary. There was Golgotha, the place of the skull, and right beside it, the Garden tomb where perhaps my Saviour's body was laid. . . . I have not words to describe our feelings as we saw the real Statue of Liberty, and the real skyscrapers as we steamed slowly into the [New York] harbor. We had seen pictures of them before. Now it seemed as if we were in a dream. . . . Toward evening we went 102 stories up by elevator to the top of the Empire State Building. We stayed there till . . . the great city's lights came on. I just cannot describe the rivers of light and the fountains of light we saw. . . . Then we tried to think that even this great city of New York cannot begin to compare with the New Jerusalem that God is preparing for His children. . . . The next day . . . dear Brother S. A. Wellman . . . took us all around the [General Conference] building and also around the Review and Herald. . . . I cannot describe how we felt. . . . Then came the General Conference session in . . . Cleveland. . . . And on Sabbath there were fifteen thousand present. And all of them Seventh-day Adventists. I think it's going to be like that in heaven, only better."

Indeed it is going to be better. Paul says, "Eye hath not seen, nor ear heard, . . . the things which God hath prepared for them that love him." Make sure that *you* are there.

"Because the preacher was wise, he still taught the people knowledge; yea, he gave good heed, and sought out, and set in order many proverbs." Ecclesiastes 12:9.

The story of Solomon's forsaking God is a sad one. It is hard to think that one who was so humble and so wise to begin with could ever fall. He gives the sad reasons in Ecclesiastes 2:4-18: "I made me great works; I builded me houses . . . : I got me servants and maidens . . . : I gathered me also silver and gold. . . . And whatsoever mine eyes desired I kept not from them, I withheld not my heart from any joy. . . . Then I looked on all the works that my hands had wrought. . . . And I turned myself to behold wisdom, and madness, and folly. . . . I hated life. . . . Yea, I hated all my labour which I had taken under the sun." Solomon came to the place where he was fed up with the world, with pleasure, and with himself. God was fed up with him, too, and sent him a message: "Forasmuch as this is done of thee, and thou hast not kept my covenant and my statutes . . . , I will surely rend the kingdom from thee, and will give it to thy servant." The message woke him up as from a dream, and we read in the book *Prophets and Kings*, "Chastened in spirit, with mind and body enfeebled, he turned wearied and thirsting from earth's broken cisterns, to drink once more at the fountain of life. . . . In penitence he began to retrace his steps toward the exalted plane of purity and holiness from whence he had fallen so far."—Pages 77, 78. It was after he repented that Solomon recorded his many proverbs. It was the forgiven Solomon who wrote, "Remember now thy Creator in the days of thy youth" (Ecclesiastes 12:1). "Solomon's repentance was sincere; but the harm that his example of evildoing had wrought could not be undone."—*Ibid.*, p. 84. As long as he lived, the thought of meeting the results of his example and influence in the judgment would haunt him like an eerie ghost from the past. The story of Solomon proves to us that self-indulgence is not the pathway to happiness. It also proves that no one has fallen too low; that if he repents he can be forgiven and be saved. If *you* would be really happy, and escape the regret and remorse that is sure to come to those who lead others astray by their example, then search your heart now, and if you need forgiveness, repent right now.

"Blessed is the man that walketh not in the counsel of the ungodly." Psalm
1:1.

We cannot help feeling a little bit disgusted with Rehoboam for
refusing the advice of the old men, and following the advice of the young
fellows who had grown up with him. But this business of not taking
advice didn't begin when Rehoboam was made king. It began when he
was just a little boy. That's when it always begins, and if you want to miss
all kinds of trouble when you grow up, you had better begin taking advice
now. Several years ago in my jungle school there were six little
girls—Sleep-sweet, Clear-gold, Clever-queen, Diamond, Brave, and
Golden-bead. It was the rainy season. The river was in flood, and its
angry, muddy waters were tearing out trees and gardens as they swirled
along. "There will be no swimming in the river today," I announced in
chapel. "The river is angry and it is too dangerous." But by afternoon
these six little girls forgot, and when the stop-work bell rang they got
their *longyis,* and started for the river. As they passed the schoolhouse the
teacher saw them and said, "Where are you little girls going? Remember,
Thara said there was to be no swimming in the river today." But the six
little girls just put their noses up in the air and went right on. As they
passed the girls' house the matron said, "Hey, where are you little girls
going? Remember, Thara said, 'No swimming today.'" But they put their
noses a little higher and went right on. At the river's edge there was a
man fishing in a canoe, and he said, "Hey, girls, it's dangerous to swim
when the river is angry."

"Oh, we're not scared. We can swim," they said. And they jumped
right in, and the man went away.

They *could* swim, and all went well for a while—till Diamond got out
too far and was caught in a whirlpool. Around and around she went. Five
frightened girls scrambled out and began to scream for help. Around and
around went Diamond, and down, down the river while five frightened
little girls followed along screaming and crying. Fortunately, the
whirlpool brought her in near a jutting rock, and Golden-bead jumped in
and pulled her out.

"I wish we hadn't come," said Golden-bead, and they all agreed.

"I don't feel good inside," said Clever-queen. And they all promised
to be good and take advice and obey after that.

" 'Because you have disobeyed the word of the Lord, and have not kept the commandment which the Lord your God commanded you, . . . your body shall not come to the tomb of your fathers.' " 1 Kings 13:21, 22, RSV.

What a lot of disobedient people we read about in the Scripture reading for today! A disobedient king, a disobedient prophet, and a deceitful old false prophet! It must be that God knew that disobedience would be one of the greatest sins in these last days. Perhaps that's why He had the men of old record so many examples of its punishment. In an old copy of the *Sabbath School Worker* I came across this story of disobedience and its terrible result.

A party of young men hired a guide and hiked up to the crater of a semiactive volcano. Then they climbed down among the lava rocks to the lowest ledge that was considered safe.

"I'm going farther down," said one adventurous young man.

"No, you're not," said the guide. "It is too steep, and it isn't safe."

"But I brought a rope for this very purpose, and I *am* going," persisted the young fellow.

"No, you're not," said the guide. "Those ashes and lumps of lava look cold, but you can never tell; maybe some of them were erupted just before we got here."

But in spite of all that the guide and his friends could say, the young fellow tied one end of his rope around a good strong rock, the other end around his waist, and lowered himself carefully and slowly down the steep side of the crater. His friends held their breath as they watched him go down, down, farther and farther. It looked so thrilling. But some of the pieces of lava *were* recent, and they were hot, and soon a tiny spark had started eating into the rope. The young fellow below couldn't see it; his friends above couldn't see it; but all of a sudden the rope parted—and the young man was instantly hurled into the depths. What a price to pay for disregarding counsel! As you can imagine, the terrible experience haunted the dreams and the waking hours of his friends for a long time afterward.

But why have to learn these lessons the hard way? Disobedience never pays. Learn to obey and take the advice of your teachers and parents in the little things now, and save yourself the sorrow and disgrace that are sure to catch up with the rebellious ones someday.

"And it shall be, that thou shalt drink of the brook; and I have commanded the ravens to feed thee there." 1 Kings 17:4.

What a loving heavenly Father we have! He is patient with us when we are discouraged and weak, and He has promised that our bread shall be given us, even if He has to tell the ravens to bring it to us.

Pastor R. A. Anderson brought a wonderful story back from Greece after he had attended a workers' meeting there many years ago. Our worker there at that time was Pastor C. A. Christoforides, and he and his family went through a very trying time while civil war raged all around them. For weeks they were cut off from supplies. At last their food was almost gone; they could not get milk for their 8-month-old baby; and they were about at their wits' end when one day there was a knock on the door. A knock could mean anything in those days, so, saying Goodbye to his family, Pastor Christoforides fearfully opened the door. There stood a soldier!

"Are you Mr. Christoforides?" he asked.

"Yes," replied our brother timidly. The soldier stepped inside, closed the door, put a pack on the floor, and handing him a note, took his leave. Trembling, Mr. Christoforides opened the note and read, "These things are for you." It was not signed. Eagerly they opened the pack. There were bread, butter, chocolate, and milk! Could it be true? Who could have sent it? It must have been God in some way or other. In a few days the soldier came again! In fact, every few days he came. He came just when they needed those things the most. Mrs. Christoforides soon got to recognize the knock, and she would say, "Did you hear that? Our raven is still alive! He has come again!" Later they learned that the provisions were being sent by an army officer who knew Pastor Christoforides, and although he was not a Christian, he felt *impressed* that if Mr. Christoforides was still alive, he would need food. So you see it *was* God sending the food after all.

Learn to cast all your care upon the God of Elijah. He is your God, too, and He can bring you help just when you need it most.

Remember, God has ten thousand times ten thousand, and thousands of thousands, of angels (see Revelation 5:11), and they are all His ministering spirits (Hebrews 1:14).

"And Elijah said unto all the people, Come near unto me. . . . And he repaired the altar of the Lord that was broken down." 1 Kings 18:30.

In answer to faithful Elijah's prayer, the living God—the Creator of heaven and earth—sent down fire from heaven to consume the sacrifice, and then sent rain to end the severe drought. Thus He demonstrated that the gods of the surrounding nations were powerless.

Again and again our living God has revealed His power on behalf of His faithful followers before the eyes of the people. In the *Review and Herald* for January 7, 1960, there was a story about a severe drought in Bombay state, India. The condition of the gardens, and of the people themselves, was so pitiful that the municipal officers called upon all the people of the town to pray to Varuna, the goddess of rain, to send rain and relieve their suffering.

Now, we had a good church in that town, and when the members heard about the call to pray to Varuna, they hurried to the officers and said, "We will pray, sirs. But we can only pray to the living God in heaven, the Creator of all things." The poor officers were so desperate that they quickly agreed that the Hindus should pray to Varuna on Wednesday and Thursday, and the Adventists would pray to their God on Friday and Saturday. During Wednesday and Thursday the worshipers of Varuna burned incense, blew trumpets, beat drums, and offered sacrifices; but no rain came. On Friday our church members began fasting and praying. They prayed for themselves. They prayed that the people of the town would see the salvation of the living God. All day Friday no rain came. Sabbath morning no rain came. But our people kept on praying. Sabbath afternoon, clouds began to appear. The people in the town gathered in excited groups and discussed the test of power. Our members kept on praying, and while they were still praying, before the sun set, it began to rain—and it rained for four days.

Thank God, He has unlimited power! He is the same yesterday, today, and forever. He longs to show forth His power for *you* too. Is there anything wrong with your altar—the one at your bedside, the one in your home? Why not repair the altar of the Lord now?

"And, behold, there came a voice unto him, and said, What doest thou here, Elijah?" 1 Kings 19:13.

In discouragement Elijah fled to Mount Horeb. And, behold, the Lord passed by and there was a great wind, then an earthquake, then a fire, and after the fire a still small voice saying, "What doest thou here, Elijah?"

We have all heard that still small voice. We call it the voice of conscience. It is the little voice by which God speaks to us. Many people only hear it saying, "Don't do that!" "It's not right!" "Do this!" But if we obey it, and train our heart to listen to it, God will lead us and guide us and comfort us with that still small voice. I can still remember the embarrassment I had when I came to America after twenty years of service in Burma and tried to carry on a conversation over a telephone. There had been no telephones in the jungle where my mission station was, and my ears were not accustomed to hearing the little voice in the telephone. It would talk and talk and talk, and I'd say, "I beg your pardon; say it again." And it would talk and talk and talk, and I would say, "I can't understand." Then I would have to ask my secretary to take the message and tell me what it said. They all laughed at me because I couldn't hear the words of the little voice in the telephone. But they didn't laugh long, for I kept on trying and listening, and in a few weeks I could understand everything it said.

If *you* ask God to speak to you by the still small voice, He will; and one of the first things you will hear God asking is "What doest thou here?" Think now—what are you doing?

Once, so the story goes, there were three men cutting stone in a Vermont quarry. A stranger approached them and said, "What are you doing?" The first man replied carelessly, "I'm cutting stone." The second man said, "I'm earning my living—$7.50 a day!" The third man said, "I'm helping to build a cathedral!" There they were—three men doing the same work, but what a difference!

Now, what are you doing? Just going to school, working for a diploma, or are you building a character that will be worth taking to heaven? There is a big difference between *having* to go to school and *wanting* to go to school, and between *having* to obey and *loving* to obey.

"Let no man seek his own, but every man another's wealth."
1 Corinthians 10:24.

One cannot help despising Ahab's actions. What a selfish man he was! He wanted his neighbor's vineyard, and when he couldn't get it he threw a tantrum. Then he arranged for his neighbor's murder and took possession of the vineyard anyhow. He deserved all the judgment that finally came to him.

We need to be constantly aware lest selfishness overwhelm us, for we read that in the last days men shall be lovers of their own selves, covetous, boastful, and proud. There is a good story told about a purse-proud old nobleman who lived in Sweden in the days when they traveled by stagecoach. You know, it was the custom to stop and change horses at an inn now and then when travelers were on a long journey. Well, this proud, rich man came to an inn one day and shouted, "Horses, landlord; horses at once."

"I'm sorry, sir," said the landlord, "but you'll have to wait till your horses are rested. I have no more fresh horses."

Just then two lovely horses were brought out of the stable and hitched to a carriage in which a quiet little gentleman was sitting.

"I thought you said you had no fresh horses," shouted the selfish man.

"These were ordered by that gentleman before you came," said the landlord quietly. Then the selfish man called to the gentleman in the carriage, "Say, my man, let me have those horses and I will pay you well for them."

"I'm sorry," replied the quiet gentleman, "I need them myself and I am ready to start."

"Perhaps you don't know who I am," replied the selfish man. "I am Field Marshal Baron George Sparre, the last and only one of my race."

"That's good," said the quiet gentleman. "It would be terrible to think there might be more like you." And he drove off.

Then the landlord turned to the haughty man and said, "There goes the king of Sweden."

I'm sorry the story ended there, for I would like to know how the selfish old man felt after that! But never mind, you can imagine it easily enough. Just be sure *you* are never selfish and demanding like that.

"And when they shall say unto you, Seek unto them that have familiar spirits, and unto wizards that peep, and that mutter: should not a people seek unto their God?" Isaiah 8:19.

Ahaziah knew better. During the reign of his father, Ahab, he had seen many wonderful works of God. He well knew that God could help, and he well knew that severe judgments were often meted out upon transgressors. He should have gone humbly to Elijah and had him inquire of God. But no! He had heard all about Baalzebub, the Philistine god in Ekron, who was supposed to be able to foretell the future. So he sent his servants off to Ekron to get his fortune told. It is a dangerous business to associate with fortune-tellers and spirit mediums. God and evil spirits can never get along together. In the *Youth's Instructor* for September 23, 1947, there was a story of Mary Jane and her experience with a spirit medium. Mary Jane lived in Minnesota. She had had nine children, but four of them had died. Then little three-year-old Robbie sickened and died. Mary Jane was not yet an Adventist, but she was a deeply religious woman. At the funeral the minister had said that her little dead children were rejoicing in heaven, but the thought brought her no comfort. Then one day a neighbor said, "Wouldn't you like to talk with your little children who are in heaven?"

"Oh, yes," said Mary Jane. "How can I do it?"

"I'll take you to our spirit medium in town, and he'll get you in touch with them," said the neighbor. Mary Jane was delighted, but before she went she felt she should have some spiritual preparation, so she read her Bible and prayed. Then she went to see the medium; but nothing happened. She went again the next week and the next, and every time before she went she read her Bible and prayed; and every time nothing happened. Then one day the medium said, "Something's wrong. What do you do before you come to me?"

"Why, I pray and—" Mary Jane began to say, but she could get no further. The medium shouted, "You pray! No wonder they won't come," and he slammed the door and left the room. Soon after that Mary Jane met some Adventists and learned the truth from them, just as it is in the Bible.

It is true—no man can serve two masters, and if you always read your Bible and seek God, you will be safe.

127

"I pray thee, let a double portion of thy spirit be upon me." "And when the sons of the prophets . . . saw him, they said, The spirit of Elijah doth rest on Elisha." 2 Kings 2:9, 15.

It's a strange thing, isn't it! You can't see the Spirit of God and you can't take hold of Him, but when He rests upon a person, you know it. For He fills him with faith and makes him fearless, courageous, kind, and patient. That's what He did for Elijah; that's what He did for Elisha; and that's what He can do for every one of us. Here's a story from a letter from Kyaw Balay, who was a leader of our work in Burma.

Away up in the Chin Hills they opened a school in a certain village. The children were very happy to come, and soon they were attending Sabbath school and singing our Sabbath school songs all around the village. But the old people did not like it. "We don't want our children to become Seven-days," they said. And they took their children out of school. Still they came to Sabbath school. The old folks were alarmed. They threatened some children and whipped some, but still they came to Sabbath school. Then one of the chief opposers, Uncle Tha Doo, became curious and said to himself, "What is it that makes these children want to go to Sabbath school?" He began to ask; he began to listen; he began to read his Bible. Then he had Bible studies with the teacher and was baptized. Then his wife, Aunty Tha Doo, became angry. She called him names; she cooked only unclean meats and fish for him; but Uncle Tha Doo never got angry. He was always patient and kind. When she put the unclean foods before him he just ate rice and salt; and when she called him names he just smiled and said, "Please read your Bible carefully and you will find it is true." Soon Aunty Tha Doo got curious and said to herself, "What's the matter with him? What makes him so kind and patient? It must be what he reads in his Bible. I believe I'll read it a little bit and see." And now *she* is different!

She is kind and patient, and she is taking Bible studies. And the village people are becoming curious. They are wondering what has happened to Aunty Tha Doo.

It's true. When the Spirit of God rests on someone, he is different, and everyone knows it. Is the Spirit of God resting upon *you?* Does anyone know it?

"He that receiveth a prophet in the name of a prophet shall receive a prophet's reward." Matthew 10:41.

Throughout the experiences of Elijah and Elisha we can see that God pours out His blessing upon those who are hospitable. The widow woman who shared her last measure of meal with Elijah, and the Shunammite woman who prepared a little room where Elisha could stay when he was in that district were both doubly blessed. Hospitality still brings blessings to all who practice it.

Listen! Two days after Hurricane Carla (1962) had left a path of wreckage for miles along the coast near Galveston, Texas, Mrs. Kirke and her two children, Danny and Betty, stood in front of their little cabin, wondering what to do. Father had gone to work in Galveston, seventy-five miles away, the morning before the storm. They had no radio; they heard no warning. Suddenly the storm was on top of them. Great waves from the ocean half a mile away rolled over and over the land. The road was broken and impassable. The neighbors had all fled before the storm, and now the Kirkes were alone, with only a little food and very little water to drink. Danny put up a flag and lighted a fire, but it was no use. The dense fog and heavy clouds made it impossible for any passing plane to see them. On the third day, Mrs. Kirke had to ration their food. Just one bowl of corn grits twice a day—no gravy, no butter. Danny and Betty were desperate. They gathered sticks and arranged them to spell the word *help* on the white sand. Then suddenly they saw some people coming. It was a Mexican family—a father, a mother, and three children, one of them a baby, all ragged, hungry looking, and desolate. "We've lost everything," said the father. "Our cabin is gone; we have had no food for three days. I ask a little food—just for the little ones."

"We too have only a little food, but you shall all have a share of it while it lasts," said Mrs. Kirke as she led them into the cabin. I'm sorry to say that Danny was sulking a little bit. He was hungry too, and tomorrow would be worse! But hardly had Mrs. Kirke finished asking a blessing when Danny left the table and rushed outside. "I hear something!" he shouted. He *saw* something too! He saw the clouds part; he saw the sunshine; he saw a plane swing low and drop a parachute with a great big bundle of food attached to it!

You see, a blessing often comes with hospitality, doesn't it?

"Servants, obey in all things your masters . . . ; not with eyeservice, as menpleasers; . . . whatsoever ye do, do it heartily, as to the Lord." Colossians 3:22, 23.

The little captive maid didn't realize that every time she appeared clean and neat and was obedient and humble, truthful and honest, kind and polite, she was witnessing for God. But she was, and Naaman and his wife often talked about her and her religion and her God, and it made such an impression on him that this great general did what the little servant girl suggested he do—and Naaman was healed!

What wonderful things can also happen when Seventh-day Adventists are clean and neat, obedient and humble, truthful and honest, and kind and polite in the places where they work. Dear old Elder Spicer used to tell a story about a Seventh-day Adventist farmer way up in the Northwest who wanted to buy some cows. Because he couldn't pay cash, the man with cows for sale asked him what security he could furnish. He showed him the papers of ownership for his car and his farm machinery. The man looked them over and said, "All right, but this is only enough security for you to buy six cows. Come tomorrow morning at ten o'clock, and we will sign the papers."

"But tomorrow is Saturday," said our brother, "and you know I am a Seventh-day Adventist. I do not do business on the Sabbath."

"You are a Seventh-day Adventist?"

"Yes."

"Oh, well, that's different! You know, I have had Seventh-day Adventist girls working for me for the past five years. And if you are a Seventh-day Adventist, you can have the whole lot of cows if you want them. It will be quite all right."

Those young women working away faithfully at their daily tasks little knew that their boss was measuring their religion and their church by the way they lived and did their work. But he was! And he felt confident that he could trust this Seventh-day Adventist man who wanted to buy the cows because he could trust those Seventh-day Adventist girls who were working for him.

When your neighbors and friends see *you* at work, at study, and at play, what do they think of your religion and your church and your God?

"Lord, I pray thee, open his eyes, that he may see. . . . And, behold, the mountain was full of horses and chariots of fire round about Elisha." 2 Kings 6:17.

In *Messages to Young People* we read: "There are three ways in which the Lord reveals His will to us, to guide us. . . . God reveals His will to us in His word, the Holy Scriptures. His voice is also revealed in His providential workings. . . . Another way in which God's voice is heard, is through the appeals of His Holy Spirit, making impressions upon the heart."—Page 156. We all have heard God's voice speaking to us as we read the Bible and as the Holy Spirit makes impressions on our heart or speaks with the still small voice. But it is not so easy to understand God's voice when He closes a door in front of us or surrounds us with some disappointment. Here was Elisha's servant surrounded by enemy soldiers. He couldn't understand God's leading in that! *Then* Elisha prayed, "Lord, open his eyes," and *then* he saw the angels! Elder C. L. Paddock tells a good story that illustrates the way God's voice is revealed in providential workings, in his book *Footprints to Success*. A ship was wrecked in the Pacific Ocean, and only one survivor was washed ashore on a small uninhabited island. He made a little hut out of the wreckage he found on the beach, put a blanket on a tall pole—hoping to attract some passing ship—and prayed every day that God would send a ship to deliver him.

The days dragged on into weeks. He still prayed and hoped. Then one day as he returned from hunting for sea birds' eggs and wild yams, he was filled with horror to find his little hut going up in flames! You can only imagine his discouragement, praying every day and hoping for deliverance, and now his only comfort was gone! But in a few hours a ship appeared in sight! It came closer and closer! A dinghy was put to shore and sailors took him aboard. The captain said, "We saw your smoke signal and figured it must be someone in distress after the recent wreck!" Of course, *then* his eyes were opened, and he thanked God many times for burning up his little hut.

When disappointment comes to you, and the day looks blue and discouraging, just pray, "Lord, open my eyes." And you too will be able to see the voice of God "revealed in His providential workings."

"We do not well: this day is a day of good tidings, and we hold our peace: if we tarry till the morning light, some mischief will come upon us: now therefore come, that we may go and tell the king's household." 2 Kings 7:9.

I like this story about the four lepers, don't you? I like the urgency they felt to tell the good news to others; they couldn't even wait till morning light! It's just like this with people everywhere who hear the good news of the gospel of salvation. They can't wait to tell others about the joy they have found; they have to begin right away. Pastor F. G. Clifford tells about a 10-year-old boy in New Guinea. He lived in a little section called Papus, and he went down to the seacoast with his big brother to work on a coconut plantation. While there he heard about the seven-day mission school not far away, and one day he slipped over to see what the school was like. He went again and again, and he decided he would rather go to school than pick up coconuts. So he joined up as a day scholar and got a slate and a songbook. He loved school; he loved learning to read and write; he loved singing and he loved Sabbath school—in fact, he loved everything on that seven-day mission. On the back cover of his songbook there were printed the Ten Commandments, one column in English and one in his own language. He learned them by heart and listened intently as the teachers explained them. Then a little fire began to burn in his heart. "How the boys and girls back in my village would love to know these things and sing these songs," he said to himself again and again. Of course, he wasn't baptized yet, and he didn't know anything about graduating or about committees that appoint people to the work. He could read and write and sing, and he knew the Ten Commandments, and the fire burned in his heart till he couldn't wait any longer. So off he went, back to his village, and the teacher just crossed his name off the class book! Several months later Missionary C. E. Mitchell found this 10-year-old boy working as the schoolteacher and preacher for that village! All he had was a hymnbook and the Ten Commandments; but the people could sing and they were having Sabbath school, and they were all ready for a big teacher to come.

I hope the fire burns in *your* heart too. Don't wait till "morning light." Begin now to help someone to be obedient, pure, and true.

"And he did that which was right in the sight of the Lord." "And the Lord was with him; and he prospered whithersoever he went forth." 2 Kings 18:3, 7.

It is simply marvelous how God prospers kings and preachers, doctors and nurses, and also boys and girls who do that which is "right in the sight of the Lord." Many years ago Elder W. R. Beach told this story about one of our young men in Italy. He was selling books in Naples and was invited to attend a workers' meeting in Florence. He bought his train ticket, but there was no room in the train. So he had to stand on the outside and hang on for dear life. As the train stopped at a station another young man climbed up and hung on right next to him.

"How far are you going?" asked the new hanger-on.

"To Florence!" replied our colporteur. "And you?"

"To Bologna. And what takes you to Florence?" he asked.

"Oh, I'm going to attend a meeting of the Seventh-day Adventists. Ever hear of them?"

"Indeed I have. I know one who lives in Bologna. I was there during the war, and one day a big bomb fell and shattered a whole section of the city. When the rescue squads got to work they found only one corner of one of the buildings still standing, and in the kitchen, still intact, was a little old lady reading her Bible. She was a Seventh-day Adventist. They must have lots of faith."

"They surely do," answered our colporteur. "I am a Seventh-day Adventist, and in my work I must have lots of faith too."

"What do you do?"

"I sell books."

"What kind of books?"

"I'll show you," said our colporteur, and holding on with one hand, he showed his prospectus with the other hand.

"That surely is a good book. I'll take one," said his newfound friend, and as he signed on the dotted line he added, "Seventh-day Adventists do have a lot of faith all right."

Yes, that is faith, but it is also an excellent example of a young man doing what is right in the sight of the Lord, and of the Lord prospering him whithersoever he goes. God will prosper you, too.

"Be not afraid of the words which thou hast heard. . . . Behold, I will send a blast upon him, and he shall . . . return to his own land." 2 Kings 19:6, 7.

The threatening letter Sennacherib sent to Hezekiah was enough to frighten anyone; then the Lord sent just one angel, and there was nothing to fear any more. At a General Conference session I heard Pastor R. E. Adams from Brazil tell a wonderful story about two men, Peter and Paul, who started out to hold some meetings. They went by train to a little town. They knew no one there, and hardly knew how to get started. But while they were still at the railway station a man came up to them and said, "Gentlemen, could I help you?" He turned out to be the mayor of the town and he owned a theater, which he gladly offered to them to use on Sunday nights. They hardly knew how they would advertise, but while they were setting up their projector, many curious children crowded around. "What are you going to do, mister?" they asked.

"Show pictures on the life of Christ," Paul replied. "Tell everybody to come."

"Everybody?" asked the children, and off they went to tell everybody! They did a good job, for the theater was well filled. The next Sunday night Paul and Peter came again and held another good meeting. But the third Sunday night, just as Paul was about to start the pictures, an angry priest walked right up to him, beamed his flashlight in his eyes, and demanded, "Who gave you authority to hold these meetings? Turn the lights on!" Someone turned the lights on, and the priest began to scold the people. "You have no business coming to a Protestant meeting. Now when I go out, everybody follow me." The priest went out, but nobody followed. He came back the second time, more angry than before. "Follow me out!" he shouted. Still nobody went. Then he came back and ordered Paul and Peter to follow him out, but just then a big giant of a man stepped up and said to Peter and Paul, "You keep on with your meeting." Then, turning to the priest, he said, "You go out, yourself, and don't come to interrupt these meetings any more." This scared the priest, and he never came back. Today we have many members in that city.

You have nothing to fear if you are on God's side.

"Then he turned his face to the wall, and prayed unto the Lord. . . . And Hezekiah wept sore." 2 Kings 20:2, 3.

How much better it would have been if Hezekiah had accepted God's plan for him. But no, Hezekiah was determined to have his own way. He wouldn't pray "if it be Thy will." He "wept sore." And God let him have his way. He lived fifteen years longer. But those fifteen extra years brought him only shame and trouble. The temptation to have our own way at any cost comes to all of us in one form or another. Elder A. S. Maxwell tells of a boy named Byron who begged his mother to get him an air rifle. His mother tried to show him that it was not good for him to have an air gun, but Byron begged and begged, and "wept sore" until, very much against her wishes, his mother bought him one. Then the trouble began, and the neighbors complained about their dogs and cats being hurt and cracked windows, till at last Mother took the gun away and hid it. "I wish I had never bought it for you," she said. "I knew it would be this way. Now I shall keep it till you have learned to be more careful." Byron begged and pleaded to have it again, but mother said, "No, not yet. I've had enough trouble over this gun to last me a long time." But Byron determined to have that gun. His mother wouldn't give it to him, so he began to look for its hiding place. He looked in the attic and in the basement, but with no success. One day he looked in the garage, and saw the end of the barrel poking over the edge of one of the rafters. It was his gun! He was going to do what he wanted with it. He sneaked off behind a tree, and holding the gun under his arm he began loading the lead pellets into the muzzle with his right forefinger. He was so absorbed in what he was doing that he did not notice his little brother Jock sneaking up behind him. Suddenly there was a "pift!" and a scream. Yes, you've guessed it. Little Jock had pulled the trigger just for fun, and now Byron's finger was bleeding terribly. He didn't dare tell Mother. He put the gun back and tied a rag around his finger, and you can imagine the rest. But that wasn't the end of his punishment. Later his hand swelled up and his finger developed an abscess. When the doctor lanced it—he found the rifle pellet.

You must learn to take No for an answer sometimes. Not everything is best for you. There is no happiness in pouting.

"Because thine heart was tender, and thou hast humbled thyself before the Lord, . . . I also have heard thee, saith the Lord." 2 Kings 22:19.

Josiah was only 8 years old when he was made king! But he was a good king. When he was 16 years old he began to seek the Lord earnestly; when he was 20 he began to destroy the idols in the land; and when he was 26 he had the Temple restored, and there followed a great reformation. God was with him at every step, because his heart was tender and humble.

Here's another story of a boy whose heart was tender and humble. Little William was going to bed, and Mother said, "Be sure to say your prayers, William."

So William knelt at his bedside and prayed, "Now I lay me down to sleep. . . . " You know that little prayer; then he added a few words of his own. "Bless Mama and Papa and bless Willie and make him a good boy for Jesus' sake. Amen." Then he looked right into his mother's face and said, "Mama, do you and Papa pray?"

"No, darling," she said.

"Well, why do I have to pray?"

"So you will be a good boy."

"Don't you and Papa want to be good, Mama?" he asked.

"Oh, yes, we want to be good."

"Then why don't you and Papa pray too?" asked William.

Mother didn't have an answer to the last question, so William went on talking. "Well, Mama," he said, "I guess God will hear the prayer of a little boy like me, but don't you think you and Papa expect too much of a little fellow like me? Do you think that God wants me to do all the praying for this whole family? It seems to me that you and Papa might help me a little." His little eyes were heavy, and in a moment he was fast asleep. He didn't even know that Mother had wiped her eyes and that Father had heard his little speech as he sat reading the paper. He didn't know that Father and Mother held hands for a long time, then tiptoed back into his room and knelt by his bed as they prayed and gave their hearts to God. After that both Mother and Father helped do the praying for the whole family.

Keep your heart tender and humble, and God will hear *you*, too.

"Thy father and thy mother shall be glad, and she that bare thee shall rejoice." Proverbs 23:25.

Almost hidden in the record of the last days of King Jehoiakim's wicked reign is the sad statement that when he was taken captive by the servants of Nebuchadnezzar, his mother was taken captive too. How true are the words of Solomon, "The rod and reproof give wisdom: but a child left to himself bringeth his mother to shame" (Proverbs 29:15). However, I am glad that Solomon also said that a wise son would make his mother "rejoice," and in the lives of our good wise men we have many examples of this. When James A. Garfield was elected president of the United States in 1880, he wrote to his dear old mother and said, "I want you to go to Washington, D.C., with me for the inauguration."

"Oh, no," she said, "I could not go. I would feel out of place with all those great people. I'll stay at home and pray for you."

But James Garfield wrote back: "Mother, I will not go without you." So they traveled to Washington together, stayed in the same hotel, and when he went to the Capitol for the ceremony, his mother was leaning on his arm. When he got on the platform he put his mother in the chair that had been provided for him, and he sat in a seat beside her. Then, after he had delivered his address and taken the oath to be true to his high office, he turned around, put his arms around his mother, and kissed her; and more than 100,000 people cheered and applauded. They all thought it was one of the most beautiful acts they had ever seen. I wish that every junior would throw his arms around his mother and kiss her today. Ellen White says in *Messages to Young People:* "When the judgment shall sit, and the books shall be opened; when the 'well done' of the great Judge is pronounced, and the crown of immortal glory is placed upon the brow of the victor, many will raise their crowns in sight of the assembled universe and, pointing to their mother, say, 'She made me all I am through the grace of God. Her instruction, her prayers, have been blessed to my eternal salvation.'"—Page 330.

I wish that every boy and every girl might do this in that glad day. Then every mother would rejoice. But for now, plan to make Mother happy today, and every day.

"Happy is the man whom God correcteth: . . . for he maketh sore, and bindeth up: he woundeth, and his hands make whole." Job 5:17, 18.

At last the punishment had come, and Judah was carried away captive. Still, through Jeremiah came the promise "I am with thee, saith the Lord, to save thee: though I make a full end of all nations whither I have scattered thee, yet will I not make a full end of thee" (Jeremiah 30:11).

God permitted great trouble to come to our people in many countries during World War II, but always God's saving power could be seen protecting His people and His work from a "full end." The country of Korea was taken over by the Japanese in 1905, and although many restrictions were placed upon our workers, by the year 1941 we had almost four thousand church members there. When World War II broke out, the Japanese Government was determined to destroy the Christian faith. Our churches were closed, our leaders arrested, our members forbidden to worship. One of our Sabbath school superintendents, Lee Tuk Hoe, was summoned by the chief of police. The officer lectured about national affairs to the men called, then announced that they must all make obeisance at a Shinto shrine to show their loyalty. They were all afraid to speak, but Lee rose and asked to be excused, because such worship was contrary to the law of Jehovah. The chief of police seemed to take no notice of him, and led them all to the shrine. Everyone else made obeisance and burned incense, but Lee refused. This made the guard very angry, but the chief of police said nothing. So they were all marched back again. Then the chief of police made another speech. He talked about loyalty and commended Lee for his courage, but said that he would have to suffer the consequences. He then dismissed the others and took Lee into another room and commanded him to kneel down. This was the customary way for a criminal to receive a beating, so Lee knelt down and began to pray to God quietly. The officer left the room and didn't come back for half an hour. Lee was still kneeling. Then the police chief spoke and said, "I hate to punish a man who is loyal to the Majesty of heaven, but as an officer I am obliged to mete out punishment to you for breaking the law. Your punishment has been to kneel for a half hour. You may go now."

No matter how much trouble God permits to come to you, remain faithful to Him and see how He will bind up *your* "wounds."

"Come, and let us return unto the Lord: for he hath torn, and he will heal us; he hath smitten, and he will bind us up." Hosea 6:1.

Today we have read one of the saddest chapters in the story of Israel and Judah. Because of their persistent sinning, their land was to be desolate, and they were to be captives of the king of Babylon for seventy years. Just before Israel was taken captive, however, Hosea reminded them of the long-suffering and mercy of God. "Come," he said, "let us return unto the Lord . . . and he will heal us; he hath smitten, and he will bind us up." Let me give you another example of how God binds up and heals after trouble has "smitten."

After World War II, Korea had only a few years of rest, for in 1950 the Communists invaded the country, and for the next two years poor Korea was torn and bruised. The capital city, Seoul, was overrun four times, and 75 percent of it was destroyed. Our college just outside the city was a shambles, and our dear people were scattered all over the country. But everywhere our believers went, the people wanted to know what this suffering meant, and our people had the answers. God's Holy Spirit was poured out upon them, and they began branch Sabbath schools and held Bible studies everywhere. In 1952, when peace again came to the land, they began to rebuild, and soon our presses were printing again and our school was full again; and the Spirit of God moved mightily on the old men and on the young men and even on the children. In a few years some of our churches had to hold two worship sessions on Sabbath. One group had Sabbath school and church in the morning and another had Sabbath school and church in the afternoon. One church had to have five worship sessions each Sabbath day! Ten years later, in 1962, the baptized church membership had grown from about two thousand to twenty thousand! The Sabbath school membership had grown from about five thousand to eighty-two thousand! There were six hundred young people enrolled in our junior academy. Our publishing house, our sanitarium, and our nurse's training school were working to capacity, and our elementary schools were overflowing!

That is the way God binds up and heals. That is what God wanted to do for Israel and Judah. When trouble and sorrow come to you, remember that God wants to do that for *you,* too.

"I am the Lord . . . that saith of Cyrus, He is my shepherd, and shall perform all my pleasure: even saying to Jerusalem, Thou shalt be built; and to the temple, Thy foundation shall be laid." Isaiah 44:24-28.

God Himself named Cyrus, through Isaiah, about 113 years before he was born, and foretold that he would make the decree that Jerusalem should be built and the foundations of the Temple should be laid. As the seventy years of captivity came near the close, there can be no question that Daniel showed Cyrus the prophecy in Isaiah, and in this way the Lord stirred up the spirit of Cyrus to do His pleasure.

Herodotus, the famous Greek historian, tells this story about the early boyhood of Cyrus. Astyages, king of Media, had a dream one night in which he saw a great river flowing over Asia. "It means that the children of your daughter Mandane will someday conquer the world," said his wise men. Eager for the neighboring Persians to be always friendly, old Astyages married his daughter to the Persian prince Cambyses. In time a baby boy was born to Mandane and was named Cyrus. When old Astyages saw the little babe, he said to himself, "I'll have him killed; then he can never conquer me." So he called Harpagus, a trusted servant, and told him to take the baby away and kill it, then to bring back the dead body so he could be sure it was dead. Harpagus asked a poor herdsman to kill the child.

As the herdsman took Baby Cyrus into his humble house, he found his wife crying. Their own newborn baby had just died! "Here," said the herdsman, "let's change the babies' clothes; then we can keep the live baby and give the wicked old king our dead baby." So they did, and no one ever knew about it till Cyrus was about 12 years old. Then one day while the children were playing soldier, Cyrus, who was playing general, punished a nobleman's son for not obeying. The nobleman's son told his father, and the nobleman told the king. The king scolded the herdsman's boy, but was so impressed with the boy's dignity that he became suspicious, and tortured the herdsman until the whole story came out. The king sent Cyrus back to his parents, hoping to keep Persia friendly. It did for a while, but when Cyrus grew up he became the general of the Persian army.

Our wonderful God knows your future and has a plan for you, too. Don't be afraid to trust Him with your life.

"So shall my word be that goeth forth out of my mouth; it shall not return unto me void, but it shall accomplish that which I please, and it shall prosper in the thing whereto I sent it." Isaiah 55:11.

God foretold through Isaiah that Cyrus would make the decree to rebuild the Temple. And although Isaiah did not live long enough to see it fulfilled, he was certain that it would be accomplished. This same living God foretold that the three angels' messages of Revelation 14 would be preached "to every nation, and kindred, and tongue, and people," and today God's Word "prospers" in all the world.

In 1885 the first group of Seventh-day Adventist missionaries to Australia was led by Elder S. N. Haskell. They settled in Melbourne and immediately began to plan for the work there. In November of that same year, while waiting for some printing machinery to arrive, Elder Haskell went to New Zealand to spy out the land. "Can you recommend a boarding house in Auckland run by some religious person?" he inquired of one of the seamen during the trip. "Yes," said the seaman. "Go to the house of Edward Hare; he has rooms."

So Elder Haskell went to Edward Hare's house as soon as he arrived. "Yes, I have a room you may have," said Edward Hare.

It wasn't long, however, before the man in the room next to Mr. Haskell came downstairs and said, "That new man is crazy! He's talking to himself all the time! You either get rid of him or I will go."

Mr. Hare went upstairs and listened. Sure enough, the new boarder did seem to be talking to himself, but as he listened a little more carefully, he realized Mr. Haskell was praying! "O God, help me to win this good man to the message. Help me to—"

Edward Hare waited to hear no more. He went downstairs and said to his wife, "That man's not crazy; that man is praying for us!" And it was only a few days until Edward Hare had accepted the message. He took Elder Haskell two hundred miles north to Kaeo, where Edward's father, Joseph Hare, and five of his brothers lived. In a few more days they all had accepted the third angel's message and were keeping the Sabbath. Edward Hare was *my* uncle, and *my* father was one of his brothers who accepted this message in Kaeo! That's the way God's Word began to prosper in New Zealand. You can put your faith in every promise and in every prophecy foretold in the Word of God.

"For we can do nothing against the truth, but for the truth." 2 Corinthians 13:8.

There were many people who told Ezra and his fellow workers that it was not possible to rebuild the Temple, and there was much opposition, but they kept at it, and it was done. Associated with Elder S. N. Haskell at the beginning of the work in Australia were J. O. Corliss and M. C. Israel, both preachers; Henry L. Scott, a printer; and William Arnold, a colporteur. They hoped to be invited to speak on the second coming of Christ in some of the other Protestant churches, but the churches were closed to them. They tried to hire halls, but the rent was too high. They pitched a tent, but the clergy of the city threatened to discipline any of their church members who attended the meetings or admitted the strangers to their homes to hold Bible studies; and sometimes Bible studies in private homes were actually broken up by disturbers. Even William Arnold went for six weeks without selling a single book! But the dear workers clung to the promise that "my word . . . shall not return unto me void," and they kept on.

Then one Sabbath afternoon Elder Haskell knocked on a door and introduced himself to the good woman of the house. "Father," she called to her husband, who was a coach builder, "there are some Americans at the door to see you." John Henry Stockton was heating a dashboard at the time, preparing to mold it. He came to the door and talked with the strange Americans so long that the dashboard was spoiled. But in spite of the ruined dashboard, he invited the Americans to come again and again, and John Henry Stockton was the first one to accept this truth in Australia. It wasn't long before the first church was organized there, and John Henry Stockton was the first ordained local elder of that church! And William Arnold, who hadn't been able to sell a single book for six weeks, sold more than one thousand copies of *Daniel and the Revelation* in less than a year! Today, after ninety-nine years, there are in all the South Pacific Division 1,220 churches, with 163,825 members.

So when people tell you it can't be done, when worldly people try to entice you to join with them, just keep on doing what God has given you to do, and it will be done!

"Then rose up Zerubbabel . . . and Jeshua . . . and began to build the house of God . . . : and with them were the prophets of God helping them." Ezra 5:2.

Whenever there has been difficult work to do, God has had His prophets right there to help the leaders. After the seventy years of captivity, when the Temple was to be rebuilt, Haggai and Zechariah were there encouraging Zerubbabel and Jeshua in the work.

In the beginning of the Advent Movement God also had a prophet—a humble little woman, Ellen G. White—and God used her mightily to counsel, inspire, and encourage the early workers. In 1875, just after our first worker, J. N. Andrews, had been sent to Europe, God revealed to Sister White that publishing houses in various countries would be sending out literature filled with the Advent message. She especially mentioned the country of Australia. Ten years went by, however, before the first group of missionaries was ready to go there. When at last they arrived, one of their first decisions was to print, and in January, 1886, only a few months after their arrival, they rented a shed and began to print a paper called *The Bible Echo and Signs of the Times.* Its light began to shine at once, and before long they were doing business in a fine building in North Fitzroy. It was there that Ellen G. White found them when she went to Australia in 1891, and as she looked over the pressroom she recognized it as one of the places she had seen in vision sixteen years before! With her encouragement the work increased, and in 1905 the publishing house moved to Warburton, forty miles from the city. If you could see the lovely building and its surroundings and the earnest group of workers there today, your heart would rejoice. They have sold millions of subscription books since they began! But just think of it, ten years before it started, the prophet was shown the publishing house in Australia!

This same prophet, Ellen G. White, has written two books especially to encourage and inspire juniors—*Steps to Christ* and *Messages to Young People.* Have you read them?

"And the elders of the Jews builded, and they prospered through the prophesying of Haggai . . . and Zechariah." Ezra 6:14.

What would Zerubbabel and Jeshua have done without the prophets? They took their counsel, and encouraged by their words of inspiration, they finished the Temple at last.

There were only about 450 church members in Australia when Ellen G. White, God's messenger, arrived to help with the work. Seeing that the publishing house was doing good work, Sister White began to urge the church members to open a training school. Two large houses in one of the suburbs of the city of Melbourne were rented, and twenty-four young people came to school. But Sister White kept advising them to look for land in the country, far from the influence of city life. So the brethren looked and looked, and finally they found a tract of 1,500 acres about seventy miles north of Sydney that could be bought for $4,500. The price was wonderfully low, but many said the land was very poor. They talked with government experts, and they said the land was worthless—"it wouldn't support a bandicoot [bush rat]."

On May 23, 1894, Mrs. White visited the site. As she walked here and there she seemed to be looking for something. Soon they came to a place where the land had been cleared, and there before them all was a furrow nine inches deep and six feet long. She spoke to Elder Starr, who was with her. "There it is," she said in effect. "There it is, just as I saw in my dream! And I heard one man say, 'This is not good land; the soil is not favorable!' But One who has often spoken in counsel was present also, and He said, 'False witness has been borne of this land.' He then described the land and said that if it was well worked it would produce an abundance of fruit and vegetables." The land was bought. The school was started in the country, and graduates from that school have gone to the Pacific Islands, to India, Burma, China, and to all the countries of the Far East. I attended that school for six years. I ate oranges, grapes, apples, vegetables, and corn that grew on that land. I have never ceased to be thankful for the prophet that God gave to the Adventist people for the building up of His work in North America, Australia, Europe, and in all the world.

Are you thankful for God's messenger too?

"From the going forth of the commandment to restore and to build Jerusalem unto the Messiah the Prince shall be seven weeks, and threescore and two weeks." Daniel 9:25.

The decree to restore and to build Jerusalem began with Cyrus; it was renewed by Darius, maybe nineteen years later, and completed by Artaxerxes eighty years after the first decree by Cyrus. The completion of the decree in the year 457 B.C. is very important, for it is the beginning of a time prophecy in Daniel that foretells the date of Christ's ministry, A.D. 27-31, and the date for the opening of the day of the judgment, 1844. Jesus Himself told His disciples about two great signs of the end of the world and of His second coming—signs that were fulfilled within this time prophecy. One was the darkening of the sun and the other was the falling of the stars. Today, May 19, is the anniversary of the day when the sun was darkened in 1780. You can read about it in Webster's dictionary (1869 edition) and a number of history books. It was noticed in all the New England States, and it lasted about fourteen hours. It began about ten or eleven o'clock in the morning and continued until the middle of the following night. It was so dark at noontime that no one could read without a candle. Birds sang their evening songs and disappeared; fowls went to roost; the cattle went into their barns; and candles were lighted in the houses. People were filled with alarm. Many thought the end of the world had come. Others thought it was the day of judgment, and they hurried to their neighbors to confess their wrongs and ask for forgiveness. Others rushed into the meetinghouses and called on God to preserve them. In the Connecticut legislature, as the darkness settled on the assembly, some believed the day of judgment had come and said they ought to adjourn, but Abraham Davenport, the speaker, said, "No! If it is the day of judgment, I want to be found doing my duty." So he ordered candles to be lighted, and they went on with their business. That night people prayed around their family altars as they never had prayed before. Many sat up all night to see whether the sun would ever shine again.

How would you have felt if you had been in the New England States on that dark day? If you keep your heart right with God, you need never fear, for these things simply say Jesus is coming soon.

145

"The hand of our God was upon us, and he delivered us from the hand of the enemy, and of such as lay in wait by the way." Ezra 8:31.

It took Ezra four months to make the trip from Babylon to Jerusalem. *The SDA Bible Commentary* estimates there were about eight thousand men, women, and children in the group that accompanied him, and they were carrying a fortune in silver and gold and brass. Ezra wanted God to have all the glory for their safe journey, so he did not ask for any soldiers to go with them. What an opportunity for hostile Samaritans or Arabs to attack and plunder their caravan! But God in His own way brought them safely through.

God still has a way to protect His workers as they travel through dangers, both seen and unseen. Elder W. H. Anderson was one of our pioneer missionaries in central Africa. He was with the group that established the Solusi Mission station in 1894. Eight months after they arrived, the Matabeles rose in rebellion, and the lives of all foreigners were in danger. The missionaries fled to the city of Bulawayo, twenty-five miles from the mission. Now and then when there was a lull in the fighting the missionaries went to the mission for supplies from the farm. It was a very hazardous undertaking, and they made these trips by night for added safety. On one occasion Elder Anderson was going for supplies. Four miles from the mission there was a shortcut to the station, but it was a rough path and a difficult one to follow in the darkness, so when Elder Anderson got to the place, he decided to stay on the wagon road which was much easier to follow. He had gone but a few yards when he heard a voice clearly saying, "Go back! Get out of here quickly; take the footpath." The voice was so urgent that he obeyed it at once and went back to the rough shortcut. No sooner was he well out of sight of the road than he heard a war party of hostile Matabeles hurrying along the road toward Bulawayo! If he had kept on the road he would surely have run right into them. But by obeying the voice, he reached the mission safely, and in a day or two was able to bring back the needed food supplies from the garden for the other missionaries in Bulawayo.

Wherever you go, whenever you travel, be sure to put yourself in the hands of God. He can bring *you* through safely, too.

"If ye turn unto me, and keep my commandments, and do them . . . , yet will I gather them . . . and will bring them unto the place that I have chosen to set my name there." Nehemiah 1:9.

Thirteen years after Artaxerxes had sent Ezra with the final decree to complete the building of Jerusalem, God began to work out His plans to have Nehemiah, the king's cupbearer, sent to Jerusalem as governor of Judah. Nehemiah became an excellent organizer.

Today is the anniversary of an important day in the history of the Advent Movement, for on May 21, 1863, just three years after our name *Seventh-day Adventist* was chosen, the General Conference was organized in Battle Creek, Michigan. There were just twenty delegates at that meeting, and John Byington was elected the first president. One hundred and twenty-two years later, in 1985, the fifty-fourth session of the General Conference was held in New Orleans. There were 2,110 delegates, and Neal C. Wilson was reelected president. In 1863 we had 3,500 church members; in 1985 we had 4,424,612 church members. In 1863 we had 22 ministers; in 1985 we had more than 14,600 ordained and licensed ministers. In 1863 our church members spoke only one language; in 1985 our church members spoke 428 languages. In 1863 our church members were all in one country; in 1985 our church members were in 184 countries. Maybe some of you were in New Orleans on the first Sabbath of the General Conference in 1985. I wish you all could have been there. It was the largest Sabbath school ever held in one city. In the afternoon at the mission program many people dressed in their national costumes representing 130 nations. What a glorious sight it was! There they were—from the Bible lands, from India, from the Far East, from Africa, from Europe, from South America, from Inter-America, from Alaska, and from the islands of the sea. You couldn't help realizing that the amazing progress reported at this meeting was not the work of men but of the living God. Everyone felt that he had had a preview of the great multitude which no man can number, who will someday stand before the throne, praising God. May God help every one of us to be there.

"The God of heaven, he will prosper us; therefore we his servants will arise and build." Nehemiah 2:20.

Nehemiah had all the faith in God, all the wisdom, and all the determination needed to make a success of building the walls of Jerusalem. Do you know that building a successful life requires those very same factors? Once upon a time, says Lora Clement in her book *Learning to Live,* there was a man who built a three-story hotel. For a number of years it was all the little town needed, but one day oil was found nearby, and the little town boomed overnight. The three-story hotel was filled to capacity day after day. The owner of the hotel saw his chance of making a fortune, so he called a contractor and asked him to add a fourth story to his hotel. "All right," said the contractor, "but first I want to see the basement."

"The basement?" said the hotel owner. "I don't want the fourth story built down there. Let us go up to the roof."

"Yes, I know," said the contractor, "but before I think of adding the fourth story, I must see if the foundations are strong enough to stand the extra weight." And down to the basement he went. He measured the thickness and the depth of the foundations, then sadly shook his head. "I'm sorry," he said, "but that foundation is not strong enough to bear the weight of another story."

The hotel owner stood there for a long time without saying a word, and no wonder, for suddenly he remembered that when he first planned to build the hotel the contractor urged him to have the foundation made strong enough for an addition sometime in the future. "There might be a boom," he had said; "you can never tell."

The hotel owner also remembered his own reply: "There's not one chance in a thousand! Why should I put extra money into a foundation for an emergency that will never come?" But the emergency had come, and he needed that fourth story. "Can you make the foundation strong enough now?" he asked the contractor. "Of course I can, but it will cost you a lot more to do it now than if you had done it at first," he replied.

You are laying the foundations of your life now. Be sure you take the advice of your parents and teachers, and build your foundations firm and strong *now.*

*"Be not ye afraid of them: remember the Lord, which is great and terrible.
. . . And it came to pass . . . that we returned all of us to the wall, every one
unto his work." Nehemiah 4:14, 15.*

I love to read this chapter telling how Nehemiah closed his ears to the
invitations and threatenings of Sanballat and Tobiah, and kept right on
with his building until at last the wall was finished.

We all have our Sanballats and our Tobiahs who are trying to stop us
from building our lives and making them successful—but they don't have
two legs! Our Sanballats and Tobiahs are *laziness* and *indifference*. "It's
too much bother!" "It's too hard." "You'll never need that anyway!"
That reminds me of another of Miss Clement's stories. This one is about
a girl she calls Ruth.

Ruth was a talented girl, but she disliked anything like hard work.
She didn't see any sense in having a program for study as long as she could
"get by." That was good enough for her. When she got into geometry,
that was the end. She just shrugged her dainty little shoulders and said
she simply "couldn't be bothered"—and dropped out of school!

Parents, friends, teachers, did their best to urge and coax her to keep
on with her studies; but it was no use. She got a clerical job. Someone
suggested she had better take up stenography. She didn't mind
typewriting so much; that was fun. But shorthand! That was too hard, so
she was contented to be a not-too-good typist.

Then she got married. "You see!" she said triumphantly to those who
had advised her to get more education, "I don't need an education to
keep house for Ray." But after a few happy years passed, and two little
children had joined their family, Ruth suddenly found herself a widow! It
took her some time to get her bearings when she was overwhelmed with
tragedy and sorrow. Then what do you think she did? She went right
back to school and began again where she had been silly enough to stop.
But it would have been so much easier if she had taken no notice of her
Sanballats and her Tobiahs and had kept right on building her walls. It
wouldn't have cost her nearly so much to have done it then.

Sanballat and Tobiah are after you, too. You had better watch out!
And do keep on building your wall.

149

"Unto thy brother thou shalt not lend upon usury: that the Lord thy God may bless thee in all that thou settest thine hand to in the land whither thou goest to possess it." Deuteronomy 23:20.

What a lot of trouble the poor people of our Bible text got into just because some of their "big" men were too "little" to realize that love and mercy and kindness were more important than business. So when the poor people to whom they had lent money couldn't pay the interest on it, the big men took their land and even made their children slaves! Here is a beautiful old legend told in India.

Long, long ago there lived a powerful king who had lots and lots of money. He called a builder by the name of Jakoob and told him to build him the most beautiful palace he had ever made, in the most beautiful place away up in the hills. So Jakoob set off with all the king's money that he needed, and he traveled till he came to the most beautiful place away up in the hills. But when he got there he found the people without food; many were sick and many were dying. Now Jakoob had a very kind heart, so he took all his own money and all the money the king had given him to build the most beautiful palace and used it to feed the hungry and care for the sick.

After a long, long time the king came to see his palace, and he found that not one stone had been laid for the building! The king was furious, and demanded Jakoob to give him the reason for this strange conduct. Jakoob told him about the poor and the sick and the hungry, and how he had fed them and cared for them till his money was all used up. The king was more angry than ever. He put Jakoob in prison and said, "Tomorrow thou shalt die." But that night the king dreamed, and in his dream he went to heaven; there he was shown the most beautiful palace he had ever seen.

"Whose palace is this?" he asked the angel.

"This is the palace of beautiful deeds, built for you by Jakoob, the wise builder," they said. "After all the buildings of earth have been destroyed, this one shall still be beautiful."

The king woke up. Then he took Jakoob out of prison and made him the most honored builder in all his kingdom.

When you grow up always remember that love, mercy, and kindness are more important than worldly gain in business.

"I am doing a great work, so that I cannot come down: why should the work cease, whilst I leave it, and come down to you?" Nehemiah 6:3.

Good for Nehemiah! I like to hear people talk like that. He was determined to build those walls, and no one could talk him out of it, nothing could turn him away from it. He stuck at it till the walls were finished. Too many people start to do something, then give up when it gets hard or discouraging.

There's a story in C. L. Paddock's book *Heroes Take Wings* that shows how near to success one can be when discouragement turns him away from his work. In the days of the gold rush in California a young prospector laid out his claim and began digging for gold. With his pick and shovel he began to dig a tunnel toward the center of a mountain. With drill and with dynamite he worked his way foot by foot through rock, limestone, and earth, hoping every day that he would find the precious yellow metal. The weeks wore on into long months of hard, strenuous work, but never a grain of gold was seen. At last his money was used up and his supplies were all gone; and overcome with discouragement, he left his pick and shovel and all of his equipment and went back home. He never went back to the mine. What was the use? There was no gold there.

Years went by. A large mining company bought the property and reopened the deserted mine. They cleared away the fallen rock and debris. They found the place where the discouraged prospector had left his tools and quit. With their modern equipment they began to dig farther into the heart of the mountain, and just six inches farther on they struck a rich vein of gold. Only six inches away from success and a fortune!

"In perfecting a Christian character, it is essential to persevere in right doing. I would impress upon our youth the importance of perseverance and energy in the work of character-building. From the earliest years it is necessary to weave into the character principles of stern integrity, that the youth may reach the highest standard of manhood and womanhood."—*Messages to Young People*, p. 45.

Have you set out to get an education? Never give up! Get it! Sickness or misfortune may make your goal seem impossible or a long, long way off, but don't lay down your tools and quit. Keep going on. There may be a rich vein of gold only six inches farther on!

"Ye shall dwell in booths . . . that your generations may know that I made the children of Israel to dwell in booths, when I brought them out of the land of Egypt." Leviticus 23:42, 43.

When at last the walls of Jerusalem were finished, the first thing the people did was to have a camp meeting. It was a joyous occasion. The people gathered branches and built shelters on the flat roofs of their houses to sleep in. During the day they had meetings where the law of Moses was read and explained, and there was lots of singing.

Have you ever attended a modern camp meeting? Have you ever heard anyone tell about the first Seventh-day Adventist camp meeting? It was in 1868, just eight years after our name *Seventh-day Adventist* was chosen, and it was held in a maple grove on the farm of E. H. Root, in the township of Wright, Michigan. The meeting place was among the trees. There was a platform for the ministers and rough boards for the people to sit on. There were two large circular tents, one containing straw for the campers to put in their tents to sleep on, and one to use for meetings in case of rain. There were seventeen smaller tents just for sleeping, pitched in a circle around the meeting place. Of course, many other campers had rooms, or slept in the barns of the nearby farmhouses. The camp had no electricity, but campfires built here and there served very well for light.

There were enough children in attendance to have their own meetings. Elder James White was their favorite storyteller; and Elder J. N. Andrews their favorite "good-night sayer," for every night he would walk around to each tent and say in his pleasant voice, "Are you all comfortable for the night? Good night. Good night." Then those who had kerosene lamps or candles put out their lights and went to sleep.

It was very primitive, but there were about three hundred regular campers and as many as two thousand came over the weekend, and many gave their hearts to Jesus there. On the way home they told and retold the stories they had heard, and began looking forward to going to camp meeting again the next year. Camp meeting does something to you. You really do get closer to God there.

I hope you can go to camp meeting this year.

"Favour is deceitful, and beauty is vain: but a woman that feareth the Lord, she shall be praised." Proverbs 31:30.

Queen Esther was the most beautiful of all the maidens in the land, but her beauty was more than skin deep. Esther also feared the Lord, and that is really why she "obtained favour in the sight of all them that looked upon her." Here is another old legend. Nobody seems to know where it came from, but it illustrates our text very well.

Once upon a time there were three girls who were always quarreling about which one had the most beautiful hands. The first one dipped her hands in the clear, sparkling water of a running brook and said, "See how beautiful and white my hands are! My hands are the most beautiful!"

The second girl gathered berries till her hands were pink, just as though an artist had painted them. "See how pink my hands are!" she said. "My hands are the most beautiful."

The third girl walked among the flowers and picked the roses till her hands smelled like perfume. "See how fragrant my hands smell," she said. "My hands are the most beautiful." Now there was another girl with them, but she never argued with the others, because she didn't think her hands were beautiful at all. Well, one day a wrinkled old woman came along. She looked like a beggar. She asked the girls for something to eat. The three girls who were always quarreling about their beautiful hands put their hands behind their backs and said they had nothing to give her. But the fourth girl gave her a chair, then ran inside and brought her some bread and milk. Then a wonderful thing happened—the poor old lady smiled and changed into an angel! Turning to the other girls, the angel said, "It is not the hands that are dipped into the brook, nor the hands that are painted with berries, nor the hands that are fragrant with perfume that are the most beautiful, but the kind hands that give to the poor."

The story may be only an old legend, but what the angel said is true. And that was the secret of Esther's beauty. Her heart was filled with sweetness, goodness, kindness, and love.

Would you like to be beautiful? Really beautiful? Try filling your heart with sweetness, goodness, kindness, and love for God and man, and then see what happens!

"And who knoweth whether thou art come to the kingdom for such a time as this?" Esther 4:14.

When the Lord needed someone with the right influence, someone He could use to save His scattered people, there was Esther—the right person in the right place at the right time.

Listen while I tell you of another young woman in the land of Queen Esther, who was also in the right place at just the right time.

In 1959 the Iraq Government took over our lovely Dar es Salaam hospital in the city of Baghdad. All the foreign doctors and nurses were sent away, and the only Seventh-day Adventist worker left in the institution was a national nurse—Sohila. When she saw the other non-Christian workers come in to staff the hospital, Sohila said to herself, "Remember you are a Seventh-day Adventist; you must be faithful and always do your very best." And she did. A few months later there was an attempted counterrevolution, and an attempt was made to kill Premier Abdul Kassem. He and several of his bodyguards were severely wounded and were rushed to the hospital that used to be ours, and Sohila, the Adventist nurse, was assigned to special duty to the Premier. She did her very best to be kind and helpful and cheerful. When Sabbath came, she got off duty as usual, and went to Sabbath school and church. The next morning when she came on duty the Premier looked at her and said, "I know where you were yesterday. You went to church, didn't you? Did you pray for me?"

"Oh, yes, sir; we did," she said. "And, sir, if you would like, our pastor, and some of our young people would be glad to come and sing to you and pray for you here, sir." The wounded Premier thought a moment and said, "Tell them to come." Three days later Pastor Behnam Arshat and a group of young people came. They sang. Dr. Fargo read the ninety-first psalm, and the pastor prayed. "Please go and sing and pray just like that for my wounded men in the ward," said the Premier; and they went. In due time the wounded men were well.

As a result of this, Seventh-day Adventists were granted full denominational rights! And today there is a fine church in the center of the city. Sohila was just the right person in the right place at the right time.

God wants you to be the right person just where *you* are today.

"The thoughts of the wicked are an abomination to the Lord: but the words of the pure are pleasant words." Proverbs 15:26.

What a thrilling story! I just love to imagine how Haman looked and felt as he led Mordecai around the town on the king's horse! Haman had come to ask the king's permission to hang Mordecai on his seventy-five-foot-high gallows! Then, thinking he was the one the king wanted to honor, he suggested the greatest possible honor he could think of. And then, after all that, to have to give this honor to Mordecai! Oh, it is just too, too good! But do you know, wicked men are still planning evil on the servants of God and reaping it upon themselves in many places in the world today.

At the General Conference I heard Elder Don Roth tell a story that thrilled me through and through. In one of the countries in Inter-America one of our evangelists went to hold some meetings in a certain town. He rented the town hall, but when his enemies heard about it, they stirred up a lot of opposition, and the use of the town hall was denied him. Then he found a privately owned hall out on the edge of the town, and advertised his meetings to be held there. His enemies were furious, but they could not influence the owner to break his contract. So they decided to hold an open-air mass meeting themselves near the hall. They planned to have loudspeakers and lots of music and noise, so they could drown out the preaching of our evangelist. On the first night of the meetings a great crowd gathered, shouting and making a terrible racket, and you can just imagine how they gloated because the evangelist's meeting would be spoiled. But just about time for the meeting to begin, a thunderstorm came up, and down came the rain—and the crowd dashed for shelter. The evangelist's hall was so near and handy that many of them crowded in and stayed for his meeting. He had never had such a good attendance before! The enemies were furious over their defeat, but there was nothing they could do about it. Many of the people who had not planned on going to all the meetings now kept on going.

How hard it is for people to learn that he who lays a snare for his neighbors' feet is in grave danger of getting caught in that snare himself. Just make sure that *you* plan no evil for any of your neighbors.

"They that plow iniquity, and sow wickedness, reap the same." Job 4:8.

So Haman was hanged on the gallows he made for Mordecai! Haman had surely plowed iniquity and sowed wickedness, and just as surely he reaped the same! The judgment of God upon men who have threatened the lives of His workers has been seen over and over.

Soon after the year 1911 Elder and Mrs. F. A. Stahl went to live in Plateria on the western shore of Lake Titicaca, Peru. The government then had made laws granting religious freedom, but there were many priests who hated the Protestants and did all they could to stir up mobs against them. On one occasion while the Stahls were visiting in the little town of Quenuani, two priests gathered a mob together, armed them with rifles, shotguns, clubs, whips, and stones, and came toward the house where the Stahls were staying. When they were about a block away the priests passed around liquor to all the mob and told them what an honor it would be if they would kill the foreign heretics. Then the priests fired off a rocket, and the mob advanced. They cut loose the horses and sent them plunging wildly down the hill. When Elder Stahl went out to try to catch them, the mob threw stones at him. One stone hit him on the head, and the blood ran down his face. Mrs. Stahl ran out and pulled him inside. They piled the furniture against the door, but the door was soon broken with the stones. "Set fire to the thatch roof!" yelled one of the priests. But the owner of the house snatched the torch and threw it away. Another torch was brought, but all of a sudden the mob turned and ran away.

"Why are they running away?" Mr. Stahl asked a friendly Indian.

"Don't you see that great company of armed Indians coming to defend you?" he asked, pointing across the plain. The Stahls looked and looked, but they could see nothing. Then they realized that God must have sent angels to deliver them. But wait a minute, the story is not yet finished. Not long after this, one of those priests died of a terrible fever, and only those who were paid to bury him went to the funeral! Then the other priest became sick and called Elder Stahl to care for him! But in spite of all Elder Stahl could do, he too died.

If you ever are persecuted for righteousness' sake, just leave the punishment of the persecutors to God.

"Though hand join in hand, the wicked shall not be unpunished: but the seed of the righteous shall be delivered." Proverbs 11:21.

In spite of the law of the Medes and the Persians, which everyone knows could not be changed, God made a way for the wicked to be punished and the righteous to be delivered. Let me tell you another experience in the ministry of Elder and Mrs. F. A. Stahl that illustrates this truth very well. Again and again the priests tried to stir up a mob to attack their mission station at Plateria. The first night the mob came they heard drums and saw a company of soldiers coming from boats at the shore of the lake toward the mission. The second time the mob came they saw soldiers standing all around the mission. The third time they came it was just the same, so they gave up and wouldn't come any more. The priests were furious, but there was nothing they could do. The people were afraid of the soldiers. Months afterward the Indians asked Elder Stahl where his soldiers were hidden. He let them look everywhere, and when they found none, they told about the soldiers they had seen when they came to attack the mission. Then Elder Stahl knew that God had sent the angels to protect him again. But that is not the end of the story. One night a messenger from an unfriendly village knocked on the door and asked Elder Stahl to please come and help a certain prominent man who was very ill.

"Of course! That is what I came for. Let us go to him at once," said Elder Stahl. "Who is the sick man?" One of them said, "He is the priest." He was the one who had tried to destroy the mission station!

Elder Stahl found him in great agony, and he was able to give the man immediate relief. However, the priest needed surgery, so Elder Stahl advised him to go to a large hospital on the coast. "Then," said the priest, "please take me to the train." So Elder Stahl gathered forty carriers and rode his horse beside the patient all the way to the railway station. And he heard the people say, "What is this we see? Has the *evangelista* taken the *padre* prisoner?" On the train Elder Stahl had the pleasure of putting the sick man to bed and tucking the blankets around him. And the power of the enemy was broken. That man never made any more attempts to destroy our mission.

That's the way God does it. Make God first in your life, and He will do things like that for you, too.

"Doth Job fear God for nought? Hast not thou made an hedge about him, and about his house, and about all that he hath on every side?" Job 1:9, 10.

God certainly did have a "hedge" around Job, but in order to prove that Job served God because he loved to, and not only for what he could get out of it, God gave Satan permission to "touch" all that Job had. And in a short time Job had lost everything. But listen to what Job said then: "The Lord gave, and the Lord hath taken away; blessed be the name of the Lord."

This test will come to every child of God sometime, in some form or other. It came to me. I know what it feels like. Mrs. Hare and I, with 12-year-old Verna May and 8-year-old Peter, were in Rangoon, Burma, when World War II broke upon us. We saw the "terror by night," "the arrow that flieth by day," and "the destruction that wasteth at noonday." More than "a thousand" fell around us, and the U.S. consul urged us to get our women and children across to India. But there were no boats running, and thousands of people were on the waiting list ahead of us. Then suddenly on January 20, 1942, the consul telephoned us and said, "We have a little freighter going to Calcutta. It is not listed with the steamship agents, but if you can get some of your women and children to the wharf by three o'clock, we'll take them across for you." That gave us just an hour and a half to pack a suitcase and roll up a bundle of bedding for each. But three of us missionary men waved goodbye to our families, and I can't tell you how we felt. You will have to try to imagine it. "They'll never get across," said a stranger beside me. "The bay is full of submarines." For more than a week our hearts were heavy as lead. Then came a letter from Mrs. Hare: "As our little freighter sailed out of the Rangoon River into the Bay of Bengal a thick, heavy fog settled down around us, and we couldn't see the sun for four days. Not until we were in the Hooghly River, on our way up to Calcutta, did the sun shine again. Then when we landed and bought a newspaper we read that two boats had been torpedoed and sunk while we were covered with the cloud!"

Trouble, loss of possessions, and destruction all around you may be your lot someday. But remember that God still has His "hedge" or His "cloud" or His "wings" under which you can hide.

"And the Lord turned the captivity of Job, when he prayed for his friends: also the Lord gave Job twice as much as he had before." Job 42:10.

I think I know how happy Job was when the trial was all over and God gave him seven more sons and three more daughters and twice as much livestock as he had before. Yes, I think I know a little bit, because I can still remember how I felt when I found my family again after we men escaped from the war in Burma. That one letter telling how they were covered with a cloud of fog for four days, and telling of their safe arrival in Calcutta, was the last word we received. The next six weeks were the blackest, most discouraging, and loneliest six weeks through which I have ever lived. The tempo of the war increased. The city of Rangoon was taken, and the enemy moved northward. We men had to walk across the border mountains into India; but when we got to Calcutta Mr. Wyman, Mr. Baird, and I learned that our wives and children were waiting for us in the hill station of Mussoorie. We couldn't send them a telegram, for the government had taken over all telegraph lines, so we got on the train and journeyed toward them without their knowing that we were alive and had escaped into India.

As we neared the house where our families were staying, we heard the children playing in the yard. Then we heard a great shout. I knew what it was; they had seen Brother Wyman coming through the gate. Then there was another shout. That was when Brother Baird came through the gate. The mothers, hearing the shouting, came running out to see what it was all about. By this time I had come through the gate, and there was more shouting! Oh, glad day! I can never forget it. There we all were, the Wymans, the Bairds, and the Hares, with arms around loved ones, all laughing and crying with joy! At last I shouted into my wife's ear. "Dear, we've lost everything—our furniture, our books, our dishes; all I could bring out was this one suitcase."

And my wife shouted back, "Oh, no; we haven't lost everything; here's Peter, here's Verna May, and now that we have you, nothing else matters." I think that was the way Job felt after his trial was over.

Keep close to God always. He will comfort you when trials come, and He is the only one who can restore your happiness.

"He [shall abide] that walketh uprightly, and worketh righteousness, and speaketh the truth in his heart. . . . He that doeth these things shall never be moved." Psalm 15:2-5.

Many of David's psalms were written after God had providentially delivered him from the hands of his enemies, so I am going to bring you a few stories from experiences during World War II, to show that we today have the same loving, merciful God who still provides for His children and delivers them.

After getting our wives and children on the little freighter that took them safely to Calcutta, we turned our attention to evacuating our church members from the city of Rangoon. Some went by train to upper Burma; some went by riverboat to the delta district. Then the day came when the enemy crossed the great Salween River, and we knew it was only a matter of a few days until Rangoon would be taken. Elder Christensen's car was all we had to take five of us men as far as the gasoline would go; then we would have to walk. "Only one suitcase and one blanket each! That's all there is room for!" said Elder Meleen, our superintendent. "Pack up the rest of your stuff and store it in the schoolroom." I think if sudden destruction took everything away it would be easier. But as I packed away Mrs. Hare's lovely dishes, Peter's toy train, Verna May's baby doll, my books, my file, and eight new band instruments that kind friends had sent for my brass band, it was like a long-drawn-out funeral in which I was preacher, undertaker, and mourner combined.

With a heavy heart and many tears I stored the belongings in the schoolroom in the mission headquarters, together with the personal belongings of the other missionary families. I had just finished my sad task when the next-door neighbor called. "Mr. Hare, I've just got a way to go overland to India with my brother. I can only take one suitcase and one rug. I have to leave everything behind. But worst of all, I can't take my car. I have to leave it, and I don't want the enemy to get it; so, Mr. Hare, please take it and use it if you can. But if you have to abandon it, pour some gasoline over it and burn it." She turned quickly to hide her sorrow, leaving me too bewildered for words.

The next day a group of workers from the delta arrived with the news that they had found a way to go by boat upriver to the border, and Dr. Walker couldn't take his car. So now there were three cars for the five of us who were evacuating the church members, and this meant that we could take some of the office equipment and perhaps be able to set up headquarters in upper Burma! Little by little it was plain that "the Lord knoweth the way of the righteous," and that He was caring for us, too.

Someday *you* may need one of God's special miracles. Walk uprightly before Him every day, and He will always be near.

PSALMS 23, 24, 27   JUNE 4

"The Lord is my shepherd, I shall not want. . . . Thou preparest a table before me in the presence of mine enemies." Psalm 23:1-5.

We saw government headquarters and military headquarters move out of the city. We saw the last riverboat leave the wharf. We saw the last train leave the station. And the next morning we five missionaries in our three cars left the mission headquarters and took our place on the road with the thousands of people who were fleeing for their lives. Mile after mile we picked our way through indescribable scenes of suffering and woe. We passed groups of burning cars. We passed hundreds of crying babies and little children dragging at the clothes of their parents. We passed hundreds of exhausted ones lying at the roadside, and hundreds of feeble ones being carried in blankets hanging from bamboo poles, riding piggyback, or carried on the shoulders of the stronger ones, till our hearts were wrung dry with sympathy. It was with a sense of relief on the second day that we neared the town of Taungdwingyi, three hundred miles away from the bursting bombs in Rangoon. But it was 8:30 p.m. and it was dark; and we were thirsty. Our waterpots had been empty since four o'clock that afternoon, and we had looked for some "green pasture" or "still waters" or even a village well where we could camp for the night. But finding none, we had pushed on to this town. The police directed us to the high school grounds to camp. We found a company of Royal Air Force personnel there evacuating some military families. They made us welcome, and while we were unpacking, Brother Baldwin went off with our waterpots to get some water. He was back in a few moments with the pots still empty. "No water till morning," he announced. "There are so many people here that there is not enough water, so they turn off the town water supply from sunset till sunrise." No water! But we must have water! Every other comfort was forgotten, and we prayed, "Lord, Thou hast promised that our bread and water shall be sure. Never mind the bread, Lord, but we must have water."

We were still praying when we heard a voice call, "Well, I declare, if it isn't Pastor Christensen!" Brother Christensen turned around and put out his hand. "Well, if it isn't Mr. Hern," he said. Mr. Hern was a young man who had attended our meetings in the city.

"And what are you doing here?" asked Mr. Hern.

"Fleeing for our lives," said Brother Christensen; and I added, "But at this moment we are dying of thirst! We can't get water till morning."

"Water!" said Mr. Hern. "We knew the water was to be turned off so I filled two cans. I'll have one here in just a moment." And as he turned to go he added, "Don't bother cooking anything. We have plenty of rice and curry left over from the evening meal." In a few moments our "table was prepared," and I wish you could have heard us give thanks for our bread and water that night—but especially for the water!

The Lord *is* a good shepherd. He does prepare a table before His children. Have *you* made the Lord *your* shepherd?

PSALM 37   JUNE 5

"Commit thy way unto the Lord; trust also in him; and he shall bring it to pass." Psalm 37:5.

If ever men committed their way unto the Lord, we five missionaries certainly did. The Lord permitted us to have enough trouble so that we had to trust in Him, but He most miraculously brought us through. Fifty miles out of Taungdwingyi Brother Christensen waved us to the side of the road. He got out of his car and said, "There's a horrible noise in that left rear wheel. Would you mind listening while I start up?" We listened, but he didn't start up; the wheel flange had broken off from the hub! We were quiet for a while; nobody wanted to say, "You'll have to burn your car." While we waited Pastor Meleen said, "I've got it! The two good cars will drive on to Yenangyaung, just thirty-two miles away. We will find a place to camp, unload one car, and come back and pick up Brother Christensen's load and take him to Yenangyaung. He can get on a bus there for Mandalay."

We drove on; we found the place to camp; we unloaded one car; and Brother Baldwin went back for Brother Christensen. "I'll be back first thing in the morning," he said as he started off. But he didn't get back first thing in the morning. Nine o'clock, ten o'clock— there was no sign of him.

"Something has happened," said Brother Meleen. "Let's go back and see what it is." We went back and found them both in the little town of Magwe, three miles off the highway.

"Mr. Baldwin's car got stuck in the sand, and he burned out the clutch," explained Brother Christensen, "so we had to be towed in here. I can store my broken car here, so I won't have to burn it, and there's a bicycle repairman who says he can repair the clutch. We can be on the road again by morning."

"Then give me the broken wheel," I said. "I saw two garages in Yenangyaung. I'll get the wheel welded." Back I went and stopped at the first garage.

"Sorry," said the man, "my welder has left me." I went to the second garage.

"Sorry, there are no welders in town; they all left three weeks ago." How hopeless it all seemed. Just then I saw Mr. Lawson, the English manager of the Nat Sing Oil Company. I told him of our predicament.

"They are right, Mr. Hare," he said. "There are no welders in town, but step into the office and explain your trouble to the boss." The boss! I needed a welder, but just to be polite, I knocked on the door and went in. Mr. Nat Sing was a pleasant Indian gentleman. He listened kindly to my story, rang a bell, and Mr. Lawson came in.

"Mr. Lawson," he said, "these men are in a tight place. Please take Mr. Hare out to our workshop—it's only twenty miles out—and have our boys weld that hub!" And inside of an hour the hub was mended!

"Thank you so much, Mr. Lawson," I said. "What is the bill?"

"There's no bill," he replied. "Just drop in and thank the boss." I went in and thanked Mr. Nat Sing, and I also took time to thank God.

That's the way our God "brought it to pass" for us. That's the way He will "bring it to pass" for *you*, too, if you will commit your way unto Him.

PSALMS 39, 41, 42   **JUNE 6**

"Blessed is he that considereth the poor: the Lord will deliver him in time of trouble." Psalm 41:1.

"It's fixed! It's fixed!" I shouted as I pulled up suddenly beside the men in Magwe. Pastor Christensen could hardly believe his eyes. He took the hub, turned it over and over, then raced off to his car; and in half an hour we heard him purring around the block.

"It's better than ever it was before," he cried as he finally drove up to us. "It's just like getting the old car back from the grave." The work on the burned-out clutch took a little longer, but by two o'clock the next day three good, strong cars drove onto the highway and headed for Yenangyaung again. We slept there that night, then early in the morning packed carefully and were ready to leave on the next stage of our journey.

"Let's call in and thank Mr. Lawson again," I suggested. We found him in his office. He was glad to see us and gave us the latest news that had come over the radio. While we were chatting together I whispered in his ear.

"Of course, Mr. Lawson, the government has commandeered all the gasoline, but I was just wondering if you might know of some private supply where we could get a drop or two." His eyes twinkled.

"Quite right, Mr. Hare," he whispered back. "Just come along with me." And he took us down a little road to his own private garage. He filled our tanks and every empty can we had! And when we pulled out of Yenangyaung we had more gasoline than when we had left Rangoon five days before! During that day we had ten unbridged rivers to cross. Because it was the dry season the rivers had only a little water in them, but the descent into each riverbed and the ascent on the other side were so steep and perilous that we held our breath as we labored down one bank and up the other.

After every crossing Brother Christensen would say, "I'm so glad that hub broke down near Magwe. If it had broken halfway up this riverbank, what would we have done?"

And after every crossing Pastor Meleen would say, "I'm so glad the clutch burned out down yonder in the sand. It never could have pulled me out of this river." And can you believe it? By the time we reached Meiktila that evening, we had actually been praising God all day long for the broken hub and the burned-out clutch.

Truly "all things work together for good" in God's way of delivering His children from trouble. Remember that—when trouble and trials come to you.

"God is our refuge and strength, a very present help in trouble." "Be still, and know that I am God." Psalm 46:1, 10.

We reached our mission station at Maymyo in northern Burma without any more trouble, and waited there for ten days, hoping that the enemy would be content with taking Rangoon, and that we could establish temporary headquarters where we were. But the enemy turned northward and was making thirty to seventy-five miles a day. We had to be gone or be made prisoners of war. So we reorganized. My car was too small for the rough roads to the border, so it was left behind, and five of us men in two cars started for the border pass. After being helped again and again by our loving God, we crossed the Irrawaddy River and found ourselves in Pakokku, at the beginning of the cart track to Tamu, three hundred miles away.

After cleaning up we went to the district magistrate to obtain a permit to travel over the road. "Gentlemen," he replied solemnly, "the road has been closed, and I have been forbidden to issue any more permits for people to go that way. You see, cholera and plague have broken out, and the poor evacuees are dying like flies. So no permits will be issued until the camps have been cleared up. The road is exceedingly rough, but cars and buses have been getting through in about five days."

Pastor Meleen looked into the magistrate's face and said, "Sir, just what might happen if we chose to proceed without a permit?" We gasped at such unbelievable frankness, and anxiously awaited the magistrate's reply.

"You would have no difficulty with my policeman at this end. Of course, at Tamu they could make you come back, but I hardly think they would." Then he lowered his voice and added, "Gentlemen, if I were in your position I think I would go without delay, but of course you understand I cannot give you a permit." We just couldn't believe our ears. It must be a dream. Real people couldn't talk like that.

Brother Baird spoke next. "Sir, how many gallons of gasoline does a car need for the trip?"

"About forty," he replied.

"We have only thirty gallons each," said Brother Baird. The magistrate took his pen and wrote an order for twenty-two gallons of gas, and handing it over, he said, "Would that help?" It did help, and in five days we were at Tamu at the end of the road at the beginning of the foot trail over the mountains to India. We never ceased to praise God for His very present help in our day of trouble.

When your day of trouble comes *you* will find that God will be your help, just as He was ours, and David's.

PSALMS 67, 73

"I was envious . . . when I saw the prosperity of the wicked." "It was too painful for me; until I went into the sanctuary of God; then understood I their end." Psalm 73:3, 16, 17.

No doubt many of us have been surprised at the prosperity of the wicked. But David is not the only one who was shown what their end was to be. God gave me a preview of the punishment of the wicked, too. Let me tell you about it.

While we were walking across the mountain pass into India when escaping from Burma, there were always two distinct groups of people at every place we camped. There were the good and the bad, the selfless and the selfish. And every day the selfish ones pushed and shoved; they wanted the best; they wanted to be first. At last we came to the town of Imphal at the beginning of the Indian road. There were big bamboo barracks for the evacuees, and the captain came in at breakfast time and called out, "Everybody be ready at eight-thirty! Buses and trucks will come and take you 104 miles to the Dimapur railway station. There you will be given free tickets to any part of India you want to go to." We clapped and we cheered, and everybody was ready by seven-thirty, because it doesn't take long to close one suitcase and tie a string around one blanket. Soon two trucks came rattling into the camp. They had canvas roofs and half walls, but no seats of any kind.

"These are ours! These are ours!" shouted the selfish ones. "We were ready first."

"OK, OK," we called back. "We can wait for the next ones."

We watched them load up, yelling, shouting, shoving, cursing. And when they got started we were glad to see them go. No sooner had they gone out of sight than three elegant passenger buses came into camp. They had padded seats and padded back rests, and there were no selfish ones left to quarrel and fight. We put the women in the front near the windows. We stacked the suitcases carefully, checked to see that everyone was comfortable; and off we went. Five miles down the road we passed the two trucks full of the selfish ones, and that's when I had a preview of the punishment of the wicked.

"Stop! Stop!" they shouted. "Put all the luggage in the trucks and let us all ride in the buses." But our driver wouldn't stop, and as we looked back at them through the clouds of dust going up and up, it looked like the smoke of their torment ascending up and up. Then I remembered the text "The last shall be first, and the first last." That is exactly how it turned out, for we arrived at the railway station two hours before they did, and got all the best seats in the train! Don't worry if you often have to be last in this old world. Someday the wicked will come to their end, and you can be among the first to go through the pearly gates into the heavenly city.

PSALM 78   JUNE 9

"Marvellous things did he in the sight of their fathers. . . . He divided the sea, and caused them to pass through." Psalm 78:12, 13.

Psalm 78 is one of the national songs of Israel, and recounts God's marvelous works in delivering His people from Egypt. We also saw God do marvelous things when we were trying to evacuate our church members from Rangoon during World War II. I remember how God opened up the way for our last two families and "caused them to pass through." With a great deal of difficulty we had gotten them aboard a riverboat headed for the delta that morning. But hardly had they settled down when the military took over the boat and ordered all passengers off. We felt terrible. However, that evening Brother Baldwin heard that the military had arranged for two evacuation trains to go north and two to go west the next morning for the people to use. So after a little conference we all thought it best for our last two families to go to the station at midnight and sleep there so they could board the train in the morning. Ordinarily the Grand Central Station was a beautiful place. It was surrounded with gardens, lawns, and parking places, but as we neared it at this midnight hour our hearts sank. For acres and acres the lawns, gardens, sidewalks, and parking places were covered with the sleeping, resting forms of thousands of people who hoped to get on the evacuee trains the next day. How could we hope to get through this mass of people and through the gates onto the platform? As we stepped in and out and around the sleeping forms, we caught sight of the soldiers with bayonets set, guarding the gates. We had no authority; we had no passes, no tickets, no permits! But we had God. We prayed as we had never prayed before; and that night we saw God work a miracle. As we came nearer to the gates the English guard recognized the ambulance uniforms and helmets Brother Baldwin and I were wearing, and we heard him call to his partner on the other side of the gate and say, " 'Ullo, buddy! 'Ere come the marines. Open up!" And the gates opened up, and we all "passed through"! Once inside we made our explanation, and the guard said, "OK, buddy, now yer in. We'll see your people get on the train all right!" And they did.

Sometimes *you* may be able to get along without authority, without passes, or without permits, but you'll never be able to get along without God. Keep close to Him today and every day.

PSALMS 84, 90   **JUNE 10**

"I had rather be a doorkeeper in the house of my God, than to dwell in the tents of wickedness. . . . No good thing will he withhold from them that walk uprightly." Psalm 84:10, 11.

God takes notice of all the volunteer work we do for His sanctuary. We may be church officers, Sabbath school officers, youth officers; or we may be only helpers—ushering at the doors, passing out the hymnbooks, or taking up the offerings. God sees it all, and someday every worker will receive his reward.

One day while we were waiting in Maymyo, in northern Burma, to see what turn the war would take, Pastor Wyman and I were walking along, when we met a stranger. He shook hands with us, but we didn't recognize him until he spoke. It was Deacon Johns from the Rangoon church! "Oh, brethren," he said, "I've been praying that I would meet some of the workers. You know, I was in government work, and I couldn't leave the city till just the day before the enemy came in." He pulled out his pocketbook as he spoke. "I was paid my last money two days before I left. It may be the last money I will have on this earth, but I folded away my tithe, for I wanted the Lord to have His share." He took out some folded bank notes and handed them to me.

But I didn't feel worthy to accept what might be his last money, so I said, "No, no, Brother Wyman is the church elder; give him the tithe."

But Brother Wyman said, "No, no, Brother Hare is the union secretary; give him the tithe."

Seeing our embarrassment, Deacon Johns took Pastor Wyman's hand, put the tithe in it, and said, "Brethren, don't worry about me. I have known the Lord too long to fear that He will forget me now." Then he put another folded note in my hand and said, "This is my Sabbath school offering. I want the Lord to have some of what may be my last money." Then he asked, "Brethren, have you any idea where my wife and children are? The government promised to fly them out three weeks ago, but I can't find a trace of them anywhere." We did know.

Just then the train whistled as it came into the station, and we said, "Deacon Johns, run for your life, and catch that train! Your wife and children are at Lashio, seventy miles away, and they are going out on the next plane." He never even said Goodbye! He took to his heels, caught the train, found his wife and children half an hour before the next plane came in, and flew out to India with them!

God does reward those who faithfully help out in church and Sabbath school and personal witnessing. Are you doing your part faithfully and well?

PSALMS 91, 92 JUNE 11

"He shall cover thee with his feathers, and under his wings shalt thou trust. . . . Thou shalt not be afraid for the terror by night; nor for the arrow that flieth by day." Psalm 91:4, 5.

The ninety-first psalm has brought comfort to thousands of God's children who have gone through the terrors of war or storm, from the days of the children of Israel down to these present days. I am sure that everyone who has ever experienced an air raid, with screaming sirens giving warning of its approach, will agree that it is indeed a "terror by night" or by day. During the days of World War II there lived in Rangoon a piano tuner by the name of Mr. Ward. He had lost his wife two years before, but his 12-year-old boy, Stanley, helped him keep the home together for his two little girls of 9 and 8 years. One morning as Mr. Ward left for work he said, "If an air raid comes today, Stanley, take your little sisters to the trench, and I'll come running home as soon as the all-clear sounds."

At 10:30 a.m. the sirens began to scream the air-raid warning.

Calmly Stanley locked the apartment and took his little sisters downstairs, across the street, and into the big covered storm drain. It was big enough—two feet wide and four feet deep. It was safe enough—covered with thick concrete slabs. But it was a smelly place and it was dark. Soon they heard the bombers overhead, and when the bombs began to burst, the little girls began to cry. Stanley put his arms around them and said, "Girls, don't be frightened. Listen! Hear how my voice echoes! This gutter is just like a cave. Come, girls, let's sing! Then our voices will echo so loud that we won't be able to hear the bombs burst." And there in that dark smelly gutter they sang: "Jesus loves me, this I know, for the Bible tells me so." And their voices echoed and echoed so much that they couldn't hear the bombs bursting overhead. When the all-clear sounded they crawled back to the road. But what an awful sight! One bomb had burst right in front of their house. It had blown the front steps away and killed half a dozen people. Their bodies lay right there among the broken pieces of the nearby houses.

"Children, we can't stay here," said their neighbor.

"Let's run! Father will find us somehow," said Stanley. They ran for four miles, till they found a small, empty bamboo house. And there their father found them a little later on, without a scratch or a bruise on them anywhere.

I think you should memorize all of the ninety-first psalm. Someday maybe you will need the comfort of its precious promises.

PSALMS 96, 97, 98   JUNE 12

"O sing unto the Lord a new song; for he hath done marvellous things: his right hand, and his holy arm, hath gotten him the victory." Psalm 98:1.

Some songs are new because they have never been sung before. But I know some old songs that have become new because of some experience people have gone through. One Friday night we had five air raids. They came at 2:30, 3:15, 4:00, 5:00, and 6:00 a.m. Nobody had slept since 2:30 a.m., everybody had been in the gutters and trenches all that time, so I hardly expected to see anyone at Sabbath school that Sabbath morning. But can you believe it? There were thirty-seven people there, early, on time! And as we called the roll we discovered that every Sabbath school member who was still in the city was at Sabbath school that morning! I'll never forget the song we sang to open our service. It was "A Shelter in the Time of Storm." And I wish you could have heard us sing it! Everyone had found God a shelter during some narrow escape, and it is wonderful how different that made the words sound. Mr. Ward and Stanley and the two little girls were there, singing with all their hearts. I wish you could have heard them.

Brother and Sister Martin were there too. He was a customs official. One day he came home for lunch and had just parked his car under the porch when the air-raid signal sounded. Down into the trench they went, and just as they got under cover, a bomb dropped right on their house and everything was burned to ashes. All they had left were the clothes they were wearing, but they were at Sabbath school that morning. Now, ordinarily Brother Martin can't carry a tune, but tune or no tune, he was singing "A Shelter in the Time of Storm"; and I wish you could have heard him.

Brother Ross was there too. He was an electrician and had only recently been baptized. One day he was at the top of a telegraph pole, repairing some wires, and when the air-raid signal sounded he shouted to his four assistants to run for cover. Down the pole he came as fast as he could, and just had time to throw himself face down into the curbside gutter. A bomb burst so close that his four assistants, still running for shelter, were instantly killed. But he escaped without a scratch, and he was there singing "A Shelter in the Time of Storm" that morning; and I wish you could have heard him sing. It was a song of experience. That's what made it sound like a new song.

If you are faithful you'll be singing a "new song" in heaven someday, and it will be a song of experience. Get that experience with God now.

PSALM 103   JUNE 13

"Like as a father pitieth his children, so the Lord pitieth them that fear him." Psalm 103:13.

What a beautiful psalm we have just read! All the goodness and mercy and love and care of God are summed up in this portion of scripture.

Some years ago I found a story in *The Reader's Digest* that beautifully describes a father's love for his child. It told of a carpenter named Bill, who had a little girl called Minna. When Minna was only 4 years old her mother died, and Bill and his little girl were left alone. They were brokenhearted, but Bill did his best to make Minna happy. He found a kitten for her to play with; he cooked and swept; he washed and mended Minna's little clothes; and at night he heard her say her prayers. Then he would kneel at his bed and pray, "Lord, help me to do what is right for her, if You see me doing wrong."

When Minna was 6 years old Bill became ill. He went to see a doctor, and when he got back he sat in his workshop a long, long time and just thought. The doctor said he had tuberculosis and wouldn't live more than six months! When Minna came to kiss him good night, he held her at arm's length and said, "Daddy doesn't want you to get his cold, dear. Anyway, you're a big girl now, and big girls don't want to kiss their daddies!" But her eyes filled with tears, and her little lips trembled. The next day he went to see another doctor, just to make sure, and the doctor made him sure. That night he thought all night long: What could he do for Minna?

The next day he advertised in the city paper. "A man with only a few months to live would like nice people to adopt his little girl, age 6, blue eyes, curls. References required." The next day a rich couple drove up in a limousine. Bill looked at them and said he had made other plans for his little girl. The woman next door saw the car drive away and said to Bill, "You've done her out of a fortune. You hadn't the right to refuse them." Other cars came and went. The woman next door said, "You ought to be reported to the authorities."

Then one day another car came. "We've just lost our little girl," said the man sorrowfully, "and we thought—"

"You are the ones," said Bill.

"When can we come and get little Minna?" they asked.

"Give me one more day," Bill said. That day he mended her toys and her clothes. He listened to her sing to her doll and her kitten. He told her about the lovely visit she was going to have with the loveliest people in the loveliest place. He heard her say her prayers and tucked her into bed that night.

"Kiss me, Daddy," she begged.

"Daddy's cold is too bad," said Bill in a trembling voice. The good people came the next morning and Minna went on her trip, leaving her father with only a heart full of loving memories.

Your heavenly Father loves you just like that. And even when you are bad He can't bear the thought of ever giving you up. He pleads for just one more day, and one more day. Won't you promise God that you will never go away from Him?

"Remember me, O Lord, . . . that I may rejoice in the gladness of thy nation." Psalm 106:4, 5.

Today is Flag Day in the United States. It is the anniversary of the adoption of the good old Stars and Stripes in 1777. It is a pleasing coincidence that the psalm we read for today is one of the national hymns of Israel. It is fitting for Christians to be good citizens and to rejoice in the gladness of their nation on earth, as well as to be good citizens and rejoice in the kingdom of heaven that is to come. Here is a story of a good citizen. I found it in *The Reader's Digest* many years ago. Ira Dutton was born in Vermont some time in the 1840s. He served with the Union forces in the Civil War; then after an unhappy marriage he tried to find peace for his troubled heart by becoming a priest in the Trappist monastery at Gethsemane in Kentucky. But nothing gave him peace, so he left the monastery, and one day in 1887, while he was in New Orleans, he picked up a magazine and read the story of Father Damien and his heroic work among the lepers on Molokai in the Hawaiian Islands. "He's getting old," said Ira Dutton to himself. "Someone will have to take his place. I will be that man." So he bought a ticket and went to Molokai. In those days leprosy was feared much more than it is today, and he well knew that he would never see his own country again.

In Molokai they called him Brother Joseph. He nursed Father Damien through his last illness and then took his place as a missionary to the lepers. Among the few things he took with him was an American flag. He erected a flagpole near the beach, and every morning he ran up his flag, and every evening he took it down. It was the only touch he had with his country and nation except for the few letters and papers that came now and then. In 1908 he saw in the papers that the American fleet was going around the world on a goodwill tour, and would be sailing around the Hawaiian Islands. "They might come past Molokai," he said to himself excitedly. "I might be able to see them!" And every morning as he ran up his flag he scanned the horizon in hope. Now someone told President Theodore Roosevelt about Brother Joseph and his deep desire, and President Roosevelt got in touch by telephone with the admiral of the fleet that was then in Honolulu. He was told to sail by Molokai so that Brother Joseph could see the fleet. And so it happened that one morning as Brother Joseph ran up his flag he saw a great gray ship coming nearer and nearer; then another and another came till at last he saw the long file of battleships all go by. And as each ship passed by, she dipped her own flag in salute to the flag of the loyal hero of Molokai.

Make up your mind to be a good citizen and rejoice in the gladness of your nation.

PSALM 119:1-56   JUNE 15

"Thy word have I hid in mine heart, that I might not sin against thee." Psalm 119:11.

The Bible is different from every other book in the world. There is power in the dear old Book of God, and our only hope of standing true and faithful through the temptations of the last days is in getting that power down into our hearts by reading the Bible every day. When I was a missionary in Burma an old man came to my dispensary one day with a severe attack of malaria. I gave him a bottle of the best medicine we knew of, and told him to take three doses each day. I even marked it on the outside of the bottle, and said, "Uncle, if you take this medicine you will be all well again in three or four days." But after four days his eldest son came to me and said, "Father is much worse. Please come and see him."

"Worse?" I asked. To myself I said, "Everybody who takes that medicine gets better. Could I have given him the wrong medicine?" As soon as our dispensary treatments were over I put a few things into my medicine bag and went with the young man to his father's house about four miles away. I climbed the bamboo ladder and looked at the poor old man lying on his mat. I saw at once that he was worse.

"I can't understand it, Uncle," I said. "You should be better by this time. Let me see the medicine bottle. Let me see if I gave you the right medicine."

"It's over there—on—the shelf," he said weakly, pointing with a trembling hand toward the fireplace. I went over to the shelf, and sure enough there was the medicine bottle, and—all at once I understood it all! The medicine was still in the bottle!

"Uncle, Uncle," I said, "this medicine is not like a charm; it has no power over malaria fever when it is here in the bottle on the shelf. You must get the medicine down inside of you where the malaria is. Come now, open your mouth; let me give you a dose." He opened his mouth, and I gave him a big spoonful of medicine. "There now," I said, "that's the way. Take another dose tonight, and three more tomorrow, and

174

three more the next day, and see if it doesn't make you better."

Sure enough, in a few days he was better, and he came down to get another bottle of medicine. "I want to keep it in my house, so that if ever the fever comes again I can take it and get better," he said joyfully.

I wonder how many of us are like that poor old jungle man. We keep our lovely new Bibles in the bookcase or on the table or maybe under our pillows, but seldom read them.

Make up your mind now to hide the Word of God in your heart, and read it every day.

PSALM 119:57-104   JUNE 16

"For ever, O Lord, thy word is settled in heaven. . . . I will never forget thy precepts: for with them thou hast quickened me. . . . Thou . . . hast made me wiser than mine enemies." Psalm 119:89-98.

How the men of old loved the words of God! What beautiful things they said about the words of God! "Thy law is better than gold and silver! Thy words are sweeter than honey! With thy precepts thou hast given me life! Thy commandments have made me wiser than mine enemies!" It is so easy to see the difference in the life of people who read the dear old Book of God and believe it and those who don't.

Once upon a time a man who didn't love and believe the Word of God was talking with a Christian doctor who did love and believe it. "I'm surprised that you put any faith in the Bible," said the unbeliever. "An educated man like you! Why, you can't even tell for sure who wrote many of the books in it. And how could anyone with any brains at all believe all those miracles?"

"Wouldn't you have faith in anything if you didn't know who wrote it?" asked the doctor calmly.

"Certainly not, my good man!" replied the unbeliever.

"Do you know who wrote the multiplication table?" asked the doctor.

"Well—er—no!"

"Yet you believe it and use it all the time, don't you?"

"Well—er—yes," replied the unbeliever, beginning to feel uncomfortable. Then a gleam of hope came to him. "Well, you see, doctor, the multiplication table works so well that no one needs to know who wrote it."

Then the doctor replied, "The same is true of the Bible. It works well too! Did you ever hear a man say, 'I was a thief, a murderer, a drunkard, a disgrace to my family; then I began to study mathematics, geology, or astronomy, and it made a new man out of me'?"

"Well—er—no!" replied the unbeliever.

"Well," answered the doctor, "I can show you not one or two or hundreds, but thousands of men and women who have become new creatures because they have loved and studied and believed the Word of God."

Ellen G. White says, "No other book is so potent to elevate the thoughts, to give vigor to the faculties, as the broad, ennobling truths of the Bible."—*Counsels to Parents and Teachers*, p. 460. Do you love the Book of God? Do you read and believe it? Then the words will give you life and make you wiser than your enemies.

PSALM 119:105-176   JUNE 17

"Thy word is a lamp unto my feet, and a light unto my path." Psalm 119:105.

The darker the night, the brighter shines the light. So, for an illustration of how the Bible becomes a light to one's path, let me bring you a story from dark New Guinea. Away back in the 1870s there was born among the cannibals in the mountains of New Guinea a little heathen baby boy. His mother named him Faole (fa-o-le). She little dreamed how bad a boy he would become. When he was 15 he killed his first man, simply because it was "fashion belong head-hunters." This murder seemed to awaken within him an unquenchable thirst for blood, and before long he had killed another man, two women, and a baby. By this time Faole had a bad reputation and was greatly feared. In a few years his mother died. That made him angry, and he went out and killed two more men. Then the government officer ordered his policemen to track him down and capture him, and eventually he landed in jail. By the time he served his sentence there was a new Adventist mission at Efogi, in his mountain district, and although he now was about 50 years old, he presented himself to the missionary and said he wanted to go to school. It was there that he found the Bible, and soon he had learned to read it. Then the light began to shine, and a great change came over him. He cleaned his body, his clothes, his house. He became a friendly man, and anyone who had trouble went to Faole for comfort. It was this Faole who befriended the Allied soldiers and was responsible for the heroic first-aiders who carried so many wounded soldiers to their base hospital. On one occasion he was trying to lead a company of Australian soldiers, who had been cut off, back through the enemy lines to their own lines, but they became hopelessly lost. Faole gathered that company of men about him and said, "Me sorry too much; me lose 'im way altogether." The men were hungry; they were tired; they were in despair, but Faole had them all kneel down while he prayed to the "big fella Master, stop along top" to ask which way to go. The prayer was finished. Faole turned in the opposite direction, as God impressed him to do, and within an hour they were safe behind their own lines! Oh, what a difference; what a change! All because the man in darkness followed the "light unto his path."

Priscilla J. Owens must have seen the power of the Bible and felt the power of the Bible when she wrote that hymn we all know and sing so often:

Give me the Bible—holy message shining,
    Thy light shall guide me in the narrow way.
Precept and promise, law and love combining,
    Till night shall vanish in eternal day.

You will need this light and the God of the light in your life, too. Read it, study it now, and it will be a light unto your path, too.

PSALMS 121, 122, 124, 125   JUNE 18

"I will lift up mine eyes unto the hills, from whence cometh my help. My help cometh from the Lord, which made heaven and earth." Psalm 121:1, 2.

Here's another story about Faole and the way God helped him. By the time Faole was baptized there was a call to open a new mission in the village of Maibikee, a two-day journey from Port Moresby on the coast, and whom do you think they sent? They sent Faole and his wife and his little children! He built a new village and new church and a new school, and the people just loved their teacher and the new way of life he brought them. Now, just over the mountain there was a heathen village. The chief of that village was very angry when he saw the change that had come to Maibikee. The people in that village didn't want their old heathen customs changed! Well, one day the heathen chief suddenly died, and the witch doctor soon decided that Faole was to blame, and that Faole and his family must die. So fifty warriors in the heathen village tightened their bows, sharpened their spears, tipped their arrows in poison, and put on their war paint, all ready to set out when night came. In some strange way the news of the coming attack reached Maibikee. The village people fled to the jungle and begged Faole and his family to come too. Faole knew of the danger, but he would not flee. He picked up his Bible and read, "The angel of the Lord encampeth round about them that fear him, and delivereth them." Then he said to his wife and children, "Don't be afraid. Just go to sleep. God will help us." They slept peacefully all night. Nothing happened that night or the next or the next. The news of the heathen threat reached the missionary in Port Moresby, and he came up to see what had happened. He found everybody in Maibikee well and happy. He went to the heathen village over the mountain, and found the men sullen and angry, and the women were laughing at them. At last the new chief explained, "You know why I did not do it. How could I kill Faole when you and a lot of other men dressed in white stood in a ring around his house all night?" That was the secret! Faole's God had sent help just when he needed it most.

When you need help lift your eyes to the God of the hills. He has promised to send you help, too.

PSALMS 148, 149, 150   JUNE 19

"Sing unto the Lord a new song. . . . For the Lord taketh pleasure in his people: he will beautify the meek with salvation." Psalm 149:1-4.

The book of Psalms closes with this exhortation: "Let every thing that hath breath praise the Lord." Singing is one form of praise, and all the reasons for praising God with singing can be summed up in the words "For the Lord taketh pleasure in his people." It is a pleasure for God to send His angels to help and protect His people, and it is a pleasure for God to receive their thanks and praise in prayer and in singing. Here is another story about old Faole and the way he praised the Lord.

When Faole was an old man he wanted to live in the mountains where he had grown up. So a new mission was opened up in the village of Enevologo, and Faole was put in charge. He built a new church, and it was about ready for dedication when the enemy during World War II came over the mountains. They killed everyone they suspected of being friends of the Allies, and burned their villages. So as they came nearer, Faole told his people to flee to the mountains. By this time Faole's children had all grown up, but in the bigness of his heart he had taken a number of orphan children into his home, so these children all went with Faole. He wanted to be near enough to keep an eye on the village, so he crossed the river and built a little hut in the jungle. One Sabbath afternoon Faole dreamed that danger was near, so before morning he took all the children into the jungle to hide. In just a few minutes enemy planes dropped bombs on the village and it was entirely destroyed. Soon after this some Allied soldiers came creeping through the jungle looking for enemy hideouts. "There's one!" whispered one of the soldiers, pointing through the undergrowth at a neat grass hut in a small clearing. The soldiers froze. They could hear the jabber of voices. "Must be an enemy officer and his staff," whispered another, and they trained their guns on the door so they could pick them off as they came out. But the next minute they heard the sound of singing: "Anywhere with Jesus I can safely go."

"It's OK, fellows," said the officer in charge. "There are no enemies there!" And there certainly were not! It was Faole and his family of orphans praising God for His goodness at morning worship. Make it a habit to sing at family worship.

PROVERBS 1   JUNE 20

"The fear of the Lord is the beginning of knowledge." Proverbs 1:7.

Knowledge is a wonderful blessing to anyone, but when it is based upon "the fear of the Lord"—"fear of" means reverence for—its results are unpredictable and without limit. In 1858, in a little windowless, mud-floored cabin, there was born a little boy. His mother, Jane, was a slave. She worked long hours and cooked for the master of the plantation. She named this boy Booker, and one of the first things Booker remembered was his mother earnestly praying, "Dear God, here I am with my children, just slaves. Look on us with pity and give us freedom, dear God; please give us freedom." There was no school for little boy slaves; there was nothing he could do, except just grow up and wait for God to answer his mother's prayers. He was only 4 years old when the Civil War began, but by the time he was 6 or 7, Lincoln had proclaimed freedom for all the slaves. Then began a new life for little Booker. Soon he was working in a salt factory with his stepfather at Malden, West Virginia. One day he saw a young man reading a newspaper to a group of people. "If I could only read," he said to himself, "wouldn't that be wonderful!" He told his mother of his great desire. She managed to buy him a spelling book. He took it with him to work; he asked everyone and anyone to explain the letters and the words. Finally his stepfather yielded to pressure and agreed to let him go to school half a day if he would get up at four o'clock in the morning and put in his work hours. The first day at school was the happiest day in little Booker's life, but it brought a little embarrassment. As the teacher called the roll Booker noticed that all the other children had two names, while he had only one. So when the teacher asked for his full name, he stammered "Booker Washington," and the name stuck with him throughout his lifetime. With his school days came the new experience of attending Sunday school. A few years later he traveled five hundred miles to Hampton Institute in Virginia, where he was able to work his way through school. He returned home to Malden, where he taught for two years, spent a year in the Wayland Seminary, in Washington, D.C., then went back to Hampton Institute as one of the instructors!

In less than twenty years a little, ignorant ex-slave boy, with a great thirst for knowledge and a heart full of love to God and his fellowmen, had become an instructor in a college! But this was only the beginning of his great lifework. After two years at Hampton he was called to open the now-famous Tuskegee Institute. It began with a rented church, a shanty, and thirty students; but it grew into a magnificent group of buildings with thousands enrolled!

"There is no limit to the usefulness of one who, by putting self aside, makes room for the working of the Holy Spirit upon his heart, and lives a life wholly consecrated to God."—*The Desire of Ages*, pp. 250, 251. And that means *you!*

"In all thy ways acknowledge him, and he shall direct thy paths." Proverbs 3:6.

The writer of Proverbs identified simple trust in the leading of God as the secret of much happiness in the Christian life. Let me tell you how this worked in the life of Booker T. Washington. After the emancipation of the slaves, and little Booker's work in a salt factory, his stepfather tried him in the coal mines. But since this kind of work gave no opportunity for Booker to study, his mother kept looking around, and finally got him a job as houseboy for a well-to-do Southern woman. The job sounded good and opportunities for study were splendid, but think of poor Booker! He had lived his life in a windowless mud-floored cabin and knew absolutely nothing about neatness, cleanliness, or order; and was his mistress strict! She made him do his work over and over again till she was satisfied. It was very discouraging at first, but Booker decided to do his very best and learn all he could about housework while he was at it.

After four years as a houseboy, Booker decided to apply for admission to the Hampton Institute in Virginia. He didn't have enough money to pay his railroad fare all the way, so he had to walk part way. When he presented himself to the lady principal and asked whether he could work his way through school, she looked at him a moment, then said: "The classroom next door needs sweeping. Take this broom and sweep it." Booker realized that this was his entrance examination. But if he knew how to do anything at all, it was to sweep and clean a room. God had directed his preparation to this end! He swept the room three times, then dusted it four times, not missing a nook or a corner. When he had finished, the principal came in, and taking a clean white handkerchief, she rubbed it over the table and some of the woodwork. Not finding one particle of dust or dirt, she quietly said, "I guess you will do to enter this institution." These were the happiest words he had ever heard. He had passed his college entrance examination! Do you see how God had directed his ways?

What do you want to be when you grow up? Tell God about it every day; then do your very best at your chores, your homework, your music, your job, and just see how God will direct *your* ways, too.

"The path of the just is as the shining light, that shineth more and more unto the perfect day." Proverbs 4:18.

In the fourth chapter of Proverbs, Solomon has been comparing the path of the just and the path of the wicked. The path of the just is the path of obedience, of obtaining an education, and of self-control. He closes the chapter with the words "Let thine eyes look right on. . . . Turn not to the right hand nor to the left," and right in the center of the chapter is the promise "The path of the just is as the shining light, that shineth more and more unto the perfect day." The light on the pathway of the just never goes out.

Many years ago there appeared in the New York newspapers a story about a lighthouse keeper, Tom Jones, and his brave wife, Mary. They were stationed on a lonely point of rock off Staten Island, called Robin's Ledge. When they first went there the place was so lonely and rocky and bleak that it was a week before Mary could make up her mind to unpack her trunk and household things. She really disliked the place, but at last they made up their minds to make the best of it. Then one night Tom got sick with pneumonia. She called the coast guard on Staten Island and they came for him in a boat and took him to the hospital. As they were carrying Tom out of the lighthouse he looked up and weakly said, "Mary, mind the light." So Mary stayed and kept the light burning. Two nights later the coast guard came back and one of the men said, "Mrs. Jones, we have bad news for you. Your husband is worse!"

"You mean my husband is dead," said Mary. "I know; I have felt it in my bones."

"Yes, you're right," said the man. "Tom is dead; Mrs. Jones, we have a relief man for the light if you want to leave, or if you want to, you can stay on as lighthouse keeper. Take a little time to think it over. There's no hurry."

"Tom's words were 'Mary, mind the light! Mind the light,' " she said, then added, "I'll stay." Mary Jones stayed eighteen years! And for all those eighteen years the light never went out.

"The bright beams of heaven's light are shining upon your pathway, dear youth, and I pray that you may make the most of your opportunities. Receive and cherish every heaven-sent ray, and your path will grow brighter and brighter unto the perfect day."—*Messages to Young People,* p. 32.

"The fear of the Lord prolongeth days: but the years of the wicked shall be shortened." Proverbs 10:27.

In Proverbs 10, Solomon is comparing the lives of the righteous and the wicked, the wise and the foolish, the obedient and the disobedient. "He is in the way of life that keepeth instruction: but he that refuseth reproof erreth," he says in verse 17; and in verse 12 of chapter 14, he says, "There is a way which seemeth right unto a man, but the end thereof are the ways of death." How careful we need be to make sure we take the counsel and advice of our teachers and parents, even if our own way does look all right to us.

I can never, never forget a certain weekend that I spent at one of our sanitariums. I will not tell you where it was, nor will I give you the real names of the people in the story, for it was too, too sad. But I was there. I saw the tears. I heard the story personally from the doctor and the matron.

Maude grew up in the country. Her father and mother were both Adventists, but the father died when Maude was just a little girl, and the mother had quite a struggle rearing her. Maude was not strong, and she became tired easily. When she was 17 years old she was fortunate to get a job at the sanitarium so she could work and attend the nearby academy. The doctor examined her carefully and said that if she was careful, she could work twenty hours a week and go to school, and in time her heart would grow stronger, but she must get her full sleep. There must be no parties or late hours. All went well for a while. Maude was a lovely girl, and was doing well. Then one night her roommate, Lucia, said, "Oh, I wish we could go skating tonight."

"So do I," said Maude. "I'm feeling fine. I don't think it would hurt me."

"Come on, then," said Lucia. "No one will ever know." So they went to the ice-skating rink and skated around until midnight. Then they came back to their room in the sanitarium. And nobody knew. At three o'clock that morning Maude was dead! The doctors did all they possibly could do, but her poor little heart was so swollen it just couldn't beat any longer.

And Lucia? Poor Lucia. "It's all my fault," she cried. "I killed her." And they had to keep her under sedatives for two days! I was there! I heard the nurses and the workers crying and wishing. I will never forget it. No matter how *right* your plans seem, make sure your teachers and parents *know* they are right. The end of the seemingly right path may be death.

PROVERBS 15   JUNE 24

"A soft answer turneth away wrath: but grievous words stir up anger." Proverbs 15:1.

In today's chapter Solomon has had quite a bit to say about words. He says, "The words of the pure are pleasant words" (verse 26). "He that is slow to anger appeaseth strife" (verse 18). Maybe the best known verse is the one we have chosen for this morning: "A soft answer turneth away wrath." Many stories have been told from all over the world that prove this statement to be true, but here is one told by Ethel Young, who for a number of years was a missionary in the Far East.

Mr. and Mrs. Mantusea lived in central Java, where Mr. Mantusea was a teacher in the government school. Mrs. Mantusea became an Adventist, but Mr. Mantusea, although he was convinced he should keep the Sabbath, was afraid he would lose his job. Every Sabbath Mrs. Mantusea took her two younger children, baby Peter and little Patricia, who was not yet of school age, with her to Sabbath school. But Christine and her two brothers had to go to school every day except Sunday, for in that country children went to school six days a week.

Now, Christine was the oldest child in the family. She had listened carefully to all that was ever said about the truths of the Bible, and in her heart she believed as her mother did; and she longed to go to Sabbath school and church with her, but her father wouldn't hear of it. "I tell you, you *are* going to *school!*" he said angrily.

One Sabbath Christine felt she just couldn't stand it any longer. She went to school as usual, but soon after answering the roll call she jumped out of the window and ran to the church. Her mother was surprised to see her, and hoped and prayed that Christine would not get into trouble. Christine did this again and again. Then her father heard about it, and gave her a hard beating. "Now will you go to school or go to Sabbath school?" he shouted as he finished beating her.

"I'm going to go to Sabbath school, Father," Christine said softly. "Jesus will help me." The father left the home in great anger.

Next Sabbath he beat her again. "If my own daughter won't obey me, they will take my job away," he said angrily. "Now will you go to school, as I tell you?"

"Father, I cannot go, whatever may happen," Christine replied softly. "Jesus would be unhappy if I did not obey Him."

"Then go to your Sabbath school! Go all your life! But don't tell me anything about it," he screamed as he left the house. And Christine went to Sabbath school. And what do you think? We heard the good news that her father has been baptized. Her three brothers have been going to Sabbath school for some time, and the oldest brother plans to be baptized.

You see, it's true. The power of God goes with a soft, gentle answer. Remember this whenever you are tempted to answer back impatiently.

PROVERBS 20 JUNE 25

"Wine is a mocker, strong drink is raging: and whosoever is deceived thereby is not wise." Proverbs 20:1.

The proverbs of Solomon contain many good verses warning us against the use of strong drink. This morning's text is one, and there are several others in chapter 23. "Look not thou upon the wine when it is red, when it giveth his colour in the cup, when it moveth itself aright. At the last it biteth like a serpent, and stingeth like an adder." The words "look not" remind me of the pictures of the three wise monkeys. One has his hands over his eyes, so he cannot see any evil; one has his hands over his mouth, so he cannot say (or taste) any evil; the other has his hands over his ears, so he cannot hear any evil. Do you know where this representation of three wise monkeys came from? It came from Japan. The original sculpture of the three wise monkeys was made on the wall of a temple in the town of Nikko, about one hundred miles north of Tokyo. Below the sculpture, in Japanese characters, are the words *iwa zaru* ("speak not"), *mi zaru* ("see not"), and *kika zaru* ("hear not"). The *zaru* means "not" when added to a verb, but the word *zaru* also means "monkey"! So the saying of the "three nots" became known as the "three monkeys."

If ever you see models of these wise monkeys for sale in the dime store or at a souvenir counter, buy one and keep it in your room. It will remind you of Solomon's advice about liquor. Don't talk about it or taste it.

Don't look at it and don't listen to anybody talking about it over the radio or on TV. And if you take the advice of the three wise monkeys you will never be deceived by liquor. A good friend of mine, Murl Vance, once worked in a typewriter repair shop. Everyone in the shop drank except Murl. They made fun of him and called him names. But Murl didn't mind. One day, however, one obnoxious fellow by the name of Johnson began to sing, "Vance is a fraidy cat; Vance is a fraidy cat."

"What am I afraid of?" asked Murl.

"You are scared to take a drink of liquor," he said, and everybody laughed a little. Then Murl had an idea and he sang, "Johnson is a fraidy cat! Johnson is a fraidy cat!"

"What am I afraid of?" shouted Johnson, getting angry and quite red in the face.

"You are scared to eat a plate of barnyard fertilizer," said Murl, and everybody just roared!

"Oh," said Johnson afterward, "you mean liquor is disgusting to you?" And no one ever taunted Murl about not drinking liquor again.

Liquor is disgusting. Never taste it; never look at it; and never listen to liquor ads.

PROVERBS 25

"He that hath no rule over his own spirit is like a city that is broken down, and without walls." Proverbs 25:28.

In the chapter we have read today Solomon refers to several things that are signs of true greatness. One of them is *humility*, and in verses 6 and 7 he says, "Stand not in the place of great men: for better it is that it be said unto thee, Come up hither; than that thou shouldest be put lower." Another sign of greatness is *kindness*. Only a great person can give his enemy food and drink (verses 21, 22). Another sign of greatness is *self-control*, and this morning's text means that a person without self-control is like a city without walls. Put these three things together—humility, kindness, and self-control—and they present a picture of a truly great person. Some time ago a teacher in a school in England asked her pupils to write an essay on true greatness. This is what one 12-year-old girl wrote: "A person can never get true greatness by trying for it. You can get it when you are not looking for it. It is nice to have good clothes. It makes it a lot easier to act decent, but it is a sign of true greatness to act decent when you have not got them, just as good as if you had.

"One time when Ma was a little girl, they had a bird at their house, named Bill, that broke his leg. They thought they would have to kill him, but next morning they found him propped up sort of sideways on his good leg, singing. That was true greatness.

"Once there was a woman that had done a big washing and hung it on a line. The line broke and let it all down in the mud; but she didn't say a word. She did it all over again, and this time she spread it on the grass where it couldn't fall. But that night a dog with dirty feet ran over it. When she saw what was done she sat down and didn't cry a bit. All she said was, 'Ain't it queer that he didn't miss nothing?' That was true greatness, but it is only people that have washing that know it."—Vincent Edwards, in *Children's Friend.*

I think that junior girl had the right idea of true greatness, don't you? Now just how great are you? Are you humble? Are you kind? Do you have self-control?

ECCLESIASTES 1, 3   JUNE 27

"The eye is not satisfied with seeing, nor the ear filled with hearing."
Ecclesiastes 1:8.

Solomon set his heart upon seeing all the works that were done under the sun. He saw the works of man, the sorrows, the pleasures, the vanities, and was bored with them all. Poor Solomon. With so much to see and hear, he was still unsatisfied! Today is the birthday of one of the world's most remarkable women—Helen Keller. Helen Keller was totally blind, yet she read far more books than most people who can see. She wrote seven books herself. She was totally deaf, yet she enjoyed music far more than do many people who can hear. For nine years she couldn't speak; yet she learned to talk and lectured in every state in America, as well as in many countries all over the world! Helen Keller could put Solomon with all of his wisdom, as well as eyes and ears, to shame.

Helen was born in 1880, a perfectly normal child. For the first eighteen months of her life she could see and hear and had even begun to say a few words, when suddenly she was struck down with a high fever that left her deaf, dumb, and blind. When she was 10 years old Anne Sullivan, a specialized teacher, came into her life, and little by little the path of communication with the outside world was opened. Her sense of feeling became so acute that she could understand what her friends were saying by placing her fingers lightly over their lips. And if she shook hands with you, she could remember you by your handshake five years later. Her life brought inspiration and courage and hope to literally thousands of people handicapped in one way or another. On one occasion a celebrated lecturer asked her what was her favorite book. "The Bible," she replied vigorously. "It is the most wonderful Book in the world. The Bible! It is beautiful."

"And why does the Bible mean so much to you?" asked the lecturer.

"It is because in my darkness the Bible makes me see the great light," she replied. What an inspiration Helen Keller has been to all of us.

Thank God for your eyes and your ears this morning, and set your heart to seek out only those things that are pure and kind and true, that your life too may be a blessing to others.

ECCLESIASTES 5 JUNE 28

"It is good and comely for one to eat and to drink, and to enjoy the good of all his labour that he taketh under the sun all the days of his life, which God giveth him." Ecclesiastes 5:18.

When God made man in the beginning, He gave him work to do. This work was intended to be a great blessing and a source of great happiness. God intended that man should "enjoy the good of all his labour." God also placed within man certain laws, and one of them is that "the sleep of the labouring man is sweet" (verse 12). God gave man a body, a mind, and a soul. In order for man to be happy and healthy he must exercise all three parts of his being.

A number of years ago a discouraged, despondent man came to see Dr. Henry Link, a famous doctor in New York. He had lost his job. Nobody seemed to love him anymore. He wanted to commit suicide and end all his troubles. Dr. Link explained that because his work was sedentary, he had only exercised his mind, and not his body. "I will give you a program of manual work," he said, "and soon you will be feeling better."

"I don't like manual work," said the man. "I don't want to work. I want to commit suicide." The doctor did his best to persuade the man to accept a program of work, but it was no use, and at last in exasperation he said, "All right, then, commit suicide. But if you do, why not do something out of the ordinary, something heroic, and get into the headlines when you die." The man liked the idea.

"What do you suggest, Doctor?" he asked. The doctor said, "I have never heard of a man running himself to death. If you want to get into the headlines, run around the block until you drop dead, and every newspaper will have it on the front page."

"That's what I'm going to do," said the man; and off he went. He went home, wrote his letter of farewell, then started running. He ran and he ran, but he couldn't drop dead. He got so tired he said, "I'll have to finish it tomorrow night." He went back home and slept better than he had for a long time. The next night he ran again, around and around; but he couldn't drop dead, and—you've guessed it—he didn't drop dead at all! He literally ran himself back to health and strength.

I hope you have work to do—wood to chop, the lawn to mow, the washing to do, or something. I even hope you have to walk to school, for that body of yours needs good, healthy exercise.

ECCLESIASTES 7   JUNE 29

"A good name is better than precious ointment." Ecclesiastes 7:1.

Solomon has said a lot about having a good name. In Proverbs 22:1 he says that "a good name is rather to be chosen than great riches." And in Ecclesiastes 9:10 he gives us the secret of having a good name: "Whatsoever thy hand findeth to do, do it with thy might."

Once upon a time, as Lora E. Clement told the story in her book *Managing Yourself*, there was a young man just out of college, by the name of Joel Prince, who got a job facing stone blocks in a quarry. "You have to face ten blocks a day," said the foreman as he handed Joel a chisel and a hammer. Joel was eager to make good, so he did his work carefully and well, but by noon he had only finished four blocks. "You are being too careful," said the foreman. "They are only foundation stones and don't have to be so correct."

Joel finished his ten blocks by the time the whistle blew, but he was not satisfied with them. "May I stay a little longer and smooth them up some more?" he asked the foreman.

"Well, all right; but there's no extra pay, mind you," said the foreman. This went on for several days, then one evening when Joel got home he found a letter waiting for him from the manager.

"Your services are no longer needed at the quarry," it said. "Report at the main office at nine o'clock tomorrow morning." Joel felt so discouraged. He had done more than his best, and he simply couldn't understand why he should lose his job.

At nine o'clock he went into the office. There was the big manager, Mr. Johnson, and his son who was the chief executive. "My son saw your blocks of stone and says you are taking too much pains with your work. If we finished off all the foundation blocks like that, they would be too expensive. The foreman says he has told you not to be so exact, but you stay after hours to finish your required number. Do you have anything to say for yourself?"

"Yes, sir," said Joe. "I have taken as my motto 'As thou hast meted out to man, so 'twill come again to thee.' I love to do them well, sir, and I'd like to have my job back."

Then Mr. Johnson smiled and said, "No, Joel, we can't use you in the quarry any more. We have a place here in the office for you."

"I'll surely do my best, sir," said Joel happily. And are you surprised to know that the day came when Joel Prince was himself a great architect? Why don't you decide to do a little better than your best, and see what a good name it will bring to you?

ECCLESIASTES 11, 12   JUNE 30

"Cast thy bread upon the waters: for thou shalt find it after many days."
Ecclesiastes 11:1.

There were so many inspirational texts in today's reading that it was hard to decide which was the best one, so I chose the first. The promise "Thou shalt find it after many days" could apply to farming, to hospitality, to missionary work, and to many things that do not show immediate results for the effort put forth.

Among American stories of the common people there is one about an outstanding person whose life was a shining example of the practice and fulfillment of this morning's text. This person is John Chapman, more commonly known as Johnny Appleseed. He was born in New England and settled in the great Ohio River valley. He loved the outdoors, and as a young man he built himself a home and started a nursery. He lived in the days when settlers were moving west, and his heart's desire was to help the settlers get established. Near him were many apple orchards, and the apples were made into cider. He noticed that after crushing the apples, the pulp and the seeds were thrown out, so he gathered bags and bags of seeds, washed and dried them, and then gave small deerskin bags of apple seeds to the settlers as they went west. Not satisfied with this, he finally gave his home to a widow and her children, tied two Indian dugouts together, loaded them with watertight bags of seed, and set off on one of the most selfless missions we have ever heard of. He planted orchards for the settlers everywhere he went. He even came back from time to time to care for the young apple trees. His greatest joy was to see little children eating the luscious fruit that his love and care had made possible. He wore no fine clothes, often went barefoot, and slept in the open, but everywhere Johnny Appleseed went he was welcome. For forty years he labored unselfishly. He established more than one hundred nurseries and helped thousands of settlers to plant their orchards. And when he finally fell asleep, the whole country mourned the passing of a good, kind, generous man. Today there are monuments to this man's labor of love on practically every farm in the Ohio Valley—not monuments of stone, but apple orchards!

Would *you* like to have loving monuments left to your memory after you have passed away? Find some kind of "bread" or "appleseeds" to "cast . . . upon the waters."

ISAIAH 5 {JULY 1}

"Woe unto them that rise up early in the morning, that they may follow strong drink." Isaiah 5:11.

I'm so glad that we find so many warnings against strong drink in the Bible, for it is one of the greatest curses to mankind. Benjamin Franklin once said, "Some of the domestic evils of drink are houses without windows, gardens without fences, fields without tillage, barns without roofs, and children without clothing, principles, morals, or manners." These are but some of the woes that come to drinkers and their children. Here is a story that tells of another woe that came to the son of a drinker.

Jack Ellis lived with his mother. He had never seen his father. He understood that his father had died when he was just a baby. When Jack grew up and went to high school his mother warned him more and more never to touch beer at any of the parties. "But why, Mother?" said Jack. "Beer is not an alcoholic drink!"

"I know it *is*, son," she replied.

"Oh, Mother, you are just old-fashioned."

"Maybe I am, but, Jack, I know beer is the devil's own brew. Let me see, next Monday is your sixteenth birthday, isn't it? Let's take a little trip and spend the day together."

Monday came, and Jack and his mother took the train for the city not too far away. "Where are we going, Mother?"

"To visit a friend," she said, biting her lips to control her emotions. Arriving at the city, they took a taxi and got out in front of the penitentiary. They rang for admittance, entered the lobby, followed an attendant down a long corridor, and stopped in front of one of the cells. "I've brought our son to see you, dear," she said to the man behind the bars. "Jack, this is your father."

"Why did you bring him here, Kathryn? It was my wish that he would think I was dead." Then speaking directly to Jack, he said, "It was drink that broke up our home, Jack—just a social glass of beer at first. But it's the devil's own brew, son. The devil is in it, and one night at a party I got drunk and killed a man; now I'm here for life."

"Oh, Mother, I wish I had never known," cried Jack on his way home. "I wish I had never known!"

"But you needed something more than my words to show you where drink can lead you, my son," said his mother.

Woe? Yes, indeed; the drinker and the drinker's children know what woe is. *You* need never know, if you will always leave the stuff absolutely alone.

ISAIAH 11   JULY 2

"They shall not hurt nor destroy in all my holy mountain: for the earth shall be full of the knowledge of the Lord, as the waters cover the sea." Isaiah 11:9.

The beautiful description of happiness and peace between people and animals given in our reading for today could have been fulfilled for the children of Israel on this earth if they had been true and faithful to God; but now it can only be fulfilled in the new earth. However, we do find many instances of love and kindness between people and animals today that help us understand what it will be like when "the wolf also shall dwell with the lamb, . . . and a little child shall lead them" (verse 6). Here's a story I found in an Australian copy of *Our Little Friend* a number of years ago.

As Tom was playing in the field one day he saw Bob going toward the river, carrying a sack. It was moving around. He could hear a faint "Yip, yip."

"What have you got in the sack, Bob?" he asked, "and what are you going to do?"

"Aw, it's just a mongrel pup; we got too many. I'm going to drown it."

"Oh, don't drown it," pleaded Tom. "Let me have him."

"You can have him, but he's no good." Tom ran forward and got the sack.

"Just be sure he doesn't get back to our place," said Bob.

"Yes, I'll make sure," said Tom as he raced home. "Oh, you poor little doggy," said Tom as he lifted a little black puppy from the sack. "You little beauty! And if I hadn't seen Bob, you would have been cold, and wet, and dead in that old river by this time." The little pup yipped and yipped and licked Tom's hands, just as if he understood all that had happened and was trying to say Thank you. "I'm going to call you Soot," said Tom, "because you are so very black." And from that moment Tom and Soot were fast friends, and everywhere that Tommy went, Soot was sure to go.

Two years went by, and Soot became a big dog. One day when Tom was crossing the river on a footbridge he tripped and fell into the water. Tom couldn't swim, but Soot could; and Soot was right there. Into the river he jumped. He grabbed Tom by his coat collar and swam with him to the nearest bank. Tom was a bit frightened and very wet, but he hugged Soot and said, "Well, Soot, that makes us even. I saved your life once and now you've saved mine. You shall have a new collar; I'll build you a new house; and what else would you like?" Soot said, "Bow-wow-wow," which, everyone knows, means "I just want to stay with you forever."

Are you looking forward to the time when all the animals and all the people will be kind to one another? Then remember to be kind to your pets and to everyone you meet today and every day!

"Trust ye in the Lord for ever: for in the Lord Jehovah is everlasting strength" [margin, "rock of ages"]." Isaiah 26:4.

At least twenty-six times in the Bible, God is called a "rock," "my rock, and my fortress," my "rock, for an house of defence," and "rock of my salvation." In the margin of our text today God is called the "rock of ages," and I think this is one of the most loved of all the names for God. It includes the meaning of all the other names and adds the assurance that God's defense and salvation are everlasting. The name has been made more dear to our hearts by the immortal and almost universal hymn "Rock of Ages." The words of this hymn were written by Augustus Montague Toplady, a Church of England minister who lived in the eighteenth century. When he was still a young man he contracted tuberculosis and died at the age of 38. One day he was taking a walk on the banks of the Severn River when he was overtaken by a sudden thunderstorm. To escape the downpour, he took cover under a nearby overhanging rock. When the storm was over, he returned to his study and wrote:

> Rock of Ages, cleft for me,
> Let me hide myself in Thee.

The beautiful hymn has been translated into many languages and has been sung on many different occasions. It was sung for Queen Victoria at her "Golden Jubilee"; and when the steamer *London* was wrecked in the Bay of Biscay, in 1866, the last sounds heard by the few who were saved were the voices of the helpless passengers singing "Rock of Ages" as the ship went down. In Constantinople when a company of Armenian Christians were being massacred they sang "Rock of Ages" in their own language. And so throughout the world this beautiful hymn containing this wonderful name of God has brought comfort, hope, and assurance to all who put their trust in Him. The Rock of Ages *was* cleft for you, too. In Him *you* can find forgiveness, peace, and salvation.

"Strengthen ye the weak hands, and confirm the feeble knees. Say to them that are of a fearful heart, Be strong, fear not: behold, your God . . . will come and save you." Isaiah 35:3, 4.

There are many ways of giving encouragement to those who are weak or tired or sick or discouraged. Today is Independence Day in the United States, and no doubt many speeches will be made reminding Americans how they were encouraged to take their first steps toward becoming a great nation. The flag with its thirteen stripes and thirteen stars had a great deal to do with this encouragement. Here is a story I read in the Oakland *Tribune* some years ago about a brave little Chinese girl and a new flag.

During the battle of Shanghai the enemy was slowly driving the gallant but under-armed Chinese forces back to the other side of Soochow Creek. One by one their forces had to retreat or surrender, till at last there was only one company of 150 men left, strongly entrenched in a concrete warehouse. At the top of the flagpole above them still waved the Chinese flag, all tattered and torn by flying bullets and bursting shells. From the roofs of the tall buildings in the international section of the city, the world looked anxiously on, wondering how long those brave men could hold out. Among the onlookers was a 12-year-old Chinese girl who timidly approached the chairman of the chamber of commerce and said, "Just look at their poor torn flag! If you'd give me a new one, I'd take it to them. They are tired and hungry, but I think they could fight better if they had a new flag."

"But the enemy would shoot you, my dear," said the man.

"But I'm so little, maybe they wouldn't," she replied. So he gave her a new flag. She folded it and put it near to her heart, under her little dress, and disappeared. The people looking on knew nothing of what was happening. Suddenly they heard a shout from the side of the enemy, and looking over they saw the torn Chinese flag slowly being pulled down. They are going to surrender, thought everyone. But just then there was a thunderous roar from the Chinese side, and looking again, the people saw a brand-new flag being pulled swiftly to the top of the flagpole. Cheer after cheer rolled across the battlefield, and hearts were brave again and arms were strong. And when at last General Chaing Kai-shek ordered their retreat, the little girl and her brand-new flag led them to safety.

Do you know anyone who is having a hard time, and needs a little encouragement? How about your taking him a new flag!

"But they held their peace, and answered him not a word: for the king's commandment was, saying, Answer him not." Isaiah 36:21.

There is a wonderful power in silence. Solomon says there is "a time to keep silence, and a time to speak" (Ecclesiastes 3:7). Amos says "the prudent shall keep silence in that time" (Amos 5:13). In today's reading Rabshakeh tried to make the Jews afraid with great blasphemous words, but they wisely "held their peace." And before long, God answered him with total destruction.

Here is the story of a heathen chief in the Solomon Islands who held his peace and was greatly blessed by God. For some time before Captain G. F. Jones went to the Solomons, old Chief Tatagu was dissatisfied with some of the heathen customs of his people. He had been the leader of many a head-hunting raid, but a feeling that there was some better way of life grew steadily upon him. His wife was about to give birth to a child, and ordinarily there would be the usual "devil string" ceremony in which strings would be trailed through the fishing grounds, and with the aid of the evil spirits many fish would be caught, followed by a devil feast. But this time Tatagu said, "No, there will be no devil strings or devil feast."

"Then we will take our own devil strings and we will have our own devil feast," said the men of the village angrily. And off they went trailing their devil strings to the fishing grounds. Chief Tatagu "held his peace," but he also went to the fishing grounds for a supply of fish. On the way evil spirits seized his canoe and rocked it as though he had run into a great storm. He could see nothing, and ordinarily he would have been filled with fear, and would have gone home and gotten his devil strings; but this time he would not give in. Then with one tremendous shake that almost upset his canoe the spirits left him. Tatagu went on to the fishing ground and had good success. He came home with a full load! The others came home with almost nothing. When his son was born, Chief Tatagu triumphantly named him Kata Ragoso, which means "without devil strings." Don't you think God was leading this heathen chief toward the light? Just about this time, in 1914, Captain Jones arrived, and the mission school was opened. Little Kata Ragoso was one of the brightest pupils in the school. He learned to speak good English and to use a typewriter. Before long he was secretary to the missionary in charge, and in due time he was ordained to the gospel ministry! I'll tell you some more about Kata Ragoso tomorrow.

Always remember that God is on the side of the one who can hold his peace and be silent when others are trying to pick a quarrel.

ISAIAH 37   JULY 6

"Now therefore, O Lord our God, save us from his hand, that all the kingdoms of the earth may know that thou art the Lord." Isaiah 37:20.

God saved Hezekiah and the children of Israel in such a way that all the world knew it was the work of a mighty God. God still works that way. Listen!

As World War II extended southward the Japanese invaded the Solomon Islands, as a stepping-stone to Australia. The Australian missionaries were ordered to the homeland, and Kata Ragoso (Without Devil Strings) was placed in charge of our work in the Solomons. He did a noble work. He selected and trained spotting units, first-aid parties, and rescue squads. With their drums information was forwarded, and the records show that more than two hundred men owe their lives to the skill and efficiency of those wonderful men. Now there was a detachment of allied soldiers on the same island where Kata Ragoso had his home, and Ragoso and his first-aiders cooperated with them in a wonderful way. But unfortunately, one day the chief officer commanded Ragoso to do certain things that his conscience would not allow. He courteously refused, and was placed under arrest.

"Don't you know there is a war on?" thundered the chief officer.

"I am sorry, sir, I must obey God first," replied Ragoso quietly. But the officer was angry. He took out his revolver and using it as a club beat him over the head with it until he fell to the ground unconscious.

"Sir," said a police boy nearby, "if he is worthy of death, there is a firing squad." And when Ragoso regained consciousness they tied his hands behind his back and stood him up near a tree in front of the firing squad.

"Now then," roared the officer, "when I count three, shoot! One—two—" but he could not say *three*. "I'll try again," he said. "One—two—" But the angel of God must have put his hand over that wicked man's mouth. He couldn't say three. In fact, he couldn't talk at all for almost two days, and Ragoso was "saved from his hand." However, with Ludi, one of his faithful assistants, he was taken back to the prison. Who but a mighty God could close a man's mouth so he couldn't say that final word?

That mighty God is your God. Make Him first in your life and in your obedience, and He will care for you, too.

ISAIAH 38   JULY 7

"The Lord was ready to save me: therefore we will sing . . . all the days of our life in the house of the Lord." Isaiah 38:20.

The Lord was indeed ready to save Hezekiah, and someday in the new earth the Lord will tell us how often He has sent the angels to save every one of us. Listen to another part of the story of how the Lord saved Kata Ragoso.

When Kata Ragoso and Ludi were put in prison the drums beat out a message over the hills and through the valleys, from village to village, "Pray—pray—for Ragoso and Ludi." And on the given night more than three hundred Solomon Island Seventh-day Adventists got down on their knees and prayed and prayed that God would release His servants. And that night as the moon rose over the mountain a tall man with a bunch of keys walked to the gate of the prison. He unlocked the padlock, opened the gate, and called, "Ragoso! Come here!"

"Yes, sir," answered Ragoso.

"Come here! Ludi!"

"Yes, sir."

"Come outside." And they stepped outside. Then the tall man locked the gate again and said, "Follow me!" He took them down to the beach, and just where the sand begins he stopped and pointed to a canoe with two paddles in it. "Take that canoe, boys, and go home," he said. Ragoso and Ludi looked to make sure the canoe was there, then turned to thank the man who had taken them out of the jail; but there was no one there! The moon was shining bright. They could see for a hundred yards or more, but the man had vanished. They have never found the man who opened the prison gate, and the guard says the keys never left the peg on which they were hung all night!

I was visiting in the Solomon Islands a few years ago. I met Kata

Ragoso. I saw the scars on his forehead where he was so cruelly beaten. I said, "Who let you out of prison that night, Ragoso?" and without a second's hesitation he replied, "An angel! The same angel that took Peter out of prison." I looked again at his beaming face as he spoke. His nose was still a little crooked where it had been broken. I thought again of the terrible blows that had knocked him unconscious, and I asked, "What if the officer had killed you that day?"

"I would rather have died than disobey God," was his calm reply. I heard that the officer who had so cruelly mistreated him was later dishonorably discharged from the service.

No matter where you are or what you are doing, if you make sure your guardian angel is by your side, you will be perfectly safe, for the Lord is ready to save *you*.

ISAIAH 39   JULY 8

"Then came Isaiah the prophet unto king Hezekiah. . . . Then said he, What have they seen in thine house?" Isaiah 39:3, 4.

What an opportunity Hezekiah had to tell the visitors from Babylon about the living God, and to show them how he worshiped Him. But poor Hezekiah made the mistake of showing them all the *earthly treasures* and all the *things* in his house, with the terrible and sad result that the king of Babylon sent soldiers, and they carried away all the *things* in his house.

Today is the birthday of one of our great pioneers—Joseph Bates. Let us take a look into his house to see what we may see. He was born in Rochester, Massachusetts, in 1792, and went to sea when he was only 15 years old. For the next twenty-one years he lived the most exciting but wicked life that you can imagine. Twice he was a prisoner of war. He cursed, smoked, chewed tobacco, and drank. He rose to be second mate, then first mate, and finally captain and part owner of a ship. He was married in 1818. In 1824 his wife placed a New Testament in his trunk on top of some novels, as he was starting off on a trip. He read the New Testament, then stopped reading novels; next he gave up tobacco and liquor, and became an ardent temperance advocate. In 1826 he was converted and joined the Christian Church. In 1828 he left the sea and settled down with quite a fortune. In a few years he heard William Miller preaching about the second coming of Christ. He believed it with all his heart. He sold his property and used up his fortune in giving the message. Then he heard of the seventh-day Sabbath from the Adventists in Washington, New Hampshire. He studied it, believed it, and accepted it with all his heart. He felt impressed to write a book about the Sabbath, but his money was gone. He had only one York shilling in his pocket, worth twelve and a half cents, but he sat down at his desk and began to write. "Joseph," called his wife, "I need some flour to finish the baking."

"How much do you need?" asked the captain.

"About four pounds," she answered, and in a short while he brought his wife just four pounds of flour. She looked at it in amazement and said, "You, Captain Bates, a man who has sailed vessels out of New Bedford to all parts of the world—you have been out and bought only four pounds of flour!"

"Wife," said the captain, "I spent for that flour the last money I have on earth."

With that Mrs. Bates began to cry, and sobbing bitterly, she said, "What are we going to do?" Let us leave the story there until tomorrow. But now, tell me, what did you see in Joseph Bates's house? Great treasures? Grand furniture? What kind of magazines were on his table? What kind of books were in his bookcase? When your friends come to visit *you*, what do they see in *your* house?

ISAIAH 40   JULY 9

"They that wait upon the Lord shall renew their strength; they shall mount up with wings as eagles; they shall run, and not be weary; and they shall walk, and not faint." Isaiah 40:31.

For an illustration of the way God sustains and strengthens His children, let me tell you some more about Joseph Bates and his good wife, who felt embarrassed because the captain had bought only four pounds of flour and they were without money. She was in tears as she said, "What are we going to do?"

Joseph Bates stood up and said, "I'm going to write a book about the Sabbath, and I am going to circulate it."

"But what are we going to live on?" said his wife.

"The Lord will open the way," answered the captain.

"That's what you always say," she said, bursting into tears again as she left the room. Joseph Bates kept writing at his desk, and he must have been praying, for in about half an hour he felt impressed that there was a letter at the post office for him. So he walked down to the post office to see.

"Yes, there is a letter," said the postmaster, "but there's 5 cents to pay on it."

"Mr. Drew," he said to the postmaster, "I'm out of money. I don't even have 5 cents to pay that postage. But I feel impressed that there is money in this letter. Will you please open it and see?"

The postmaster opened the letter—and there was a $10 bill! Joseph paid the postage then went right down to a store and bought a barrel of flour and some potatoes and sugar and other things they needed and asked that they be delivered to his wife. "Mrs. Bates will probably tell you that the supplies don't belong to her," he said, "but don't pay any attention to what she says. Just unload them on the front porch anyway."

First he went to the printing house to make arrangements about printing his book; then he went back home. Mrs. Bates met him at the door. "Joseph, just look out there," she said. "I told the man it didn't belong here. But he said this was the address he had been given. Where do you suppose it all came from?"

"Why, the Lord sent it," said the captain, and we can imagine the smile on his face.

"Oh, yes, the Lord sent it; that's what you always say," she teased, for she could hardly believe it was true.

"Then read this letter and see," he said. She read the letter and then had another cry! But this time it was a happy cry, because it was plain as could be that the Lord had not forgotten them and that His promises are sure. When Joseph Bates was ready to have his book printed, the money came in for that too—and in good time. Joseph Bates simply made God and His work first; and God never forgot him.

You will need to have your strength renewed someday. You will need to run and not be weary. Make God and His work first in your life, and everything will be all right.

"I am the Lord, that is my name: and my glory will I not give to another, neither my praise to graven images." Isaiah 42:8.

I love to see how Isaiah compares the living God with man-made idols, and I love to collect stories of what only the living God could do for His children.

In the days when the Advent cause was young some of the members took up a collection to buy James and Ellen White a horse and buggy. It was arranged that several of the men who had horses for sale would bring them to a certain place on Monday morning for Elder and Mrs. White to choose the one they wanted. Now you wouldn't expect the God in heaven to be interested in a small matter like choosing a horse, but He was; and Sunday night He gave Mrs. White a vision. She saw three men holding three horses. As she looked at the first one the angel said, "Not that one." As she looked at the second the angel said, "Not that one." Then as she looked at the third one, a beautiful dappled chestnut, the angel said, "This is the one for you."

The next morning they went to the place and saw the three men with the three horses, exactly as Sister White had seen it in the vision; and they chose the dappled horse. His name was Old Charlie, and he did much to make their traveling pleasant and comfortable.

Boys and girls today can hardly realize what traveling was like in those horse-and-buggy days. There were no smooth paved highways such as we have now, and over the dirt roads, often rutted and rocky, it was difficult to make more than twenty or twenty-five or at best thirty miles in a day.

On one occasion Elder Loughborough and another minister borrowed the horse and buggy to go to a meeting some distance away. There had been a heavy rain, and they came to a place where a bridge had washed out. The creek looked pretty deep. People nearby said others had crossed over all right, so Elder Loughborough decided to try. His friend preferred to cross over on a small footbridge. Old Charlie went cautiously into the water, but it was too deep, and soon the buggy and Old Charlie were floating downstream. Brother Loughborough cried out to God to save him and the horse and buggy. Just then the buggy wheels struck a rock. Old Charlie looked around as if to make sure it was still right side up. Brother Loughborough called out, "Charlie, you've got to get me out of this!" Old Charlie gave two or three lunges, gained a footing, and drew the buggy up out of the creek. Quite a group of people had gathered when they saw that Elder Loughborough was going to try to drive over, and when they saw Old Charlie get safely across, they gave a shout and a cheer for the good old brave horse. Can you imagine an idol or a heathen god foreseeing things like this, and directing in the choosing of a horse? Isaiah must have seen many providential acts that only the living God could perform.

What a wonderful God we have! Take even your little problems to Him. He will see you through.

ISAIAH 43 JULY 11

"When thou passest through the waters, I will be with thee; and through the rivers, they shall not overflow thee." Isaiah 43:2.

God's promise of deliverance has been fulfilled again and again to many people in many places, but I will tell you about the time Captain Joseph Bates fell into the river. Elder and Mrs. James White and Joseph Bates had been traveling from one company of believers to another in New York State, and they planned to finish up their meeting in Port Gibson in time to catch the riverboat for New York City, where they had a Sabbath appointment. However, the meeting lasted longer than they expected, and by the time they got to the river landing, the big riverboat had gone. There was a smaller boat there that was to stop at some of the smaller towns on the way, so instead of waiting at the landing for the next big boat, they decided to start off on the smaller one, then transfer to the next big boat when it overtook them. All went well, and in due time the big riverboat came near. They called to the captain, but he would not stop. So they decided to pull alongside and jump onto the deck of the bigger boat while it was moving. It seemed easy to do. Brother White jumped aboard; then they helped Mrs. White aboard. Brother Bates had his money for the fares in one hand and his wallet in the other hand, but just as he made the jump from the smaller boat, it moved a little farther away. He missed his footing and fell into the muddy water of the river. He was a good swimmer, but as he fell into the water his hat came off, and as he was grabbing for his hat he lost the money in his hand. Seeing what had happened, the captain of the riverboat slowed up, and Captain Bates, dripping wet, was pulled up on deck! Captain Bates couldn't go to New York sopping wet like that, so they got off at the next stop and spent the weekend with some believers there. It was a surprise visit all right, but it was such a blessing to one good sister who was healed in answer to prayer, and to the others with whom they spent the Sabbath, that Brother Bates felt sure the Lord had overruled the misfortune of his falling into the river, and made it a blessing.

The precious promise of our text for today was written for you, too. Memorize it and keep it in your heart.

"Then shall thy light break forth as the morning, and thine health shall spring forth speedily." Isaiah 58:8.

Isaiah 58 contains one of the many strange yet undeniable truths of the Bible, such as the truth Jesus taught when He said, "Whosoever will save his life shall lose it: but whosoever will lose his life for my sake, the same shall save it." One thing this chapter teaches is that if we do missionary work for *others*—giving food and clothing to the poor, visiting the sick, comforting the discouraged, helping people to overcome bad habits—then *we* will obtain an inner joy and improved health! If you look around, you will find that those who think of others and put others first *are* the nicest and happiest people you know. Here is an example given by the famous Dr. Link.

A well-educated woman who had worked in a bank for years became despondent. She felt so miserable that she feared she was going to have a nervous breakdown. Her doctor asked, "Who is the young woman who works beside you in the bank?"

"Dorothy," she replied.

"Dorothy who?"

"I don't know."

"Where does she live?"

"I don't know."

"What is she working toward?"

"I don't know."

The doctor understood at once that plain selfishness was robbing her of joy and health. He said, "I can help you if you will promise to do exactly as I say."

"I'll do anything," she said.

"All right," said Dr. Link. "First, get acquainted with Dorothy. Find out where she lives. Invite her over to your house for supper. Find out what she is aiming at in life, and do something to help her. Second, get acquainted with the milkman and his family, and see if there is something you can do to help them. Third, get acquainted with your newsboy. Find out what he hopes to be when he grows up. In two months come back to see me."

At the end of two months she didn't go back, but she wrote a ten-page letter to the doctor with not one word about her gloom or sadness. It was ten pages of joy! She had helped Dorothy with her Latin, and Dorothy had passed her college exam with honors. One of the milkman's children had whooping cough, and she had looked after the child now and then to let the poor mother get a little rest; now they were good friends. "Where have I been all my life?" she wrote. "I didn't know there was a joy like this!"

It's as true as it can be. Selfishness leads only to unhappiness, but helping others gives you an inner peace and improved health.

ISAIAH 60   JULY 13

"Arise, shine; for thy light is come, and the glory of the Lord is risen upon thee." Isaiah 60:1.

Jesus is the light of the world. All who believe on Him and accept Him receive the light, and in turn become lights. There is nothing more useless in the dark than a lamp that won't shine! There is nothing more disappointing to God than to see a junior whose light has gone out. The words of Isaiah are for all of us— "Arise, shine; for thy light is come."

Several years ago in Oakland I heard evangelist G. R. West tell this story: At a certain railway crossing somewhere in America a flagman was stationed. By day he waved a red flag to warn automobiles of approaching trains, and by night he waved a red lantern. He was a faithful man and was always at his post of duty. One night, however, there was an accident. An automobile started across the tracks and a train crashed into the back end of it. Fortunately, no one was killed. As soon as the car owner recovered he sued the railway company for damages, claiming that he had not been warned of the approaching train. When the case came to court, the flagman was called to the witness box.

"Were you there on the night of the accident?" asked the judge.

"Yes, sir," answered the flagman.

"Did you see this man coming down the road in his car?"

"Yes, sir."

"Did you wave your lantern?"

"Yes, sir," again answered the flagman. Because of the flagman's testimony the case was dismissed. As they went out of the courtroom, one of the railway officials thanked the flagman for his testimony.

"You answered your questions so well that our company does not have to pay damages," he said.

"Yes," answered the flagman, "but you cannot imagine how scared I was all the time for fear the judge would ask me if my lantern was lighted."

Oh, ho! I wonder what happened after that. Evangelist West didn't say, but, juniors, we are all in danger of letting our light go out.

God forbid that anyone should lose the way or lose eternal life because your light has gone out! You have the light. "Arise, shine"!

ISAIAH 63   JULY 14

"In all their affliction he was afflicted, and the angel of his presence saved them: in his love and in his pity he redeemed them; and he bare them, and carried them all the days of old." Isaiah 63:9.

In the sixty-third chapter of Isaiah, the prophet gives a striking description of the coming Messiah—"mighty to save," with His blood-stained garments, as of one who had "trodden the winepress alone." No one else could help, so His "own arm brought salvation." We talk of salvation being free, but what a price in suffering it cost the Saviour! In an old *Sabbath School Worker* I found this story.

One day, way over in China, a little girl was brought to a missionary doctor. Her leg had been badly burned, and not having any medical care, the calf of the leg had grown fast to the under side of the thigh. So she couldn't straighten out her leg and therefore she couldn't walk.

"Can you do anything for her?" asked her anxious parents.

"Yes," said the doctor, "I can cut away that scar tissue, but I will have to graft some skin to the raw surfaces so it can heal properly."

Then turning to the father, the doctor said, "Will you let me take some skin from your arm?"

"Very well," said the man, and he offered his arm for the operation. But when the doctor had washed and scraped the arm and had picked up his knife, the man drew back and said, "No, no; I cannot bear it."

"Then," said the doctor to the mother, "will you let me take some of your skin for your little girl?"

"No, no," she said. "I could not bear it."

Then the doctor turned to his assistant and said, "Then you must cut some skin from *my* arm. We must do something for this little girl."

"No, no," said the assistant. "I couldn't bear to hurt a good kind missionary."

"Then I will have to do it myself," said the doctor. And with a sharp instrument he cut a piece of skin from his own arm, divided it into five pieces, and grafted it onto the raw surface of the little girl's leg. In time her leg healed, and she was able to go home and run about like other children. But she always carried with her the marks of the missionary doctor's great love—five little patches of white skin on her brown leg!

Always remember that Christ suffered and was afflicted for *your* salvation.

JEREMIAH 9   **JULY 15**

"I am the Lord which exercise lovingkindness, judgment, and righteousness, in the earth: for in these things I delight, saith the Lord." Jeremiah 9:24.

Jeremiah was called to be a mouthpiece for God in the most difficult time in the history of Judah. Again and again other prophets had been sent to warn the people of their sins, but they had hardened their hearts. Jeremiah was called when he was only a young man, maybe 19 or 20 years old, just at the time Judah was to be taken away captive for their sins. How earnestly he pictures God exercising "lovingkindness, judgment, and righteousness." Yet in spite of it all, when it is *too late* he hears them cry, "The harvest is past, the summer is ended, and we are not saved" (Jeremiah 8:20). No wonder his heart was crushed with sadness (verse 18).

I also know how it feels to hear people crying, "Too late! Too late!" During the early months of World War II five of us missionaries were fleeing to the border of India in two cars. As we left the town of Pakokku, after crossing the Irrawaddy River, Pastor W. W. Christensen waved us to a stop at the side of the road. We pulled up behind him and went to see what was the trouble. We found him in conversation with a well-to-do Indian woman and her family. She was saying, "Oh, Pastor Christensen, this is the way you said the end of the world would be. No one can tell whether he will live to see another day. Won't you take me to the river and baptize me now? I would then feel that all is well with my soul."

And I heard Pastor Christensen say, "It's too late now, lady. It's too late now. Can't you remember? Six weeks ago I was kneeling in your home with you and your children, pleading that the Spirit of God would help you make your decision then. You had been coming to the tabernacle meetings. You knew our message is right, but you wanted to wait for others to take their stand. Now, lady, we are fleeing for our lives.

We will pray that God will bring you safely into India, so we can study and get ready for baptism then."

And I saw that well-to-do Indian woman sink to the ground and cover her face with her sari, as she sobbed, "Too late! Too late! Why didn't I get baptized six weeks ago? There was time then; but now it's too late." It is impossible to forget things like that.

Is the Spirit of God speaking to your heart now? Do you hear Him warning you of some sin or pleading for you to make some important decision? Do it now, while there is balm in Gilead, and while there is a physician there. Someday the harvest will be past and the summer ended.

JEREMIAH 10   JULY 16

"The way of man is not in himself: it is not in man that walketh to direct his steps." Jeremiah 10:23.

How much we human beings need directing! The best time to ask God for direction is at the beginning of the day, and the best place to do it is at the family altar. Satan knows this, and he does his level best to crowd out time for family worship. "The family that prays together stays together" is a true saying; and do you know what happens to the families that don't pray together? You will find the answer in verse 25. Meg Mudoon tells a story in *The Good-Deeder* that illustrates very well our need for God to direct us.

Fifteen-year-old Albert lived in a small Newfoundland settlement overlooking the vast Atlantic Ocean. One fine promising morning he readied his rowboat for a day in the fishing area some distance away. The fish were really biting that morning, and for some hours he was kept busy pulling in the codfish and stowing them in the stern of his boat. Then, glancing to windward, he noticed a bank of fog coming his way. It was only a matter of minutes before he was completely enveloped in it. He could barely see the prow of his boat, and all directions looked alike. Then suddenly he realized that he was alone on the bosom of the great ocean. It was a frightening feeling. He felt for his compass, for with its help he could still find his way home. But his compass was not in his pocket! He had forgotten to bring it! "Don't forget your compass," his mother always said. "A body has no business out on the sea without a compass." Of course, he had *intended* to bring it. No one would deliberately leave his compass at home. But this time intentions were not enough. He was alone, without his compass, just when he needed it most. He dropped anchor and prepared to sit it out, hoping that no storm would spring up before the fog lifted. It might be two hours; it might be ten; it might be longer. He remembered hearing about two experienced seamen who had been lost in a fog and had never returned home. How much he did need a guide to point him homeward now! His mother would see the fog and she would be praying. Albert prayed too. He had plenty of time to pray. He prayed again. Then—could it be true? He could see the prow of his boat clearer! The fog was lifting! It was! At last he could see the coastline. It was still day. He rowed and rowed, and made it safe and sound before night. Do I need to say he never forgot his compass after that? The *first* thing he thought of when starting off on a fishing trip was his compass. And *before* pushing off from the jetty he checked to see that it was safely in his pocket.

Good intentions are not enough. Make sure you commit your way unto the Lord and get your directions from Him every morning. It may be dangerous to put off your decision until tomorrow.

JEREMIAH 24   JULY 17

"I will give them an heart to know me, that I am the Lord: and they shall be my people, and I will be their God." Jeremiah 24:7.

In the reading for today the Lord gave Jeremiah a vision of two baskets. One was filled with good figs; the other was filled with bad figs. In this way the Lord assured Jeremiah that not all the people of Judah were bad, and He promised to give them a heart to know God, and to bring them back into their own land again. This is what we all need—a heart to know God.

In the early years of the Advent movement Elder and Mrs. White always had a great interest in boys and girls. They believed that juniors needed to be saved, as well as adults. Once they were holding meetings at Monterey, Michigan, and a number of boys and girls were at the meeting. Elder and Mrs. White both knew that they all had to overcome fear throughout their Christian life, so when Elder White made the call he invited those juniors who wanted to be Christians, and who desired the prayers of God's people, to come and occupy the front seats. This was not easy to do. But Elder White knew that their overcoming one fear would help them overcome other fears, and he also knew that God could give them a heart to know Him and obey Him.

One by one the juniors went forward until nearly all in the Sabbath school were sitting on the front seats. Later Elder White talked with the juniors about baptism, and in a few days arrangements were made to hold a baptism in a little stream nearby. Now among the ten girls who were to be baptized first, there was one very timid girl. She had been afraid of water all her life. She couldn't even watch her friends being baptized, but stood there with her face turned away. Mrs. White spoke to her and tried to encourage her to follow the example of her Saviour. Then Elder White came over and stood beside her. He prayed that God would take away her fear of the water. "In the name of the Lord, move forward," encouraged Elder White. And the girl calmly entered the water and was baptized. The next morning that girl was the happiest girl you can imagine. "I'm so happy you didn't leave me alone just because I was afraid," she said. Soon after this five junior boys were baptized, and they were the happiest juniors in Monterey.

Has God given *you* a heart to know Him? Pray for it, and He will surely give you one, and He will cast out all your timidity too.

"Therefore now amend your ways and your doings, and obey the voice of the Lord your God." Jeremiah 26:13.

The priests and the false prophets didn't like the preaching of Jeremiah. They didn't like being called sinners, and they didn't like his prophesying that Jerusalem would be destroyed. So they arrested him and decided to kill him (verses 8, 11). But even in the court Jeremiah lifted up his voice, and called them to repentance. That there *are* sinners among God's people is sad, but it is true.

Elder and Mrs. White on one occasion went to hold some meetings in the little church at Washington, New Hampshire. Again they made a special appeal to the juniors and young people. There was one young man there who didn't respond. The real reason was that he knew his father chewed tobacco, even though he was the choir leader in the church! The father managed to keep this habit a secret from the church people, but as the boy worked with his father he knew very well what made those brown spots on the snow where his father spat. At the Sabbath morning service Sister White was appealing to the brethren to amend their ways and obey the voice of the Lord. "Oh," said the young man to himself, "I wish she would speak to my father and tell him about his sin. I am sure no one has told her."

Just then Sister White turned to the father and said in effect, "Brother, I was shown your case. You are a slave of tobacco." Then she went on to describe the way he was trying to hide his sin.

The face of the young man lighted up. "Only an angel could have told her that," he said to himself. "Indeed, this message is from God." God was with them. Many of the older ones confessed their sins, and thirteen young people took their stand for Christ. To show you how earnest they were about it, they wanted to be baptized right then, even if it was the middle of winter. The river was frozen over and they had to cut through two feet of ice to get to the water. The temperature was -10° F., but twelve of those young people were baptized, and suffered no ill effects. Most of those young people became workers in God's cause.

As God looks at you does He see some secret sin that is spoiling your Christian life? Something nobody knows about but you? Mend your ways and your doings right now, and know the joy of obeying the voice of the Lord your God.

"Behold, I am the Lord, the God of all flesh: is there any thing too hard for me?" Jeremiah 32:27.

The Lord spoke encouragement to Jeremiah when the future seemed discouraging and altogether impossible. It was hard for the people to see how God could permit them to be carried into captivity, then bring them back again into their land to dwell safely. But it was not too hard for God to do, and we know that He did it.

Ever since the world began God has been doing that which seemed impossible to human beings. Also, throughout the history of the Advent movement God has been continually doing the impossible. When Ellen Harmon was just a young woman, before she was married to James White, she was given a vision one night from the Lord in which she was shown that she must go to Portsmouth, New Hampshire, and bear her testimony there. Now, it was hard for a young woman to have to stand before older people and point out their weaknesses and their shortcomings, but Ellen did not hesitate. She had no money to pay her fare on the train, but she believed God had told her to go, and that He would open up the way somehow. So she and her sister got ready to go. Their home was not far from the railway station. They heard the first bell ring, giving the passengers only fifteen minutes to board the train. Ellen put her hat on and walked to the window. Just then a man drove up in a great hurry, and as he ran to the house he called out, "Is there anyone here who needs money? I was impressed that someone here needed money." Ellen and her sister explained that they had to go to Portsmouth, but didn't have the money to pay the fare. "I have come twelve miles to bring you this money. I could not hold my horse back; he seemed driven to go faster and faster." The man put enough for two return tickets in their hands. "Here, jump into my wagon and I'll take you to the station." They arrived just in time to board the train and find seats before the train started! Impossible? No! Not for God.

Someday God will impress *you* to go to an academy and perhaps later to college. You may have no money, but don't sit down and say it can't be done. Get your hat on and go to the window, for God opens the windows of heaven for those who make Him first in their life. Nothing is ever too hard for Him.

"The Lord is merciful and gracious, slow to anger, and plenteous in mercy." Psalm 103:8.

The Lord had been very long-suffering with the people of Judah, but at last their punishment had to come, and in today's Scripture reading we learn of the fall of Jerusalem, the burning of the Temple, the capture of King Zedekiah, and the taking of the last group of the children of Judah into captivity. In order to be really happy we all have to learn to make God first, and to make obedience to God the most important thing in our life. To measure our obedience, God gives us home rules and school rules.

In a *Youth's Instructor* Lois Christian Randolph told one of the saddest stories I have ever read. It was wintertime at one of our colleges. The little lake nearby was frozen over, and the students were looking forward to the time when the ice would be thick enough for skating. Finally one Saturday evening the principal announced: "All students who wish to skate will please meet at the gymnasium. We shall go down to the lake as a group, and when the whistle blows we shall return as a group. Flares have been placed at the limits of the safe ice. Beyond the flares the ice is not safe. Do not go beyond the flares. Your skating privileges in the future depend upon your observing this rule."

When they gathered at the gym, the dean of men again gave the warning: "Do not go beyond the flares. It is unsafe."

For two hours 120 or more young people had an intensely enjoyable time skating in the moonlight. Then a shrill call of "Help! Help! Help!" sent a chill to every heart. Two of the teachers went quickly in the direction of the sound and were able to rescue a young woman who had broken through the ice just beyond the flares. It took longer to recover the body of the young man with her, and in spite of efforts to revive him, the doctor at last pronounced him dead.

Just then one of the girls called, "I can't find my roommate!" They telephoned the boys' dormitory to see whether the roommate's skating partner was there; but no, he too was missing. It took the rescuers forty-five minutes to find their bodies. They worked and worked to restore them to consciousness, but it was hopeless. Three lives were lost because they had not learned that obedience is the only way to be happy.

How do you measure up? Do you obey cheerfully?

"Daniel purposed in his heart that he would not defile himself with the portion of the king's meat, nor with the wine which he drank." Daniel 1:8.

Daniel stands out as one of the greatest examples given us in Bible history. Only 18 years old when taken captive, he was filled, nevertheless, with a holy determination to be a vegetarian and an abstainer from strong drink. His three companions did likewise, and after a ten-day test they were "fairer" and "fatter" than the other young people who ate and drank everything; and they were "ten times better" mentally than all the king's wise men!

This kind of record has been achieved by Seventh-day Adventist youth many times in many countries of the earth since then. Did you ever hear of Calvin Hansen? I had the pleasure of meeting him in 1962 in Colorado. He was a blond, blue-eyed, 25-year-old Seventh-day Adventist! He is a vegetarian, a nonsmoker, and a nondrinker. For three years running he had carried off the championship of the annual Pike's Peak race. In 1959 his record was twenty-six miles up and back in four hours and fifteen minutes. Well, on September 7, 1961, Cal was one of sixteen runners who entered the Mount Whitney, California, race. The summit of Whitney is 14,495 feet, and the course up and down was a rugged twenty-one miles. Of the sixteen, Cal was the only Seventh-day Adventist, but there were two other vegetarians—Mrs. Katherine Heard, 59 years old, and Leslie Milson, a 34-year-old carpenter. There also were two boys, 12 and 13 years old; the rest were experienced athletes but nonvegetarians. Only two of them smoked cigarettes. It is apparent that cigarette smokers don't specialize in races of this kind. Well, I hardly need to finish the story; you've guessed already. Cal Hansen came in first, covering the entire twenty-one miles in four hours, nine minutes, and twenty-two and a half seconds. And Les Milson came in second! Many of the nonvegetarians had cramps in their leg muscles, but the vegetarians had none. Coach Rudy Fahl says that meat leaves poisons in the system and causes muscles to ache, and he also warns against smoking and the use of alcoholic beverages, white sugar, and white-flour products. This instruction also sounds familiar to us Adventists.

Did you ever sing "Dare to Be a Daniel"? I hope you will do more than sing it. Imitate Daniel, and you too can be fairer and healthier, and ten times better than the king's wise men.

"In the days of these kings shall the God of heaven set up a kingdom, which shall never be destroyed." Daniel 2:44.

The promise of the kingdom Jesus would establish has been the hope of prophets, apostles, and all the faithful for centuries.

Today is the birthday of one of the founders of the Advent message in modern times—Elder J. N. Andrews. He was born July 22, 1829, in the little town of Poland, Maine. In the early days of 1844, when the Adventists believed and preached that Christ was coming in October of that year, John Andrews was only a lad 14 years of age. One day (as Elder W. A. Spicer tells the story) he was accompanying a Mr. Davis who was going to hold a meeting somewhere in Maine. Of course, there were always plenty of people who ridiculed and mocked anyone who was religious, so there was a mob of angry men gathered at the meeting place who were determined to stop the preaching. When jeers and shouts could not make Mr. Davis stop preaching, one man rushed forward with a big black snake whip to beat him. Now young John was of a timid, retiring nature, but he wasn't going to let his friend suffer alone, so he jumped in front of him, and said to the man with the whip, "You know it says in the Bible we are to bear one another's burdens. If you whip Mr. Davis you will have to whip me too."

The ruffian with the whip was taken aback with this little speech. He hesitated a moment, then said, "Well, it would be too bad to beat a little boy." Then he turned and went away—and the mob followed! When John was 17 years old he accepted the Sabbath truth. When he was 20 years old he joined Captain Bates and James White in preaching the Sabbath and the second coming of Christ. He became a mighty preacher, and when he was only 23 years old, J. N. Loughborough was converted to the Sabbath truth under his preaching. John Nevins Andrews was one of our most able writers. He was the General Conference president from 1867 to 1869, and our first missionary to Europe, in 1874. He was mighty in the knowledge of the Scriptures, and he could repeat the entire New Testament by heart. What a man of God he was! But once he was only a junior who simply loved the Lord with all his heart. Maybe God has a mighty work for *you* to do too.

"Our God whom we serve is able to deliver us from the burning fiery furnace, and he will deliver us out of thine hand, O king." Daniel 3:17.

When it has pleased God to do so, He has made people, houses, villages, churches, books, and even boats fireproof. Here is a famous story from the Solomon Islands during World War II days, about a boat that would not burn. The Australian missionaries in the Solomon Islands had all been ordered home, and the British Government had taken over our three mission launches, the *Dadavata,* the *Portal,* and the *G.F. Jones.* The Japanese were coming nearer and nearer, determined to use the islands as a steppingstone toward their attack on Australia. The British officer in charge had been successful in cutting off the enemy scouting patrols, but he knew the day would come when he would have to retreat before superior gunboats. One day a runner brought the news that a large fleet of enemy boats was coming, and it was time for the officer to go. There was nothing else he could do, so the officer gave the order to start the engines of the three launches, and get ready to go. The engines of the *Dadavata* and the *G. F. Jones* started easily enough, but the engine of the *Portal* simply refused to turn over. They tried and tried, but it was no use, and rather than let the launch fall into enemy hands, the officer reluctantly gave the order to burn it. Two five-gallon cans of gasoline were poured over it; the officer himself lighted a bundle of waste and threw it into the cabin of the launch. Immediately there was a roar, as a sheet of flame leaped as high as the masthead. Satisfied that the flames would do their work, the officer left with the other two launches. As our SDA Solomon Islanders saw the flames leaping high, they fell on their knees and prayed, "O God, *Portal,* 'e boat belong God; don't let 'im burn."

And as if in immediate response to their prayer, the flames died down and went out! Convinced that God was keeping the boat for His work, they swam out and poled and dragged the *Portal* into the mouth of a little creek and hid it among the mangroves. Hardly had they done so when fourteen enemy gunboats went by! Our brethren worked all night and took the engine to pieces. They distributed the parts among the people for safekeeping, and covered the *Portal* with palm trees and branches till no one would know a boat was there.

Perhaps someday God will put out some destructive fire for *you.*

"To the intent that the living may know that the most High ruleth in the kingdom of men, and giveth it to whomsoever he will." Daniel 4:17.

God worked miracle after miracle for Nebuchadnezzar, and there was no possible doubt about who was in charge of the affairs of men. Even so, in the affairs of the nations today, God is permitting and directing toward His own plans for man. In the battle of the Solomon Islands the enemy came and hindered the work of God for a time; but then the tide turned and the enemy was driven out. One day in May, 1945, the American forces landed on one of the Solomon Islands and brought with them Pastor Norman Ferris, who had been a missionary to those islands for more than twenty years. When the Solomon Islanders saw him, there was great shouting and jubilation. In just a little while he saw a group run to the beach and launch a big canoe.

"Where are you going?" he asked.

"We go catch 'im *Portal,*" they said.

"But the *Portal* has been burned. The government has informed us," said Pastor Ferris.

"Government, 'e no know. *Portal,* 'e boat belong God. 'Im, 'e no burn. We get," the men said. And in a day or two, there was the *Portal,* tied up to the jetty! The rigging and the awnings were burned, but the body of the ship was all right. Pastor Ferris was delighted. He jumped on board and went to the engine room. Then despair settled down on him. Every removable part of the engine was gone!

"What can we do without an engine?" he said.

But the men smiled and said, "Engine, 'e all right; we get 'im." And with their drums they sent out word to the people to bring back the parts of the engine. And for the next three weeks the parts came in. Some had buried their pieces for safekeeping. Some had worn them around their necks. But when they knew Pastor Ferris was back, in came all the bits and pieces, and not so much as a half-inch screw was missing! The parts were cleaned and put together. New rigging and awnings were put in place. The *Portal* was painted, refueled, and stores were put aboard. The boys pulled with all their might on the starting rope. And the engine started! And the *Portal* put to sea! A miracle? Yes, not only on the boat but also upon the hearts and lives of our dear believers there. Who can doubt that the living God was directing in the affairs of those men?

Keep close to God; make Him first in your life.

"I have even heard of thee, that the spirit of the gods is in thee, and that light and understanding and excellent wisdom is found in thee." Daniel 5:14.

When people talk well about someone, they build up that person's reputation by what they say. People talked well about Daniel, and what a wonderful reputation he had! Belshazzar heard that Daniel was wise, and that the Spirit of God was with him, to give him understanding of mysterious dreams and writing. People everywhere are talking about Adventists. Do you know what they say? Do you know what reputation we Seventh-day Adventists have? A colporteur went to a country home in Europe, far from any Adventist church.

"Have you ever heard of Adventists?" he asked.

"Oh, yes," was the reply, "we know they keep Saturday; they don't eat pork; they don't smoke or drink; and they don't dance!"

Mr. James and his family moved into a house next door to Mr. Chinnock in Sebastopol, some time ago. One day a neighbor said to Mr. Chinnock, "Do you know anything about the man who has moved next door to you?"

"Why, yes," said Mr. Chinnock, "I know him well. He goes to the same church I do."

"Oh, so he's an SDA," said the neighbor, with a smile. "Well, that's good. Now I won't have to lock my chicken house at night."

Elder Henry Brown told of a bus company in a certain town in Europe that was having trouble with its conductors stealing the passenger fares they collected. One of the directors said, "I'll tell you what you need. If you could get Seventh-day Adventist conductors you'd have no more trouble with stealing. But you must give them Saturdays off. They would rather lose their job than work on Sabbath!"

"What church do you belong to?" asked a hospital nurse of a man who had a badly broken leg.

"I am a Seventh-day Adventist," he said.

"That explains it," said the nurse. "I understand now why you don't curse and swear."

"Do you know, I like it here," said a patient in one of our sanitariums to another patient. "I like these people. I like the way they do things. In fact, if it were not for their religion, I could be a Seventh-day Adventist myself."

"You'll find it's their religion that makes them that way," her friend answered.

Say, what are people saying about *you?* What kind of reputation do you have?

DANIEL 6 JULY 26

"My God hath sent his angel, and hath shut the lions' mouths, that they have not hurt me." Daniel 6:22.

Many stories are told of how angels have protected those who put their trust in God. Here is one from Tanzania in Africa.

Joy Buckle was a lovely junior Christian girl. Her father was the manager of a large cattle ranch sixty miles from the town of Arusha. Mr. Buckle was a strong, fearless man who often had to take his flashlight and gun to drive lions away from the cattle at night. He often told Joy exciting stories of his experiences with lions, and he always added, "Joy, if you ever meet a dangerous animal in the wilds never show fear. Just remain calm." Now that sounds easy when you are with someone who has a gun or when you are in a safe place. But—

Well, one day Joy went to Arusha to see some friends, and after a lovely visit they started to bring her back to her home in their car. It had been raining heavily, but the road was well paved, and all went well until they came to the four-mile dirt road that went from the highway to the ranch. They had gone only a little way on the dirt road when the car got stuck in the mud. "Never mind," said Joy, "I can easily walk from here. You go back. I'll be all right." With great difficulty the car was turned around, and off it went, leaving Joy alone—but not really alone. Her angel must have been with her. She wrapped her sweater around her head to keep it dry, and began singing to keep herself company. Suddenly, only a few hundred yards down the road, she saw a huge male lion. His tail was twitching back and forth like a big tomcat getting ready to pounce upon a mouse. "That looks like a very hungry lion," said Joy to herself. Then the words of her father came to her mind. "Never show fear; just be calm." She wanted to scream, but that would do no good. She wanted to run, but the lion could run faster than she could. There were only two things she could do. She could pray and she could go on down the road, and she did both. Her prayer brought courage to her heart. Her father's words "Never show fear" came again and again to her mind. Straight toward the lion she went, and when the lion saw her coming he slunk off into the long grass at the side of the road. She did not look to see where he had gone, but with her heart pounding like a steam engine and her knees trembling, she walked straight home! As she entered the house, all she could say was, "Mother, kneel down with me and let us thank Jesus for saving me from the lion." Just a week later a man was taken from his garden nearby and eaten by a lion, probably the same lion that Joy met on the road.

Is your angel near you every minute? Better make sure. Satan's lions are everywhere, seeking whom they may devour.

DANIEL 7   JULY 27

"I beheld till the thrones were cast down, and the Ancient of days did sit. . . . The judgment was set, and the books were opened." Daniel 7:9, 10.

If only we could always remember that angels are making a record of all we do and say, and that in the judgment the books will be opened, I think we would always stay close to Jesus and choose what is right. The president of one of our great American universities used to tell this story about a boy who didn't choose to do what is right.

This boy was in the seventh grade, and was always giving his teacher trouble. The teacher tried in every way to get him to cooperate, and had even sent him to the principal's room for punishment on many occasions. Well, one day this boy was sent up to the principal's office again, and the principal just didn't know what to do. At last he gave the boy a sheet of paper and told him to write down all the bad things he could remember that he had done that year. The boy wrote for five minutes, and the sheet of paper was nearly full. "Is that all you can remember?" asked the principal. "There are more than that." Then he took out his record book and showed it to the boy. "Look at that, and that, and that," he said. "Now copy out all you have missed, and make the list complete." The boy wrote and wrote, and at last the list was complete and the boy's misdeeds were many and black. "Now make another copy, and after each bad deed, explain why you did it." By the time it was finished, the boy was tired and hungry, and wanted to go home, but the principal said, "Now take pen and ink, and make an exact copy of what you have written, to take to your mother."

"Oh, please, don't let my mother know anything about this," said the boy.

"Why not?"

"Because I don't want her to know what kind of boy I am in school."

"Oh! So your mother thinks you are a good boy in school?"

"Yes."

The principal thought for a while then said, "I'll tell you what I will do. Do you think you could be the kind of boy your mother thinks you are?"

"I will try, sir," said the boy.

"Then I'll put this record in an envelope and put it in my safe, and if you are not sent to me any more this year, I will burn it. But if you are sent to me again, then you will have to copy it, and we will send it to your mother. Is that fair?"

"Oh, yes, sir; and I will try."

And he *did* try; he *was* good. He found he had much more fun being good, and he became a loyal friend to his teacher and principal.

Thank God, He has given us a way by which the records of our sins can be forgiven. Keep your record clean in heaven; then when the books are opened, you need not fear.

DANIEL 9   JULY 28

"Whiles I was speaking in prayer, even the man Gabriel . . . said, O Daniel, I am now come forth to give thee skill and understanding. . . . For thou art greatly beloved." Daniel 9:21-23.

By studying the book of Daniel, chapters 8 and 9, the early Adventists were led to believe that Jesus would come the second time, on October 22, 1844. They thought the sanctuary that was to be cleansed was this earth, and great was their disappointment when the day went by and Jesus did not come. In Port Gibson, New York, a little town on the Erie Canal, there lived an Adventist by the name of Hiram Edson. The little company of Adventists there looked to him as their leader. They were together on the day of disappointment, and there was great weeping when Jesus didn't come. "Have the Scriptures failed?" they asked. "Is there no reward for the saints? Is there to be no judgment day?"

"Not so," said Edson. "There is a God in heaven. He has not failed. Sometime soon the mystery will be solved, and this dark secret shall be made as plain as day. Let us go out to the barn and pray." They went out and prayed, and soon they felt the assurance that God loved them, that their prayers were heard, and that soon light would be given. After breakfast Hiram Edson said to one of the men, "Let us go and comfort the others with the assurance we have received." So they started off, taking a shortcut across a field where Edson's corn still stood in the shocks. About halfway across the field Hiram Edson was stopped, as if someone had put his hand upon his shoulder. As he turned and looked up at the gray skies, there flashed upon his understanding the meaning of the sanctuary in heaven. He saw that Christ, our High Priest, was minister of the heavenly sanctuary and that its cleansing required the movement of Jesus from the holy place into the Most Holy Place. This was the event that was to take place in 1844, and Jesus' coming would be later.

"Brother Edson, what are you stopping for?" called his companion.

"The Lord is just answering our morning prayer," said Edson. As they walked and talked it over, it became clearer and clearer. God had given them a new light, and with this new light the Adventist believers were lifted out of their disappointment and greatly comforted.

If ever you are heavyhearted and disappointed, lift your heart to God. He will send light somehow and make things plain for you.

DANIEL 12   JULY 29

"Thy people shall be delivered, every one that shall be found written in the book. . . . And they that be wise [teachers] shall shine . . . as the stars for ever and ever." Daniel 12:1-3.

Long, long ago, according to an old parable, there was an ancient old king who ruled over an ancient old kingdom. One day wishing to honor the most worthy citizen in his realm, he sent his ministers of state throughout his land to search for those they thought were the most worthy citizens. Then he set a day when they were to appear before him, at which time he would choose the one he thought most worthy of them all. At last the day came. The plaza was crowded with important people, and the king sat upon his throne. The first minister approached the throne and presented a great lawyer, a man by whose skill good laws had been made, and liberty and justice given to all. And the crowd clapped and applauded, for he was a very worthy citizen. The next minister presented a great financier, and told how he had brought security to the trade of the kingdom; and again the crowd clapped and applauded. The third minister bowed and presented a great doctor, whose skill had conquered disease and saved the lives of thousands of people. Again the crowd clapped and applauded. Then the fourth minister approached the throne with a little old lady on his arm. Her hair was white. Her back was bent. Her clothes were old and shabby. The king was shocked and visibly annoyed.

"Who is this woman?" he demanded, "and what right hath she to be classed with these illustrious men?"

"O King," said the minister, "when these great men were just little boys this woman was their teacher." Nobody clapped or applauded. There was a moment of deep silence. Then the king stood up, walked down from his throne, and with tears in his eyes he placed the wreath of honor around the neck of the little old lady. She was indeed the most worthy citizen in his kingdom!

Many of our great workers in the cause of God today owe their success to the skill, the patience, and the understanding of the teachers they had when they were little boys and girls—their schoolteachers and their Sabbath school teachers! Plan to be a teacher someday—in a school or in Sabbath school—for God is going to honor teachers in a special way, and they "shall shine . . . as the stars for ever and ever."

"I will heal their backsliding, I will love them freely: for mine anger is turned away from him." Hosea 14:4.

Hosea lived in the darkest period of the kingdom of Israel; it is probable that the book of Hosea was written just before the nation was taken captive by Assyria. It is full of pleading for Israel to turn from their idols and repent. It also contains many precious promises and assurances that God would forgive them and receive them. Forgiveness for those who have rebelled and been enemies is one of the most beautiful things in the world.

During the Revolutionary War there lived in Pennsylvania a faithful gospel minister by the name of Peter Miller. There was a man living nearby who was very bitter toward Mr. Miller. He openly abused him and also his followers. As time went on, this enemy of his got into trouble with the government. He was arrested, found guilty of treason, and sentenced to death. As soon as Miller heard of his sentence, he set out on foot and went to General Washington to beg for the man's life.

"I am sorry," Washington said, "but your prayer for your friend's life cannot be granted."

"My friend?" said Miller. "He is not my friend. I have not a worse enemy living than that man!"

"What?" said Washington. "Do you mean to tell me that you have walked sixty miles to try to save the life of your enemy? That puts the matter in a different light. I will grant the pardon." As soon as the pardon was made out, Peter Miller set off at once for the place, fifteen miles away, where the execution was to take place. He got there just as the man was being led to the gallows. The prisoner saw Miller coming, and he said, "Here comes Peter Miller! He has come all the way from Ephrata to have his revenge by seeing me hanged today." But Peter Miller rushed forward and thrust the pardon into the hand of the executioner and said, "Stay! Stay! I have a pardon from General Washington!" The life of his worst enemy was not only spared; it was altogether changed by this manifestation of Christian love.

That's the kind of love God has for every one of us. Whenever you slip and make mistakes, repent and confess quickly. God will forgive your backslidings and always love you, too.

"Blow the trumpet in Zion; sanctify a fast; call a solemn assembly; gather the people. . . . Assemble the elders; gather the children, even nursing infants." Joel 2:15, 16, RSV.

Joel prophesied of the last days, and in this verse I think he has given us the blueprint for attendance at the eleven-o'clock church service— elders, children, and infants, or, as we would say, *families* sitting together to worship God in church. We have Sabbath school, where we study the lesson in age groups; we have special children's meetings at camp meeting and at summer camps; but for the regular, every-week worship, I believe that God wants us to worship Him sitting together in families. God said to Abraham, "In thee shall all *families* of the earth be blessed" (Genesis 12:3). To Jeremiah, God said He would "be the God of all the *families* of Israel" (Jeremiah 31:1). One of the most beautiful things I have seen is a family sitting together when I get up to preach in a church.

When William Cady was a 10-year-old he went with his mother and little brother and sister to spend a summer at his uncle John's farm. He saw many wonderful things, but the most wonderful was a big bottle with a perfect apple inside. The apple was bigger than the neck of the bottle, and yet the apple wasn't bruised.

"Aunt Sarah," he said, "how did the apple get into the bottle?"

"That is Uncle John's secret," she said. "Ask him."

He asked Uncle John, but all he would say was "Keep your eyes open, Willie, and see if you can find out." The next summer Willie came back, and still kept looking everywhere to see whether he could find out how Uncle John got the apple into the bottle. One day he saw something shining up in an apple tree! He looked closer, and there was a little apple poked inside the bottle!

"I know Uncle's secret! I know Uncle's secret!" shouted Willie as he raced back to Uncle John. "You put the apple in the bottle when it was little, and then it just grew inside the bottle," he said. And his uncle said, "You're right, Willie. That's exactly how it was."

I hope *you* sit with your family during church service, for I've noticed that boys and girls who sit in church with mother and father *grow up* in the church and *stay* in the church.

"Behold, the days come, saith the Lord God, that I will send a famine in the land, not a famine of bread, nor a thirst for water, but of hearing the words of the Lord." Amos 8:11.

Not one of us can fully realize what a priceless treasure we have in the Bible—the Word of God. David likened it to a "lamp" and a "light" (Psalm 119:105) that would show us the way to eternal life. Paul likened it to a "sword" that would protect us from the temptations of the evil one (Ephesians 6:17), and Moses likened it to "bread" that would give life to those who read it (Deuteronomy 8:3). What else do we need to take us safely into heaven? This priceless treasure is ours, yet we read it so little!

Edgar A. Guest tells a story about a rich woman who lived in New York. Her husband gave her a beautiful brooch set with pearls for which he paid $30,000! It was her pride and joy, but one day while visiting friends in Detroit she lost it. Frantically she advertised for it, offering a liberal reward for its recovery. She called on the police to help her. They made a check of all the pawnshops where secondhand jewelry is often sold; but all to no avail. The brooch was lost. Now, in Detroit there lived a poor woman who earned a living for herself and her daughter by washing clothes. One day she was walking along and she saw a brooch on the street. She picked it up, but she had no idea of its value. It was a pretty pin, she thought, so she pinned her collar together with it. She didn't read the papers, so knew nothing of the lost brooch or the reward that was offered for its recovery. Six years went by, and the washerwoman still wore the pretty brooch in her collar, though in some way one of the beautiful stones had dropped out and been lost. At this time her daughter was graduating, and she thought she would get another little stone put in the brooch, then give it to her daughter for a graduation present. She took it to a jeweler and asked how much it would cost. The jeweler looked at the brooch carefully, then said, "Yes, madam, we can match that pearl for $2,000!"

The good woman's eyes bugged out as she gasped, "And to think that for six years I've been wearing a fortune on my collar and didn't know it!"

In life's journey you will need a light, a sword, and bread. Before the famine comes, make this priceless treasure yours, now!

"As thou hast done, it shall be done unto thee: thy reward shall return upon thine own head." Obadiah 15.

The Edomites were the descendants of Esau, and they were always bitter and cruel toward the descendants of Jacob. They wouldn't let the Israelites pass through their land when they were on their way into the land of Canaan. They were continually attacking the Jews and joining their enemies when they went to war against them. And they rejoiced when Nebuchadnezzar destroyed Jerusalem and took the Jews captive. Obadiah prophesied that their cruelty would return upon their own heads. And it did. Have you noticed that a bully always gets back, in one way or another, the torment he serves up to others? Here is a story I found in Daphne Lacey's lovely book *Sunshine Stories:*

Once upon a time there was a little hunchback boy named Davie. He was a pitiful little boy—his legs were too thin; his arms were too long; and his back was crooked. But there was nothing wrong with his head, and he was very strong for his size. Well, the first day he went to school Tom, the class bully, began tormenting him. "Hello, what have we here? A hunchy! Ha, ha, ha! Look at his arms and legs! Why, he looks like a spider!" And I'm sorry to say that many of the other boys joined in laughing with Tom.

Poor Davie ran away from his tormentors. He couldn't help being a hunchback. The teacher scolded Tom, and after a while the teasing stopped. But Davie was left out of his schoolmates' games and other activities, and he was very lonely. The second week in school Tom was bragging about how well he could climb. Bullies always brag. "Come and I'll show you," he shouted as he ran toward a big oak tree. He could climb! And up he went. "Tom, you'd better come down," someone called. "You'll fall."

"Oh, no I won't! Watch me go out on this limb," he said, and he pulled himself slowly out toward the leafy end of the limb.

"Come down! It'll break," shouted someone again.

"No, it won't," shouted Tom. But suddenly the bough bent, and Tom's face went white as he felt himself slipping.

"Help! Help! I'm going to fall," cried Tom. They all held their breath. There was a dreadful silence; then like a flash Davie the hunchback rushed forward.

"Hold on, Tom," he cried. "I'm coming; you'll be all right." Davie pulled his small crooked body from limb to limb. He could climb, too! And how! He reached the branch where Tom was swaying helplessly. "Don't look down! Just hold on," he encouraged. Then he stretched out his arm and caught Tom's collar and pulled and tugged. "There now, take another hold," he said, and Tom did as he was told. Inch by inch with Davie's help he got back to the solid limb, and soon they were both on the ground.

"I'm sorry I treated you so shabbily," said Tom, but no one could hear him, for everybody was cheering wildly for Davie.

If you are ever tempted to bully someone or to pick on someone you had better think first, for as you do, "it shall be done unto thee."

JONAH 1, 2 AUGUST 3

"Arise, go to Nineveh. . . . But Jonah rose up to flee unto Tarshish from the presence of the Lord." Jonah 1:2, 3.

Throughout the years men who have chosen not to believe in God or the Bible have delighted to ridicule the story of Jonah and the whale. But to the one who believes in God and in His Word there is nothing impossible about His making a "big fish" large enough for the purpose of preserving Jonah inside the fish until he got back to the seacoast again. Indeed, here is a story found in the *Literary Digest* for April 4, 1896, that shows it is possible for a man to be swallowed by an ordinary whale and still live. One day in February, 1891, the whaling ship *Star of the East* launched two small boats with men and harpoons to go after a huge whale not far off. The men were successful in harpooning the whale and capturing it, but as it struggled, one of the boats was struck by the tail of the whale and shattered to pieces. The men were thrown into the ocean. Eventually all but two of the men were saved by the men in the other boat, and later the body of one of the two lost men was found. But the other, James Bartley, could not be found anywhere. It took them a day and a half to get the huge whale onto the deck and cut up. Then they cut open the big stomach, and there was James Bartley, unconscious but still alive! For several days he was delirious, and it was three weeks before he recovered his reason and could tell about his terrible experience. But he lived for many years afterward. The only noticeable effect on him was that his skin was tanned by the action of the gastric juices.

In the book *Jonah and the Whale*, by Charles G. Bellah, other experiences of men, huge fish, and even of a horse being found in a whale's stomach are given. So I have no trouble in believing that the big fish swallowed Jonah. I even believe that Jonah himself wrote the story of his experience, and that he wrote it for you and me, so we might know it is no use trying to run away from God or from duty.

JONAH 3, 4   **AUGUST 4**

"Arise, go unto Nineveh. . . . So Jonah arose, and went unto Nineveh, according to the word of the Lord." Jonah 3:2, 3.

In his book *The Hand That Intervenes* Elder W. A. Spicer tells the story of a modern Jonah. En-meg-ah-bowh was a young Indian from eastern Canada who went with some early missionaries to open up work among the Chippewa Indians in northern Minnesota. He married a Chippewa maiden, and promised her people that he would remain with them. But the work was very discouraging, and after a while the white missionaries went back, leaving En-meg-ah-bowh alone. Before long he was so discouraged that he decided to go back to his former work at Sault Sainte Marie, on the Straits of Mackinac.

"Will you go with me?" he said to his wife.

"I am ready to go with you and die with you," she said. So he obtained passage on a sailing ship from Duluth, and the captain promised that if all went well they would arrive in Sault Sainte Marie in three days. But all did not go well. A few hours after leaving they ran into a dead calm, and at five o'clock a terrible storm, with wind blowing on them from the wrong direction. The captain was worried. "In twenty years," he said, "I have never seen anything like this. I am afraid there is something wrong with us." En-meg-ah-bowh's face went white. He felt that he knew what was wrong. He knew that he was fleeing to "Tarshish." Nothing could be done, so the captain had to turn around, and with great difficulty the ship got back to Duluth.

"I believe that we are the cause of our almost perishing in the deep water," said En-meg-ah-bowh's wife to her husband.

"I fully agree," said En-meg-ah-bowh.

"Will you try to go again?"

"Yes. Have we not paid our passage?"

"Then I shall follow," she said softly.

The next morning at two o'clock the wind was right once more, and the ship set sail, but about the same time and at the same place they ran into another dead calm followed by an even worse storm. The thunder and lightning and the waves were terrifying. The captain threw part of the cargo overboard to try to face the storm, but it was no use. He had to turn the ship around and return to Duluth.

"Now what will you do?" asked En-meg-ah-bowh's wife of her husband.

"I will stay in 'Nineveh' and preach the gospel," he said. And he did. He stayed for forty years among the Chippewas.

It's true. You cannot run away from God and be happy. When God gives you some duty to do, do it.

MICAH 4   AUGUST 5

"They shall beat their swords into plowshares, and their spears into pruninghooks: nation shall not lift up a sword against nation, neither shall they learn war any more." Micah 4:3.

This prophecy is one of several prophecies that reveal God's original plan for Israel—the plan that they would become His agency for the salvation of the world, bringing the light of the gospel, and peace and happiness, to all nations. However, literal Israel failed, so the prophecy can only be fulfilled by spiritual Israel—God's chosen people today—and by the setting up of the kingdom of Christ. Nevertheless, there have been many attempts to bring lasting peace to the nations of the world. The Palace of Peace was erected in The Hague, capital of Holland, in 1899, and many peace conferences have been held there. After World War I the League of Nations was organized (January 10, 1920) with fifty-nine nations joining, and after World War II the United Nations was organized, with forty-six nations signing the charter in 1945. The headquarters of the United Nations is now in New York City, and by 1984 there were 160 nations as members.

Remember when the dove brought a twig from an olive tree back to Noah in the ark? Noah regarded that as a sign that the wrath of God had passed and that there was peace between God and the world again. Ever since then the dove with an olive branch in its beak has been the symbol of peace. Perhaps the most famous peace monument is *The Christ of the Andes,* erected high up on the border mountains between Chile and Argentina in South America. In 1900 these two countries were quarreling over a rich strip of land that lay between them. They were on the verge of war when they were persuaded to submit their dispute to the king of England. He called together a group of experts and they wisely recommended that part of the land belong to Chile and the other part belong to Argentina. Both nations cheerfully accepted the decision, bitterness passed away, and good will took its place. Cannonballs were melted and made into a statue of Christ twenty-six feet high. This was placed on a cement foundation twenty-two feet high, on which was placed a huge granite hemisphere to represent the world. There, high up on the border mountains stands this statue today. In the left hand the figure holds a cross, and the right hand is lifted in blessing. A copy of this statue has been erected in the Palace of Peace in The Hague.

Remember that you belong to God's chosen people of the last days. Make sure you are a messenger of peace in your home, in your school, and in your church.

NAHUM 1   *AUGUST 6*

"The Lord is slow to anger, and great in power . . . : the Lord hath his way in the whirlwind and in the storm." Nahum 1:3.

Today is the anniversary of the first use of an atomic bomb in war. August 6, 1945, was a fearful day—100,000 people lost their lives, and practically all the buildings in the city of Hiroshima, Japan, were destroyed by just one bomb. Before the war we had about ninety members in the Hiroshima church. Many of them scattered into the country during the war, but there were forty-two Seventh-day Adventists in Hiroshima when the bomb burst, yet not one whose name was on the church books lost his life! Brother S. Morita, a dentist, was the church elder at the time. The military police and the "thought control" police kept a constant watch over him and his activities, but finally they arrested him and put him in prison for fourteen months! Then, satisfied that he was not connected with a spy ring, they released him. During his imprisonment he spent much time reading the writings of Mrs. White, and when he got back to his home he felt impressed to move out of the city to a small village eight miles away. And he was there when the bomb fell! After the explosion he went into the city as soon as possible, to see whether he could be of any assistance to our church members. The destruction and the suffering he saw were indescribable. The houses around his former city home were all destroyed, and everyone in them had been killed. He came to the home of an elderly sister of the church, and to his surprise, it was still standing! He found her house open, and there she was—giving first aid to more than thirty people who had crowded inside! However, the city was on fire, and since the fire was coming that way, they had to vacate. In time Mr. Morita was able to account for all the church members. Though their homes were lost, their lives had been saved. God is indeed great in power, and He can cover His children when storms rage, when bombs burst, and when fire burns.

Give God first place in your heart. You will need Him in the tempests of the last days.

HABAKKUK 3 AUGUST 7

"His brightness was as the light; he had horns coming out of his hand [bright beams out of his side (margin)]: and there was the hiding of his power." Habakkuk 3:4.

Habakkuk lived and worked in a time of deep apostasy. He prophesied the coming of the Chaldeans, and in chapter 3, verses 3 to 16, he gives a description of the Lord coming in judgment and for the deliverance of His people. These verses also are descriptive of the coming of Christ to usher in the reign of righteousness. At that time the hands that were pierced on Calvary will be honored for what they stand for.

In the book *Christ and the Fine Arts*, by Cynthia Pearl Maus, there is a copy of a beautiful painting called *Praying Hands*, and this lovely story is told about it.

Albrecht Dürer was born in Nuremburg, Germany. When he was just a young man he went away to study painting under a great artist. While there he found a friend somewhat older than himself who was also studying painting. They were both poor, so they decided to room together to save expenses. It was a great struggle, however, to get odd jobs to pay their expenses and still study art, so one day the older man suggested that it would be better for him to work full time and support them both; Albrecht could study full time and would soon be able to earn a living with his paintings. Then Albrecht could earn the living, and the older man would give his full time to studying art. Reluctantly Albrecht agreed, for he thought he should be the first to make the living. His friend went to work in a restaurant, washing dishes and scrubbing floors. The hours were long and the work was hard, but he was happy to think that someday his chance to study would come.

At last the day came when Albrecht sold his first wood carving and brought home sufficient money to last them a while. "Now it is your turn to study," he said to his friend, "and I will be the breadwinner." Joyfully his friend took up his brushes and went back to study, but the hard work had stiffened the muscles and enlarged the joints of his hands, and although he tried hard and long, he knew that his hands had lost their skill, and he would never be a great painter. One day Albrecht came back to his room and heard the voice of his friend in prayer. He saw those work-worn hands folded reverently, and a great inspiration came to him. "I can never give back to those hands the skill they have lost," he said to himself, "but I can paint them, and show to the world the feeling of gratitude and love that I have in my heart for his noble deed." And he did.

Someday in the art gallery you may see a copy of the painting he made of those hands. When you do, remember the beautiful story. And someday I hope you will see the Saviour's hands with beams of glory shining from them. Then you will remember His love for you forever!

ZEPHANIAH 2   AUGUST 8

"Seek ye the Lord all ye meek of the earth . . . : it may be ye shall be hid in the day of the Lord's anger." Zephaniah 2:3.

Zephaniah lived in the days of Josiah, king of Judah. He prophesied the coming judgment on Israel and also pleaded with them to seek the Lord, to seek righteousness, to seek meekness, that they might escape punishment.

The story of the Advent message in all the world is full of experiences in which those who have sought God and made Him first in their lives have been "hid" in the day of destruction. Let me tell you the experiences of Brother Morita's son and daughter when the atomic bomb fell on Hiroshima. Two days ago I told you how Mr. Morita moved out of the city into the country and thus escaped death among the 100,000 victims in the city. Well, his son went into the city each day to work in a factory, and his daughter, Setsuko, went each day to the girls' high school. On August 6, 1945, Mr. Morita's son was working with a group of men around a heavy, reinforced table. There was a blinding light, then a terrible crash. The factory was demolished. Almost every workman in the factory was killed. Somehow the Morita boy found himself under the table, perfectly protected from crashing walls and beams, without a scratch! Setsuko was in school when suddenly a huge ball of fire seemed to enter the room. The eighty girls in her room remained in their seats, but Setsuko jumped up and pressed herself against a pillar in the center of the room. In the crash that followed, the whole building collapsed, crushing to death most of the 350 girls attending the school. The pillar to which Setsuko clung remained standing, and although the debris tumbled down all around her, she was unscathed and able to climb out to safety. You can only imagine the parents' joy when the son and daughter both found their way back home that night.

"The tempest is coming, and we must get ready for its fury. . . . Thousands of ships will be hurled into the depths of the sea. . . . Human lives will be sacrificed by millions. . . . Disasters by rail will become more and more frequent; confusion, collision, and death without a moment's warning will occur. . . . The end is near, probation is closing. Oh, let us seek God while He may be found, call upon Him while He is near!"—*Messages to Young People*, pp. 89, 90.

HAGGAI 2   AUGUST 9

"The desire of all nations shall come: and I will fill this house with glory, saith the Lord of hosts." Haggai 2:7.

You will remember that Haggai was one of the prophets who was among the first exiles to return to Jerusalem. He helped Zerubbabel the governor and Joshua the high priest in rebuilding the Temple. Among his inspiring encouragements was the prophecy that "the desire of all nations"—the Messiah—would come and fill the Temple with glory. He did come. Soon "the desire of all nations" is coming again, the second time, and God is using missionaries and evangelists everywhere to get people ready for that great day. And in places where we do not have enough missionaries the Spirit of God is using many strange ways to bring the truth to people who *desire* to know God. Listen:

Away up in northern Uganda in central Africa there lived a man named Eriya Musoke. One day he thought he would like to visit a relative

150 miles away on the other side of Lake Kyoga. When he reached his relative's home he saw a little book on the table written in the Luganda language. The name of it was *Is the End Near?* He picked it up and began to read it.

"Where did you get this book?" he asked.

"A colporteur sold it to me," his relative replied.

"Can I have it?"

"No. That is my book."

"But *you* can't read and I can."

"Still, you can't have it, but you can read it while you are here," said his relative. So Eriya stayed five days and read it over and over, till he almost knew it by heart. When he got back to his home he hunted up a Bible, bought it for 20 cents, and began to read it. Soon he came to Matthew 24. He remembered reading about that in the little book. His heart burned within him. "It's true! It's true!" he said. "Jesus is coming again soon!" Before long he was keeping the Sabbath and telling his friends all about it. I will tell you some more about Eriya tomorrow, for it is wonderful what the Spirit of God can do for a man who *desires* to get ready to meet Jesus.

Are you getting ready for the coming of the "desire of all nations" too?

ZECHARIAH 4   AUGUST 10

"Then the angel that talked with me answered and said . . . , Not by might, nor by power, but by my spirit, saith the Lord of hosts." Zechariah 4:5, 6.

Zechariah was another prophet who encouraged Zerubbabel and Joshua in rebuilding the Temple after their return to Jerusalem from Babylon. The poor Jews were so discouraged by enemy opposition and lack of resources that the finishing of the Temple seemed humanly impossible. Zechariah encouraged them by saying the rebuilding of the Temple was a divine plan and that the work would be accomplished by the Spirit of God.

The Spirit of God is with us today, still doing things that seem impossible with men. Pastor M. E. Lind was the president of a mission station in Uganda. One day he sat in his office with his faithful assistant, Luka Kaddu, translating Sabbath school lessons, when the mailman came and left some letters. Among them was a letter addressed "to the missionary who keeps the Bible Sabbath, Mbale." Pastor Lind smiled and opened it. It was from a man away up in northern Uganda. "I have been preaching the Bible Sabbath," it said, "and now there are two more keeping that day. Can you come up?" It was signed Eriya Musoke.

"How far away does this man live, Luka?" asked Pastor Lind.

"About 160 miles. It is a good letter. Shall I go up?" said Luka.

"No, not now. We are too busy with the Sabbath school lessons. We will write to him and send him some tracts." Two weeks later there came another letter addressed to the missionary who keeps the Bible Sabbath. It said, "Now there are four of us keeping the Sabbath. Can you now come up?"

"Shall I go up now?" asked Luka.

"No, Luka, I can't spare you now," answered Pastor Lind. "We are just starting an evangelistic effort." In two weeks there came another letter. This time it was addressed to Pastor M. E. Lind. It said, "Now there are twelve of us keeping the Sabbath. Can you now come up?"

"I am going, sir," Luka said; and Luka went. He stayed about a month, and when he got back Pastor Lind said, "Well, Luka, did you find twelve people keeping the Sabbath?"

"No," said Luka, "there were eighteen! And when I left, twenty-eight! And they want you to come up." So Pastor Lind went up.

"Eriya," he said, "how did you find out about the Sabbath?" And Eriya told him about finding the little book in his relative's house.

"And how did you find the Seventh-day mission?"

"Well," said Eriya, "one day I had to go to the town five miles away on an errand for the chief. I was riding the chief's old bicycle, and when I got to the city I found policemen inspecting all bicycles.

" 'Have you brakes?' they asked. I said 'Yes, but they don't work.'

" 'Have you a bell?'

" 'No,' I said; so they took me off to jail. There was nothing to do in jail, so I just sat there and talked with the jailer.

" 'Do you know anyone who keeps the seventh-day Sabbath?' I asked.

" 'Yes,' he said. 'There is a seventh-day Sabbath missionary near Mbale,' and that is how I got your address." Today Eriya has eight Sabbath schools with more than five hundred keeping the Sabbath!

But it was not Eriya's might or power that accomplished this. It was the Spirit of God.

"Bring all the tithes into the storehouse . . . , and prove me now herewith, saith the Lord of hosts, if I will not open you the windows of heaven, and pour you out a blessing, that there shall not be room enough to receive it." Malachi 3:10.

Malachi probably ministered during the second period when Nehemiah was governor of Jerusalem. The people were lukewarm and indifferent toward God and His worship, and God used Malachi to call them to repentance. We know Malachi best for his appeal to be faithful in returning the tithes and offerings to God, and for reminding us of the guarantee God gives that great blessing will result.

Here is the greatest story of tithe-blessing I have ever heard. In 1913 a young man by the name of Clyde Harris and his brother opened a little box factory in Milton, Oregon. The following year Clyde was married, and in a remarkable way a few months later he and his wife became Sabbathkeepers, were baptized, and joined the Seventh-day Adventist Church. They were all-the-way people, and had no trouble giving up tobacco, tea, and coffee. What they believed was right, they did, and that's all there was to it. He regarded paying tithe to be as basic as keeping the Sabbath, and they always gave more than the tenth, to be sure they were doing their part. God blessed them so much that after they had been running their box factory for three years they added a sawmill to their business. God still blessed, and Mr. Harris added fruit farms to his business. Again and again God rebuked the devourer for their sakes, and they always had good crops. Soon Mr. Harris moved his plant to Pendleton to be near the railway. Then he added a furniture factory and made arrangements for students from nearby Walla Walla College to work there and earn part of their school expenses. God blessed more and more until in 1951 his factory produced $4 million worth of goods and was employing 650 workers! In all of their thirty-nine years of operation there was only one depression year, 1932, when they did not show a profit, and they have never been unable to pay their workers.

As Brother Harris approached retirement age he began to think of the future. What would he do with his $9 million business? One day he called in Elder Scriven, the conference president, and Elder C. J. Nagele, the conference treasurer, and told them to get the papers ready, for he had decided to give the whole business to the church! And he did! And God is still blessing the business.

"Thou shalt call his name Jesus: for he shall save his people from their sins." Matthew 1:21.

One of the sweetest stories I have ever heard was told about this text, by Elder L. H. Christian, one of the great builders of the Advent cause in Europe. It happened back in 1925, in the country of Poland, after World War I. Our little church in one small town had been used as a barracks and had suffered much at the hands of the rough soldiers. So when one of our SDA soldier boys came back to his hometown, he found the windows of the church all broken, the doors torn from their hinges, the yard all overgrown with weeds, and the congregation scattered to the four winds. It broke his heart to see that the light of the church had gone out; but what could he do? He was only a soldier boy with very little education. But he had a Bible, and he could read, and as he prayed that God would rekindle the light of truth in that little town, God talked to him in a dream and said, "Arise and build!"

"O Lord, I don't know how!" he pleaded.

"My word builds," came the voice, and when he awoke, he couldn't forget those words. The more he thought of his dream, the more he was impelled to do something. So he repaired the church and pulled up the weeds. Then he took his Bible and decided to go from house to house and read to anyone who would listen. When the woman in the first house invited him in, he read the first chapter of Genesis, had a short prayer, and invited her to the church service the next Sabbath morning. As he went on to the next house he felt that the story of Creation wasn't very inspiring, so decided to try the New Testament next time. So after being invited in at the second home, he read the first chapter of Matthew. In just a minute he realized he had made a terrible mistake because he was lost in a wilderness of big names. But he kept courageously on, and soon came to the verse that says, "Thou shalt call his name Jesus: for he shall save his people from their sins."

"That's just what I need," said the woman. "I need a Saviour." The young man had prayer and invited her to the church service next Sabbath. And thus he went from home to home, and when Sabbath morning arrived, the people came to the church. He had no hymnbooks; he couldn't preach; so he simply read from the Bible. But it was just what the people wanted, and they came the next Sabbath and the next and the next. After two and a half months the conference president came to that little town, hoping he would find one or two of the church members still faithful. Instead, he found forty-one people keeping the Sabbath and waiting for baptism! That is just what the world needs. It needs a Saviour.

You need a Saviour too. Give Jesus first place in your heart, and He will save you from your sins.

MATTHEW 2   AUGUST 13

"The angel of the Lord appeareth to Joseph in a dream, saying, Arise, and take the young child and his mother, and flee into Egypt." Matthew 2:13.

At the General Conference session in 1962 Pastor Walter Schubert told of a young man who was the only Seventh-day Adventist in his family. He loved to read his Bible, but his mother didn't like this new religion, and she watched angrily while he read his Bible. One day while he was away from the house she took his Bible and hid it under the mattress of her bed. When the young man came home and couldn't find his Bible, he said, "Mother, did you borrow my Bible to read?"

"Me borrow your Bible!" she replied angrily. "As if I would read that!" That night the young man prayed that God would help him find his Bible, and that night he dreamed. In his dream he saw an angel, and the angel said, "Your mother has hidden your Bible under the mattress of her bed. You will find it there." The next morning he went to his mother's room and lifted up the mattress.

"What are you doing?" asked his mother.

"I'm getting my Bible," he said.

"How did you know it was there?"

"Last night an angel told me in a dream that you had hidden it there," he replied.

His mother was speechless! "There must be something to this new religion after all," she said to herself. The next Monday night she went to the meeting with her son, and when Pastor Schubert made a call, she went forward without any hesitation. Later both she and her husband were baptized and became church members.

Keep your heart right with God. Maybe someday He will send an angel to talk to you in a dream.

"Bring forth therefore fruits meet for repentance." Matthew 3:8.

When we have been disobedient, unkind, dishonest, or discourteous, we must do more than feel sorry; each one of us must bring forth the fruits of repentance; that is, we must show by our *actions* that we are sorry and that we are trying to correct our mistakes. In a long-ago copy of the *Youth's Instructor* I found this story:

A train was waiting at the station, almost ready to start. Standing near the platform of one of the coaches was a man carelessly dressed. He was lame. He looked as though he had neither wealth nor influence. "All aboard, Limpy," shouted the conductor.

"Time enough, I reckon," replied the stranger.

"Get on, Limpy!" The lame man made no reply, but quietly walked in and took a seat. In a few moments along came the conductor.

"Your ticket, quick," he said to the stranger.

"I don't pay," replied the lame man.

"We'll see about that," said the conductor as he moved on down the aisle, collecting his tickets. "I'll put you off at the next station."

"Do you know the man you were talking to just then?" asked a man nearby.

"No, sir."

"That is Peter Warburton, the president of this railway company."

"Are you sure?"

"Yes; I know him well." The color rose in the conductor's face. He knew he was in for trouble now. When he came back he stopped beside Mr. Warburton, placed his books and tickets in his hands, then said, "It serves me right, sir. I resign my place."

"Sit down, young man," said Mr. Warburton. "You have indeed been very impudent, and if you had treated a passenger that way, the company reputation would have been injured. Remember, you cannot judge a man by the clothes he wears, and even the poorest passenger should be treated courteously. Take up your books. If you change your course of action, I shall tell no one about it."

That's it—change your course of action. You may make a mistake, but you should not make the same mistake over and over again. Make it right, then change your course of action and don't make that mistake again.

"Man shall not live by bread alone, but by every word that proceedeth out of the mouth of God." Matthew 4:4.

The precious Word of God is likened to a light, because it shows the way into the future; to a sword, because it protects us from the temptations of Satan; and to bread, because it supplies us with spiritual life and growth.

Many years ago during my service in Burma, there came a little old grandma into my dispensary. She waited till all the other patients had gone.

"Have you got fever?" I asked kindly.

"No, not that," she said. "I'm starving, I tell you!" Then she told how her son had gone to Moulmein to work in a lumber mill. He had promised to send her money every month.

"But he hasn't sent me any money at all in his letters," she wept, "and when you go to the city, I want you to—"

"How often does he write you, Grandma?" I interrupted.

"Every two weeks I get a letter," she said.

"And doesn't he send anything in those letters?"

"Only some crazy little bits of paper with English printed and written all over them," she replied almost angrily.

I was immediately interested in those crazy little bits of paper, so I said, "Grandma, go home and get all of his letters and all of those crazy little bits of paper and bring them to me. I want to see them." The next morning she came with them all wrapped carefully in a banana leaf, and I think you have guessed it. Each of those "crazy bits of paper" was a money order for ten rupees!

"Grandma, Grandma," I said, "all you have to do is to take these to the post office and put your thumbprint on them and the postmaster will give you ten rupees for each one of them." I wish you could have seen her face.

"I can? He will?" she gasped. Then, hugging the money orders to her heart, she said, "And there I was starving! With all this fortune in my hands!"

And we might add: Why are so many juniors starving spiritually with the precious bread of heaven in their hands? Are *you* reading the Bible faithfully?

*"Blessed are ye, when men shall revile you, and persecute you. . . .
Rejoice, and be exceeding glad: for great is your reward in heaven." Matthew
5:11, 12.*

Ever since Satan started the war in heaven, those who have taken his
side against God have persecuted those who have chosen to love God
and follow Him. In a copy of the *Review* Pastor S. M. Samuel, of the
North Nyasa Field in central Africa, tells this story.

During an evangelistic effort in a town in eastern Africa, among
those who joined the probationary class was a young woman named
Nyangwira. At the end of the year she was promoted to the baptismal
class.

She told her husband about what she had learned and tried to
persuade him to come with her, but he became angry. "I don't want this
kind of religion in my home," he shouted, "and if you keep on I'll kill
you." Nyangwira, however, kept on. Sweetly, patiently, gently she
refused to brew beer, and her husband's anger increased. Another year
end came. She was to be baptized at the camp meeting. Before going to
camp meeting she knelt before her husband, as respectful wives do over
there, and told him she was now ready for baptism.

"I have told you not to get baptized," he said. "And you have to obey
me." He went to the wall and picked up a large hunting knife. Shaking it
in her face, he said, "The day you are baptized I will kill you." Nyangwira
was determined to obey God rather than man, whatever the cost, so off
she went to camp meeting and was baptized. When she got back she went
to the wall where the hunting knife hung, and picking it up, she took it to
her husband.

"Have you been baptized?" he said angrily.

"Yes," replied Nyangwira. "Here is the knife."

"Are you ready to be killed?"

"Yes, I am." But her courage completely unnerved him, and he put
the knife away and said no more! The Spirit of God was with Nyangwira.
She entered the colporteur work shortly after this and brought the light
of the gospel to many homes. Not only did God bless her here and now
but there is laid up for her a rich reward in heaven.

Do not fear persecution. Let people call you names if they will. Be
sweet, kind, and gentle, and God will bless you here on earth too.

"After this manner therefore pray ye: Our Father which art in heaven, Hallowed be thy name." Matthew 6:9.

Do you know why Jesus taught His disciples to say, "Our Father which art in heaven"? I think it was because He didn't want them to be afraid or nervous when they prayed. If Jesus had taught them to say, "King of kings" or "Great Ruler of the universe," they might have been scared. I would be nervous about talking to even the president or a senator of our country. But few are afraid to talk to a father. I am a father. I have two sons and two daughters, and they are not afraid to talk to me!

One day when my eldest son, Lenny, was just a little fellow 4 years old he awoke at four o'clock in the morning, crawled out of his crib, sat on top of me, then started: "Daddy, Daddy, Daddy! Please, Daddy, will you make me a toy car? And paint it green all over and put a toot-toot on it like an engine train, and a seat in it for the pussy cat to ride on? Will you, Daddy? Huh?"

I was so sleepy that I said, "I'll do anything if you will only let me sleep!"

Later on he ran off down the stairs to his little friends Barnabas and Stephen. "Daddy's going to make me a toy car. He said he would," he shouted. And *all* day long, *every* time I saw him, he said, "You are going to make me a toy car, aren't you, Daddy? You said you would!"

At last the day was done and he lay asleep in his crib.

"Isn't he sweet!" said his mother as we looked fondly at him.

"Yes," I said, "when he is asleep! He has toy-carred me all day long." But I *was* his father and I *did* love him and I *had* promised, so while the little fellow slept I went downstairs and worked till midnight. I made him a toy car with a toot-toot on it like an engine train; I painted it green all over, and made a seat in it for the cat to ride on, and I put it right beside his bed where he could find it in the morning.

God is King of kings, but He also is our heavenly Father! Never be afraid to tell Him everything, or to ask His help for every occasion. He *is* your Father; He *has* promised to supply all your need; and He *will!*

"Judge not, that ye be not judged. For with what judgment ye judge, ye shall be judged." Matthew 7:1, 2.

It is so easy to criticize or condemn. Like a flash you can decide that someone has done wrong. But you'd better be careful! You had better look at both sides of the question and find out all the circumstances before you judge, because things are not always what they seem to be at first sight. Not long ago at a church youth meeting, I was showing some color slides on Burma and New Guinea. A friend had taken me to the church quite early, and I had the projector and the tape recorder all set up and checked over before the people began to come in. More and more people came in, and it was just about time for the meeting to begin when in came a tall woman dressed in a fur coat. She brushed heavily along the back of the pew where I was sitting, and bumped my head as she went by! "Dear me," I said to myself, "what a clumsy person!" I was afraid she would bump into my equipment and knock it over, but fortunately she didn't, and she finally found a seat in front of me.

The meeting began. I gave my talk and entirely forgot about the clumsy woman until my friend said, "I want you to meet our faithful *blind* sister. She comes to every meeting." And he introduced me to the tall woman in the fur coat! My face went red at the thought of my unspoken judgment. How glad I was that nobody knew what I had thought! My heart nearly stood still!

"I'm sorry you couldn't see the pictures," I finally stammered.

"But I can hear," she said cheerfully, "and what you said and the music in the background made a very enjoyable evening for me." I suppose she has forgotten all about that meeting by this time, but I will *never* forget how near I came to making a regrettable judgment. I'm going to be doubly careful evermore.

"That which we do to others, whether it be good or evil, will surely react upon ourselves, in blessing or in cursing. . . . Everyone who has been free to condemn or discourage, will in his own experience be brought over the ground where he has caused others to pass; he will feel what they have suffered because of his want of sympathy and tenderness."—*Thoughts From the Mount of Blessing,* p. 136.

Won't you promise God that you too will be careful about what you say and how you judge?

"A certain scribe came, and said unto him, Master, I will follow thee whithersoever thou goest. And Jesus saith unto him, The foxes have holes, and the birds of the air have nests; but the Son of man hath not where to lay his head." Matthew 8:19, 20.

A little boy from a Buddhist home in Hawaii was enrolled in the Adventist kindergarten. Day after day he came and enjoyed every activity—the games, the songs, the stories. But the stories about Jesus, he loved the best. It was a new name for him and a new kind of teacher—born as a baby in a manger, because there was no room for Him in the inn. Day by day the story told how He grew up and went around doing good to everybody. Then came the day when the teacher told the story about the scribe, and she solemnly said: "Jesus said: 'The foxes have holes, and the birds of the air have nests; but the Son of man hath not where to lay his head.' Just think! Poor Jesus had no place He could call His own."

The little boy listened carefully and took it all in, and when the story was finished he went up to the teacher, caught hold of her hand, looked earnestly into her face, and said, "Teacher, this Jesus—didn't He have any home?"

"No, sonny, not here."

"And you say He's coming back here again?"

"Yes, very soon."

The little fellow looked very pleased and said, "Then, Teacher, you tell Jesus when He comes again that we have plenty of room for Him at our house!" Precious little lad! No wonder Jesus said, "Of such is the kingdom of heaven!"

Would you find plenty of room in your house, too, for Jesus when He comes again? But you don't have to wait till He comes. You can make room for Jesus now, in your heart.

Mabel J. Rosemon wrote a beautiful song. The chorus says:

"Dear Saviour, come to me, I'll ever welcome Thee. Within this heart of mine Thy dwelling place shall be; O Saviour, come to me, for there is room for Thee; Within my heart there's room for Thee."

"They that be whole need not a physician, but they that are sick." Matthew *9:12.*

Jesus called Himself a doctor to those who were sick with sin. This helps us to understand how He could hate sin but love a sinner. We know that a doctor often has to hurt or operate on patients because he loves them and wants them to get better. So God permits us to be punished for our sins, and punishment of every kind hurts! But God only lets us get hurt so we can get rid of sin and be good again.

One day when I was in Burma I went to our Awbawa village school to give the half-yearly examinations. After school the village sick people flocked into the school for treatment. There were some with sore eyes, some with malaria, and some with teeth to be pulled.

While I was hard at work another poor man came groaning up the ladder with a big boil on his wrist. "Quick, Doctor!" he said to me. "Get your knife, cut it deep, and squeeze all the matter out."

"It will hurt you if I cut it!"

"Never mind if it does hurt," he said.

"Do you like people to hurt you?" I asked.

"Of course I don't," he said, "but I can't sleep and I can't work. Come on, Doctor, get your knife and cut it." Then he added, "If you think I'll wriggle around too much, call those six big men over there and have them sit on me so I can't move." And I did that very thing; and when he couldn't move, I lanced the boil. It *did* hurt, and he groaned with pain.

"Shall I stop now?" I asked.

"No, keep on till it's all finished," he cried.

I squeezed it, and he groaned again. "Shall I stop now?" I asked.

"No! Keep on till it's all finished," he said. So I kept on hurting him until it was all finished; and I put a nice clean bandage around his wrist. Then the men got off him, and he sat up. For a moment he looked at his sore arm. Then he moved over beside me and took my hand in his—the hand that had cut him—and stroking it, he wept out his joy, "Oh, thank you, Doctor. Thank you so much."

And that's just the way it is with God. He hates sin, but He loves us. And sometimes He has to let us get hurt in order to take away our sin. Next time you have to be punished or corrected, remember this and say, "Thank You, Jesus. Thank You so much. Please help me not to sin again."

"Whosoever therefore shall confess me before men, him will I confess also before my Father which is in heaven." Matthew 10:32.

I will always remember the day when Ohn Bwint decided to be baptized. He was my biggest boy in school, and he had been at our mission school for four years. One night he knocked on my office door and said, "Thara, I want to go home."

"But, Ohn Bwint," I replied, "there are only three weeks before school closes!"

"Yes, but Thara, I want to be baptized at camp meeting time, and I want to ask my parents' permission to be baptized."

"Oh, that's different," I said. "Of course you can go." And off he went, radiant and happy. But when he came back the joy had gone out of his face. "I can't do it, Thara," he sobbed. "My father says that if I am baptized he will disown me and tell the devils I am dead!"

Each person has to make his own decision to follow Christ and be baptized, so I just said, "Keep your heart right, my boy, and the right time will come someday." School closed. The camp meeting was held. On the last Sabbath seven big boys from the school were baptized. We sang, "Happy day, happy day, when Jesus washed my sins away." And it was a happy day for everyone but Ohn Bwint. He sat alone, weeping.

Late that night he knocked on my door once more. "Thara," he sobbed, "I'm going home again. I'm going to tell my father that even if he does disown me, I must be baptized. As I saw the boys going into the water today, it seemed I could see heaven open, and I could imagine Jesus standing before His Father, saying, 'This one is Mine, Father; look at the nailprints. I paid the price for him. And this one too, Father; and this one too. He's not ashamed to confess Me before men; I'm not ashamed to confess him before Thee. But not that one under the bush over yonder, Father; he is afraid of being disowned. Not him!' " Ohn Bwint broke down and cried. "I couldn't stand it! To think that Christ was ashamed of me! I must go and tell my father that I must be baptized." Ohn Bwint went. He came back again and he was baptized, and a happier boy you couldn't find anywhere.

Do you want the joy of having Jesus claim you as His own? All you need do is to confess Jesus before men, here on earth. Confess Him where you are, and He will surely confess you before His Father in heaven.

"Come unto me, all ye that labour and are heavy laden, and I will give you rest." Matthew 11:28.

The invitation to come to Jesus is for all. Many have come to Jesus and found freedom from the slavery of sin, and rest for their poor tired souls. But there are some who keep struggling along, bound with bad habits, longing to be free, but failing to realize that what they need is Christ.

In an old copy of the *Youth's Instructor* Miss Lora Clement tells a story that illustrates their pitiable condition very well.

Once upon a time, away over in Africa, the king of one tribe was taken prisoner by a bitter enemy and carried off to his distant territory. There he was chained to a heavy iron weight but allowed to move about as he wished. Of course, his movements were slow and limited to the distance he could drag or carry the heavy weight. How he longed to be free and to return to his own tribe again! One day a European traveler passing through the country saw the poor man and pitied him. He dared not try to help him openly, however, because he was closely watched, but he did get permission to give the poor captive a Bible. The captive king wasn't interested in the Bible. He wished the traveler had given him food or clothing or money. He put the Bible to one side and never looked at it. Three years went by, and then one day, bored with nothing to do, he picked up the Bible and looked through it. All of a sudden he felt something hard inside the back cover. He felt it and pulled at it, and what do you think? It was a file! Slowly he made his way to the woods, then began to file away on his chain. He worked and worked till at last the chain fell off—and he was free! At once he set out for home, traveling by night to keep out of sight, and before long he was safe at home again. But just think, he could have been free three years before! He had endured three needless years of slavery just because he didn't look inside the Book!

Are you tied up to some bad habit? Are you enduring slavery to sin? Jesus invites you to come to Him. He is the way, the truth, and the life, and He will give you rest. It is not enough just to *have* a Bible. You need to *read* your Bible and *find* Christ in it. Only Christ can make you free.

"I say unto you, That every idle word that men shall speak, they shall give account thereof in the day of judgment." Matthew 12:36.

Idle words! Gossip! How easy it is to talk without thinking! Nina Willis Walter tells a story, in an old *Youth's Instructor*, that I have retold many, many times. Sam, Curly, Red, Gail, and Lee were all in the same Sabbath school class. They also had a club called Scouts for Jesus. One day a new boy, Eddie Jones, and his mother came to town and moved into a little house nearby. A few days later Sam, president of the club, said, "Has anyone asked the new boy to join our class?"

"No, fellows; it's all off with Eddie Jones," said Curly. "We don't want him in our club, and I'll tell you why. He's a thief!"

"What did he steal?" demanded Gail.

"He stole the bottle of milk right off our front porch!" said Curly. "Believe me, I told him plenty; and he brought it back."

"You mean a big boy like one of us stole a bottle of milk?"

"And that's not all. I watched him out of the corner of the window, and he no sooner got into the street than he went next door and stole Mr. Andrews' milk. He's a thief, all right."

"Wait a minute," said Sam. "Let's not call him names until we figure out why he did what he did. You fellows wait right here. I'll be back soon." Before long, Sam was back, and the fellows crowded around to hear his report.

"OK, fellows, here's the story. Eddie's mother is sick. They are all out of cash after moving here, but Eddie's mother is a nurse and she'll soon get work when she gets better. Eddie has been looking everywhere for a job. They are renting their house from Mr. Andrews, and this morning Eddie saw him on his way to the train. He asked Eddie to please tell the milkman not to leave any more milk till he got back, and to pick up the bottle of milk on his porch and use it."

"Somebody please kick me," moaned Curly. "Mr. Andrews' house and our house are painted the same, and I suppose he just . . ."

"Yes, he just—and Curly, *you* just— Say, fellows, what about asking Eddie Jones to join our class and our club?" And four fellows shouted, "Yes!"

Is your tongue quick on the trigger? Better tie a knot in it! Or you'll have a hard time in the judgment.

"The kingdom of heaven is like unto treasure hid in a field." Matthew
13:44.

In Matthew 13 the kingdom of heaven is likened to several things
that show how valuable and precious it is. In verses 3 to 8 it is likened to
seed that brings forth an abundant harvest to all who receive it. In verse
46 it is likened to a pearl of great price that was worth all that a man
possessed. In verse 44 it is likened to treasure hid in a field, treasure worth
more than everything a man had. I wonder if we realize how valuable the
kingdom of heaven is, how close it is to us, and how easy it is for us to
obtain. According to a story by Russell H. Conwell, there once lived an
old Persian sheik by the name of Ali Hafed. He owned a large farm not far
from the Indus River. He was a very wealthy and contented man. But one
day a Buddhist priest visited him, and as they talked together the priest
told him about diamonds that were more precious than gold.

Once Ali Hafed had heard about diamonds, that was all he wanted.
"I want a mine of diamonds," he said, and he lay awake at night dreaming
about it. Eventually he sold his farm, left his family in the care of a
neighbor, and went off in search of a diamond mine. He searched
through the Mountains of the Moon in Africa, wandered through
Palestine, then on into Europe, but he couldn't find a diamond mine
anywhere. At last his money was all spent, and he was in rags. In his
wretchedness and despair he threw himself into the bay at Barcelona,
Spain, and drowned himself! But that is not the end of the story. One day
the same old Buddhist priest came to visit Ali Hafed's successor. As he
entered the house he saw a flash of light on the mantel. He rushed up to it
and shouted, "It's a diamond! Has Ali Hafed returned?"

"No! Ali Hafed has not returned; and that is not a diamond," said the
man. "It is only a pretty stone I found here in the garden."

"But it is a diamond," said the priest. And it was indeed. They went
into the garden, stirred up the white sands, and found more of the
valuable gems. Thus was discovered the famous Golconda diamond
mine! Think of it! There were priceless diamonds all around him, hidden
in his field, all within reach, but Ali Hafed didn't recognize them.

The precious, priceless kingdom of heaven is all around you, within
your reach. Have you made it yours?

"And when he [Peter] saw the wind boisterous, he was afraid; and beginning to sink, he cried, saying, Lord, save me. And immediately Jesus stretched forth his hand, and caught him." Matthew 14:30, 31.

I think it was more than the boisterous waves that made Peter sink. I think there was a little bit of a show-off spirit in Peter, which made him take his eyes off Jesus and turn around to see whether the other disciples were admiring him. That unlovely show-off spirit always causes boys and girls to *go down* in the estimation of their companions. Uncle Arthur tells a good story about a show-off in *The Children's Hour,* Book I.

Jerry was a well-developed 10-year-old lad. He could do everything well, but unfortunately, he was always calling for attention and praise by saying, "Watch me hit this ball" or "Watch me ride my bike!" "Watch me" seemed to be a part of him, and nobody liked to hear him brag. Well, one day he was at the seaside for his vacation. His folks hired a rowboat, and Jerry could handle it quite well. But he spoiled it by always saying, "Watch me!" "Watch me!" "Watch me!"

One lovely morning he shouted, "Watch me race the boy in that boat!" He bent his back and pulled hard, but one oar slipped out of the oarlock. Jerry tipped over backward, his feet went up in the air, and the oar fell into the water and went floating away. But Jerry was a bright boy. He picked himself up, looked around, then moved one of the oarlocks to the back of the boat. He put the one oar that was left in it, and moving it from side to side with a twisting motion, began moving forward. "Watch me!" "Watch me!" he called triumphantly. But just then the oar slipped out of the oarlock and Jerry lost his balance and fell headlong into the sea. Fortunately, there were lots of people around. One rescued Jerry, another pulled the boat to the beach, and another saved the two oars. It was a sorry picture, but suddenly someone in the crowd shouted, "Watch me!" And everybody laughed. Jerry went red, then he laughed too. But Jerry really was a bright boy, and that day he caught on to one of the best ideas he ever had. He stopped saying "Watch me" and never said it again.

Listen in to yourself, and if you find yourself saying "Watch me! Watch me!" then *you* stop it too.

251

"Great is thy faith: be it unto thee even as thou wilt." Matthew 15:28.

Over and over again Jesus performed miracles *according to the faith* of the people who came to Him for help. Jesus was always pleased when He found someone with "great faith."

Here is a story that everyone should know. About 130 years ago there was a man in England whose name was George Müller. He had unusually great faith in God. In his heart he had a great burden to make Christian homes for the poor orphan children in Bristol. He believed God wanted him to do this work, and he believed that God would help him do it. And to make sure that God was doing it, he decided he would never ask anyone for money; he would just pray, and if the money came in, then he would know for sure that God was doing the work. So George Müller prayed—and along came the money. He rented one house and filled it with orphans. Every day he prayed. More money came in. He rented more houses and filled them with orphans. By 1841 he had ninety-six orphans in his houses. He kept praying, and within sixty years he had built five of the largest orphanages in the world, and had cared for more than ten thousand orphans!

One day George Müller told the Lord he would like to give his two thousand children a little treat, for it was his birthday, and he would like to provide each of the children with a banana. But two thousand bananas would cost a lot of money. He looked in the safe to see how much money he had, then went to town to see whether he could buy two thousand bananas. Can you imagine his surprise when he got there, to find that a firm of importers of bananas had already sent a shipment of bananas to the orphanage. When he got back and counted them, there were four thousand instead of two thousand! So the orphans had two bananas each instead of only one! George Müller is a wonderful example for us all. God honored his life of prayer and faith.

We have a mighty God, with whom all things are possible. But how much faith have you? "Without faith it is impossible to please him" (Hebrews 11:6). And remember, "Prayer is the key in the *hand of faith* to unlock heaven's storehouse, where are treasured the boundless resources of Omnipotence."—*Steps to Christ*, pp. 94, 95.

"If any man will come after me, let him deny himself, and take up his cross, and follow me." Matthew 16:24.

We often speak of the things we have to give up, and the things we have to suffer to be real Christians, as "the cross" we have to carry. Did you ever think your cross was too big and too heavy? Listen. Margaret White Eggleston tells this story in her wonderful book *Seventy-five Stories for the Worship Hour.*

There came a day during World War I when Turkey entered the war as an ally of Germany. With the declaration of war came the decision that Turkey would rid her land of the hated Armenian Christians. The poor Christians were driven from their homes and marched off to some unknown destination in the Arabian Desert. Many died on the way. Many became slaves of the Arabs. Some of the Arab masters were kind, but some were very cruel. In the nearby countries of the Western Allies the Americans set up relief camps, and to these camps many refugees found their way. One day among the refugees that came to one of these camps was a young Armenian girl. As she waited in line to see the doctor everyone saw she was in terrible pain.

"Lean on me," said one person next to her. "I am strong."

"I cannot lean," replied the poor girl.

"Have you been hurt?"

"I am bearing the cross," she said. "I know now how Jesus suffered." Just then a nurse came by, and seeing how sick the girl looked, she bent over to help her.

"Wait," said the girl, "I must show you first." She then slipped her loose dress from her shoulders and showed them the form of a cross that had been burned across her shoulders with a red-hot iron. It was swollen and terribly inflamed.

"Day by day they added to my cross," she explained. "They would ask me 'Mohammed or Christ?' and when I said 'Christ,' they brought the hot iron and burned the cross bigger and bigger. I thought I would surely die for Christ. Then, miraculously, I escaped and found my way here." Lovingly she was led to the hospital and tenderly cared for. She will bear her cross as long as she lives.

Now, how big is *your* cross? How heavy is *your* cross?

"This is my beloved Son . . . ; hear ye him." Matthew 17:5.

To Moses and Elijah was given the greatest honor human beings could know—the privilege of comforting and strengthening Jesus before He was crucified. Both Moses and Elijah had experienced much suffering and disappointment. Once Moses prayed, "Please, let me go over and see the land of Canaan." But God said No. Once Elijah prayed, "Let me die." But God said No. God had something better for both of them.

While we were on our mission station in Burma, I gave my 7-year-old Lenny a little steam engine one Christmas. It was a real engine. You could put water in it and fire under it, and it turned a wheel and it whistled. Oh, it was marvelous! How excited he was about it. That afternoon, however, a letter came from his three little cousins—Edwin, Wilfred, and Buddy—saying that in February they were coming up to spend three months with us, and they added, "We got a Mechano set for Christmas." As soon as I read that letter, in my imagination I could see Lenny's engine turning a Mechano merry-go-round. But that was two months away, and in two months Lenny's engine might be all broken. So I said, "Son, let's put the engine away till your cousins come with their Mechano set. Then it will still be new and you'll have more fun." But he couldn't see two months ahead, and he said, "No, no, Daddy, I want to play with it now."

I thought it over carefully. I was sure I was right, so I said, "I know it will be better this way, son." And we put the engine away. Poor Lenny cried. He couldn't understand. But the weeks passed quickly. The cousins came. They unpacked their Mechano set. I brought out Lenny's brand-new engine. In a little while the engine was turning a Mechano merry-go-round, and four little boys were squealing with delight.

"Now aren't you glad that I put the engine away, Lenny?" I asked. And what do you think he did? He jumped onto my knee, threw his arms around my neck, hugged me tight, and said, "How did you know it would be better this way, Daddy?"

Really, parents and teachers and God do know what will be best for you in the future, and if ever they have to say No to some of your plans, take it kindly. Someday you will know it was best.

"Where two or three are gathered together in my name, there am I in the midst of them." Matthew 18:20.

Grandma Batty always went to prayer meeting, and usually she was the only one there besides the minister. Everybody else seemed to be too busy to go. But Grandma Batty said, "Anyway, I'm number two! And that means that the Lord will be there too." So she was always there. But one day Grandma Batty broke her leg and had to stay in bed. Her little grandson found her weeping on the afternoon of prayer meeting day.

"What's the matter, Grandma?" he asked.

"Bobby, I can't go to prayer meeting tonight; and I'm number two, and if I don't get there, maybe the Lord won't come either, for the Bible says, 'Where two or three are gathered together in my name, there am I in the midst of them.' "

Bobby's eyes opened wide as he took it all in, then he said, "Don't worry, Grandma; I'll go and say my prayers with the minister. I'll be number two tonight. Then God will come, won't He?" And after supper, instead of just playing around, Bobby marched bravely down the street toward the church. On the way he met old Peter Quirls.

"Hi, Bobby. Where are you going?" he asked.

"Granny broke her leg and can't go to prayer meeting, so I'm going to be number two and say my prayers with the minister, so the Lord will come too," said Bobby. Right into the church went Bobby.

"Granny can't come tonight," said Bobby to the minister. "So I came to be number two, so the Lord won't be disappointed." Tears came to the minister's eyes.

"All right, Bobby," he said; "let us pray." Bobby said his little prayer, then the minister prayed. He prayed as he had never prayed before, and as he prayed old Peter Quirls came up to the front, and he prayed, for out of curiosity he had followed little Bobby to see what he would do. What a lovely prayer meeting they had together. The Lord surely was there, and as they rose from their knees Peter Quirls said, "Pastor, I'll never be absent from prayer meeting again. I'll be number three." Then Peter told everybody else about little Bobby's prayers, and they all began to come to prayer meeting.

Say, won't you be number two or number three at family worship or in prayer meetings?

"If thou wilt enter into life, keep the commandments." Matthew 19.17.

Jesus told the rich young ruler of a simple way to enter into eternal life. The way is *simple,* to be sure, but it is not *easy,* and the young ruler soon found that out—and he went away sorrowful. Then Jesus said to His disciples, "It is easier for a camel to go through the eye of a needle, than for a rich man to enter into the kingdom of God."

In this verse Jesus was using a common Eastern proverb that implied impossibility. But let me tell you something interesting that I know about camels. When I was a junior boy we lived for about a year in a town called Broken Hill, on the edge of the great central desert in Australia. My father raised up a church there. I was always fascinated by the camel caravans that took supplies to the mining settlements far across the desert sands. I was always interested to see how the camels were loaded each morning. The men simply spoke a word that the camels understood, and they all got *down on their knees!* Then, while they were on their knees, the boxes, the bundles, the lumber, and the iron sheets were loaded on the saddles, and tied securely. When they were all loaded, the camels got up from their knees and started on their journey. During the day if anything went wrong with one of the loads, so it became uncomfortable, that camel would flop down on his knees, and the master would straighten it up again. Then, at the end of the day, when they reached the journey's end, all the camels would get down on their knees and wait patiently till the men took off their burdens; then, without a care, they would eat and drink and rest for the night.

I think that is the way we can carry our burdens successfully. In the morning we can get down on our knees and ask the Lord to place upon us just the right amount of duty; then during the day if ever anything goes wrong we can fall on our knees and call for help. At night when the day is done we can fall on our knees once more and ask the Lord to take off all our cares and forgive all our mistakes and sins. Then we can lie down to sweet refreshing sleep.

Whether a person is rich or poor, I think that's the only way anyone can keep the commandments and find the way to life eternal.

"Is it not lawful for me to do what I will with mine own?. . . So the last shall be first, and the first last." Matthew 20:15,16.

In many ways Jesus taught the people what the reward of a meek and unselfish spirit would be. In the parable of the workers in the vineyard, the "last" were not last because they were lazy, but simply because no one had hired them earlier in the day. To me it is quite evident that after they were hired they worked hard. They made no demands, but trusted the master to pay them what was right. And he did. In an old copy of *Our Little Friend* Sue M. Cole told a lovely story about a reward that came to a little girl who was always last.

In a faraway country where there was suffering and hunger, welfare workers began to distribute bread to the hungry children. Little Sally went to the bread line, but there were people there when she arrived, and when others came they pushed in ahead of her, so that she was the last in the line. Of course, the bigger loaves were taken first, and when Sally got to the basket there was only a small loaf left for her. "That will do for Grandma and me," said Sally sweetly to the woman in charge. "We thank you so much." The next day Sally was last again, and got the smallest loaf that was left. The next day it was the same, but Sally always smiled and said Thank you. The woman in charge took notice of her kind, unselfish ways. The next day the woman played a lovely little trick. She made a special small loaf and put it right on top of all the loaves in the basket. As usual, the bigger loaves were taken first, and Sally got the small loaf. But when she got home and Grandma cut into it, there was a folded piece of paper money right in the middle of it! The next day Sally took the money back, and when the gate opened she called out, "Lady, there must be a mistake. There was some money in the loaf I got yesterday."

"It was not a mistake," said the woman. "I put it there for you."

"It isn't fair." "Wish I had taken the small loaf now," said a dozen voices.

"You could have taken it if you wanted it," said the woman. "I put it right on top. But Sally is the most unselfish of you all. Now she can buy some warm clothes for winter."

Really, now, how *meek* are you? Do you push and shove to be first or are you content to be last sometimes? Remember, in God's plan, someday, the "last" are going to be "first."

"Son, go work to day in my vineyard." Matthew 21:28.

Today, September 1, is the anniversary of the beginning of World War II in 1939—a day that many of your parents and grandparents will always remember. It is interesting to notice that the parable of the two sons in our Scripture reading today contains the reason for all wars, and trouble between men or nations. The second son said, "I *go*, sir," but he *went not.* He did not keep his word! He did not live up to his promise! He was not trustworthy. He could not be depended on! Another story from *Our Little Friend,* by Margot Lucille Ridge, illustrates the point very well.

Ken came home angry one day. "I'm not going to belong to their old club any longer!" he said.

"And why?" asked his big brother Dirck.

"They didn't vote for me to be president, that's why. They voted for Merv Kingston."

"And why?" said Dirck.

"He's responsible," they said. "I suppose that means that I am not!"

"Wouldn't they give you some other office?"

"I should say not! If I can't be president I don't want to be in their club at all."

"Maybe they did mean you were not dependable, Ken," said Dirck. "Better keep your eyes open and see." Ken went out to water the garden, but the hose was not there. "Who's taken the hose?" said Ken to himself. Then suddenly he remembered—*he* had left it at Mr. Conley's place when he was washing his car a few days ago. He started off to get it, and met Red Watkins.

"Any word from your uncle about Milt getting that job?" he asked. "Remember, you promised to write."

"No. Haven't heard yet, but I'll let you know as soon as I do," stammered Ken. As Red went off he said to himself, "Why did I forget to write that letter? Never mind, I have $1.35 in my bank; I'll telephone Uncle tonight." As he got back with the hose the postman was putting the letters in the mailbox. "There's one for you," he said.

"For me? Who would be writing to me? It's not my birthday or anything," said Ken. He tore the letter open and read: "Kenneth Crain: Three books charged to your library card No. L32479 were due June 30. A fine of 1.12 must be paid within three days or we shall be obliged to notify the guarantor."

"Oh, dear!" groaned Ken. "That takes nearly all my money, and I've just got to telephone Uncle. What can I do?" With a red face he went to Dirck for help.

"Sure, I'll help you out. I think you will learn someday, all right," he chided.

"I guess I don't rate to be president of the club yet, do I?" said Ken. He surely didn't.

Do you? Are you really dependable? Do you keep your word? Do you faithfully fulfill all your promises?

MATTHEW 22   SEPTEMBER 2

"Thou shalt love the Lord thy God with all thy heart, and with all thy soul, and with all thy mind." Matthew 22:37.

How good and how just is our heavenly Father! He never requires us to do anything impossible. He just expects us to serve Him with *all* our heart and soul and mind. The 2-year-old, with all his heart; the 10-year-old, with all his heart; and the 20-year-old with all his heart. I love to serve a God like that, don't you?

One day over in Burma I stepped into the head teacher's house for a few minutes. It was dinnertime, and I found Thara Myat Po with his little 3-year-old son, Solomon, sitting at the table. Little Solomon looked up into his father's face and said, "I love you, Daddy."

The father smiled and said, "How much do you love me, Solomon?"

The little fellow stretched his chubby arms as far apart as he could and said, "This big."

"Then," said the father, "if you love Daddy that big, you jump up and bring me a drink of water." Solomon jumped up and ran over to the waterpot, but the waterpot was too high! For just a moment he looked at it, and then looked at the tin cup that hung on a nail near the waterpot; but it was too high also. Then without a moment's hesitation he stood on his tiptoes, with his little stomach pressed flat against the post and his little arm reaching toward the cup. He could just touch it. But he did all he could for all he was worth, and while his little finger made the cup go *tinkle, tinkle, tinkle,* he called, "Daddy, Daddy, Daddy!" Joy filled the father's face as he quickly rose from the table and walked over to his little boy. Then he lifted him in his arms till his little hand could reach the cup and dip the water. Then he put him down on the floor again, and the little boy took the cup of water to the table. I saw the father drink the water and heard him say, "That's the sweetest cup of water I've ever had in all my life."

That's the way it is with you and your Saviour. He wants you to love Him with all your heart and soul and mind. That is, He wants *you* to obey Him all you can, for all *you* are worth.

MATTHEW 23 SEPTEMBER 3

"Ye pay tithe of mint and anise and cummin, . . . these ought ye to have done." Matthew 23:23.

God Himself established the principle of supporting His work by the tithe of the income of His people. And our text this morning shows that Jesus had no idea of changing that plan. Tithe-paying has always had the blessing of God upon it, and it still does.

Once there was a boy named Samuel. When he was 16 years old he set off to find a job in New York City. On the way he met an old canal-boat captain who was a friend of the family. "Be sure you start right, lad," he said, "and you will get along fine. Let me pray with you and then I'll give you a little advice." After a fatherly prayer the old man asked Sam what work he would try to get.

"I can make soap and candles," said Samuel. "Father taught me to do that, and I will try to find that kind of work."

"Good," said the old man. "Someday someone will be the leading soapmaker in New York. You can be that man as well as anyone. I hope you are. Be a good boy; give your heart to Christ; give the Lord all that belongs to Him of every dollar you earn. Make a good soap; give a full, honest pound; and I'm sure you'll be a rich man someday." Samuel went to the city. He found work in a small soap factory. He remembered the advice of the old friend. He paid an honest tithe. Soon he was a partner in the business; then the owner. Then he decided to give the Lord two tenths of every dollar. His business kept growing. Soon he was giving three tenths to the Lord, then four, then five! Before he died he was the leading soapmaker in New York, and his soaps and toilet preparations could be bought all around the world. Maybe you've heard of him—Samuel Colgate!

Why don't *you* take the advice of the old canal boat captain. First, give yourself to God; second, pay a faithful tithe; third, be thoroughly honest with your fellowmen. Then see what God can make out of *you*.

MATTHEW 24   SEPTEMBER 4

"Nation shall rise against nation, and kingdom against kingdom: and there shall be famines, and pestilences, and earthquakes, in divers places." Matthew 24:7.

How good Jesus is to give us so many signs to tell us that His second coming and the end of the world are near. That day need not come upon us like a thief! Here is a pathetic description of the distress and famine that followed the war in Algeria. Ninety percent of the European population and a million Muslims fled to France. The harvest was left to rot, factories were plundered, and 60 percent of the laboring classes were without work, without money, and without food. Our welfare workers from Denmark quickly collected twelve tons of clothing and food, and soon our Adventist welfare headquarters were set up in our three dispensaries in Algeria. One day a young man came to one of the dispensaries asking for work. His clothes were worn; he looked thin and hungry; but he said he would rather work than receive charity. So although there really was no work for him, the manager told him to come the next morning at eight o'clock and he would give him work. The man came at 6:30 a.m.

"Why did you come so early?" asked the manager.

"I must leave my home before my children are awake. They ask for bread, and I have nothing to give them. It breaks my heart." He was only one father among the thousands of starving Algerian families.

Jesus is indeed coming soon. The poor, starving children around the world are signs that this is so. Are you ready for Jesus to come?

"Then shall the King say unto them on his right hand, Come, ye blessed of my Father, inherit the kingdom prepared for you from the foundation of the world." Matthew 25:34.

I have had a preview of the dividing of the "sheep" from the "goats" at the time of Christ's coming. When we were walking over the border mountains between Burma and India, in our escape from the war, we camped every evening and found that there were always two distinct kinds of people in the group. The good people liked to be together and the bad people liked to be together, so that on one side of the camp the people were kind and helpful, and every night they sang songs of praise to God. But on the other side of camp they were unkind and selfish. They pushed and shoved, cursed and swore, grumbled and growled, murmured and complained. Nobody told the people what side of the camp to go to; they just went where they wanted to go. But I could see that the good people always stayed together in one part of the camp because they had always been good and they could only be happy among good people. And the bad people gathered together in their part of the camp because they had always been bad and they could only be happy among bad people. They couldn't be happy among good people. One evening when we had just finished our soup, some of the good people called out, "Mr. Hare, won't you play your trumpet for us?" So I took my trumpet out of my bundle and began to play "Take the Name of Jesus With You." Now, sitting on a rock near me was a man who stayed on the other side of the camp. When he heard me begin to play, I wish you could have seen him. He listened for just a few seconds to see whether I might play "Roll Out the Barrel" or something like that, and when he recognized that I was playing a hymn he dropped his spoon and his plate, clapped his hands over his ears, and ran off to the other side of the camp, shouting, "I don't belong here! Let me get out of here quick!"

Truly, bad people can't be happy with good people; and bad people could never be happy in heaven. Do you want to be at the right hand of Jesus when He comes, and hear Him say, "Come, ye blessed of my Father"? All you need do is to get on the *right* side with the *good* people now, and stay there every day. Then when Jesus comes you will be there.

"What, could ye not watch with me one hour?" Matthew 26:40.

Peter and James and John did not know that Jesus was about to endure the most important hour in His ministry on this earth when He entered Gethsemane with them. If they had only known that they could have been the most privileged of all men on earth, to be able to encourage and comfort the Saviour when He struggled in the darkness to make His final decision to die for mankind, they would not have failed the Lord Jesus by going to sleep. John could have spoken words of comfort to the Saviour, but he went to sleep and an angel had to do it. Peter could have lifted the Saviour's head and held it lovingly on his breast, but he went to sleep and an angel had to do it. Jesus longed for human sympathy, but His dearest, closest, most favored friends failed Him. They must have been ashamed about it for neither John nor Peter ever mentioned it in his writings.

You and I have been chosen to witness faithfully for Jesus in the very last days of the earth's history. Will we measure up to our privilege or will we fail Him by going to sleep? In his book *More Sermons in Stories* William Stidger tells a little story that I think will help us keep awake. Fifteen-year-old Ron was busy putting a model airplane together one evening when there was a knock at the front door. His mother opened the door, and a boy about Ron's age asked whether Ron could come out for a while.

"Who is it?" Ron asked his mother.

"I don't know his name," she replied.

"Well, what kind of sweater does he have on?"

"I didn't notice."

"Oh, well, tell him I'm too busy," said Ron, and he went on with his work. The mother went to the door and said, "Ron says he's too busy." But the boy answered, "When Ron knows it's me, he won't be too busy!" Then the boy ran around to Ron's window and called, "Hi, Ron! It's me! Come on out!"

"Oh, sure!" cried Ron, "if it's *you!*"

That's the way it is with us. We're too busy to do missionary work for our teachers and leaders, but if we knew it was Jesus calling us to be true and faithful, how easy it would be then to watch with Him for one hour.

"What shall I do then with Jesus which is called Christ?" Matthew 27:22.

Try to imagine how the people felt, and what they did, and what they said, as they turned their eyes upon Jesus hanging on the cross at Calvary that day. The centurion was there. He was a hardened man. He had seen many criminals put to death, but as he looked upon Jesus he cried out, "Truly this was the Son of God."

Joseph of Arimathea and Nicodemus were there. They believed on Jesus secretly, but were too timid to follow Him openly. But as they looked upon Jesus, suddenly they were ashamed of their timidity. They boldly went to Pilate and begged the body of Jesus, and after that they gave their wealth to the church, that the cause of Christ might triumph in the world.

Peter must have been there—Peter who had gone to sleep and had denied his Lord three times. But as he looked upon the compassionate Saviour his heart was broken with repentance. Out into the darkness he went; he sought the very place where Jesus had agonized in the Garden, and kneeling in the same place, poor old Peter wished that he could die. But he came out of the Garden a new Peter, never again to deny his Lord. He truly followed Jesus even to the cross.

The thief was there, and as he looked upon Jesus he believed. While the multitude mocked, he expressed his faith openly, and said, "Lord, remember me when thou comest into thy kingdom." I wonder whether Barabbas was there; I wonder what he did and said.

The priests were angry and jealous. The people were astonished and afraid. But there was one happy man on Calvary that day—"Just to think, I had the privilege of carrying His cross! Me! I came to Jerusalem hoping to see Him and hear Him, and—think of it—they let me carry His cross!" All the way back home he must have told everybody he met. When he got there he must have gathered his children and grandchildren around him and said, "Listen while I tell you about the day I carried the cross for Jesus."

Don't you wish *you* could have had that honor? Only Simon the Cyrenian carried the Saviour's cross of wood, but *you* can carry His cross of humility and service! Won't you do it gladly?

"All power is given unto me in heaven and in earth. . . . And, lo, I am with you alway, even unto the end of the world." Matthew 28:18-20.

God has given unto us the "going" and the "teaching" and the "baptizing"; the obeying, the being kind, the overcoming of temptation; but we must always remember that the power to do these things belongs to Christ. We need never be without that power, however, because Christ has promised to be with us "alway, even unto the end of the world." We can see electric bulbs and electric wires, but we cannot see electricity. We know the electric power is there, however, because when we turn the switch the light shines. Even so, we can see junior boys and girls, and although we cannot see the power of God, we can know the power is in them, because they shine!

Once a little boy was flying a kite, when an old man came along.

"What are you doing, my boy?" he asked kindly.

"I'm flying a kite, mister," the boy replied.

"Kite?" said the old gentleman. "Where is your kite?"

"Up there beyond the tops of the trees. Can't you see?" said the boy pointing.

"No, I can't see anything away up there. Are you sure you have something on the end of that string?"

"Oh, yes, mister. It's there all right. Look! can't you see it over there?" The old gentleman looked, then shook his head.

"No, I can't see anything at all. How do you know you've got something up there on the end of the string?"

"Aw, mister," said the boy, "I can tell by the pull."

That's just the way it is with all of us. If the power of Jesus is in your life, you will be able to tell by the "pull." Is your life *pulling* toward obedience, respect, truthfulness, and faithfulness in your school and in your home? It should be, and it can be. Just make Christ first in your life, and everyone will know it.

"Every soul is surrounded by an atmosphere of its own—an atmosphere, it may be, charged with the lifegiving power of faith, courage, and hope, and sweet with the fragrance of love. . . . By the atmosphere surrounding us, every person with whom we come in contact is consciously or unconsciously affected."—*Messages to Young People*, p. 417.

"And in the morning, rising up a great while before day, he went out, and departed into a solitary place, and there prayed." Mark 1:35.

Jesus kept the Morning Watch! Do you? Jesus got up early and went to a quiet place to pray. You do not have to get up early and go to some special place to keep *your* Morning Watch; you can do it right in your own bedroom. As soon as you awake, with your very first thoughts, say in your heart, "I am not my own, I belong to Jesus." Then take your Bible and read your Morning Watch text; then drop to your knees and ask Jesus to be with you all day, to help you to be good. Then get dressed and see how frequently those first thoughts will come to your mind through the day.

Carl kept the Morning Watch. His mother reminded him, "Someday those texts will shine like jewels in the dark." One evening Carl went to the library to look up some facts for his homework. He found the book he needed, and curled up in a comfortable chair in the corner to read. Then, because he was only a junior, he went sound asleep. At nine o'clock the bell rang. Everybody left the library. The librarian put the lights out and locked the front door, but Carl slept on with his book on his lap. It was midnight when he woke up. For a minute he didn't know where he was. Oh, yes! He had gone to sleep in the library. But there was smoke in the air. His eyes stung! He was choking. There was fire somewhere! For a second or two panic seized him. Then his Morning Watch jewels began to shine in the dark. "What time I am afraid, I will trust in thee." "Fear thou not, for I am with thee." He said aloud, "I will trust." His brain cleared. He was thinking now. There's a telephone! Of course! In the darkness he felt his way to the librarian's table. Could he find it in time? The smoke was getting worse! There it was! He called Mr. Randolph, his employer. "I'm locked in the library and there is a fire somewhere!"

Almost by the time he found his way to the front door, he could hear the sirens of the approaching fire brigade. "Good work, lad!" they said, as they came in and soon got things under control. And by the time he could explain, Carl was the hero of the day.

"But, Mother," he confided afterward, "I couldn't have done it without those 'jewels in the dark.'"

Are *you* keeping the Morning Watch?

"The sabbath was made for man, and not man for the sabbath." Mark 2:27.

We can never fully tell what a blessing the Sabbath has been to the people of God. Mrs. John Baerg wrote a wonderful story about a Sabbath blessing a few years ago in our Sabbath school *Missions Quarterly.*

Down in Brazil there lived a poor man named Rui. He was a humble water carrier, and he was so poor that he even had to borrow the can in which he carried water. Then he heard about the seventh-day Sabbath and decided to keep it. Although he was earning hardly enough money to buy food for his family, Rui decided to pay tithe. His faithfulness to God made him faithful and honest and happy in his work. Soon he had so many customers that he bought his own water can and began to save a little each week in a small bank on the kitchen shelf. Soon it was full, and he bought a little donkey. Soon the bank was full again, and he bought another donkey. He taught his older son to help him in the water business. Soon the bank was full again, and Rui bought a store, and turned the water business over to his son.

After the sun sets on the evening after Sabbath, he puts up a sign that says, "First day of the market." Sunday evening he puts up another sign: "Second day of the market"; and so on till Friday evening when he puts up the sign "Sabbath." Then he closes his store, and as the sun sets he gathers his family and they all sing as the Sabbath begins. Since there are mother and father and thirteen children in the family, the whole village knows when Sabbath begins. Pastor Baerg was spending the weekend with Mr. Rui's family not long ago, and since they were all ready, Pastor Baerg suggested they begin to sing. "No, no, Pastor," said Mr. Rui, "if we sing now, it will throw the village folks out of time, for we always sing at a certain time, and the village folks set their clocks and their watches by our Sabbath songs." No wonder God blessed Mr. Rui and his family! No wonder Isaiah says, "Blessed is the man that doeth this, . . . that keepeth the sabbath from polluting it, and keepeth his hand from doing any evil" (Isaiah 56:2).

Are you faithful and regular in welcoming the Sabbath too? Try it, and see what blessing God will pour out upon *you.*

"Whosoever shall do the will of God, the same is my brother, and my sister, and mother." Mark 3:35.

The late dear old Brother Spicer used to say, "The Advent family is a good family to belong to." And it surely is! There is something about doing the will of God that binds people together even closer than blood relationship. A few years ago Mrs. Hare and I were traveling on the S.S. *Aorangi* to Australia, where I had a program of Sabbath school institutes to attend. As our boat left Vancouver, British Columbia, there was quite a group of Adventists at the wharf to see us off. An hour or two later our boat touched in at Victoria, and there on the wharf we saw another group of Adventists. They were seeing off Brother and Sister Postles and their three children, who were going to New Zealand. We were introduced and, of course, were in each other's company quite frequently after that.

"Are they relatives of yours?" asked Mr. Blakers, a fellow passenger.

"Oh, no!" I said.

"Then they must be old friends."

"Never saw them before."

"Then how come you are so friendly?"

"Why, we belong to the same church!" I explained.

At Honolulu there was another large group down to meet us. They welcomed us with song and with leis, as the Hawaiian people do, took us ashore and later brought us back in style to the boat.

"Just who are you, Mr. Hare?" asked friend Blakers. "Are you some prince traveling incognito?"

"Oh, no!" I said. "They are just members of our church!"

At Fiji there was another big delegation down to meet us. At Auckland, New Zealand, there were some more, and at Sydney there was a big crowd.

"Just what I expected," said friend Blakers. "Everywhere the boat stops there is a big delegation down to meet the Hares! I do declare, before I take my next tour, I'm going to join up with the Adventists! Then I'll have people at every port to welcome me." Many of our traveling workers and church members and hundreds of our soldier boys have experienced the same warm Advent family tie.

Do you belong? Better join up before you take your next-world tour!

"With what measure ye mete, it shall be measured to you." Mark 4:24.

C. L. Paddock tells an unusual story in his book *Don't Rope Those Calves* that illustrates the solemn truth contained in our Morning Watch text today. There was once a farmer who had rented a certain farm for years. He was a good farmer—he kept the soil well fertilized; he struggled to keep down the weeds; he kept the buildings well painted and in good repair; and he had no trouble renewing his lease year after year. However, one day the agent came to see him and said, "The son of the owner is getting married and he plans to live here on the farm, so when your lease expires this year you must look for another place."

The poor farmer was terribly discouraged. He begged again and again for the owner to change his mind and let him lease the farm again. But it was no good. "All my care and my faithful work for nothing!" he grumbled to himself, and the more he thought about it the worse he felt, till one day, just for spite, he decided to take revenge. He went around gathering up weed seeds—seeds from the worst weeds he could find! Then one dark night just before he had to vacate, he moved up and down over the nice clean fields and sowed the weed seed all over them. "There now! That will serve him right!" he said.

The next morning the agent came while he was still doing his chores. "You'll be glad to know," he said cheerfully, "that the owner's son has changed his plans and is going to live in the city; so you can lease the farm again." The poor farmer could hardly believe his ears! He stood there speechless for a moment or two, then realizing what he had done, and the days of toil and trouble it would take to undo what he meant for revenge, he began to tremble, and said, "What a fool I've been!"

The dear Book of God says: "Recompense to no man evil for evil. . . . Avenge not yourselves, but rather give place unto wrath: for it is written, Vengeance is mine; I will repay, saith the Lord" (Romans 12:17-19). And this is God's way.

Life is too short for hate and cross words. You are sure to get back what you sow anyway, so why not sow kindness, courtesy, and helpfulness? Then the reaping will be so much more pleasant.

"They come to Jesus, and see him that was possessed with the devil, . . . sitting, and clothed, and in his right mind." Mark 5:15.

The power of God is just as great today as it was two thousand years ago. A few years ago when Pastor M. D. Howard was superintendent of the Haiti Mission, he wrote a remarkable story in our *Missions Quarterly* about casting out evil spirits. There was a certain evil woman who was envious of a certain younger woman; she wanted the young woman's job. So she went to a devil priest and paid him 350 gourdes ($70) to torment this woman's soul with evil spirits. For a year and a half the poor young woman was frequently thrown about by the evil spirits, who made her cry and shout and say all kinds of terrible things, so that she couldn't work. Then the mother took the young woman to another devil priest for help, and for eight months he tried all kinds of incantations to free her from the evil spirits, but to no avail. She just got worse and worse. Then someone told the anxious mother that the Seventh-day Adventists had power over the evil spirits; so she sent for the elder of our church there. He came and explained that he had no power, but that the power belonged to Jesus, and if they would turn to Jesus and give their hearts to Him, He would cast out the evil spirits.

"We will. We will. Please help us. Tell us what to do," said the mother.

"First we must take off all these devil charms," said the elder. So the mother took them all off. But this made the evil spirits furious, and the poor girl was thrown around till she cried out with pain and fear. Then the elder sang a hymn and read a psalm and prayed. And while he prayed, peace came to the heart of the young woman, and she was calm. She was so happy that she went to prayer meeting that week. But fearing that the evil spirits were not finished with her yet, a group of Adventists went to her house a few days later to pray again. While they were there a strange woman who had traveled many miles by bus arrived, and as she came in there was a most awful noise, as when an angry mob is present. The poor girl was seized again. Then the evil spirit spoke. "I am Lucifer," it said. "For eighteen months I have been after this girl. Today I brought three hundred evil spirits with me, but unfortunately for me, you Adventists got here first, and we found the house surrounded with the angels of Jesus." The Adventists sang, read another psalm, and prayed. They commanded the evil spirit in the name of Jesus to depart. And it departed. And the dear woman has been free ever since.

We don't speak of people being possessed with devils here in Christian lands. But I have seen some juniors throw tantrums and get into fits of temper, and I'm sure it's not the Spirit of Jesus that makes them do that. Do you need some evil spirits cast out of you? Jesus can do it.

MARK 7   **SEPTEMBER 14**

"That which cometh out of the man, that defileth the man. For from within, out of the heart of men, proceed evil thoughts." Mark 7:20, 21.

How many good-looking juniors are spoiled by the meanness and unkindness that comes forth out of their hearts and from their lips! In *Our Little Friend* some time ago there appeared this story about a good-enough-looking boy named Pat. Not too far away, but in the same town, there lived a poor little old lady in a poor little old cabin, but Pat never bothered to become acquainted with her. He and Jeanie, his sister, had seen her gathering sticks in her wheelbarrow frequently, and now and then they saw her counting her pennies very carefully when she bought her groceries at the store. They never learned her name, but I'm sorry to say, Pat called her "Old Mrs. Penny Pincher."

"There she goes again," he called one day. "Old Mrs. Penny Pincher picking up sticks."

Jeanie said, "You shouldn't talk like that. It's real mean of you."

But Pat just laughed and said, "When it's dark tonight I'm going over to Old Mrs. Penny Pincher's and I'm going to scatter her sticks all over the yard."

"That's a mean, shabby trick to play on a poor old woman," said Jeanie. And when the snow began to fall that afternoon she made up her mind that she was going to run over and help the poor old woman put her sticks carefully inside, where Pat couldn't touch them. It didn't take her long to reach the little cabin, and she was just going to knock when she heard voices inside. "She must have company," she said to herself. She was so close that she could hear what the little old woman was saying.

"Dear Father—"

"Why, she's praying!" said Jeanie, as she held her breath.

"Please let these sticks of wood keep me warm until my boy comes home in the morning. My Jim will have money, and he won't let me go cold and hungry any longer."

Jeanie couldn't stand to hear another word. She raced back home and told Pat what she had heard.

Pat's face went red, then white. "Suppose we put our allowance together and buy her a sack of coal," he said at last.

"Let's do," said Jeanie. Mother filled a basket with food. Then over to the little cabin they went. They put their gifts quietly down, knocked on the door, and hurried softly away.

"I wish I hadn't been so mean," confessed Pat. "I feel so much happier this way."

Are *you* ever mean and unkind? Give your heart and your lips a good bath, and come clean. It really is more fun.

MARK 6   SEPTEMBER 15

"And he called unto him the twelve, and began to send them forth." "And they went out, and preached that men should repent." Mark 6:7, 12.

In 1858, only fourteen years after the early Adventists began to keep the Sabbath, a converted Polish Catholic priest, M. B. Czechowski, attended some tent meetings in Ohio and accepted the Sabbath truth. After about six years he wanted the Seventh-day Adventists to send him to Italy as a missionary. When he was told there were not sufficient funds he became impatient and went to the first-day Adventists; and they sent him to Europe. But, strange to say, as he traveled around through northern Italy and into Switzerland, he preached not only the second coming of Christ but also the seventh-day Sabbath! A company of Sabbathkeeping Adventists was organized near Basel, Switzerland, and in a few years they sent one of their men to America to become acquainted with the American Sabbathkeepers. In a few more years they sent another representative, Adlmar Vuilleumier, to plead for help, with the result that in 1874 the General Conference selected J. N. Andrews to be their first overseas missionary. He was sent to organize the work in Europe.

Today, September 15, is the anniversary of the day that he sailed! What a lot has happened since that day when we "began to send . . . forth" our overseas missionaries! And what strange ways God has chosen to open up the way for the message to be preached! One Sabbath morning, soon after J. N. Andrews arrived, the little company in Basel was having Sabbath school when there was a knock on the door. The lady of the house opened the door, and there stood a beggarman.

"Come in," she said. He came in and sat down—and listened to the Sabbath school lesson!

"These people are keeping the Sabbath like the Jews," the beggarman said to himself in surprise. Then he remembered another group of Sabbathkeepers he had met in Elberfeld, Germany. As they talked together after the Sabbath school lesson he remembered that the leader's name was Pastor Lindermann! J. N. Andrews wrote down the name and the town, and the next year he found the Sabbathkeeping Adventists in Germany. Pastor Lindermann had begun to keep the Sabbath from his own study of the Bible, and did not know of any other Christians keeping the Sabbath till J. N. Andrews found them.

What a wonderful God we serve! Study hard, for if time lasts He may need to send you forth, too.

MARK 8   **SEPTEMBER 16**

"What shall it profit a man, if he shall gain the whole world, and lose his own soul?" Mark 8:36.

Do you remember about the image Nebuchadnezzar saw in his dream? Then you will remember that the toes of the image were of part iron and part clay, which showed that the smaller kingdoms into which the Roman Empire broke up would never join together to make another worldwide empire. Someday in a history class you will learn the names of those kingdoms: Ostrogoths, Visigoths, Franks, Vandals, Suevi, Alamanni, Anglo-Saxons, Heruli, Lombards, and Burgundians. Well, now, listen. In the year A.D. 768 Charlemagne became king of the Franks (later called French), and in his heart he decided to conquer his smaller neighbor nations and rule the whole world. So he conquered the Lombards in Italy, the Saxons in Germany, and after fifty campaigns he was made emperor of Rome in A.D. 800. He then ruled practically all the western part of the Roman Empire. But he died in 814, without his dream of a world empire coming true, and was buried in a large marble tomb.

Nine hundred years went by, then one day his tomb was opened. There was his skeleton, still clothed in kingly robes, sitting on a marble slab. His golden scepter was still in his skeleton hand. On his knee was an open scroll, and a bony finger was pointing to the words "What shall it profit a man, if he shall gain the whole world, and lose his own soul?"

Never be deceived by worldly ambition or wealth. The salvation of your soul is worth more than anything else in all the world. Make your soul's salvation the first and most important aim in your life.

MARK 9   SEPTEMBER 17

"If any man desire to be first, the same shall be last of all, and servant of all." Mark 9:35.

Truly great men take pleasure in serving others, and the faithful performance of helpful little acts that no one else takes time to do is a sign of true greatness. Sister White says: "The youngest child that loves and fears God is greater in His sight than the most talented and learned man who neglects the great salvation. . . . Those who feel that they are God's servants will be men who can be trusted anywhere. Citizens of heaven will make the best citizens of earth. A correct view of our duty to God leads to clear perceptions of our duty to our fellow men."—*Messages to Young People*, p. 329.

Some years ago a man was walking down a busy street in New York City when he saw a black man walking along carrying two heavy suitcases. Immediately his heart prompted him to help. He put his hand on the man's shoulder and said kindly, "Pretty heavy, brother, isn't it? Here, let me take one; I'm going your way." There was no use to protest, and soon they were walking along together. The bighearted man learned that his newfound friend was walking from the railway station to a hotel several blocks away because he couldn't afford a taxicab, and that made his helpful deed all the sweeter. He arrived at the hotel before he learned that the man was Booker T. Washington, who later became the famous founder of the Tuskegee Institute. And who was the big-hearted man who carried one of the suitcases? He was Theodore Roosevelt, who later became one of the greatest of American presidents. In the Mount Rushmore National Memorial in South Dakota his head is carved in imperishable granite along with Presidents Washington, Jefferson, and Lincoln!

Always keep your eyes open and faithfully do the helpful little things that you can find to do for others.

"And Jesus . . . said . . . , What wilt thou that I should do unto thee? The blind man said unto him, Lord, that I might receive my sight." Mark 10:51.

My heart goes out to everyone who is blind. Think of poor old Bartimaeus sitting in darkness day after day, year after year, only being able to listen to the happiness of those who could see. How discouraged he must have felt! *Then* Jesus came and changed his night to day. It is hard even to imagine his great happiness when he looked up and saw the lovely face of Jesus. In our modern times we often hear of people who have been blind for a few years having an operation and being able to see again. But here is a story from L. A. Hubbard, who was connected with our Kwahu Hospital in Ghana, West Africa, that tells of a miracle in answer to prayer that brought sight to a young mother named Theresa. She came to the hospital to have her baby, and all went well till the evening after the baby was born. Then Theresa became hot with fever, began to go stiff, and had a kind of fit that doctors everywhere dread. Dr. Hyde was called, and everything possible was done with medicines, treatments, and prayer, and after three days the fit gradually went away and her fever cooled down. But then they noticed unnatural movements with her hands; she had to feel around for the baby's hands and feet. She had to feel around for the food on her tray. They quickly called the doctor, and tests showed that the fit had left poor Theresa completely blind. It was a terrible shock to all the hospital staff. They called in the relatives; then they all knelt in a circle around her bed and prayed. They prayed that God would forgive all their sins and that He would lead Theresa to know more of His will for her, and if it would be to His glory, that He would perform a miracle right there.

They rose from their knees. But they didn't need to ask whether she had been healed. There was a light in Theresa's eyes. "I see! I see!" she said, and a wave of joy and happiness swept through the whole hospital.

There is another kind of blindness that many juniors have. *"I don't see* why I can't go," they say. *"I can't see* why this, and why that." If *you* ever get this kind of blindness, pray God that you can receive your sight too. Then you will be able to understand that your parents and teachers know what is best for you.

"Have faith in God. . . . When ye pray, believe that ye receive them, and ye shall have them." Mark 11:22-24.

Paul tells us to come *boldly* unto the throne of grace, that we can find help in the time of need (Hebrews 4:16). But unless we have *faith* in God and in His promises, we can never be bold and courageous in prayer. One day some years ago, away over in Burma, I was working at my desk when a timid little boy came in and stood beside me. He stood first on one leg then on the other, and opened his mouth to speak, but the words simply wouldn't come.

"Come on, sonny," I said, "tell me what you want! Don't be scared. I won't eat you!"

He opened his mouth with a tremendous effort and said, "Please, Thara—I—please, Thara—I—want a new shirt!"

"All right," I said. "We have plenty of cloth and plenty of big girls to sew shirts for little boys. That's nothing to be scared about."

"But, Thara, I—I haven't any money!"

"Oh, oh!" And come to think about it, I would be scared to go into a shop and ask for a shirt, too, if I didn't have any money, wouldn't you? I soon made arrangements to put his shirt on his account, and away he went as happy as could be. I was still thinking about how scared he was, when another little boy burst into my office, put two-pice down on my desk, and blurted out, "Please, Thara, two pice' worth of soap!"

Now, I was the director of the mission. I didn't sell soap in the store. I had big girls spend regular hours in the store selling soap and pencils. But he was so earnest, so bold, so courageous, and he had his money! I just didn't have the heart to tell him to come back some other time, so I got up and gave him the soap.

"Thank you, Thara," he said pleasantly, and off he went as happy as could be.

When *you* get on your knees to pray, are you timid about your requests to God or are you bold? Have *faith* in God, and in His promises, then *you* too can ask and receive.

"The stone which the builders rejected is become the head of the corner." Mark 12:10.

During the building of Solomon's Temple great big stones were brought in from the quarry to be built into the foundation. Among these huge stones there was one that didn't seem to fit, so it was rejected and laid to one side. But when they finally came to the last corner of the foundation they found that the rejected stone was an exact fit, and it had already been tested with all kinds of weather, so it became the chief cornerstone!

What a perfect illustration this is of Jesus the Messiah. How many people today reject the only One who can help them build a strong character in this world and give them eternal life in the world to come!

The story is told about one of the soldiers of Alexander the Great who was searching for booty in the ruins of the palace of Darius. He was a simple fellow, and he knew nothing about the precious stones. He found a leather bag containing priceless unset jewels, but he did not recognize the great value of the shiny little stones. So he shook them out onto the rubbish heap and eagerly claimed the leather bag! He girded it onto his belt and went around boasting to everybody about the splendid bag he had found in which he could carry his food. Poor, simple fellow, he threw away a fortune and got only a leather bag!

Be sure *you* don't make the same mistake. Make Christ the chief cornerstone in the foundation of your life.

"Heaven and earth shall pass away: but my words shall not pass away."
Mark 13:31.

In the year 1949, while in the city of London, England, I went to the British and Foreign Bible Society to obtain a new copy of the Bible in the Karen language of Burma. My old copy had been lost during the war, and it seemed impossible to get one from Burma. Four years had passed since the war ended, but I was shocked to see so much destruction still visible as I approached the building. I went into the salesroom and made my request. The salesman went to a shelf and came back with a Karen Bible.

"Can you read it?" he asked.

"I surely can," I replied and opened it and began reading. The salesman was delighted. "Just a moment," he said. He disappeared for a minute or two then came back with the manager of the Bible Society.

I told them of my twenty years of mission service among the Karens. I told them I had sold hundreds of copies of the precious Karen Bible. Then the manager said, "Mr. Hare, let me show you around." He took me upstairs. He showed me the room where nearly one thousand translations of the Bible were on the bookshelves. He showed me the "Mary Jones Bible," one of the first to be published. Then he took me into the huge pressroom and told me to look out of a window on the west side.

"What do you see, Mr. Hare?" he asked.

"Just heaps of broken brick buildings," I replied. We went to a window on the north side and another on the east side. It was just the same—nothing but piles and piles of bricks from the broken-down buildings that had been destroyed.

Then the manager, with tears in his eyes, said, "Mr. Hare, all during the war, while the bombs fell all around us and destroyed these buildings, our presses kept running! The windows were smashed and we had to board them up, but we kept on printing the Word of God!" Then we came down to the front lobby of the building, and there in great letters a foot high all around the top of the walls I read the words "Heaven and earth shall pass away, but my words shall not pass away." I think I know why those presses kept running, don't you? There is miracle power in the Word of God. Make that power yours.

"And immediately, while he yet spake, cometh Judas, one of the twelve. . . . And he that betrayed him had given them a token, saying, Whomsoever I shall kiss, that same is he." Mark 14:43, 44.

Because of the mean, despicable act of betraying the Lord Jesus, we are apt to conclude that Judas was all bad—a horrible, ugly, selfish, covetous thief. But wait a minute. Don't be too fast to judge. Judas was a Judean. He believed Jesus was the Messiah, and he actually *volunteered* to follow Jesus! Jesus didn't want Judas to get the idea that this would bring him wealth and honor and fame on this earth, so He said, "The foxes have holes, and the birds of the air have nests; but the Son of man hath not where to lay his head." Then we read in *The Desire of Ages,* "The disciples were anxious that Judas should become one of their number. He was of commanding appearance, a man of keen discernment and executive ability, and they commended him to Jesus as one who would greatly assist Him in His work. . . . When he came into association with Jesus, he had some precious traits of character that might have been made a blessing to the church. If he had been willing to wear the yoke of Christ, he might have been among the chief of the apostles."—Pages 294, 295. He was capable and so clever that the disciples made him their treasurer! How then could this promising man become the betrayer? You can read why in *The Desire of Ages:* "Judas was blinded to his own weakness of character, and Christ placed him where he would have an opportunity to see and correct this. As treasurer for the disciples, he was called upon to provide for the needs of the little company, and to relieve the necessities of the poor. . . . But while listening daily to the lessons of Christ and witnessing His unselfish life, Judas indulged his covetous disposition. . . . Often when he did a little service for Christ, or devoted time to religious purposes, he paid himself out of this meager fund. In his own eyes these pretexts served to excuse his action; but in God's sight he was a thief."—Page 717.

So you see that Judas hardened his heart when he had opportunity to do good, refused to heed the Saviour's counsel, and followed his own selfish, covetous practices until his very name became repulsive.

In one of the large slaughterhouses in Chicago there is a well-trained, clever black goat. Do you know what his job is? Well, it is hard to drive sheep down a narrow passageway to the place where they are killed, but sheep will always follow a leader, so this old black goat mixes around with sheep, then starts off down the narrow passageway, and the sheep follow him down, down to their death. Do you know the name given to the black goat that leads sheep to their destruction? It is "Judas!"

When Jesus said, "One of you which eateth with me shall betray me," one by one the disciples asked, "Lord, is it I?" "Is it I?"

Would you like to know what to do so that *you* will never be a Judas? When your mistakes are pointed out, confess them, and stop following your own selfish ways!

"Selfishness is a deadly evil."

"Selfish interest, if given room to act, dwarfs the mind and hardens the heart; if allowed to control, it destroys moral power. Then disappointment comes."—*Messages to Young People*, pp. 308, 150.

MARK 15   SEPTEMBER 23

"He saved others; himself he cannot save." Mark 15:31.

No truer statement was ever made than that Christ could not save Himself. Jesus came to save mankind, and the price of man's salvation was the precious blood of Jesus. Christ *could* have come down from the cross, but He would not. That is why every sinner can find pardon for his sins and receive the gift of life—eternal life! The Ahoada County Hospital in east Nigeria was staffed by Seventh-day Adventist doctors and nurses. At one time I heard Nurse Maria Moletta, who had just returned from a visit there, tell this story about Dr. DeShay, who was the physician in charge at the time. The doctor had worked a full, heavy day in the seventy-bed hospital. There was morning worship with the staff, and there were visits to the hospital inpatients, two or three hours in surgery, and the usual host of patients in the afternoon clinic. And by the time the day was done he wa␣ ␣oking forward to a good night's rest, when suddenly he ␣␣ard th␣ noise of an approaching group of ␣␣␣␣ ␣.

"Master, Maste␣," they called plaintively. "Our friend is dying. Please come and help!" Quickly Dr. DeShay ran outside, and there at the gate, carried in a blanket, was a poor man who was bleeding in spite of the rough bandages they had put on him.

"Yes," said the doctor, "I can help; and I will, but this man needs some blood. Who will volunteer to give this man a pint of blood?" But there was no response. They were all afraid. "Will no one give a pint of blood to save this man's life?" he asked again. But still there was no response. "Then," he said turning to his assistants who had come to help, "take a sample of my blood and see whether it is compatible, and prepare this man for an immediate operation." The doctor's blood *was* compatible, so he had his assistants draw one pint of his blood and give a transfusion to the patient. Then the doctor operated, and he saved the man's life. He waited long enough to make sure that all was well, then went out to the group of fearful friends with the glad news "He lives! He lives"; and a clamor of thankful voices arose. Thus another life had been saved with blood.

Have you taken advantage of the blood of Jesus that was shed for you? "If there had been but one lost soul, Christ would have died for that one."—*Christ's Object Lessons*, p. 187.

MARK 16   SEPTEMBER 24

"Go ye into all the world, and preach the gospel to every creature." Mark 16:15.

The word *gospel* means "good news," and wherever the gospel is preached, it makes people happy. Not everyone can preach this good news from a pulpit in a church, but everyone can preach it in his daily life by speaking words of kindness and good cheer, which will make people happy. Kind words passed along throughout the day make a lot of people happy.

One morning the manager of a big city store said to one of his department heads, "Mr. Parker, you keep things running smoothly in your section. I like the way you do it."

The kind words didn't cost the manager anything, but they made Mr. Parker very happy, and it wasn't long before he said to one of his salesgirls, "Miss Belle, you have a very successful way of handling difficult customers. I'm so glad you are in my department."

Miss Belle's eyes sparkled with pleasure, and when she went to lunch she couldn't help saying to the girl who filled her order, "It's so good of you to be so prompt. Now I'll have time to do a little errand during this noon hour."

The heart of the little waitress sang all the rest of the day, and when she got home that evening she said to her young brother, "Jimmy, I'm so proud of you—working on your homework the way you do. It isn't every girl who has a brother she can be proud of."

Jimmy looked up in surprise, and all he could say was, "Aw, now!" But there was a warm glow in his heart, and the next day he said to his teacher, after she had explained a problem to him, "You sure know how to make it clear. I wish I knew as much as you."

The tired look vanished from her face. When the teacher bought her newspaper on her way home, she smiled at the newsboy and said, "Billy, you surely are dependable. You'll make a good businessman someday."

And Billy whistled all the way home. At supper he said, "Mother, you sure are a good cook; a fellow can't help working hard—with a supper like this and a mother like you waiting for him at home." And Mother smiled and wasn't quite so tired. Thus many people were made happy, yet nobody thought he was preaching the good news.

When Jesus said to go and preach the good news, He meant *you,* too. Are you doing it?

LUKE 1   SEPTEMBER 25

"The angel said unto him, Fear not . . . , for thy prayer is heard." Luke 1:13.

An angel came to Zacharius. Maybe Zacharius had been praying for a son; or maybe for the Messiah to come. In either case, the angel came to tell him that his prayer was heard. John the Baptist was born to make people ready for the ministry of Jesus on this earth; and six months later Jesus was born. When the angel appeared to Zacharius he said, "Fear not." And when he appeared to Mary he also said, "Fear not." Do you know, when people want to get ready for Jesus to come, Satan always tries his hardest to make them afraid. But I am glad to tell you that there is always a power connected with loving Jesus that helps people overcome all fear.

In Ethiopia, three days' journey from our Gimbie Mission station, there lived a witch doctor up on the hillside overlooking a village. He had several children. His third son, Alemu, had the care of the sheep and the goats. "Did you listen to that stranger down by the river?" asked the witch doctor angrily one day as Alemu brought the sheep back from the river.

"No, Father," said Alemu. But he did not tell him he had heard a few words that had made him hungry to hear more, and had caught a glimpse of a picture that was more beautiful than anything he had ever seen. The next day he lingered a little longer, and the next day a little longer. He couldn't sleep at night. "Heaven," "Jesus," "no more sickness," "no more fear"—the words kept ringing in his ears. The next day as he lingered his two big brothers came down the hillside and grabbed him and dragged him back to his father.

The witch doctor shouted, "Didn't I tell you that this Jesus power would spoil my power to bewitch!" Then he cursed Alemu, beat him severely, and shut him up in the hut. But what he had heard was so beautiful. It must be true. As he thought about Jesus his heart was filled with peace; he was not afraid anymore. He knew what he would do. The mission was only a three-day journey away. He could find his way there; then he wouldn't be tired or hungry again. One night he slipped away into the darkness and became a pupil at our school.

Has the hope of seeing Jesus taken all fear from your heart?

LUKE 2 SEPTEMBER 26

"How is it that ye sought me? wist ye not that I must be about my Father's business?" Luke 2:49.

Wonderful Jesus! He was only 12 years old, but He knew already what He was going to be when He grew up; and there He was, doing His Father's business! A few years ago I heard Elder M. V. Campbell tell a thrilling story about a 12-year-old boy in Rome who also was determined to be about his Father's business. He had just been baptized and was selling books to earn his way through school. God had blessed him, and he already had 50,000 lira saved up. One day he came to a very big house. For just a second or two he was tempted to go past it. But he remembered that he had promised to go to *every* house. So he went to the house and rang the bell.

"I would like to see the lady of the house," he said politely to the maid who opened the door.

"You mean you want to see the countess?" she asked in surprise. "You cannot see her."

"But I have something so important to show her. I'm sure she would want to see me," he pleaded. And he was such a gentleman that the maid finally took him into the front room. When the countess came he gave her his canvass. The countess was thrilled.

"What are you going to be when you grow up?" she asked.

"I want to be a minister," he said.

"Oh, you mean a priest?"

"No, I mean a minister—a Seventh-day Adventist minister. I am selling books to earn my way through school," he said.

"Now, look here, sonny," said the countess, "if you will agree, I will adopt you as my own son. I will give you a million lira and I will educate you for the priesthood."

The boy looked kindly into the woman's face and said, "Countess, many years ago there was a man named Judas who sold his Lord for thirty pieces of silver. But I would not sell my Lord for 1 million lira." When the countess saw his earnestness, she didn't say any more. She just bought his books. That's all we know for the time being, but of one thing I am very sure. The countess will never forget that junior boy who had made up his mind to be about his Father's business.

What are you going to be when you grow up? Have you made up your mind yet?

LUKE 3   SEPTEMBER 27

"He that hath two coats, let him impart to him that hath none; and he that hath meat, let him do likewise." Luke 3:11.

When John the Baptist spoke to the people who came to hear him in the wilderness he summed up a Christian's duty to friends, neighbors, and the world. Whatever we have, God has given it to us to share; and when we share, God always gives back a greater blessing than we had before. Here is a story that appeared a while back in the *Review and Herald.*

Many years ago there was a young man by the name of George Bolt who was a desk clerk in one of the large Philadelphia hotels. One evening an old man came in and asked for a room. "I'm sorry, sir," said George, "but every room is taken for tonight."

The man turned as if to go out, but paused to say, "I'm sorry too, because my wife is ill and I need a room. I have not been able to find one anywhere tonight."

"I am very sorry, sir," said George. "There isn't a room left." The old man started to walk away, but George called him back. "Wait a minute, sir," he said. "I did not say you couldn't have a room. I just said there wasn't a room vacant in the hotel. But if your wife is ill, and if you will accept it, you shall have my room. I can sleep on one of these chairs when I go off duty. Please follow me." And George took the old couple to his own room and made them comfortable.

Early the next morning the old man called the hotel manager on the telephone and said, "You have a clerk named George who was on duty last night?"

"Yes, we do," said the manager. "George Bolt. May I ask what you want him for?"

"Want him for?" said the old man. "I am John Jacob Astor, and I am going to build the biggest hotel in America. I want that boy for my business manager. For years I've been looking for a man who knows how to be kind to strangers." You may have heard of the famous Waldorf-Astoria Hotel, and the equally famous George Bolt who was manager of that hotel for forty years. George didn't have two rooms; he had only one, but he gladly gave it up for the night and received a forty-year blessing.

Try sharing with those in need and see what God will do for you!

LUKE 4   SEPTEMBER 28

"And, as his custom was, he went into the synagogue on the sabbath day, and stood up for to read." Luke 4:16.

Jesus always went to church on Sabbath. No doubt His mother took Him when He was little, and He just kept on going every Sabbath, rain or shine, hot or cold, until it became His habit, or custom. There are thousands of Seventh-day Adventists who have the same habit. They simply couldn't think of staying away from Sabbath school for anything. Among the many inspiring acquaintances I made during my visit to Brazil in 1956 was that of an influential lawyer named Americo Coelho. Now *coelho* is the Portuguese word for "rabbit," so as I was introduced to him, I smiled and said, "Our names are almost the same; mine is Hare!" He was then 73 years old and had been an Adventist for thirty-three years. For most of that time he had taught a Sabbath school class in the little Victoria church in the state of Espirito Santo (Holy Spirit). He had been so highly respected for his honesty and his integrity that once when there was a vacancy in the position of secretary of state, he was asked to fill the position until a new secretary could be elected. In addition to this, he also had served eight years as a judge in the court of Victoria. On one occasion the president of Brazil was to visit the city of Victoria, and elaborate plans were made for his reception and entertainment.

"Mr. Coelho," said the chairman of the committee, "as one of our prominent citizens we want you to be one of the honored ones to meet the president at ten o'clock on Saturday morning, and you will sit on the platform with him when he addresses us."

"I'm sorry, gentlemen," said Americo Coelho, "but I have another appointment, and I cannot be there."

"But this is the president of our country!" they urged.

"Yes, I know," he replied, "but I am teacher of a Sabbath school class at that time, and I must be there." And Americo Coelho was there.

I can well imagine the kind of welcome Jesus, the King of kings, will give him when he goes to Sabbath school in the New Jerusalem. Can't you?

Do *you* have the go-to-church-on-Sabbath habit?

LUKE 5   SEPTEMBER 29

"They that are whole need not a physician; but they that are sick. I came not to call the righteous, but sinners to repentance." Luke 5:31, 32.

In order that we can readily understand how Jesus can hate sin but at the same time love the sinner and have mercy on him, Jesus likened Himself to a physician. In our scripture today we have read of the healing of the leper and also of the man who had the palsy. How kind and sympathetic Jesus was to these poor sufferers! Truly He was the loving physician. In the front lobby of the Johns Hopkins Hospital, in Baltimore, there is a beautiful marble statue of Christ called *The Divine Healer*. I have seen it several times. On the base of the statue are carved the words "Come unto Me, all ye that labour and are heavy laden, and I will give you rest." The hands are outstretched in blessing, and the face, filled with tender sympathy, is looking down in love. Many people visit the Johns Hopkins Hospital just to see that statue, and everyone who sees it is impressed with the Saviour's mercy revealed there.

Well, there is a story told about a certain infidel who heard people talking about the statue, and about the way they felt when they saw it. He heard so much that he determined to go and see it for himself. He went. He looked at the statue, but felt nothing. It was only a piece of cold marble to him. And he was disappointed, for in spite of his unbelief, he had secretly hoped to feel the charm that others talked about so enthusiastically. He looked at it from one side, then the other, and with disappointment showing on his face, he was about to leave the building when a child's hand slipped into his and a sweet voice said, "Don't go away disappointed, mister; you haven't seen Him from the right place yet. Come, I'll show you where to look." And the child led the man to the foot of the statue and said, "There, mister; now kneel at His feet and look up!"

It does make a difference how you look at the Saviour. If you are weary and heavy laden, if you have made mistakes, if you are so discouraged that you don't feel like trying any more, why don't you kneel at His feet and look up! "The Lord is nigh unto them that are of a broken heart; and saveth such as be of a contrite spirit" (Psalm 34:18).

LUKE 6   SEPTEMBER 30

"Give, and it shall be given unto you; good measure, pressed down, and shaken together, and running over. . . . For with the same measure that ye mete withal it shall be measured to you again." Luke 6:38.

It may be only a coincidence, but after giving His disciples the beautiful promise in Luke 6:38, Christ's next words were "Can the blind lead the blind?" This morning I want to tell you about a blind woman who has given good measure to thousands of both blind and sighted people all over the world, and has received again the same kind of generous abundant blessings wherewith she has tried to bless others. Fanny Jane Crosby was born March 24, 1820, in southeast New York. When she was only 6 years old she lost her eyesight through a mistake made by a family physician. It was a sad day for everyone in the family when it was learned that the little girl would never see again. But God had bestowed upon her the gift for writing poetry, and she soon found a way to write verses without seeing with her eyes. When she was only 8 years old she wrote:

O what a happy soul am I!
Although I cannot see,
I am resolved that in this world
Contented I will be.

Fanny never complained, and as the years went by she wrote about six thousand hymns. Some that we sing over and over again are "Jesus, Keep Me Near the Cross," "Tell Me the Story of Jesus," "Jesus Is Tenderly Calling," "Safe in the Arms of Jesus," " 'Tis the Blessed Hour of Prayer," "Rescue the Perishing," "Pass Me Not, O Gentle Saviour," and "I Am Thine, O Lord." When you sing "When my lifework is ended, and I cross the swelling tide" you cannot help feeling the pathos of the closing words in the chorus—"I shall know Him by the print of the nails in His hands." Only a blind person would think of identifying the Saviour by feeling the nailprints. You can also feel her touch in the lovely song "All the Way My Saviour Leads Me." And you cannot help sharing her great joy expressed in the chorus of the hymn "Saved by Grace" where she says, "And I shall see Him face to face, and tell the story—saved by grace." Fanny Jane Crosby blessed the world by giving of her talent, good measure, pressed down, and running over.

What are *you* doing to bless the world with *your* talent?

LUKE 7   **OCTOBER 1**

"This is he, of whom it is written, Behold, I send my messenger before thy face, which shall prepare thy way before thee." Luke 7:27.

Jesus Himself said John the Baptist was to prepare the way for Him, and Matthew adds these words to the testimony of Jesus on the occasion: "If ye will receive it, this is Elias, which was for to come" (Matthew 11:14). John was indeed doing the same kind of work that Elijah had done. He was doing it just before the first coming of Christ, and he was partly fulfilling the prophecy of Malachi 4:5. This prophecy indicates that the same kind of work will be done in the spirit and power of Elijah before the *second* coming of Christ. We believe this is being done by those who are preaching the three angels' messages of Revelation 14. Search throughout the world, and the only people you will find preaching the three angels' messages are the Seventh-day Adventists. This day, October 1, is the anniversary of the day in 1860 when our denominational name, "Seventh-day Adventist," was chosen. As you know, there were many Adventists in the various churches before 1844 who believed in the second coming of Christ. But in that year one group of Adventists began to keep the seventh-day Sabbath. Little by little the Adventists from the other churches joined with the Sabbathkeeping

Adventists until, after fourteen years, there were about three thousand members among one hundred groups. Then a meeting was called in Battle Creek, and the choosing of a legal name for the publishing house and for the denomination was discussed. Many names had been used to refer to the group—"the brethren," "the little flock," "the remnant people," "Sabbathkeepers," and "The church of God," but finally David Hewitt suggested "Seventh-day Adventist," and it was voted and accepted.

Do you remember the name David Hewitt? He was an interesting person. When Joseph Bates first visited Battle Creek he went to the postmaster and asked who was the most honest man in town. And he was directed to the home of David Hewitt. At that time he was a merchant who sold small household articles from a wagon as he drove around town. He was so honest that the whole town knew him as the most honest man in town. He was the first convert in Battle Creek, and had the honor of suggesting our denominational name.

Are *you* an honest Seventh-day Adventist?

LUKE 8   OCTOBER 2

"Return to thine own house, and shew how great things God hath done unto thee." Luke 8:39.

Some of the most wonderful results in soul winning have followed the humble, personal testimony given among friends and relatives. Because the two healed demoniacs went around showing what great things God had done for them, about nine months later, when Jesus came to that part of the country again, more than four thousand people flocked to hear Him and stayed with Him for three days (see Mark 8:1-10).

Pastor Antonio Nogueira, from Brazil, tells this story of the wonderful results of the personal testimony of a young man in that country. In a certain town there lived a young man who was full of life and very talented. His mother was a Seventh-day Adventist, but he had no time for God or religion. He gave himself entirely to the world—its pleasures and its evils. Then one terrible day he discovered that he had leprosy! As there was no hospital for lepers in that town, he was confined to his own bedroom by the doctor who was treating him. The loneliness was awful! His worldly friends forgot him, and he was tempted to take his life. Then one day a colporteur came along and sold him a book. He read it and it changed his life. He became a Seventh-day Adventist, and his heart burned within him to tell his worldly friends about his newfound faith. But how could he do it? A missionary gave him a Picture Roll. He looked at it, prepared a talk on each picture, then hung it out of his window. One day as one of his former friends passed by, he paused out of curiosity to look at the picture. The converted leper told him about the picture and asked him to stop again the next time he was passing. That friend told others, and others came. They in turn told others, and still others came. The earnestness with which the young man told about the satisfying love of God appealed to them, and by the time his leprosy was cured, there were forty-two people ready for baptism. And they all worship together now in the little Adventist church in that town. It is true that there is no preaching more powerful than the simple telling of what God has done for you.

Has God given *you* happiness, faith, satisfaction, and hope? Go tell your friends what great things God has done for you.

LUKE 9   OCTOBER 3

"No man, having put his hand to the plough, and looking back, is fit for the kingdom of God." Luke 9:62.

I can never forget the day that Thara Peter and I opened a school among the Karens at Ohn Daw, on the banks of the beautiful Salween River in Burma. We had been doing dispensary work there for three years, and the jungle people weren't afraid of us anymore. Many were asking, "When are you going to open school?" So the mission appointed a fine young Karen man from the Meiktila Training School, whose name was Peter, to be the teacher. With great enthusiasm we went around everywhere proclaiming, "Next Monday morning at nine o'clock we are going to open school. Be sure to come next Monday morning!"

"Ugh, ugh! Sure, sure!" they said as they heard the happy news. So next Monday morning we opened school. I mean, we opened the schoolhouse—but nobody came. "Maybe they will come tomorrow," said Peter. "You know the jungle people don't know the days of the week very well." So we opened school again the next day, but nobody came. The next day we went to a village eight miles away where we knew for sure we would get two students, and sure enough they were ready. So we brought them back, and the next morning we really did open school.

And while Peter taught the two students, Ton Pein and Naw Too, I went out to gather in some more; but no more came. The next day Peter taught school again with two students while I went out to gather in some more; but again no one came. And no one came the next day or the next or the next, and poor Peter taught school with only two students for three weeks! Then he became so discouraged that he decided to quit. So early one morning he put his bed bundle and his box on his head and went off to the little river steamer landing one mile away. He had had all he could take. He wasn't going to do this one more day! The steamer came, the gangplank was put down onto the sandy bank, and then this morning's text came to Peter's mind: "No man, having put his hand to the plough, and looking back, is fit for the kingdom of God." For just a second he hesitated. Then he thought of me there all alone, and he said to himself, "I can't turn back! I won't run away." And he came back, bless his heart, and taught school with those two students one more day. Then something happened. The next day two more students came; the next day, one more; then two more; and by the end of the next week we had ten students! The next year we had twenty-six students; the next year thirty-four; the next year sixty-three; and later there were more than two hundred in the school!

Have you put your hand to a plow? Stay by it through thick and thin. A blessing must surely come at last.

LUKE 10   OCTOBER 4

"Behold, I give unto you power to tread on serpents and scorpions, and over all the power of the enemy: and nothing shall by any means hurt you." Luke 10:19.

Many promises of comfort and encouragement were given to the seventy disciples Christ sent forth to preach the gospel and heal the sick. It would be foolish for anyone to be presumptuous and deliberately handle serpents and scorpions, and then expect God to fulfill the promise given in our reading for today. But when one is as careful as he can be, and yet accidentally falls into danger, then he can indeed claim this promise. And many experiences have been related to show that God's promises are fulfilled.

Here is a story Elder L. B. Halliwell told in a mission pamphlet many years ago, about two colporteurs in Brazil who claimed this promise.

They were delivering books to the people who lived on the cattle ranches, where they had taken orders some time before. They had heavy packs of books on their backs, and when they came to a big gate that opened into the property of one of these ranches, they opened it and went through. When the gate didn't shut by itself one of the colporteurs stepped into the tall grass to pull it shut—and was immediately bitten just above his ankle by a bushmaster snake. His friend picked up a stick and killed the snake, but what could he do for his suffering companion? They had no medicine with them, and the only thing he could do was to make a fire, then cauterize the wound with the red coal at the end of a burning stick. And this certainly didn't guarantee a cure! But the man who had been bitten said, "No! I'm going to claim that promise in Luke 10:19. This is either the Lord's work or it is not. If it is His work, and He desired that I shall deliver these books, then I am going on; but if He does not wish me to do so, then His will be done." So saying, he picked up his pack and went on his way. The wound never even swelled! And in a few days there was no trace of the bite! The promise had been fulfilled indeed, and the young man went forward with new assurance that God was with them while they were doing His work. Remember this promise; you may need to claim it someday.

LUKE 11   OCTOBER 5

"Ask, and it shall be given you; seek, and ye shall find; knock, and it shall be opened unto you." Luke 11:9.

Our loving God is an all-powerful God with whom nothing is impossible. He does the giving, the finding, and the opening for us. *But* we have to do the asking, the seeking, and the knocking. Here is a story from Pastor M. F. Grau that illustrates the point very well. During the pre-Christmas season a certain large store advertised that a live Santa Claus would give away children's toys at a certain hour, and that the program would be televised. So a fond mother took her 7-year-old Johnny to the store, hoping that he would receive something. The program started. The master of ceremonies took child after child up to Santa and gave his name. Then the child would make his request and receive his toy. It was very exciting! Soon the master of ceremonies noticed Johnny, so he took him up to Santa Claus and told his name. "And what do you want, Johnny?" asked Santa. But Johnny was speechless. He was too timid and shy to say a word. "Would you like a bicycle?" said Santa. Johnny nodded his head, but said nothing. "Or would you rather have a train?" Again Johnny nodded his head, but wouldn't say a word. "Maybe you would prefer a wagon," encouraged Santa. Still Johnny only nodded his head and kept silent. The master of ceremonies smiled and said, "Johnny, you have us all confused. We don't know what you really want. Here's a lollipop for you to suck on while you make up your mind." And while Johnny ate his lollipop the program went on, and child after child received a toy. Toward the end of the program the master of ceremonies gave Johnny another chance, but he still was afraid to ask. "Oh, well, son," said Santa at last, "you'll never get it if you don't ask for it." And the program went off the air. Johnny could have had a bicycle or a train or a wagon—if he had asked for it. But because he wouldn't ask, all he got was a lollipop.

What would you like God to give you? Victory over a bad habit? Strength to say No to temptation? Ability to get good grades at school? Grace to be sweet and patient? Ask and you will receive.

LUKE 12   OCTOBER 6

"Be ye therefore ready also: for the Son of man cometh at an hour when ye think not." Luke 12:40.

Many of the sermons Jesus preached and the parables He told are focused on the importance of our being ready for His coming. In the scripture for today He warns us of covetousness, assures us of His loving care for us, then tells us to seek first the kingdom of God.

After this there follows the parable of the servants waiting for the return of their master; then comes our Morning Watch text: "Be ye therefore ready also: for the Son of man cometh at an hour when ye think not."

Here is a beautiful story to illustrate being ready. I have read it in several books and heard many speakers tell it. A traveler visiting in Switzerland one day came across a beautiful home in the midst of a beautiful garden on the shore of a beautiful lake. It looked so inviting that he thought he would like to visit awhile with the owner. So he knocked on the garden gate, and soon an aged gardener appeared. He opened the gate and bade him enter. The aged man seemed glad to have a visitor and he showed the visitor all around the wonderful garden.

"How long have you worked here?" asked the traveler.

"Twenty-four years," said the old gardener.

"How often has your master been here during that time?"

"Four times."

"When was he here last?"

"Twelve years ago."

"Does he write to you often?"

"Never once!"

"Then from whom do you receive your wages?"

"From his agent in Mailand."

"Does the agent come here often?"

"He has never been here."

"Then who does come?"

"I am almost always alone, except for an occasional visitor like yourself."

"Yet you keep the garden in such perfect order, just as if you were expecting your master to come tomorrow."

"Not tomorrow, sir; as if he were coming *today*," said the old man.

If every one of us could only get ready to meet the Master, then stay ready, just as did the gardener, wouldn't that be wonderful! I'm going to try. Won't you try too?

LUKE 13   OCTOBER 7

"Strive to enter in at the strait gate: for many, I say unto you, will seek to enter in, and shall not be able." Luke 13:24.

The Greek word translated "seek" in today's text also means "desire." So a careful study of this verse indicates that many people would desire to enter in at the strait gate that leads to life, but would not be able to because to "desire" is not enough; a person must *strive* to enter in. God makes no precious promises to lazy people. He wants people who will serve Him with all their heart and soul and strength, people who not only desire to read their Bible and come to church but who also will do something about it.

I like this story about a happy old couple in Brazil. The little old man earned a few cruzeiros by cutting firewood for his neighbors, and the little old lady, with hands all wrinkled and trembling, washed clothes. They could barely make a living. They could neither read nor write, but one day they heard about Jesus' love and began to attend Sabbath school. This was all so new to them—the singing, the lesson study, and the happy faces of those who put their hands up to show they had studied their lesson seven times. How they wished they could read, and learn better, and be able to put their hands up for studying seven times. They more than *desired;* they did something about it. And one Sabbath, sure enough, they put up their hands for studying their lesson seven times. And they were the happiest couple in all the Sabbath school that day. The next Sabbath up went their hands again—and the next and the next. The teacher could hardly believe it, for she knew they could not read, so that Sabbath afternoon she went to visit them.

"You must have learned to read," she said to the little old man.

"No," he replied, "I can't read."

"Then your wife must have learned to read."

"No, she can't read."

"Then," said the teacher, "how is it you can study your lesson seven times?"

The little old folks looked at each other and smiled a big smile and said, "Our neighbor has a nice little boy. He can read very well. He comes every day and reads the lesson to us."

"What a nice little boy he must be," said the teacher, "but does he come every day? Doesn't he miss sometimes?"

"Oh, he comes every day all right," said the little old man, "and I don't think he will ever miss, because, you see, we pay him!" Well, that's what I call *striving* to enter in. They *desired* to learn about Jesus so much that they were willing to pay a little boy to read their lesson to them. It makes me ashamed to think how little I *strive* to enter in.

Don't you think you ought to *strive* a little harder too?

LUKE 14   OCTOBER 8

"Whosoever exalteth himself shall be abased; and he that humbleth himself shall be exalted." Luke 14:11.

Wonderful are the ways of our loving God. He notices when you let others go first, and the times when others received the honor or the credit that should have been yours, but which you so unselfishly let them have; and then, in His own way and in His own time, He lifts you up and gives you more glory than you ever deserved.

During the Civil War there was a fine old soldier that everyone loved, called General O. O. Howard. He was put in command of a special division during General Sherman's last campaign, to take the place of a retiring general. When the war was over a great parade through the city of Washington, D.C., was planned. The former general of Howard's division insisted that he should ride at the head of the division in the parade, because even though he had retired he had served longer with that division than had General Howard. General Sherman didn't know what to do. He called General Howard in and said, "I know you are in the command of that division, and it is your right to lead in the parade. But, you know, Howard, you are a Christian, and you can stand the disappointment better than the former general. So would you mind letting him have that honor?"

"Oh, well, General, if you put it that way," said General O. O. Howard, "that's all right with me. Let him have the honor. Let him ride at the head of the division."

General Sherman smiled and said, "I thought you'd do that, Howard. Now, I want you to report to me at nine o'clock in the morning and ride by my side at the head of the whole army!" Oh, what an honor! But it could only be given to one who was humble.

What is your humility rating? Are you ready yet to be exalted?

LUKE 15   **OCTOBER 9**

"There is joy in the presence of the angels of God over one sinner that repenteth." Luke 15:10.

If there is one great truth that Jesus tried to impress upon the hearts of His hearers above all others it is that our heavenly Father is always more than ready to forgive the sins of those who come to Him in humble repentance and make confession. Here is a story I have heard again and again about a modern prodigal son.

Jim was a good boy when he was little, but as he grew up he got into bad company. He lied, he stole, and he got into all kinds of trouble. Again and again his heartbroken father and mother pleaded with him to make things right and go straight. But the more they pleaded the worse he got, till one day in a fit of anger he shouted, "I've had enough! I'll never darken your door or come into your house again as long as I live." He packed a few things in a suitcase and ran off. But life away from home was not so rosy as he thought it would be. It is not easy for a young man who is not honest to keep a job, and it wasn't long before he was down and out.

The still, small voice that had often tried to make itself heard now spoke louder than ever before. "Go back home! Say you're sorry!"

"I'm too ashamed to go back," he argued with the little voice. "Father and Mother could never forgive me. I've lied; I've stolen; I've dishonored them."

"Go back! Go back!" said the voice.

"They would never receive me—"

"Go back! Go back!" repeated the voice.

At last he thought of a plan. He took a pen and a piece of paper and wrote a letter. "Dear Father and Mother," he wrote, "I've been a terrible disgrace to you. I've lied and stolen and spoken so rudely to you that I am afraid you can never forgive me. I would like to come back home and say I'm sorry, but I am afraid I have sinned against you so much that you would never let me in the house again. I'll be on a train on the first day of the month; if you can forgive me, put a blanket on the clothesline, and as the train goes by I'll see it and know I can come back to tell you how sorry I am." He mailed the letter, and on the first day of the next month he took a train that went past his home. As he neared the familiar scenes—the woods, the factories, the parks—his heart beat faster and faster, "Would they—?" At last the train rounded the last bend. There was his home! And on the clothesline were hanging, not one, but seven blankets!

Our heavenly Father and our earthly parents are just like that. Why be miserable with a heavy sinful heart? Go back and say you're sorry. And you'll find joy on earth while waiting for joy in heaven.

" 'He that covereth his sins shall not prosper: but whoso confesseth and forsaketh them shall have mercy.' The conditions of obtaining mercy of God are simple and just and reasonable. The Lord does not require us to do some grievous thing in order that we may have the forgiveness of sin. We need not make long and wearisome pilgrimages, or perform painful penances . . . ; but he that confesseth and forsaketh his sin shall have mercy."—*Steps to Christ*, p. 37.

"He that is faithful in that which is least is faithful also in much." Luke
16:10.

Nothing is small in God's sight. He sees the faithfulness or the
unfaithfulness with which we do our tasks. Young people who do their
work faithfully seldom realize that anyone is taking notice, and maybe
they will never know the influence of their faithfulness.

Over in Paris there were some Seventh-day Adventist young people
working for a certain airline. We don't know their names; we don't know
what work they were doing; but we do know something about the
influence of their faithfulness. Listen to this. The youth congress in Paris
was just over. And as you can imagine, the youth leaders had had a hectic
time getting the young people on their way home again. At last Pastor
Watson went out to the airport to fly back to London. He went to the
desk to check in. He pulled out his wallet, took out his reservation
slip—but there was no ticket! Where could—? Then he remembered.
His ticket was in his other coat pocket, packed in a trunk that had been
sent by freight to London. "Sorry," said the agent, "but you must have a
ticket." He tried to telephone the office in London where he bought the
ticket to get confirmation, but the office was closed for a holiday! As
Pastor Watson searched his pockets again, he pulled out the SDA youth
congress brochure.

"I've been attending a youth congress," he explained.

"I've read about it in the papers," said the agent. "Are you an
Adventist?"

"Yes, I am," replied Pastor Watson.

"Well, that changes things," said the agent. (Now listen!) "I have
some Seventh-day Adventist young people working for me. I can trust
every one of them, so I know I can trust you, too." He immediately wrote
out another ticket, and handing it to Pastor Watson, said, "If you don't
send me your ticket after you get home, I'll be out of pocket just that
much, for I'm paying for this ticket myself. But I'm not worried. I know I
can trust a Seventh-day Adventist." I wonder whether those faithful
young people know about this yet?

Say, how does your faithfulness measure up in regard to those really
count-for-something activities, such as mowing the lawn, doing the
dishes, making the beds, keeping your clothes hung up and your bedroom
neat and tidy? There are no unimportant things with God.

*"And one of them . . . turned back, and with a loud voice glorified God
. . . , giving him thanks. . . . And Jesus answering said, Were there not ten
cleansed? but where are the nine?" Luke 17:15-17.*

Today people are just about as ungrateful as were those we read about
this morning. Only about one person in ten takes the time and effort to
say Thank you. We are inclined to take all that God does for us, and what
our parents and teachers do for us, for granted, as though the world owed
us a living and we ought to be paid just for being in it. We are quick and
eager to grumble and complain, but how many of us stop long enough to
say Thank you?

There is an old legend that tells of two angels who were sent down to
earth on a special mission one day. To one was given a large basket, and
he was told to gather up all the "thanks" he could find. To the other was
given a small basket, and he was told to gather up all the grumbles and
complaints. "I don't think I'll have much to do," said the angel with the
small basket. "The earth is so beautiful with an abundance of food, with
flowers, with birds and sunshine. Surely no one will be grumbling or
complaining today! I'll be able to help you gather up the thanks. I'm sure
there will be many of them."

But it was not that way at all. As evening came they met, and the
angel with the large basket had gathered scarcely enough thanks to cover
the bottom; and the other angel had carried back three full loads of
grumbles and complaints!

Feel the pleasure, perceive the fragrance, see the brightness in this
little thank-you story from away over in Ethiopia.

"What can we do for you?" The doctor in our Addis Ababa hospital
was talking to a patient standing in line.

"Oh, nothing, thank you," he said. "I was a patient here a few
months ago, and I was cured. So I just came back to kiss the hospital
ground and to thank the doctors and the nurses." Do you wonder why the
hospital workers went around with a song in their hearts all the rest of the
day? There is magic in a sincere little word of thanks. Why don't we use it
more? If you want to feel that kind of magic, just think of half a dozen
things your father, mother, brothers, and sisters have done for you. Then
give each one a nice, sweet Thank you and just see what happens!

"Men ought always to pray, and not to faint." Luke 18:1.

To teach the disciples to be persistent, Jesus told the parable about the widow who would not give up making her request to the unjust judge. How much we all need to learn the lesson of sticking at something until it is completed. Too often we get tired and quit.

The story of Christopher Columbus gives us a splendid example of persistency, or just plain stick-to-itiveness. Columbus was born in Genoa, Italy, in 1451, and as a boy he loved to watch the sailing ships as they entered and left the port. When he was 19 years old he went to sea, and after an eventful seven years, he settled in Lisbon, Portugal. By this time thinking people believed the world was round, and little by little Columbus got the idea that he could find his way to India by sailing due west, instead of going all the way around South Africa. He tried to interest the king of Portugal in the undertaking, but he would not think of such a foolish thing. But Columbus would not give up. In 1484 he went to Spain and offered his services to King Ferdinand and Queen Isabella, and little by little he persuaded them to finance the expedition. On August 3, 1492, he set out with three sailing ships and eighty-seven men. In nine days he reached the Canary Islands and then the excitement began. A week went by. They kept going. Two weeks went by. The men had never been out of sight of land for so long. They were getting homesick.

"The men are discouraged; they want to go back," said the mate to Columbus. "What shall I tell them?"

"Tell them to sail on!" he replied. And two more weeks went by.

"The men are sick and weak. God wouldn't even know where we are if we died. I'm afraid the men will mutiny," said the mate. "What shall I tell them?"

"Tell them to sail on! Sail on!" said Columbus. Then he added, "If in three days we do not sight land, then we will turn back." They sailed on, and the second night, at two o'clock in the morning of October 12, 1492, they saw a light! And on that day they landed at San Salvador in the Bahamas. Because of the fearless persistency of Christopher Columbus, a new world was found that day.

Today is the anniversary of that day! It is a good day for you to get out your "persistency" and clean it up, to make sure it is working.

"Lord, the half of my goods I give to the poor; and if I have taken any thing from any man by false accusation, I restore him fourfold. And Jesus said unto him, This day is salvation come to this house." Luke 19:8, 9.

The day that Zacchaeus saw Jesus, the day salvation came to his house, was the greatest day in all his life. He would never forget that day. There is a beautiful little legend told about Zacchaeus in his old age. They say that he continued to live in Jericho and was a very humble and godly man. Every morning at sunrise he would leave his house and go for a walk. When he returned, his face was always radiant and his heart was filled with joy and peace. His wife often wondered where he went and what he did on these morning walks, but he never told her. So one morning out of curiosity she followed him. Down the main road he went till he came to the sycamore tree into which he had climbed that day when he first saw Jesus. He picked up a water pot that he kept there, went to the nearby spring, filled it with water, then brought it back and watered the tree. He didn't want that tree ever to die. He pulled the weeds from around the foot of the tree, then looked up into the branches where he had sat on that wonderful day. And as he looked he relived that wonderful experience. He remembered the great joy that filled his heart as he saw his blessed Saviour and heard those wonderful words—"This day is salvation come to this house." He wanted to remember that happy day always; and he did. And that is why he was so humble and godly.

Can you remember the day you first gave your heart to Jesus? Can you remember the day you were baptized? Can you remember how happy you were? Think of those days often; talk about them often. Never let them die, and your face will be radiant and your heart filled with joy and peace too. In *Steps to Christ,* on page 117, Ellen G. White says: "Have there not been some bright spots in your experience? Have you not had some precious seasons when your heart throbbed with joy in response to the Spirit of God? . . . Are not God's promises, like the fragrant flowers, growing beside your path on every hand? Will you not let their beauty and sweetness fill your heart with joy?"

"Render therefore unto Caesar the things which be Caesar's, and unto God the things which be God's." Luke 20:25.

Jesus taught that it is our duty to give our allegiance to the rulers of the country in which we live, and there is nothing I love to see more than a group of juniors, either in school or at summer camp, pledging allegiance to the flag of their country. I love to hear juniors in this country say: "I pledge allegiance to the flag of the United States of America and to the republic for which it stands, one nation under God, indivisible, with liberty and justice for all." God has set up rulers and governments, and He desires that we obey them so we might have liberty. I suppose the most popular statue in America is the Statue of Liberty, "The Lady With a Torch," on Liberty Island in New York Harbor. Have you ever seen it? The statue was a gift from the French people to commemorate the establishment of American independence, in which France had given help. The statue was dedicated October 28, 1886. The "Lady" is made of copper sheets over an iron framework and weighs 225 tons. From her feet to the top of the uplifted torch measures 152 feet. She stands on a pedestal about 150 feet high, so the torch shines out more than 300 feet above the sea. The figure is only made of metal, but the spirit of "The Lady With a Torch" has an indescribable power over all who look upon it. I remember when we were coming back home as refugees after the war. It was early morning as we came into the harbor, and suddenly we heard a great shout. Instinctively everyone knew what it was for, and twelve hundred passengers and three hundred sailor boys crowded to the decks to see "Old Liberty." Some were crying; some were praying; two little ladies began to sing "Praise God from whom all blessings flow"; and we all joined in. One sailor waved his hand affectionately and shouted, "Oh, Mother, I'd like to jump right over to you and put my two arms around your neck and give you a big kiss, I would." And everybody cheered because that's the way everybody felt. I can never forget that day, and every time I see that statue it makes my heart tingle.

Say, juniors, open your eyes wide. Try to realize what liberty and justice for all really means. Then see that *you* cheerfully render to Caesar the things that are Caesar's.

"And he saw also a certain poor widow casting in thither two mites. And he said, Of a truth I say unto you, that this poor widow hath cast in more than they all." Luke 21:2, 3.

God measures our gifts to Him, not by the amount of the gift, but by the relation it has to what we have left. The poor widow had nothing left; that's why her gift was greater than all the others.

I found a touching little story in an Australian missions-appeal magazine not long ago, told by Grace E. Boehm, about a little Solomon Islands boy named Gileni. Gileni's father, Pastor Oti, was a Solomon Islands worker who went to the New Guinea islands of Mussau, Emirau, Manus, and Bougainville as a missionary. He was particularly successful in opening up new work among primitive peoples, and spent half his lifetime bringing happiness and hope to unenlightened people. His children were born on these islands, which were foreign to them, and they knew very little about their own relatives. When Gileni was about 12 years old Pastor Oti was given furlough back to his home island, and on their way the family arrived in Rabaul, at the union mission headquarters. Sad to say, several members of Pastor Oti's family were desperately ill with dysentery, and although the missionaries did all they possibly could, it was too late to save Gileni's life, and he was buried beneath the palms in the nearby village cemetery. A few days later Pastor Oti brought Gileni's little suitcase to Mrs. Boehm, and said, "Please take these things and give them to someone who has need of them. Gileni does not need his books or his clothes anymore, and it makes us sad to look at them." In an envelope right on top of his clothes were four ten-shilling notes. Gileni had saved it, and it was all that he had. His father could have used the money, but he said, "Gileni wanted to be a missionary someday, but since he cannot be a missionary now, I'm sure he would want his money to help someone else to be a missionary in his place." So Gileni also gave all that he had. And no doubt, because of his offering some little boy was helped through school, and is now a missionary to those who still sit in darkness.

Would you like to know how large *your* offerings are? Don't measure your giving by what you put into the envelope, but look at how much you have left.

"Satan hath desired to have you, that he may sift you as wheat: but I have prayed for thee, that thy faith fail not." Luke 22:31, 32.

Poor old Peter surely needed someone to pray for him. He thought he was strong, but he was weak. He said he was willing to go to prison and even die for the Lord Jesus, but he denied Him thrice. Sometimes there is a big difference between what we *are*, and what we *think* we are, and what *others* think we are. I was talking to a 12-year-old girl in one of my baptismal classes one day, and I asked, "Are your parents Christians?"

"I don't think so," she said. "They go to shows; they read novels; they quarrel and fight; and we never have family worship."

"Oh, but," I said, "haven't I seen them at church?"

"Oh, yes," she said, "they are church members!" No doubt that father and mother thought they were Christians, but their daughter thought they were not. Who do you think was right? It was something like that with Peter. The people in the high priest's courtyard had three counts on him. First of all, Peter looked like a Christian. He was clean and tidy. He wasn't smoking or drinking. He was different.

"Are you not a Christian?" asked the servant girl.

"I am not," said Peter. Then along came a relative of the man whose ear Peter cut off. He had seen Peter keeping company with Christ. This was the second count they had on him.

"You must be a Christian," he said. "I saw you in the garden with Him."

"I am not," said Peter. Then someone else came along with the third count.

"You surely are a Christian," they said. "You talk like one." And Peter cursed and swore and said, "I don't know Him." They said Peter was a Christian. Peter said he was not. Who do you think was right? If you look in Mark 3:14 you will find that Peter was an ordained minister. If you read Luke 10:17-23 you will find it was probable that Peter was among those whose names Jesus said were written in heaven, and Peter had been following the Lord Jesus for three and a half years. I think Peter was a Christian, all right, but he had sinned and he needed to repent. Thank God, he did repent; and then he knew and everybody knew he was a Christian.

Say, do you look like a Christian? Do you go to church with Christians? Do you talk like a Christian? Do you think you are a

Christian? Do your parents and your brothers and sisters think you are a Christian? Better check up and see what they think. You may need to do a little repenting.

LUKE 23 OCTOBER 17

"Then said Jesus, Father, forgive them; for they know not what they do." Luke 23:34.

How could Jesus plead forgiveness for the people who had turned against Him? "He came unto his own, and his own received him not." He came to save them, and they mocked Him and spat on Him. He came to give them eternal life, and they crucified Him. Then He prayed, "Father, forgive them!" How could He do it? But the wonderful truth is that He did do it, and to those who open their heart and invite Him to come in He offers the same loving forgiveness.

At a Fall Council not long ago I heard Elder A. H. Roth tell an almost unbelievable story about a humble layman who had this marvelous forgiving spirit. Abelino lived in a country not far away, and his heart burned within him to do some missionary work in a nearby town. So he got some tracts and started off. He knocked on the first door, and as soon as the man saw he was giving away Protestant papers, he shouted, "We're not interested," and slammed the door. He went to the second and the third house, and was treated just the same. Then an angry mob gathered. They threw him to the ground, beat him with clubs, and threw stones at him. When they went away, poor Abelino limped to a house at the edge of town. Here the people were kind to him and let him stay for the night. In the morning he could hardly walk, but he went right back to the first house again. "Maybe he will listen this time," he said to himself. But the man was more angry than before, and soon the mob appeared again and beat him so unmercifully that they thought he was dead. But he was not dead, and somehow he managed to get back again to the house where they had been kind to him. You won't believe it, but the next morning Abelino went back the third time to the same first house.

"You again?" said the astonished man. "I thought we killed you yesterday. How many lives have you got?"

"If you only knew how much Jesus loves you," said our brother. "I want to tell you about it so much that I am willing to die if only you will listen." The man had never seen or heard of anything like this before.

"Come in," he said.

"Gather your friends and let me tell them too," said Abelino. And the astonished man gathered eleven men who were in the mob that beat him, and Abelino told them of the love of Jesus. "We've never heard anything like this before," they said. "Come again!" Abelino went again and again, and he formed a branch Sabbath school. Soon there were seventy members coming every week. Then they sent for a conference worker to come and organize a regular Sabbath school, and when he arrived, there were 104 people keeping the Sabbath!

There is a divine power in a forgiving spirit. Do you have a forgiving heart?

LUKE 24   OCTOBER 18

"Why seek ye the living among the dead? He is not here, but is risen." Luke 24:5, 6.

When Jesus rose from the dead He rose to a new life. All who are baptized are "buried with him . . . into death: that like as Christ was raised up from the dead . . . even so we also should walk in newness of life" (Romans 6:4).

I love to tell about people who have found a new joy in living when they walk as Jesus walked. I found a sweet story in an old *Reader's Digest* that illustrates this perfectly. It told of a little old lady who was just too sick and weak to walk. She had her chauffeur drive her out to the cemetery where her son was buried. She stopped at the office of the clerk, and said, "I am Mrs. Adams. You may remember that I have been sending you $5 every week for the past two years to put flowers on my son's grave."

"Oh, yes! I remember," said the clerk.

"Well, I came here today because the doctors say I can only live a few more weeks, and I wanted to have one last look at the grave, and I wanted to thank you."

The clerk listened, then said, "You know, ma'am, I am sorry you kept sending the money for flowers." Mrs. Adams was shocked.

"Sorry!" she gasped. "Why?"

"Because," said he, "no one ever sees them."

"Do you realize what you are saying?" said Mrs. Adams angrily.

"Oh, indeed I do. I belong to a visiting society. We visit state hospitals and places like that. The people there dearly love flowers, and they can see them and smell them. Only living people can enjoy flowers, lady."

Mrs. Adams was too shocked to reply, and in a moment drove off. Some months later the clerk received another visit from Mrs. Adams, but this time *she* was driving the car! And this time she was well and very much able to walk. There was a wonderful smile on her face as she said, "I take the flowers to the people myself. You were right; it does make them happy, and it makes me happy, too. The doctors don't know what is making me well—but I do! I have something to live for now."

It's true! And if *you* are not getting real satisfaction in living, maybe you need to find a new way of life.

JOHN 1   OCTOBER 19

"I saw the Spirit descending from heaven like a dove, and it abode upon him. . . . He that sent me to baptize with water, the same said unto me, Upon whom thou shalt see the Spirit descending . . . , the same is he which baptizeth with the Holy Ghost." John 1:32, 33.

As the years have gone by since the baptism of Jesus, people have come to regard doves, or pigeons, as symbols of the presence of the Holy Spirit, and in front of many of the big churches in Europe today you will find flocks of pigeons. Tourists love to watch them and feed them.

Pastor Jovan Slankamenac sent this surprising story to be used in a missions paper a number of years ago. In a town where there was a big church with a nice flock of pigeons our Seventh-day Adventist believers built a church. It was a simple church building because they could not afford anything grand. So it had no steeple. There was only a sort of attic between the ceiling and the roof, and for ventilation there was a round hole in each end of the attic. The people in that town had never seen such a strange-looking church. Many of them laughed and many of them wagged their heads in scorn. Well, one day one of the pigeons from the flock at the big town church, while flying around, discovered the nice little opening into the nice little attic above the nice little Adventist church, and he went right back and told all the others about it! And what do you think? One sunny morning the whole flock of pigeons flew away from their home in the big church tower and flew right over to the Seventh-day Adventist church and moved right into the attic! At first the surprised people thought it was only a temporary visit the pigeons were making, but the pigeons stayed there! Then the people said to one another, "The Holy Spirit has left the old church and has gone over to the Adventists! We must go and see what is going on there too!" And many people from the town came to see and to listen, and many of them stayed and became members of the Adventist Church!

Now, of course, no church really needs pigeons, and you don't need pigeons, but every church and every Christian most certainly needs the Holy Spirit. Have you opened your heart to let it become the temple of the Holy Spirit?

JOHN 2   OCTOBER 20

"The zeal of thine house hath eaten me up." John 2:17.

In our Scripture text for today we have read about the beginning of miracles that Jesus performed (verse 11) and also about His great enthusiasm (zeal) as He began His ministry by cleansing the Temple. Today is the anniversary of one of the most enthusiastic events in Adventist history—the day when our missionary ship, the *Pitcairn*, began its voyages taking missionaries to the South Pacific Islands. The story of the *Pitcairn* really begins when a 16-year-old boy, John I. Tay, became interested in the tale of the mutiny on the ship *Bounty*. He read about it and became curious about Pitcairn Island and its people. In 1874 John became a Seventh-day Adventist, and his heart burned to take the truth to Pitcairn. In 1886 his opportunity came, and he was able to sign up as a ship's carpenter and go to Pitcairn Island. He stayed there five weeks. The islanders began keeping the Sabbath and wanted to be baptized, but since he was not an ordained minister, he could not do it. But he promised that he would send someone to baptize them as soon as possible. When John Tay returned to America his story caused great rejoicing, and the Adventists were convinced that the time had come to send missionaries to the South Pacific. An attempt was made to send Elder A. J. Cudney to Pitcairn to baptize the people there, but the ship he was on was wrecked, and Pastor Cudney was lost at sea. Then the Adventists began talking about having their own missionary ship. In

1890 the General Conference authorized the building of a ship, and gave the Sabbath schools the privilege of raising the money. Talk about enthusiasm! Fathers and mothers, grandfathers and grandmothers, boys and girls, began saving dimes and nickels and dollars as they had never saved before, and in six months they had gathered $12,000! The ship was built! It was named the *Pitcairn*, and on October 20, 1890, it set sail with its first group of missionaries on board—Elder and Mrs. E. H. Gates for Pitcairn, Elder and Mrs. A. J. Read for Tahiti, and John I. Tay and his wife for Fiji! In all, this wonderful missionary ship made six voyages to the South Pacific Islands carrying missionaries. Then in 1900, because steamship connections had greatly improved, the brave little ship was sold. But the influence of those ten enthusiastic years during the life and service of the *Pitcairn* will be felt throughout eternity.

Have *you* felt any enthusiasm for missions because of it?

JOHN 3   OCTOBER 21

"For God so loved the world, that he gave his only begotten Son, that whosoever believeth in him should not perish, but have everlasting life." John 3:16.

As we think for just a few moments on the words of John 3:16—one of the best-loved verses in all the Bible—we can only say, "Behold, what manner of love the Father hath bestowed upon us" (1 John 3:1). We know that Jesus would have gone through the agony of Calvary just to save one sinner. He would have come to earth and lived and suffered and died just for you or just for me, even if there had been no other sinners! And He would have done all this just for love! In Miss Lora Clement's precious book *Let's Talk It Over*, I found a beautiful story about this kind of love. *Here is a story of such love*

Rena was in a serious accident and had lost a lot of blood. She was rushed to the hospital, and a call was made to the family to come and give her some blood. After tests were made, it was found that only 12-year-old Danny had the same type of blood, and he agreed manfully to give his blood to save his sister's life. The transfusion was given. Rena was operated on and was soon out of danger. But Danny lay in a bed, white as a ghost, and looked almost scared to death. "You saved Rena's life, Danny. Don't you feel proud of that?" said a nurse as she tried to cheer him up. But he could only say Yes in a squeaky little voice that could hardly be heard. A little later the supervisor tried to cheer him up.

"We think you were very brave, Danny. You have done a beautiful thing for your sister." But Danny slid down under the covers and he wouldn't say a word; they could tell he was crying.

"Doctor, please come and try to cheer Danny up," said the supervisor. "He's acting so strange."

So the doctor came along. "Hello there, son. What's the trouble?" he said, and pulled the covers off the boy's face.

When Danny saw the doctor he swallowed hard and said, "Doctor, how soon do I die?" "You die, Danny? You are not going to die. You'll be OK in just a little while; then you can go home." Danny blinked and looked so relieved that suddenly the doctor understood. "Didn't anyone in this great big hospital tell you that giving blood wouldn't hurt you?" he asked.

"No, sir. I thought I was giving my life," said Danny.

Now just think for a moment. When Rena recovered would she ever try to think of things she could do to please Danny? If Danny ever wanted a button sewed on, or a shirt ironed, would she ever say, "Oh, go on; do it yourself"? You know she wouldn't. She would do all she possibly could to show Danny how much she loved him for saving her life.

And that's what Jesus did for you—He gave more than His blood; He gave His life! Will you love Him as much as Rena loved Danny when she got all well again?

JOHN 4   **OCTOBER 22**

"Whosoever drinketh of the water that I shall give him shall never thirst. . . . The woman saith unto him, Sir, give me this water, that I thirst not." John 4:14, 15.

When Jesus talked with the woman at the well, we all know that He was talking about the spiritual water of life, a knowledge of the truth that would result in eternal life in heaven. And we all know what it means to be hungry and thirsty for righteousness. If ever there were people who searched and studied the Scriptures to find this truth, it was the early Adventists. In fulfillment of the first angel's message of Revelation 14:6 and 7, many messengers arose around the world between 1831 and 1844 and began to preach the coming of the judgment and the second coming of Christ. There were men such as William Miller, Charles Fitch, Joseph

Bates, and James White in America; Edward Irving in England; Joseph Wolfe in Europe and Asia; and even little children in Scandinavia, where old people were not permitted to preach. As the Adventists in America eagerly and earnestly studied the prophecies of Daniel 8 and 9, they came to the conclusion that the prophecy of the cleansing of the sanctuary meant that Christ would come on October 22, 1844. As that day drew nearer and nearer they "drank" more eagerly and earnestly of the "waters of life," and got ready for Jesus to come and take them to heaven. At last they whispered to one another, "Tomorrow is the last day! We shall never see the sun set again, or hear the unbelievers cursing and scoffing again. Tomorrow we will see Jesus!" Then tomorrow came. They dressed in their best clothes and gathered in the meetinghouses.

The unbelievers trembled. "Suppose it *should* be the last day!" they said to themselves; but outwardly they were as mean as could be toward the trusting ones. In the meetinghouses the faithful ones watched and prayed. Twelve o'clock! But Jesus hadn't come yet; three o'clock, four o'clock, six o'clock! At last the sun set, the day was past and Jesus had not come. The disappointment almost crushed them.

"Go up! Go up! Why don't you go up?" shouted the unbelievers.

And the children asked, "Why didn't He come, Father? Why didn't He come?" Of course, they soon learned that Jesus had not failed them. They soon learned that cleansing the sanctuary meant the beginning of the judgment connected with the cleansing of the heavenly sanctuary. But today is the anniversary of that sorrowful day, always referred to in the history of our church as the day of disappointment. It is a good day to remember. But *every day* is a good day in which to make sure your sins are confessed and that you are *ready* for the judgment.

JOHN 5   OCTOBER 23

"Search the scriptures; for in them ye think ye have eternal life: and they are they which testify of me." John 5:39.

Almost two hundred years ago there lived in Wales, Great Britain, a 10-year-old girl by the name of Mary Jones. In those days Bibles were very scarce and very expensive. The nearest Bible that Mary knew about was at Mrs. Evans' farm two miles from where Mary lived. One day Mary dressed up and walked to the farm that had a Bible. There she asked Mrs. Evans whether she might read the Bible for herself for a little while. "Of course you may, if you're very careful," said Mrs. Evans. And Mary was left alone in the front room with the Word of God. She was almost afraid to touch it. Then she carefully opened the Bible, and among the first words she read were "Search the scriptures . . . , they are they which testify of me."

"Oh, I will! I will," cried Mary. "If only I had a Bible of my very own!" And as she went home that day she determined that she was going to work and save every penny she possibly could till she had enough to buy a Bible. Can you guess how long it took her? Six years! Then one sunshiny day she set off for the little town of Bala, twenty-five miles away, where she heard that Dr. Thomas Charles had some Welsh Bibles for sale. She walked barefoot, to save her shoes and stockings, but there was a song in her heart because she would soon have a Bible of her very own. She stayed that night at a Mr. Edwards' home, and very early the next morning she went across the street to Dr. Charles's house. She put her money in his hands, then tremblingly asked for a Bible. She looked so hopeful that Dr. Charles hardly knew what to say. At last he sadly shook his head and said, "I'm sorry, Mary, my child, but there's not another Bible for sale. I have a few Bibles here, but they have all been paid for. There is not one left!" Mary couldn't hide her disappointment; she just broke down and cried. Dear old Dr. Charles couldn't bear to see her crying, and at last he said, "Dry your tears, Mary. I will let you have one of these Bibles; someone else can wait."

Mary walked the twenty-five miles home again, rejoicing at having a Bible. But Dr. Charles couldn't forget Mary's tears. He went to London and there told the story of Mary Jones and her Bible to his friends, with the result that they all determined that everybody who wanted a Bible should have one. And in 1804 they formed the British and Foreign Bible Society. This society has printed millions and millions of Bibles since then. When Mary Jones died they put her Bible in a glass case in the society's building. I was there a few years ago and saw it. And as I looked upon that precious, well-worn book I determined to read the Word of God more and more.

Won't you do that too?

"I am the bread of life: he that cometh to me shall never hunger; and he that believeth on me shall never thirst." John 6:35.

If you eat about four slices of bread a day, then in the past year you have eaten at least eighty loaves of bread! And if you are 12 or more years old you may have eaten nearly half a ton of bread in your lifetime, all by yourself! It is because we all know how necessary bread is for physical life that Jesus called Himself the "bread of life." There can be no spiritual life without Jesus. The Bible also has been likened to bread. But the life is not in the paper on which the Bible is printed; the life of the Bible is in Jesus the Saviour, of whom it tells. As healthy, growing juniors get hungry for ordinary bread, spiritually healthy juniors get hungry to read about Jesus in the Bible.

Many exciting stories have been told about what some people have done to keep their Bibles from being taken away from them during times of persecution. Many years ago there was a family named Schebolt who lived in Bohemia (Czechoslovakia). During this time the rulers and the priests didn't want the common people to read the Bible for themselves. A law had been made prohibiting the people from owning or reading a Bible, and frequently soldiers were sent to search the homes of anyone suspected of having one. One day when Mrs. Schebolt was making bread one of the children came running in from outside and said, "The soldiers are coming!" Mrs. Schebolt wasn't about to give up her precious Bible. She thought quickly, and then opened the dough she had just put in her bread pan, put the Bible in, closed the dough over it, and popped it into the oven. The soldiers came; they searched the house; they even looked into the oven; but they didn't find the Bible! When they had gone and the danger was past, Mrs. Schebolt pulled the Bible out of the loaf of bread, none the worse for its baking! The baked Bible was in the possession of the grandchildren who lived near Maumee City, Ohio, for many years.

How much do you love your Bible? How hungry are you for the Bread of Life your Bible tells about?

"If any man thirst, let him come unto me, and drink." John 7:37.

If you have ever been really thirsty, then you can understand how essential it is for our spiritual thirst to be satisfied too. We might live for thirty or forty days without food, but a person can live only seven to ten days without water. Man's body is two-thirds water, and it requires about one ton of the precious liquid in food and drink every year. Many stories have been told about thirsty people, but here is one that shows how thirsty people were sustained by the water of life, which only Jesus can give.

During World War II the newspapers told of a ship that sank near Trinidad. It was not a large ship, and it carried only nine passengers and a crew of fifty. But among the passengers were two missionary families coming home on furlough from West Africa, and in those two families there were four children. Four rafts succeeded in picking up all but seventeen of the crew. In the captain's raft, which was just a small one, eight by ten feet, there were eighteen people, and among them were Mrs. Bell and the four missionary children. It's hard to sit still, all cramped up hour after hour, but these children did! It's hard to have only one cracker and a swallow of water for a meal, but there was no grumbling. It was frightening to see the sharks swimming all around them, but 7-year-old Carol said, "It's almost like being Daniel in the lions' den." Some of the seamen didn't know about Daniel, so Mrs. Bell told the Bible story about him. The men loved it. So Mrs. Bell told Bible stories every day. After a few days the captain died, and finally the drinking water was all gone. What could they do? The children had the answer. "Why, we'll pray for rain," they said. So Mrs. Bell prayed. And it rained. They all filled their empty water bottles. Mrs. Bell prayed for it to stop raining so they could get dry again, and it stopped raining. Then an airplane found them and dropped them some food. Days later a convoy picked them up and took them to Barbados. Every man on the raft agreed that it was the faith of those little children that had kept them all alive.

You seldom suffer with thirst; you have plenty of water to drink every day. And why let your spiritual life get all dried up? You can read about Jesus and think about Jesus and talk to Jesus every day. Be sure you do it.

"I am the light of the world: he that followeth me shall not walk in darkness, but shall have the light of life." John 8:12.

In another verse Jesus said, "Ye are the light of the world." Now, we all know Jesus was not talking about physical light, but about spiritual light; and we all know equally well that nobody can do deeds of love, purity, kindness, and truth unless Jesus lives within him and shines out of his heart. Here is a story that appeared in the *Youth's Instructor* a long time ago, and it illustrates this fact very well. A certain good man brought an Indian, Chief Eagle Eye, from the northland to the United States to be educated and sent back as a teacher to his own people. Chief Eagle Eye had never ridden on a train before. "What make him go?" he asked excitedly. "No dogs pull! Nothing pull!"

The man showed Chief Eagle Eye the engine and said, "Fire inside! Fire make him go!"

From the station they rode in a taxi to the hotel. There was no steam engine pulling the taxi, and Chief Eagle Eye was still puzzled. "What make him go?" he asked again, and the man replied, "Fire inside."

Arriving at the hotel, they went up to their room in the elevator, and Chief Eagle Eye felt afraid. "What make him go? Fire inside?" he asked.

"Yes," replied his friend. "Fire inside."

In the room the man switched on the light. "Ugh," said Chief Eagle Eye, "where light come from? You no strike match." The man switched off the light. "Ugh, where light go? You no blow out." The man unscrewed the bulb, turned the switch on, and told him to put his finger in. Chief Eagle Eye put his finger in, then nearly jumped out of his skin. "Ugh! Fire inside! Fire inside!" he said.

One day the man called Chief Eagle Eye on the telephone, and by this time he knew the answer. "Ugh," he said, "fire inside. Little box he talk." Then one day there was a terrible thunder and lightning storm and all the city fuses were blown. The room was in darkness and everything stopped. Eagle Eye thought for a moment, then said, "Light, he gone. Up and down basket, he dead. Little box, he no talk. What matter? No fire inside?" Chief Eagle Eye had discovered the reason, all right. And if ever you see a junior whose light has gone out, a junior who is unkind, impure, or dishonest, it is simply because there is no "fire" inside.

"One thing I know, that, whereas I was blind, now I see." John 9:25.

The haughty Pharisees refused to believe that Christ had opened the eyes of the man who had been born blind. To refuse to believe the words and the work of Christ is spiritual blindness, and that is even worse than physical blindness. For the eyes of the physically blind who believe will see throughout eternity, but the eyes of those who refuse to believe will not see beyond this short life on earth. The man who was born blind rejoiced, because whereas he was blind, now through the power of Christ he could see.

Do you know that this same power is being manifested today? Listen! Over in Angola, in a little village not far from our Bongo Mission Hospital, there lived a man by the name of Manjata. According to the story told by Dr. Roy Parsons in a world missions paper, Manjata had worked hard, and he owned a farm, two bullocks, and a plow. His only son, Dolino, had grown to manhood, and Manjata should have been the happiest man in the village; but he became blind. He was unable to work in the fields. For three years Manjata's wife did the work and cared for him, but he was unable to repair his house. He had to live with his son. But Dolino was not kind to his poor old blind father. You can hardly believe how mean he was. He secretly sold his father's farm, his plow, his bullocks, and even the corn that had just been harvested. Then one night while his father and mother were asleep Dolino went away with his family to a faraway village, leaving poor old Manjata and his wife to get along as best they could.

Two more years went slowly by and old Manjata wished he could die. Then an Adventist man, Samuel Bongue, bought a garden near Manjata's house. Now Samuel had worked in the dispensary years before, and when he saw Manjata's eyes he said, "Why, Manjata, you have cataracts! The doctor at our Bongo hospital can operate and make you see again!" Manjata believed, and Samuel brought him to the hospital where Dr. Roy Parsons operated on his eyes. In ten days off came the bandages, and he could see! He stayed at the hospital for nearly one month, rejoicing every day. By that time his spiritual eyes were open too, and Manjata went back to his village a new and happy man.

Because you have eyes that can see, don't be satisfied. Pray that your spiritual eyes will be able to see too. That is what counts most.

"The sheep hear his voice. . . . And when he putteth forth his own sheep, he goeth before them, and the sheep follow him: for they know his voice." John 10:3, 4.

The voice of God sounded like thunder at Mount Sinai, and also when He glorified Christ on the last day of His public ministry (John 12:28, 29). But when God spoke to Elijah He used the still, small voice of the Holy Spirit. It is the still, small voice with which we are most familiar. "Another way in which God's voice is heard is through the appeals of His Holy Spirit, making impressions upon the heart."—*Messages to Young People,* p. 156. Many people have had such clear, distinct impressions that they were almost like an audible voice. Sometimes the still, small voice gives reproof, sometimes instruction, and sometimes encouragement.

I will always remember one time when I heard the "voice of God." It was in the early days of my ministry in Burma. I had learned the language. That was easy. I was having success in my dispensary. That was easy. But I couldn't get the jungle people interested in the gospel. They wouldn't come to Sabbath school. I took my trumpet and a bag of medicines and a Picture Roll to a village, and sheer curiosity made them listen to the first meeting. But when I came the next week, as I had announced, the village was empty except for three old grandmas who wouldn't even listen to me when I began to tell about Jesus with the Picture Roll. I was so discouraged. I sent Mrs. Hare and our dispensary helper back home by canoe, but I walked home through the jungle. I wanted to be alone. I had tried everything I could to get them interested in the gospel, but nothing seemed to do any good, and in the agony of my heart I cried, "Lord! I can't do it!"

Then I heard it, just as clear as a voice. It was the voice of God—I know it was—and it said, "I know you can't. I've been waiting for you to realize that *you* don't have the power to change hearts. That's My work. I alone have that power. Just be faithful sowing the seed. I will give the increase. 'My word shall not return unto me void.' "

Oh, what wonderful words! My discouragement vanished. "Yes, Lord," I said, "I can keep sowing the seed, and I will." And I did. And as the voice had promised, before long the change came.

When you talk to God, take time to wait and listen to see what the voice of God will say to you.

317

"Jesus wept. Then said the Jews, Behold how he loved him!" John 11:35, 36.

Verse 5 of today's Scripture reading tells us that Jesus "loved Martha, and her sister, and Lazarus." And when the messengers went to call on Jesus they said, "He whom thou *lovest* is sick." The love of Jesus is the most wonderful love in all the world. It is so wonderful that sometimes it is hard to understand. Jesus could have gone to Lazarus as soon as He was called, and He would have performed a miracle and healed his sickness, and everybody would have been happy. But in His great love Jesus waited until Lazarus was dead. Then He went. And then He performed a much greater miracle. He raised Lazarus from the dead! This in turn produced much greater happiness. That's the way Jesus loves everybody. His love is likened to a father's love, a mother's love, a friend's love. Writers have used many words to describe it. They have called it great, wonderful, and everlasting, but Paul sums them all up when he says, "The love of Christ passeth knowledge." Poets and musicians have written countless songs about the love of Jesus, but perhaps the most loved and the most widely known is "Jesus loves me! this I know, for the Bible tells me so." Those precious words were written by Anna Warner, a Sunday school teacher at West Point, New York, in 1852. She wrote the hymn for the little children in her Sunday school, little dreaming that the whole world would fall in love with it. It was first published in London in 1853, and soon after spread round the world. You will remember that we date the beginning of our Sabbath schools also from the year 1852. So that lovely little song is just as old as our Sabbath schools, and it is interesting to know that wherever our missionaries go, as soon as the name of Jesus is known, and a Sabbath school is formed, that beautiful song is translated into the language of the people first of all; and fathers and mothers, grandfathers and grandmothers, little and big children, all join in singing "Yes, Jesus loves me; yes, Jesus loves me; the Bible tells me so." Always remember that Jesus loves everybody—the people who are kind and who love Him and those who are mean and do not love Him.

Yes, He loves *you*, too, when you're good or when you're bad. He dislikes the bad things you do, but He always loves you.

"And I, if I be lifted up from the earth, will draw all men unto me." John 12:32.

Because Jesus died on the cross, multitudes of every kindred, tongue, and people have been drawn to Him. If Christians lift up Christ in their own life—if they are kind like Jesus, patient like Jesus, thoughtful like Jesus—then all people will be drawn to Him.

In the *Youth's Instructor* a number of years ago I found a story about a little Christian nurse called Annabelle who did this very thing in one of our sanitariums, and found that it was true. There was a very fretful woman patient brought to a room on Annabelle's floor. She was sick and she was restless, but Annabelle did all she could to make her as comfortable as possible, and as she patted the woman's hands sympathetically when she came to say good night, she smiled and said, "Would you like me to pray for you before I go?"

"No," answered the woman sharply.

"Well, then, have a restful sleep and pleasant dreams," said Annabelle with a smile as she went out.

"She's so cross and unreasonable and unappreciative," she confided to Grace, her roommate, that night.

"Forget it, honey," said Grace. "Tomorrow will be a new day, and maybe she will be different." Tomorrow came, but the woman didn't sweeten up one bit. She was just the same the next day and the next and the next, and Annabelle found it all she could do to be sweet. But she was always kind and patient with her. Finally the woman got better and went home. Annabelle was almost glad to see her go. A year went by. Then one day Annabelle received a pressing invitation to come and visit in this woman's home. She almost dreaded to go, but what a surprise awaited her! A gracious, charming woman welcomed her. "You were so kind to come," she said. "Do you remember the night you asked me whether I would like to have you offer a prayer and I said No? I have never forgotten your kindness and cheerfulness in spite of my peevish impatience. You are a Seventh-day Adventist. Please tell me what Adventists believe. I would like to be the kind of Christian you are."

Would anyone want to be the kind of Christian you are? They will if you lift Jesus up in your life.

"What I do thou knowest not now; but thou shalt know hereafter." John 13:7.

Jesus did many things and said many things that the disciples could not understand at the time, but even as Jesus promised, in the words of our Bible text for today, the time surely did come when they understood not only what He said and did but also why. I think many of the answers to our prayers are hard to understand now, but I am sure that in the "hereafter" we shall know and understand.

Moses prayed, "O Lord God, . . . let me go over, and see the good land that is beyond Jordan."

But the Lord said, "No, thou shalt not go over." But some time *after,* Michael the archangel came and resurrected Moses and took him to heaven! Then Moses understood why God had said No. It was because He had a better answer for him.

Elder Steen Rasmussen used to tell a story about six Seventh-day Adventist miners in Yugoslavia. One day as they were being paid their wages the manager said, "Men, I have to lay off twenty men. So do not come back to work till we call you again."

"But, sir, we have wives and families. Why don't you lay off only the single workers?" they pleaded. But it was no use; the manager wouldn't listen; and the men went home discouraged. They prayed about it at home and pleaded with God to help them get their work back again. The next day they went back to the manager of the mine and begged to be reemployed, but without success. They must have felt that the Lord had forgotten them or had turned a deaf ear to their prayers.

But a few days *after* their dismissal, a terrible explosion occurred in the mine where they had been working, killing scores of the workers, including the men who were working where they had been! Then, of course, they understood why God had permitted them to be laid off, and they praised His name for saving their lives.

When you have committed your way to the Lord, trust Him to give you the right answer even though you may not understand it now. You will surely know "hereafter."

"Let not your heart be troubled: ye believe in God, believe also in me. In my Father's house are many mansions: if it were not so, I would have told you. I go to prepare a place for you. And if I go and prepare a place for you, I will come again, and receive you unto myself; that where I am, there ye may be also." John 14:1-3.

The promises recorded in John 14 sustain and support all whose hearts are troubled. They fill their hearts with hope, because the day will come when there will be no more sorrow, no more tears, and no more death.

As an example of the sustaining hope the words "I will come again" can give, let me tell you about General MacArthur. Douglas MacArthur was born in Little Rock, Arkansas, January 26, 1880. He graduated from the U.S. Military Academy at West Point in 1903. After a colorful and successful career he was appointed military adviser to the newly created Philippine Commonwealth in 1935. On December 7, 1941, the enemy suddenly attacked Pearl Harbor, in Hawaii, thus forcing the United States into World War II. In the face of superior forces, the U.S. division in the Philippines suffered temporary defeat, and in March, 1942, General MacArthur was ordered to Australia to become commander of all the South Pacific troops and to make preparation to liberate the islands from the hand of the enemy. As he left Corregidor by night in a Navy torpedo boat, he said to the Filipinos, *"I shall return!"* What wonderful words! They were whispered from trench to trench, from village to village, from prison camp to prison camp, from hospital to hospital. "He will come again!" The people knew Douglas MacArthur. They believed he *would* come, and in a little more than two years, on October 20, 1944, he *did* come back. His return struck terror to the hearts of the enemy but brought great rejoicing to the suffering people. Step by step his troops marched forward; island after island was liberated; and in six months the Philippines was free! Only those who were there can picture the rejoicing. Prisoners were released; families were reunited. People wept for joy and danced in the streets.

It will be better than that when Jesus comes again. He said He would come. Believe it. He *will come* someday, and it must be soon. What a day of rejoicing that will be!

"I am the vine, ye are the branches: He that abideth in me, and I in him, the same bringeth forth much fruit: for without me ye can do nothing." John 15:5.

The longer you live, the more you will realize that you need power and life from the Lord Jesus in order to make a real success of anything, for without Him you "can do nothing."

There is a lovely story told about a little girl and her mother who were staying at a hotel in Switzerland. The mother insisted that the little girl keep up her piano practice while they were on vacation, so every day right after lunch the little girl would go to the piano in the lounge room and do her five-finger exercises and play her one-finger tunes. Over and over for a whole half hour she would do them, till the guests couldn't stand it; and one by one they would get up and leave the room. As the days went by, the guests became very weary of the performance, but they were too polite to complain. Then one day one of the guests came and stood beside the little girl for a moment, then said, "Move up a little and make room for me." She moved up and the guest sat down beside her. "Now play those exercises again and I'll play with you," he said. And while she strummed away on her same five-finger exercises, the guest put his arm around the little one and with his two skillful hands improvised a most beautiful melody. The guests heard the difference at once! Who could it be? They had seen the little girl sitting down at the piano as they left, but she couldn't be responsible for this beautiful harmony! One by one the guests returned. They saw the man sitting beside the little girl. They saw them playing together. "Who is that man?" they asked the hotel manager.

"The great pianist Josef Hofmann," he whispered. "He is spending his vacation here under another name just to have a little rest." The little girl alone nearly drove them crazy. But the little girl and the great pianist together produced pleasing, delightful music.

That is the way it is with us. Alone we often play the wrong notes and do not get the time right. At best our efforts are not at all melodious or satisfactory, but if we will "move up a little" and make room for the Master in our life, then His life and ours together will produce sweet harmonies.

"I will see you again, and your heart shall rejoice, and your joy no man taketh from you." John 16:22.

There is such a difference between the clean, satisfying joy of a Christian and the transitory pleasure that the world offers and that so often is mixed with regrets. Jesus said, "Your joy no man taketh from you." But in Job 20:5, we read: "The triumphing of the wicked is short, and the joy of the hypocrite but for a moment." A number of years ago while we were living on our Karen mission station in Burma, our three little nephews—Edwin, Wilfred, and Buddy—and their mother came to visit us. One day 7-year-old Wilfred was blowing soap bubbles in a room next to my office. He was having tremendous success and wanted me to share in his pleasure. "Oh, Uncle, come and see," he called with great enthusiasm. "What a beauty! Oh, Uncle!" But I was very busy and made no response. "Oh, Uncle, there's another! What a beauty! Oh, Uncle, there's another! What a beauty! Oh, Uncle, come quickly!" His enthusiasm was so contagious that at last I stood up. "Come on, Uncle! There's another. Oh, what a beauty." I went to the door, and encouraged by my movement, Wilfred shouted still louder. "There's another, oh, Uncle!" I opened the door, but as I did so I heard him say, "Aw, Uncle, it's busted!" That reminded me of that verse in Job that says the joy of the hypocrite is but for a moment. Probe into the reasons for the great army of alcoholics that are found in our land, or into the background of the thousands of suicides we have every year, and you will find that the pleasures of life for these unfortunates proved disappointing, and that laughter and excitement yielded only fleeting satisfactions, and they sought a way of escape. They reached for the beautiful bubble, but it "busted" before they even touched it!

Don't you be disappointed. Make God first and last and best in your life, and no man will be able to take your joy from you. David says, "In thy presence is fulness of joy; at thy right hand there are pleasures for evermore" (Psalm 16:11). And Seventh-day Adventist young people the world around bear witness to the fact that those who find their recreation where Jesus can be present do indeed have fullness of joy in physical and mental activities, unmarred with the sorrows of regret and remorse.

"The world hath hated them, because they are not of the world, even as I am not of the world. I pray not that thou shouldest take them out of the world, but that thou shouldest keep them from the evil." John 17:14, 15.

What a beautiful thought—that Jesus prayed for His children! And this prayer—that His children who are *in* the world should not be *of* the world in thought or word or action—has been granted again and again down through the centuries.

A good example of this was given by the students of Oakwood College when it was first founded. An old plantation was bought near Huntsville, Alabama. The land was worked out and the buildings were run down, but worse than that, the nearby neighbors were definitely hostile toward having a school near them sponsored by Northerners. However, Principal S. M. Jacobs and his students went to work with a will, and they soon had the buildings in shape for use and the farm doing as well as possible. Then one day one of the neighbors who was most bitter in his tirades had a terrible misfortune. His barn caught on fire and burned down. His work animals and farm machinery were all destroyed. The next morning Principal Jacobs called the boys together for worship, and after prayer they briefly discussed the neighbor's plight.

"Would any of you boys volunteer to give him a helping hand?" he asked. Every hand went up. They promptly hitched the horses up to the cultivators and drove over to the neighbor's place.

"What do you want?" the farmer asked angrily.

"Why, we've come to plant your corn," said Mr. Jacobs. It took a few seconds for the angry man to get the idea.

"Is that the kind of people you are?"

"That's the kind of people we are," they answered.

"Well, just a moment before you get started," said the man. "I've said some mighty hard things against you people for starting that school. Now I ask you to forgive me for all I've said."

"We have forgiven you long ago. That's why we are here," said Mr. Jacobs. And they went to work. They planted the corn and stopped at noon to eat their lunch.

"Oh, no, you don't," shouted the farmer. "My wife has dinner ready, and we'll all eat together today." As you can imagine, the grateful farmer told the story all around, and that was the end of the hostility and the bitter words. That's the spirit this bitter old world needs.

"If my kingdom were of this world, then would my servants fight, that I should not be delivered to the Jews: but now is my kingdom not from hence." John 18:36.

Seventh-day Adventists are loyal citizens in whatever country they live. They are honest. They pay their taxes, salute the flag, sing the national anthem, and repeat the pledge of allegiance. They believe that the principles of government were established by God, and in harmony with the teaching of Christ they are proud and happy to "render to Caesar the things that are Caesar's." However, they also believe that there are certain things that are God's, and they are equally as loyal in rendering to God the things that are His. In 1863 the General Conference organization was made a legal body. This was in the midst of the Civil War, so as soon as possible a statement was drawn up giving the reasons for Seventh-day Adventists' being noncombatants, and the next year, 1864, J. N. Andrews was sent to Washington, D.C., to present our position to the Provost Marshal General. He was kindly received by Brigadier General James B. Fry, and we were finally classed with the Quakers and granted exemption from bearing arms.

Our men who were called up by the draft were assigned to hospital and other noncombatant duties. During World War I, however, our position was not well enough known to benefit all of our men who were called up, with the result that a number of them suffered court-martial and imprisonment for keeping the Sabbath. After the war E. N. Dick, who had been a Marine during the war, felt we ought to do something about preparing our young men for hospital work in the event of a future war, with the result that our Medical Cadet Corps was founded. Those who organized the Corps chose for their motto "God First Always." The Medical Cadet Corps has given intensive basic and medical training to thousands of our young men, with the result that all who take the training are readily classed 1AO and are given noncombatant duties. Today we have the Medical Cadet program in all of our North American conferences as well as in Japan, Korea, Indonesia, the Philippines, Brazil, and the British colonies. In a few years you boys should be planning to take the Medical Cadet Corps training.

"When Jesus therefore had received the vinegar, he said, It is finished: and he bowed his head, and gave up the ghost." John 19:30.

From the foundation of the world, from the time when God had created man, Christ had been coming nearer and nearer to the time when His paying the price for man's salvation would be accomplished. For four thousand years all heaven had looked on at the great controversy between Satan and his forces and Christ and His forces. What sadness there was when Cain killed Abel, and when the world mocked at Noah, and when Israel worshiped idols! But what great rejoicing there was when Enoch walked with God, when Noah and his sons entered the ark, when faithful Abraham went forth, and when Moses chose to suffer affliction with the people of God rather than to enjoy the pleasures of sin. Then Jesus came; Mary, Martha, Lazarus, Peter, James, John, and a few more than a hundred others believed on Him. But His own nation received Him not. They mocked Him. They spat on Him. They crucified Him. But there on the cross, the price of man's redemption was paid, so that whosoever would believe on Him could have eternal life.

There's a lovely story told about a little boy who made a boat. With his father's help it was shaped and painted. He put a mast in it and put some sails on it, then proudly took it to the park to sail it in the lake. He had a long string tied to it, and joyfully he watched his little boat sail farther and farther out on the water. Suddenly the string slipped out of his hand, and he could not bring his boat back. He called for help, but there was none, so he ran home to bring his father. By the time they got to the lake, however, the little boat was gone. Someone had found it and taken it. The little boy was heartbroken.

One day while downtown he saw *his* boat in a toy shop window. Of course it was his boat. He could tell by the size, the paint, the mast, and the sails. But rather than start an argument with the shop owner, he went in and bought it. He paid the price for it. Then he went home, hugging his little boat to his heart while he said, "Dear little boat, how I love you! You are mine, twice mine, for I made you and now I have bought you."

That's what Jesus says about you and me. "O how I love you. You are Mine, twice Mine, for I made you and I have bought you!" Won't you believe Him and accept Him?

"Jesus saith unto him, Thomas, because thou hast seen me, thou hast believed: blessed are they that have not seen, and yet have believed." John 20:29.

The name of Thomas has come down through the years as one who would not believe unless he saw with his own eyes and felt with his own hands. Remember, Jesus blessed those who believed on Him without seeing! Once upon a time, the story goes, a young man who didn't believe in God was traveling on a boat. On the same boat there was a godly old minister who was also a passenger. One day they got into conversation, and the young man ridiculed the idea of anybody believing anything he hadn't seen.

"You believe many things you haven't seen," said the old minister.

"No I don't," said the young man.

"You believe there is a country called England, don't you?"

"Of course!"

"But you have never seen it."

"No, but others have."

"Oh, I see," said the minister. "Then it's only the things you have seen or that someone else has seen that you believe."

"That's it," said the young man confidently. The old minister looked at him with a half smile on his face and said, "Have you ever seen your brain?"

"Well—er—"

"Has anyone else ever seen your brain?"

"No, but—"

"Do you believe you have a brain?" asked the old man; and the young man went away feeling very uncomfortable.

I like the answer a good old fisherman gave to a man who asked him how he knew there was a risen Saviour. He said, "I go fishing on the lake very early in the morning. By and by I see the glory and brightness of the sunrise reflected in the windows of the homes on the lake shore. I don't have to turn around and see whether the sun has risen. I know it has risen because I can see the reflection of it.

"So, when I see love, kindness, thoughtfulness for others shining in the faces of men and women, and being given out in their words and actions, I can tell by the reflection that there is a risen Saviour."

Do *you* believe in a risen Saviour? Can others see His reflection in *your* life?

"Cast the net on the right side of the ship, and ye shall find. They cast therefore, and now they were not able to draw it for the multitude of fishes." John 21:6.

Near the beginning of His ministry Jesus performed a miracle, and Peter, James, and John caught a "multitude of fishes" in their net. Now, after His resurrection, near the end of His ministry, just before He ascended, He performed another miracle for the discouraged fishermen, and they caught 153 great fish! Notice that on each occasion there was absolute obedience to the command of Jesus. Do you know that Jesus is always the same—yesterday, today, and forever—and where He finds absolute obedience He can still work miracles?

A few years ago I was visiting our Sabbath school workers in Brazil, and as we flew from Fortaleza to Belém, Pastor Mario Rasi pointed out the location of a village where another miracle had been performed for a family of faithful Adventist fishermen. These men caught their fish in a big trap made with bamboo poles, in such a way that when the tidewaters rose, the fish could get in very easily, but they couldn't get out. There were fourteen traps in all, belonging to fourteen different families of fishermen. Soon after our Adventist fishermen were baptized they had a severe trial. No more fish came into their trap! A whole week went by; still no fish! A whole month; no fish! Soon they owed the equivalent of $350 at the grocery store.

"It's because you're keeping the Sabbath," taunted their friends. "Come on, give up your Sabbath and you'll catch more fish."

But our good believers said, "We will not deny our Saviour. We'll die first." They got down on their knees and told the Lord they were determined to be true, and they asked for His help. Then one Thursday night a huge fish weighing two hundred pounds got into their trap! They knelt down right there on the shore and thanked God. Friday morning there were three fish that size in their trap, and by sunset Friday there were six more huge fish in their trap! But our men wouldn't touch them.

"No," they said, "not till after the Sabbath." Their friends called them fools.

"They will break your trap if you don't take them out," they said. But our people kept the Sabbath, and Saturday night they found in their trap twenty-two large fish and four hundred pounds of smaller fish—five thousand pounds in all! They worked all night getting the fish ready for market. They paid off all their debt, put a good nest egg in the bank, and supplied half the cost of a new chapel in their village!

Don't be surprised if God tests your obedience sometime. Be sure you keep true, and He could perform a miracle for you, too!

"Ye shall be witnesses unto me both in Jerusalem, and in all Judaea, and in Samaria, and unto the uttermost part of the earth." Acts 1:8.

A witness for Christ is someone who says or does something that brings honor to the Saviour's name. Mary, the sister of Martha and Lazarus, did something for Jesus that has been told wherever the gospel has been preached.

Now let me tell you about another young woman who lives away over in New Guinea, who also has done something kind for Jesus, which has been told round the world. She was one of the daughters of Faole, whom you read about on June 17-19. She had gone to school at one of our missions and had been trained to do dispensary work there. Later on she was married, and with her husband she moved to one of the out-stations far up in the Owen Stanley Mountains.

One day during the war an American pilot crashed into the jungle not far from Faole's home village. Faole's first-aiders found the pilot unconscious with both legs broken. Tenderly they carried him into the village. They had no dispensary, but Faole's married daughter took over. She gently straightened his legs and put them in bamboo splints as well as she could. She sewed up his wounds with a needle and thread, and tenderly nursed him back to health and strength again. Frequently they had to move because of the nearness of the enemy, but they took the pilot with them. Then after seventy days they were able to carry him through the jungle to his base hospital.

"Officer," said the pilot to the doctor in charge, "I want you to give this good woman anything she may desire. Never mind the cost. Put it to my account. I am alive and back here with my friends because of her excellent service." They asked Faole's daughter what she would like for caring for the pilot, and what do you think she said?

"Sir, if I can have anything I want, please give me a medical kit with everything in it so that I can help someone else who may get injured."

The physicians couldn't believe their ears. They had never heard of such devoted witnessing. She got the medical kit, and most likely she has forgotten all about her kind deed by this time. But the pilot hasn't forgotten, and the medical officers at the base hospital haven't forgotten, and they have told the lovely story all around the world.

You are a witness for Jesus too. How far around the world will your story be told?

"During His ministry Jesus devoted more time to healing the sick than to preaching. . . . His voice was the first sound that many had ever heard, His name the first word they had ever spoken, His face the first they had ever looked upon. Why should they not love Jesus, and sound His praise? . . . The followers of Christ are to labor as He did."—*The Desire of Ages,* p. 350.

ACTS 2   NOVEMBER 10

"I will pour out of my Spirit upon all flesh: and your sons and your daughters shall prophesy, and your young men shall see visions, and your old men shall dream dreams." Acts 2:17.

What a wonderful experience the early Christians enjoyed when the Holy Spirit was poured out upon them on the day of Pentecost. Peter said it was a fulfillment of Joel's prophecy (Joel 2:28). Now Joel likened the work of the Holy Spirit to the early and latter rains that produced a bountiful harvest (verses 23 and 24). Zechariah 10:1 tells us to "ask . . . of the Lord rain in the time of the latter rain"; so does James 5:7. So we believe that in these last days there is going to be a mighty outpouring of the Holy Spirit, and I believe that the wonderful things we are seeing in Korea, the Philippines, New Guinea, and Africa are the beginnings of this latter rain.

The Spirit of God is using the workers and the laymen, but here is a story of how the Holy Spirit used a little 8-year-old girl in the city of Tunis to do a great work for Him. She was the daughter of our church pastor there, and when her father first moved to the city she got acquainted with the little girls who lived on her street and played with them. Now the chief of police lived on the same street, and he had a little girl the same age. The pastor's little girl and the policeman's little girl soon became good friends. Every day they played together, but on the Sabbath the pastor's little girl went to Sabbath school, of course. Then on Sabbath afternoon, in her Sabbath clothes, she went to visit her little friend.

"Why didn't you come to play with us today?" she asked.

"I went to Sabbath school today," said the pastor's little girl. "You see, today is the true Sabbath, so that's why I don't play." Then she told them all about Creation and how God made the Sabbath on the seventh day. The policeman's daughter told her father and mother that evening, and they were very interested. The next day, the policeman's daughter brought home the news that the Adventists didn't eat pork. The chief of police was so interested that he told the other policemen when he went to work.

"Why do they believe Jesus is coming soon?" the chief of police asked his little girl one evening.

"I don't know. I'll ask my friend tomorrow," she said. And her little friend asked her father, and the pastor wrote down a few texts on a slip of paper. Then the pastor's little girl told the policeman's little girl all about it and gave her the piece of paper. Then the policeman read the texts and told his fellow policemen the next day. And that's the way it went, step by step, day by day, till at last the policeman asked for Bible studies, and today five policemen and their families are members of our church there!

It's time for the Holy Spirit to be poured out everywhere. Are you ready for the latter rain to be poured out upon you?

ACTS 3   *NOVEMBER 11*

"Silver and gold have I none; but such as I have give I thee: In the name of Jesus Christ of Nazareth rise up and walk." Acts 3:6.

What a wonderful gift the poor lame man received the day that Peter told him to walk! The ability to walk was much more precious to him than silver or gold. No wonder the happy man leaped up and down as he praised God!

Today is the anniversary of another day, in 1918, when something more precious than silver or gold was given to the people of this world. For four long years sixteen nations with 65 million soldiers had been fighting in World War I; more than 8.5 million had been killed or had died of wounds. Another 21 million had been wounded, and nearly 8 million had been taken as prisoners of war. At last, at the eleventh hour, on the eleventh day of the eleventh month, the peace treaty was signed.

For two minutes, as that eleventh hour swept around the world, all traffic stopped and everybody remained silent in gratitude for the peace that had been restored. Then, after taps sounded out over the radios, people went wild with joy. Whistles blew, bells rang, car horns honked, and millions of people everywhere leaped up and down with joy. People wanted to remember that happy day always.

They called it Armistice Day, and during the next few years monuments were built in the great cities of the world, and the bodies of unknown soldiers were buried in many special places so the people could remember the millions of soldiers who died to bring back peace again. France's unknown soldier was buried under the Arc de Triomphe, and above the grave a flame representing sacrifice is kept burning day and night. England's unknown soldier was buried in Westminster Abbey in London. The United States's unknown soldier was buried in Arlington National Cemetery, on November 11, 1921. Ten years later a marble tomb was erected; on it are the simple words: "Here rests in honored glory an American soldier known but to God," and sentries, who are changed every hour during the day and every two hours during the night, keep guard over the tomb.

Wherever you are, be sure to thank God for peace, and make up your mind to have a place in Christ's eternal kingdom, where there always will be peace.

ACTS 4   NOVEMBER 12

"By the name of Jesus Christ . . . doth this man stand here before you whole." "Neither is there salvation in any other: for there is none other name under heaven given among men, whereby we must be saved." Acts 4:10, 12.

It matters not one bit whether a man is a Pharisee or a scribe, a publican or a sinner, a lame man or an able-bodied man, a Jew or a Gentile. There is only one way to be saved, and that is to believe on the name of the Lord Jesus Christ. I am reminded of a story William Stidger tells in his inspiring book *More Sermons in Stories,* about a friend of his who fell down into a well. Fortunately, the well was dry, with only a little soft mud in the bottom of it; but it was thirty feet deep and quite a distance from his house. He yelled and shouted for an hour, hoping to attract somebody's attention. But it was no use; nobody heard and nobody came to help him. At last the seriousness of his position came to him, and as he began to get chilly and numb, he was terrified. He tried to think, but he couldn't. Then he tried to pray, and as he *looked up,* there above him at the top of the well was a circle of light with a star clearly visible in the sky. The sight of that star brought hope to his fearful heart, and he said to himself, "The only way out of this dark, miserable well is *up,* up toward that star." He took out his pocketknife and dug two toeholds in the clay walls of the well about a foot up from the bottom. Then he cut two more a foot or so above them, then two more and two more. Then step by step, with his toes in the toeholds, he kept on climbing up. It took him five hours to climb up and out, but there was no other way, no shortcut. The only way was "up," and he kept going up until he made it. And so it is with us—the only way out of this world of sin, sorrow, and temptation is to believe on the precious name of Jesus. Whether you are weak or strong, baptized or not, whosoever believeth on Him shall not perish but have eternal life. Have you made Jesus your Saviour?

ACTS 5   NOVEMBER 13

"They brought forth the sick into the streets, and laid them on beds and couches, that at the least the shadow of Peter passing by might overshadow some of them." Acts 5:15.

Today is the anniversary of the falling of the stars in 1833, which fulfilled one of the Saviour's own prophecies about the nearness of His second coming. It is a good day for us to think about what kind of shadow we cast over people as we go by, for we certainly want to be ready for Jesus when He comes again; and our shadow, or influence, has a great deal to do with the condition of our heart and our mind. Peter was so humble, so good, so kind, so cheerful, so Christlike, that wherever he went the sick were healed and people were happier and felt better. Maybe you have not realized yet that you have a shadow, or an influence, that makes people feel glad to see you or upset when they see you. Your influence can make them better or worse; it can encourage them or discourage them.

I well remember the first time I realized that I had a shadow. I was 19 years old, a junior in college, and on my way back to school I was spending a weekend in Mount Gambier. I had lived there when I was a boy 11 years old, and Pastor Brown wanted me to preach on Sabbath and take the young people's meeting; and, of course, I was thrilled. I stayed in Pastor Brown's home, and in the evening we sat around the fire with Mr. and Mrs. Brown, 10-year-old Lionel, and his two little sisters. As we talked together about the good old days I felt young Lionel's big eyes looking at me all the time, and when it was time for the little folks to go to bed he said, "Oh, Dad, can't Eric sleep with me in my bed tonight?" And when I nodded my assent, he went bounding happily away. But he was sound asleep when I finally crawled in beside him, and he didn't know anything about it till he woke up and found me in bed with him in the morning.

"Eric," he sputtered in surprise, "did you sleep with me?"

"Sure," I said.

"All night?"

"That's right," I said. Then we talked a little while, till it was time to get up. I got up first, poured some water from the big pitcher into the porcelain basin, and washed my face. Then I went to the window to open it, so I could throw my dirty water out—for that's the way we did long ago. When I got back to the basin, Lionel sprang out of bed, put his hands on the basin, and said imploringly, "Aw, Eric, can't I wash my face in your water?" My heart nearly stood still. I didn't know what to do. But I couldn't disappoint him, so I let him wash in my water. And as I saw him, I suddenly realized that this little boy wanted to be like me, and I lifted my heart to God and prayed, "Dear Lord, help me so to live that it will always be safe for boys and girls to wash their faces in my water."

Your shadow will fall on someone today. Make sure your influence will help someone to be ready when Jesus comes.

ACTS 6 NOVEMBER 14

"And Stephen, full of faith and power, did great wonders and miracles among the people." Acts 6:8.

Stephen was a wonderful man. His faith, his courage, and his good works were amazing to all. But the secret was very simple—he was full of the Holy Ghost (Acts 6:5).

There have been many, many Stephens in the work of God all around the world. Let me tell you about one away over in Burma. His name was Ohn Bwint. Ohn Bwint came from a village thirty-eight miles away. He was one of the first students in our mission school. After four years he was baptized, and when he had finished the sixth standard (grade), Hte Po, the headman of La Po Ta village, eighteen miles away, made such an insistent plea for a teacher that we had to let Ohn Bwint go there. Now Ohn Bwint was full of faith and the Holy Spirit, too, and at the end of his first year he came to camp meeting with five bullock wagons filled with people, and Hte Po, the headman, was ready for baptism. Ohn Bwint went back to La Po Ta for the second year. Now we had a custom on our mission of calling in all the workers from our outstations the first Sunday in each new quarter for a workers' meeting. They brought in their school reports, medical reports, and Sabbath school reports; received their wages and their supplies; then returned, refreshed and encouraged, to their outstations. The end of the third quarter in Ohn Bwint's second year found the whole country under flood. It had rained heavily for three weeks. The great Salween River had overflowed its banks and covered the whole country with water and mud right back to the foothills. Our other outstations were on the riverbank, and we were able to bring the men in by launch and canoe, but La Po Ta was eighteen miles inland. It was impossible to think of Ohn Bwint coming in till after the flood had gone down. Nevertheless, on the first Sunday of the fourth quarter, according to our regular custom, in came Ohn Bwint!

"However did you make it?" we asked. "Wasn't the whole country under water?"

"Oh, yes," Ohn Bwint replied cheerfully, "but it wasn't so bad in the hills. I had to swim across twenty rivers in the little valleys between the hills, then when I came to the plains I had to walk through mud and water, often up to my neck, for six miles. But I brought in my report on time!" You won't be surprised to know that in time Ohn Bwint was ordained to the ministry and was used by God to raise up several churches. What inspired Ohn Bwint to be so faithful? The same Spirit of God that inspired Paul to say, "None of these things move me, neither count I my life dear unto myself, so that I might finish my course with joy" (Acts 20:24).

Won't you pray that God will fill you with His Holy Spirit and make you a faithful Stephen, too?

"And they stoned Stephen, calling upon God. . . . And he kneeled down, and cried with a loud voice, Lord, lay not this sin to their charge." Acts 7:59, 60.

When Jesus was being crucified He prayed, "Father, forgive them; for they know not what they do." Nothing could be more Christlike than to pray this kind of prayer for people who are determined to persecute you or destroy you. Stephen offered this kind of prayer for his enemies, and all through the years there have been followers of the Lord Jesus Christ who have prayed in this same Christlike spirit.

Many years ago, during the fearful Mau Mau rebellion in Kenya, East Africa, many of our African Seventh-day Adventists were persecuted and tortured because they had adopted the white man's religion. The Mau Mau leaders were trying to force all Africans to take an oath that included obscene acts and a promise to worship the Mau Mau leader. Gakui, a teen-age girl who had been at our mission school only one year, was determined not to take the oath, come what may. Her heathen parents coaxed her to do it for their sake, and the Mau Mau threatened her with death if she refused. However, she succeeded for some time in hiding in the bush whenever the Mau Mau came to her village. Then one day a neighbor woman betrayed her, and she was seized and taken to the ceremonial hut some distance away.

"Will you take the oath?" they demanded.

"I cannot," she replied. "I am a Christian."

They slapped her face in fury. "Do you want to die?" they shouted.

"I don't want to die," she replied, "and I know Jesus will save me. I know He will." The men beat her with clubs till she fell to the floor unconscious. There were other young people to take the oath, so they dragged her body over to the wall of the hut. Gradually she regained consciousness, and in horror watched other young people perform filthy acts and swear the terrible oath. "O God," she prayed, "save me, save me!" And as she prayed she felt strong hands grip her feet, and she was pulled slowly but steadily through a hole in the wall. Once outside, she rose carefully to her feet, and quietly slipped away to the home of an Adventist family who hid her until the trouble was over. When the government officials asked Gakui to come and identify her tormenters and lay charges against them, she quietly said, "No, I don't want to do that. They did not realize what they were doing. I have hope that they will be Christians someday." What a lovely spirit! The officers examined the walls of the ceremonial hut, but there were no signs of the hole through which she had been pulled. God does not let anything hinder Him when He performs His miracles. He only needs to find a Christlike spirit in the life. Then He can do anything. Have *you* that Christlike spirit?

ACTS 8   **NOVEMBER 16**

"And the people with one accord gave heed unto those things which Philip spake, hearing and seeing the miracles which he did." "And there was great joy in that city." Acts 8:6, 8.

The reason that Philip had power to bring great joy to the city of Samaria was because he was filled with the Holy Spirit. And wherever we find men filled with the Spirit, we find miracles, people accepting the truth, and great joy. At a council meeting not long ago I heard Elder Fridlin, president of the Southern European Division, tell a wonderful story from one of the countries in Southern Europe.

In a certain town there lived a very poor shoemaker who was a good man and wanted to do what was right. One day he listened to the Voice of Prophecy broadcast on his radio and was convinced that it was God's truth. He listened every week and was thrilled with what he was learning about the Bible. Then one day a colporteur came along and tried to sell him a book.

"I don't need a book," said the shoemaker. "I listen to the Voice of Prophecy broadcast, and I believe they have the truth."

"This book is published by the church that broadcasts the Voice of Prophecy," said the colporteur, "and I belong to that church, too."

"You do?" exclaimed the shoemaker.

"Yes," said the colporteur. "It is the Adventist Church!"

"Oh, well then, I want to understand more. I will buy a book. Will you come and explain it to me?"

"I surely will," said the colporteur; and he visited the shoemaker nearly every evening. The shoemaker rejoiced over one truth after another, but when it came to the Sabbath he said, "Oh, no. I couldn't keep Sabbath. That is my biggest day for business." Our colporteur tried to persuade the man to step out by faith and see what God would do for him. But no, he was sure he would starve if he closed his shop on

Saturday. When the first Sabbath came, although his heart told him it was God's rest day, he deliberately went to work. He opened his shop, got out his leather, but his hammer was not there! He looked everywhere for it, but it was nowhere to be seen. At last he said, "It seems I'll have to keep this Sabbath anyway." So he went home.

When he went to work the next day, there was his hammer, as plain as could be, right on his workbench. "Well, now! Where was that hammer yesterday, and where has it come from now?" he wondered out loud. Next Sabbath he went to work again. This time he had locked his hammer in the drawer and it was there all right. "Ah," he said, "now I shall work, and no one will stop me." But as he brought his hammer down on the very first blow, the hammer head broke into two parts! So he had to go home again!

"It must be a sign from the Lord that the Sabbath is true and that He wants me to keep it," he told the colporteur.

"I think so too," the colporteur replied. A few months later this good man and his wife were baptized, and after the baptism the pastor presented him with a brand-new hammer that had never worked on Sabbath. He said, "I am sure you and your hammer will both enjoy keeping the Sabbath after this." And they did.

Are you filled with the Spirit? Are you bringing great joy to your community?

ACTS 9   NOVEMBER 17

"Now there was at Joppa a certain disciple named . . . Dorcas: this woman was full of good works and almsdeeds which she did." Acts 9:36.

To be full of good works and almsdeeds is almost the same as to be full of the Holy Spirit, for it is only the Holy Spirit who can make us kind and thoughtful toward the needy. What a blessing Dorcas was to the church in Joppa and to the needy ones there! But Dorcas got sick, and she died. Peter raised her to life again; but we don't know how many more years she lived to bless that little town. At last she died again, and was buried. But her reputation and her great spirit of helpfulness have lived on in the lives of other women, and are still found in the wonderful welfare workers of the Christian church. Let me tell you of just one present-day Dorcas, to show you what I mean.

A few years ago the church members at Worcester, Massachusetts, decided they should start a welfare center. "Anything can happen any time," said their pastor, "and we should be ready to do our part." So Mrs. Myrtle Meyer was elected as Dorcas leader, and for years the Dorcas women gathered clothing, bedding, and supplies of all kinds. They had more than enough for the needy in their community. But "anything could happen," said Myrtle Meyer, so they kept putting things away and kept getting ready for a catastrophe. Tuesday, June 9, 1953, was an ordinary day at the welfare center. Nineteen families had been cared for. The place was cleaned up and the women went home. Just as Mrs. Meyer reached home a terrible thunderstorm broke. The wind roared; the lightning flashed; the rain poured down. Then there was an ominous quietness for a while, till in the distance an awful roar was heard. "It's a tornado, Myrtle!" shouted her husband. "The radio says there's destruction all around us. Hundreds of people have been killed and wounded. Thousands are homeless!" Myrtle Meyer waited for no more. This was the hour they had prepared for. She hustled off to the welfare center. When morning came, the hospitals were full; thousands were homeless; children were crying with hunger. All was confusion and chaos except in one building—the welfare center. There Mrs. Meyer and her Dorcas women were all in uniform and ready. A big sign was put up in front of the church—"Relief Center"—and eggs were cooking in the kitchen. Then the needy began to come. They needed clothes, and they were given clothes. Newborn babies needed layettes, and they were given layettes. Whatever they needed was there, ready; and when they needed more sheets and blankets, the people in the homes that had not been destroyed took them from their own beds. The "green-clad angels" worked in turn all day and all night for the first few days. They fed five hundred to seven hundred people a day. Bakeries gave them bread; a dairy donated all the milk they needed. One store gave one hundred pairs of slippers; a furniture factory came up with a truckload of baby carriages, cribs, and high chairs. They gave them to the Dorcas women to dispense because they were ready.

Are you full of good works and almsdeeds? If you are, you can be sure of a resurrection someday, and after that—eternal life.

"And Cornelius said, Four days ago . . . I prayed in my house, and, behold, a man stood before me in bright clothing, and said, Cornelius, thy prayer is heard. . . . Send therefore to Joppa, and call hither Simon, whose surname is Peter." Acts 10:30-32.

How many times we read and hear of the Holy Spirit leading, guiding, and bringing people together by the use of dreams and visions to hear the gospel story! Here is one sent in by Pastor J. M. Miranda, telling about one of his experiences as a missionary in Angola.

Pastor Miranda, with his wife and a group of workers, was conducting evangelistic meetings in a district about seventy-eight miles from Nova Lisboa, their headquarters mission station. They went to the location in the mission pickup and divided the villages between them so that every house would receive a personal invitation to the evening meetings. The home of the king of the tribe was in Pastor Miranda's territory, and he and his three wives listened with great interest as Pastor Miranda spoke about salvation through Jesus Christ. They closed their visit with prayer; then just before leaving, Pastor Miranda asked the king whether he had anything to say. The king replied, "Yes. A few days ago I had a dream. I saw a great multitude dressed in white, singing hymns as they were marching toward the great city of heaven. I wanted to go with them, but one of the glorious multitude told me I would have to have a passport to go with them. But he said there are people on a mission station that has four buildings, in Nova Lisboa, who can give you a passport, and soon a white man and a teacher from the Quioco tribe will come to your village. They will tell you what to do and how to get the passport to go to heaven."

The king paused, and Pastor Miranda said, "Today your dream is fulfilled. I am here, right in your village. Our mission in Nova Lisboa has just four buildings and my assistant pastor is of the Quioco tribe!" Needless to say, the king attended the meetings and joined the baptismal class, where he was getting ready to bury his past in the waters of baptism.

Stay close to God. In the last days the Holy Spirit is to be poured out on all flesh. Who can tell, maybe God will direct you to go to the help of someone, someday, by a dream.

"And they sent forth Barnabas. . . . For he was a good man, and full of the Holy Ghost and of faith: and much people was added unto the Lord." Acts 11:22-24.

Did you ever wonder why they called Barnabas a *good* man? He was a rich man, but he wasn't good because he was rich. He was a successful evangelist, but he wasn't good because he baptized many people. He was of the tribe of Levi, but his goodness didn't come from social standing. If you read about him carefully you will find one outstanding fact about Barnabas—he was kind and thoughtful of others. That's why they called him a good man. Barnabas sold his property and donated the proceeds for the support of the needy in the Jerusalem church; Barnabas befriended Paul, the converted persecutor, and helped him to get started in the ministry; Barnabas stood by his young cousin, John Mark, who had failed during his first missionary trip, and gave him another chance to make good. Good old Barnabas! No wonder everybody said he was a good man.

Once upon a time there were two brothers called Ahmed and Omar. They were both rich; they were both educated; and they both wanted to do something that would cause people to remember them forever. So Omar erected a great stone obelisk in the desert near a road that passed from one country to another. Upon it he carved his name in big, deep letters among many beautiful designs. The hot winds blew and the desert sands gathered around it, but after a year or two, no one ever stopped to admire the great stone pillar or to read the name. But Ahmed found a place in the desert where he could dig a well, a well that would cheer the thirsty travelers. Around it he planted date palms, to make cool shade for weary pilgrims and to provide sweet fruit for the hungry. He carved no name, but as the years went by, lo, everyone stopped at the well, and everyone rested in the shade of the trees, and everyone remembered the name of Ahmed, for he was a good man, one who had made kindness to others first in his life. Did you know that "goodness" is one of the fruits of the Spirit (Galatians 5:22)? And it is the "goodness of God" that leads to repentance (Romans 2:4).

Are you a good junior? I don't mean rich; I don't mean clever; I mean good—to others.

"When Peter was come to himself, he said, Now I know of a surety, that the Lord hath sent his angel, and hath delivered me out of the hand of Herod." Acts 12:11.

Stories of how God has delivered His people from the hands of wicked men and from prison have been told from many countries, from the time of Peter down to the present time. In his wonderful book *Jungle Flower,* Pastor Kalee Paw tells this marvelous story of deliverance in the land of Burma.

One Friday evening in the month of September, 1956, twenty-one armed bandits surrounded our Karen boarding school and kidnapped ten of our young people—six young men and four young women. The bandits took them across the Salween River, then forced them to carry the food and clothing they had stolen to their camp about fifteen miles away in the mountains. The next day one young man was sent back with a note demanding twenty-five thousand rupees and saying that if the money wasn't brought, the nine remaining prisoners would be shot. It was raining; the mosquitoes were bad; they were given no shelter; and a bowl of rice and a sprinkle of salt twice a day was their only food. You can't wonder that some of them began to cry. But Mo Chit Aye, a young woman teacher, took control and said, "Now listen, children. It won't do us any good to cry. We are Seventh-day Adventists, and Seventh-day Adventists don't cry; they sing. Come on, let's sing." One by one the others joined in, and as they sang the bandits listened and listened.

"What kind of people are you?" asked the bandit chief. "Everybody else that we capture curses and swears, but you sing."

"We are Seventh-day Adventists," said the young teacher, "and after we sing we are going to pray. And we are going to pray for you, too, for Jesus told us to pray for our enemies."

"You needn't think your God can deliver you out of my hands," scoffed the bandit chief. "Nothing can deliver you but money, and if we don't get the money we will shoot every one of you."

But day after day our young people kept on singing and praying. About a week later one of the girls was released to take back the final word that if the money was not produced in three more days, the eight remaining prisoners would be shot. Our poor people could find no more money. All they could do was to pray, and they prayed that the great God of heaven would preserve the lives of our young people. Our young people in the bandits' camp sang and sang, preached and preached, and prayed and prayed every day, and those wicked men listened and listened and listened. Every day the captives thought this would be their last. But after three weeks a messenger from the great district bandit chief brought a message to the bandit who held our young people captive, and it said, "Release immediately the eight Seventh-day Adventist young people you are holding as prisoners."

"All right! All right! I will," shouted the bandit angrily. He called our students to him and said, "Follow me. I'll show you what I was going to do today." He led them to the back of the camp to where eight newly made graves were dug! "I was going to stand each of you by one of those graves and shoot you into it," he said. "But your God has delivered you out of my hands."

Then he led them to the trail and let them go back to school!

The God who can deliver is your God. Stay close to Him. You may need Him to deliver you someday.

ACTS 13   NOVEMBER 21

"It was necessary that the word of God should first have been spoken to you: but seeing ye put it from you, and judge yourselves unworthy of everlasting life, lo, we turn to the Gentiles." Acts 13:46.

Acts 13:46 is one of the saddest verses in the Bible. God chose the children of Israel to be His own people. He planned to make them the most enlightened people on the earth, physically and mentally. They were to be the head and not the tail. They were to be light bearers to the whole world. But again and again they turned from God and worshiped idols. They rebelled against the leadership of God and demanded a king, so they would be like the other nations. When the Saviour of the world was born among them, they crucified Him; and when Christ's messengers preached the last message to them, and gave the last invitation, they contradicted and blasphemed. If they had only known that this was the last message to be given them as a nation, if they had only realized that this was their last chance to excel as a nation, and that after this the invitation would be given to people among all nations, how different their history could have been. This danger of putting off until it is too late comes to all of us.

There is a story told of a Persian prince who, when he grew to manhood, divided his future life into four periods—ten years for travel, ten years for government work, ten years for pleasure, and ten years for God. He thought his plan a good one, but the trouble was that he died during the first ten years! If he had only known, how much more wisely he could have planned.

There is another story told about a young man from a foreign land who came to Chicago as a tourist and rented a room in a hotel. Soon after getting settled he took a walk around the shopping section and got lost. He wandered around trying to find his way back, but in his excitement he had forgotten the name of the hotel and the name of the street. He was too embarrassed to appeal to the police for help, and at last he had to take another room. He tried for five days to find the first hotel where his luggage was, but nothing looked familiar. Finally he was compelled to ask the police for help. They telephoned around to some of the hotels and soon found his name in the register of the hotel *next door* to where he had been staying! He was so near, but he was lost!

God wants you to be one of His special children. He wants to bless you physically and mentally and spiritually above all others, so you can be a light bearer to the world.

Make sure you have accepted Him now. Don't put it off until it is too late. It is too sad to think of being almost saved, but lost.

ACTS 14   NOVEMBER 22

"There sat a certain man at Lystra . . . who never had walked: the same heard Paul speak: . . . Stand upright on thy feet. And he leaped and walked." Acts 14:8-10.

I love to think of the joy and happiness that must have come to the man Paul was able to heal. He had never walked before when he obeyed the words of Paul. Try to imagine him sitting there day after day, year after year, watching the happiness of others who could run and walk and play, but not having any of the happiness for himself. No wonder he leaped and walked when he was healed.

I know some juniors who have never walked with a Sunshine Band or walked with an Ingathering group or walked with a literature group, and they do not realize how much happiness they are missing.

Once upon a time, according to a story in an old copy of the *Youth's Instructor*, there was a timid girl who had never walked out Ingathering.

But one year she decided she would have to get over her timidity, so she took a bundle of magazines and some Ingathering leaflets and started off.

"If I'm too scared to ask for money," she said to herself, "I'll give them a paper anyway."

She went down the street and selected the poorest looking house of all for her first call. She knocked on the door, and when a woman with a baby in her arms opened it, she was so scared she couldn't do anything but say, "Please take these papers." And she put the whole bundle of them in the woman's hands and fled in embarrassment. The woman didn't want the papers, but she took them, and put them up on top of a kitchen cabinet. Weeks went by, and one cold winter day she sat shivering with her baby in her arms.

"If only I had some paper I could paste it over those cracks in the wall," she said. Then she remembered that bundle. "Just the very thing," she said, and soon the pages were pasted over the cracks in the walls. How much more comfortable her room was now! Another day as she sat rocking her baby her eye caught the heading of an article on a page of a paper on the wall. "That's interesting," she said, and read it to the end of the page. Then she looked all over the wall till she found the rest of the article. Day after day, week after week, she read the articles pasted on the wall, and as she read she accepted the truth of what she read, and in time she found her way into the church. The day she was baptized, the minister asked to see the hands of those whose first contact had been through literature, and this woman told her story.

If the timid girl who had never walked before only knew, wouldn't she be happy! She will know someday; then her joy will be full.

If you have never walked before, start now, and you will be really happy.

ACTS 16   **NOVEMBER 23**

"A vision appeared to Paul in the night; There stood a man of Macedonia, and prayed him, saying, Come over into Macedonia, and help us." Acts 16:9.

In response to the pleading call for help that came to Paul in a vision, Paul and Silas took the gospel overseas to a new continent. In response to this same plea thousands of young people have gone to the mission fields of the world. As a young man I heard the same call, and with my good wife I joyfully went to Burma to labor among the spirit-worshiping

Karens; but I was greatly disappointed. I found that my "man of Macedonia" didn't have his arms out. My spirit worshipers didn't want the gospel. They were quite satisfied with their ignorance and superstition. They called me a *dawtaka*—an evil spirit that eats babies. With my trumpet and a Picture Roll and a bag of medicines I could get them, out of curiosity, to listen to me once; but the next time I would find the village empty. I invited them to come to Sabbath school; but nobody came. Nobody came for six weeks.

Then I decided to have a Sabbath school in a nearby village. I visited every house, treated every sick person, and told them to come to the headman's house when they heard the trumpet play. And they came this time—two hundred of them. They clapped their hands and said, "Fine, fine. Now sing for us." We sang two songs, and I was just reaching for my Picture Roll when they clapped their hands again and said, "Fine, fine! Now tell your wife to dance for us."

I was so discouraged. I turned to Acts 16 and 17 and studied Paul's experience again. I was surprised to find that his trip to Macedonia took about a year, and that he only preached in three cities! In Philippi he was beaten and put in jail; in Thessalonica there was a riot, and he had to escape from the city by night; and in Berea there was another riot and his friends had to send him out of the country into Greece! But Paul was *not* discouraged. He sang in prison at midnight, and made a second and even a third trip into this difficult field.

I fell on my knees and asked God to show me what made the difference. Why was Paul not discouraged at his terrible experiences? And God showed me. The man of Macedonia was the *symbol* in a *vision.* You know, in a vision a *woman* means a church; *animals* mean kingdoms and nations. And Paul understood that this *Macedonian man* meant "the Lord had called" them to preach the gospel in Macedonia (verse 10). What a difference it made to Paul. He was helping the Lord Jesus save souls! The dear Lord Jesus, whom the people spat upon and crucified! Of course, Paul could do anything for *Him* and suffer anything for *Him.*

And when I understood that the Lord had called me to Burma to *help Him* preach the gospel there, it made a world of difference to me, too. Little by little the indifference of the people gave way; many souls were added to the church; and my twenty years among the Karens were the happiest years of my life.

When you are called to do Ingathering or literature work, don't expect the people to have their arms out waiting to welcome you; but go forth to help the Lord Jesus save souls, and you will see what a difference it makes to you.

*"The brethren immediately sent away Paul and Silas by night unto Berea.
. . . These were more noble . . . in that they received the word with all readiness
of mind, and searched the scriptures daily." Acts 17:10, 11.*

How thankful we are for the noble Bereans, who studied their Bibles
every day. What a wonderful example they have given to all Christians.
All down through the years there have been Bible-reading clubs and
Bible-reading awards called by the name Berean. But remember, the
Bereans did more than just *read* their Bibles; they *searched*, and that
means they *studied* the Word of God.

Long ago in a Sabbath school paper Pastor J. B. Cooks told of an
experience he had in South Africa that illustrates perfectly the difference
between only reading the Bible and studying the Bible. When he was a
boy 13 years old he lived in that part of Africa where there are diamond
fields. Because his mother was a widow it was necessary for him to get
work when he finished grade school and save money so he could go to
high school. So with a partner he chose a piece of unclaimed ground and
began digging for diamonds. Each week they found enough diamonds to
pay expenses to live well, but the fortune they dreamed of never turned
up. Now, diamonds are generally found in a layer of gravel near the
surface. So young John and his partner worked the gravel thoroughly
right down to the basic dirt. They noticed that their neighbors were
digging deeper, but thought only that the surface gravel over there was
deeper than their own. They did not think of digging a hole to see
whether there was more gravel under what appeared to be the basic dirt,
and when they had thoroughly worked the surface gravel, they moved
on.

Later on, someone else came along and dug a hole on their old plot.
They found more gravel deeper down, and in that gravel was the fortune!
Many thousands of dollars' worth of diamonds were actually dug from
that plot of ground. If John and his partner had only dug a little deeper
they could have found that fortune! But they had been satisfied to skim
over the surface; so they missed it.

There is a "fortune" in the Word of God, but you have to search for
it. You have to dig for it. Skimming over the surface and getting the story
will give you some blessing, but the richest blessing comes when you
study, when you think, when you compare one text with another, and
when you compare your life with the ideas found in the Word of God.

"When Paul had laid his hands upon them, the Holy Ghost came on them, and they . . . prophesied." "So mightily grew the word of God and prevailed." Acts 19:6, 20.

I think that among the many, many things we have to be thankful for is the Spirit of Prophecy in our church. All through the years God has spoken to His people and led them by His servants the prophets. In the early Christian church there were prophets, and they prophesied; and the work of God grew mightily and prevailed.

When this Advent Movement began in 1844 God needed a prophet He could use as a mouthpiece so He could lead and encourage His people. Among the early Adventist preachers there was a young man by the name of Hazen Foss. He was an eloquent speaker and well liked by all who knew him. One night God gave him a vision. In the vision he saw the Advent believers traveling on a straight, narrow path high above the world, leading to the heavenly city. A light was shining from the beginning of the path all along the way, so that the travelers would not stumble. Jesus was leading the company, and as long as the travelers kept their eyes on Jesus they were safe. But some lost sight of Jesus; then their light went out and they were left in darkness. He watched and watched till he saw the righteous dead rise from their graves and be caught up to enter the city of God with the faithful Advent travelers. Then the voice of God said to Hazen Foss, "Make known to others what I have revealed to you."

But Hazen Foss was afraid people wouldn't believe him, and that it would hurt his influence; so he would not. The vision was shown to him the second time, and again he was told to make it known to others; still he would not.

Then God chose a young woman only 17 years old and not very strong. Her name was Ellen Gould Harmon. She was given the same vision; she heard the same voice commanding her to make it known to others; and although she was timid and weak and her voice not strong, she courageously began to tell what she had seen. And as she talked her voice was strengthened. Outside the room where the meeting was being held, listening to her message, was Hazen Foss!

"That's it. That's it," he said to the man standing beside him. "That's the vision that was given to me. I was told to tell it to others, but I refused."

348

The next morning he met Ellen, and said to her, "I heard you talk last night. I believe the visions are taken from me and given to you. . . . I am a lost man. You are chosen of God. Be faithful in doing your work, and the crown I might have had, you will receive."

Don't you feel sorry for Hazen Foss? But aren't you thankful that Ellen Harmon accepted the responsibility and became the mouthpiece of God for this Advent Movement? What a blessing she has been and still is to each one of us!

Are you careful to follow the instruction God has given through her?

ACTS 18   **NOVEMBER 26**

"Be not afraid, but speak, and hold not thy peace: for I am with thee, and no man shall set on thee to hurt thee: for I have much people in this city." Acts 18:9, 10.

Again and again when Paul was preaching, mobs of angry people, shouting and blaspheming, rushed upon him. But again and again God delivered him, and this time He appeared to Paul in a vision and gave him the beautiful promise found in our Morning Watch text. This same promise has been fulfilled again and again for God's faithful Adventist preachers. Over in the Far East, between Java and New Guinea, there is a little island called Alor. Pastor J. A. Raranta held a series of meetings there. The people on the island were Moslems, Catholics, and Protestants, and strange as it may seem, this time it was the Protestants that stirred up trouble.

One night the headman of the city got a mob of strong men together. He armed them with sharp knives, clubs, and axes and sent them to break up the meeting and kill Pastor Raranta. The pastor saw them coming. They were yelling and shouting, sharpening their knives and swinging them over their heads. But Pastor Raranta kept on preaching, trusting in the Lord for help. He was halfway through the meeting when they entered the building. Then something wonderful happened. They took one look, then turned around and ran back to the leader.

"That place is filled with people bigger and stronger than we are," they said. "We've never seen anything like it before."

The headman was angry and called them cowards. He decided he would lead the mob himself on the day there was to be a baptism; then they would kill the pastor for sure.

The day came. Seven were to be baptized. A large group of interested ones gathered by the quiet river. In the midst of the service the mob rushed down to the bank of the river. The pastor quietly invited them to watch the service first, before making any trouble. They quieted down and watched, and as they watched, the Holy Spirit came upon them and made them so weak that they couldn't even stand up after it was over. Pastor Raranta invited them to give their hearts to Jesus and obey His Word. For a while they couldn't even talk. Then the headman said, "The Adventists are being led by God. I can't do anything against them. In the future I am going to leave them alone." Then one by one the mob picked up their knives and axes and went quietly away.

What a wonderful God we have! What a wonderful promise He has given us! Keep close to Him. You may need this promise to be fulfilled for you some day.

ACTS 20   NOVEMBER 27

"But none of these things move me, neither count I my life dear unto myself, so that I might finish my course with joy." Acts 20:24.

Good old Paul! What a man he was! He knew that bonds and afflictions awaited him, but nothing could intimidate him. Nothing could make him turn back. He was determined to finish his course with joy, and he has inspired thousands of others to do the same. One of the most inspiring books I have read recently is *These Fords Still Run,* by Barbara Westphal. It is the story of Elder and Mrs. Orley Ford, who have given forty-five years of service to the Indians in Peru and Inter-America. It was my privilege to meet them at the General Conference session in San Francisco. I was at the meeting the night Inter-America gave its report. I saw them receive the heartfelt honor of their division and I heard Elder Ford say, "Were we to begin life anew we would only choose to follow the same course. The Lord has been so precious to us in giving us good health through the years and in saving our lives in many times of extreme peril. I have been shot at many times, handcuffed and chained to a soldier guard, and thrown into dirty dungeons. On one occasion I was stoned and beaten to unconsciousness and left for dead. But here we are, as good as new. On one occasion while I was away from home Mrs. Ford's life was miraculously spared from death when twenty thousand Indians on the warpath began looting and burning. We leave three little mounds, monuments to our little ones, laid away out there in lonely graves waiting to see us again. It is our desire to continue until the work is finished. Although officially retired, as all old Fords finally must be, I find in the used-car lot that the older the car the greater its sales value. So, as the oldest Ford on the road, I take courage and feel that I don't need to be retired but just need a retread. We have greatly enjoyed our work out there where darkness and poverty cause the light to shine with greater brilliance. We have lived with these people, treated their sick, conducted their marriages and their funerals, and we love them and desire to go home together with them. After hearing the wonderful reports here of what others are doing and have gone through, we feel that our lot has been too easy and our efforts insufficient. So we hope that these Fords will still run a little longer."

Aren't you proud of wonderful missionaries who want to finish their course with joy like that? Now, how are you going to finish your course some day? I can tell you the answer—it will be exactly the same way you finish your chores, your homework, and your schoolwork now.

Are you satisfied with that kind of finish?

ACTS 21   ·   NOVEMBER 28

"What mean ye to weep and to break mine heart? for I am ready not to be bound only, but also to die at Jerusalem for the name of the Lord Jesus." Acts 21:13.

What a noble spirit of devotion is often expressed in the words of Paul! Just think of it—Paul, the man who used to imprison, persecute, and kill the followers of the Lord Jesus, is now ready himself to be imprisoned and to die, if need be, for the Lord Jesus Christ! The words of our text have inspired young people all around the world with the same spirit of devotion to the cause of the Saviour of mankind.

Did you ever hear of Felipe Corcoro? Felipe was born in the Philippine Islands, and in company with some other young men whose one object was to get rich, he went to California. There he found the truths of the gospel; and this gospel was to him more precious than silver or gold.

With the truth there came an intense longing to bring the message to his own people. So after being an Adventist only a few short years, he set sail for the Philippines again. Before long all his father's family had accepted the third angel's message and a new church was built in their village. Felipe then became a colporteur, and with his heart burning with love and enthusiasm, he decided to go to the darkest part of the island—to the Bontok tribe in the mountains.

"We would advise you not to pass along that road alone," said the keeper of the gate at the beginning of the mountain road. "It is dangerous to go alone. The Bontoks are bloodthirsty head-hunters, you know."

Of course, Felipe knew there was danger. The day before, he had mailed a letter back to the office, enclosing two pesos for his Sabbath school offering. In his letter he said, "This is all I have left. I could use it to buy a seat on the bus, but I will walk. I want Jesus to have that money. You may not see my face again, for somehow I feel that I may never return. But for Jesus' sake I am determined to go. Farewell."

Poor Felipe; he never returned. While on that mountain road he was attacked by four young Bontok men and killed. His lower jaw was severed from his head as a trophy of their manhood, and his body was thrown into the river below. Two weeks later his body was found, and the sad news was brought to our Philippine college. What do you think our young people did when they heard of Felipe's noble devotion? Five young men stood up and said, "We will go in his place."

How great is the spirit of devotion to the work of God in your heart? God may not require you to go to prison or to die for Him, but it would please Him to see you serving Him where you are.

ACTS 22   **NOVEMBER 29**

"The God of our fathers hath chosen thee, that thou shouldest know his will, and see that Just One, and shouldest hear the voice of his mouth. For thou shalt be his witness unto all men of what thou hast seen and heard." Acts 22:14, 15.

In the Scripture reading for today Paul tells the story of his dramatic conversion. The process of conversion differs with different people. With some it is quick and sudden, like that of Paul. He could always point to the time and the place of his conversion. With others it is so gradual that they cannot remember any particular time or place when they were converted, as in the case of Samuel and of Timothy. In the book *Steps to Christ* we read: "A person may not be able to tell the exact time or place, or trace all the chain of circumstances in the process of conversion; but this does not prove him to be unconverted."—Page 57. I was so happy when I first read that paragraph, because like Samuel, I was born in an Adventist family; and like Timothy I had known the Scriptures since I was a child; and I couldn't remember a special day when I was converted, as some of my schoolmates could. Those words make it very clear. The passage goes on to say: "Who has the heart? With whom are our thoughts? . . . Who has our warmest affections and our best energies? If we are Christ's, our thoughts are with Him, and our sweetest thoughts are of Him."

Billy Sunday, the well-known evangelist, had the simplest rule whereby we can tell positively whether we have been converted. He said, "If a sheep falls into a mudhole, it tries to get out as quickly as possible, but if a pig falls into a mudhole, it is in its glory, and stays there as long as it can." So when a Christian makes a mistake, if he feels miserable and tries at once to make it right, that person has a changed heart; he has been converted. Only a converted heart hates sin. But if a person does something wrong and is not found out, if he says "Goody, goody! Nobody knows! Nobody has found out! I'll do that again sometime," what would you say about that person's heart?

Now think a moment. Do you really hate sin? And do you hate yourself till you have made things right? Have you been converted? You may be able to remember the time and the place when you withdrew your affections from the world and fastened them upon Christ, or you may not; that is not the proof of conversion. But if you hate sin and love Christ, then you have been converted.

ACTS 23   NOVEMBER 30

"Men and brethren, I have lived in all good conscience before God until this day." Acts 23:1.

A conscience is a strange thing. You can't see it or smell it or taste it, but you can hear it; and everybody has one. Isaiah called it "a word behind thee, saying, This is the way." Elijah called it "a still small voice." An old Indian who had become a Christian called it a "three-cornered thing" that pricked him whenever he did wrong. Let us thank God this morning for the voice of conscience, and pray that it will never, never stop speaking to us.

Once upon a time when streetcars were drawn by horses, a junior boy took a ride without paying his nickel. The little voice kept telling him that to do this wasn't right; but the voice was so small that he tried to forget it. But he couldn't. Forty-five years went by; then he sent the company twenty cents in stamps. And at last he had peace.

Once upon a time a woman took two towels from a hotel room in which she was staying. For twenty years the little voice told her to make it right. At last she sent the hotel a dollar bill, then she could sleep peacefully again.

Once upon a time a girl cheated in an algebra examination. She passed the test, but she was unhappy. "Make it right. Go and confess," said the little voice; but she was too ashamed. She grew up and traveled across the sea to Africa, but she couldn't get away from that voice. One day she couldn't stand it any longer, so she wrote a letter to her teacher: "Twenty-five years ago . . . I cheated in an algebra examination. It has troubled me ever since. I have decided that my peace of mind is worth more than my pride, and I am therefore confessing my wrong. Please forgive me."

Once upon a time a 13-year old boy in Veedersburg, Indiana, stole a watermelon. When he grew up he was converted, and the voice of conscience got after him. The man from whom he stole the melon was dead, so he sent this letter to the man's daughter: "I am on my way to heaven, and have run up against that melon. It has grown so large that I cannot get over it. Please forgive and forget."

There is something very interesting and also something very sad about this voice of conscience. The more we listen to it and obey it, the nearer it will draw us to God, for it is the voice of God's Spirit. But if we rebel and refuse to obey it, its voice will become weaker and weaker till we can hear it no more, for God has said, "My spirit shall not always strive with man." And when through deliberate disregard the little voice ceases to speak, then we have sinned against the Holy Spirit. And since there is no other voice to call us to repentance, this is the sin that cannot be forgiven. (See Matthew 12:31.)

How is your conscience? Do you keep it well oiled and in good working order?

"And as he reasoned of righteousness, temperance, and judgment to come, Felix trembled." Acts 24:25.

Paul was only a minister of the small early Christian church, which was hated and despised by the worldly Jews, but when he stood before the greatest rulers in the land and explained his faith in Christ, they trembled.

In the book *Education* we read: "Many a lad of today, growing up as did Daniel in his Judean home, studying God's Word and His works and learning the lessons of faithful service, will yet stand in legislative assemblies, in halls of justice, or in royal courts, as a witness for the King of kings."—Page 262. This prophecy has been fulfilled many, many times. Again and again in times of war our young men have been called to witness for their faith before high military officers, and God has given them words to speak and courage to speak them, so that glory and honor have come to His name.

In England three of our men were brought before their commandant because of difficulty in getting their Sabbaths off.

"I too am a Christian," the commandant said, "and in civil life I am strict about Sunday observance. But now, in the army, I just forget my Sunday."

The eldest of the three men replied, "Sir, the Sabbath is not *our* day; it is God's and we cannot change His law."

The officer became angry. "You are a bunch of cowardly hypocrites," he shouted. "You are not fit to live. I'll turn the machine guns on you. Christians! Bah! You'd sit on your bed and read your Bible all day Saturday, and if the hospital should catch on fire, you'd just fold your hands and pray."

"No, sir," our young man replied, "if such an emergency arose, we would work all day and all night if necessary. Punish us if you must, sir. We are not afraid to suffer in prison.

"We do not drink or smoke; we do not eat meat or drink tea or coffee. Prison would deprive us of nothing. We do not go to shows, play cards, or gamble. If it would be all right with you, you could put us in the guardhouse every Saturday, and we would be ready for business as soon as the sun sets."

The captain was astonished. "Is this man telling the truth?" he asked their officer.

"He is, sir" was the reply.

"Well, then, call in all the noncommissioned officers at once," he ordered.

When they came in he said, "Do you see these three men? From now on, a half hour before sunset on Friday, no matter where they are or what they are doing, send them back to the barracks."

And for all the rest of the time they were in the army they had no trouble.

Make sure you put God first in your life. He will give you words to speak and courage to speak them someday if you are called to stand before rulers.

ACTS 25   DECEMBER 2

"And when they bring you . . . unto magistrates . . . , take ye no thought how or what thing ye shall answer, or what ye shall say: for the Holy Ghost shall teach you in the same hour what ye ought to say." Luke 12:11, 12.

After being kept in prison for two years Paul was brought before another ruler, Festus, who succeeded Felix as governor of Judea. Again the Holy Ghost gave him just the right words to say. Paul appealed to Caesar and thus took his case out of the hands of the local rulers and placed it in the hands of the highest authority in the Roman Empire.

Again and again the Holy Ghost has given our young men the right words to speak as they have stood before their military officers appealing for permission to keep God's Sabbath day.

Take, for example, the young man who was secretary and stenographer to the president of the Latin Union Conference just before World War I. He was called into the French Army, and went to his captain and asked for Sabbath privileges. The captain flew into a rage and shouted, "Are you a fool? Do you think you are going to run the French Army?"

"Sir," said the young man respectfully, "I do not wish to dictate to the army and I do not think I am a fool, either. I only believe my first duty is to obey God."

"In the army you have to forget all other authority and give supreme allegiance to the army," replied the captain.

"I can't do that in disobedience to God, sir."

"Then I'll draft you to the worst fortress in Africa, where they have the worst climate and the worst criminals."

"I can go there, sir, but I cannot disobey God."

"Then I'll take you to the colonel and have him sentence you," said the captain. And to the colonel they went.

"So you think you can't do any work on Saturday, do you?" asked the colonel kindly.

"Yes, sir; I must obey God." The colonel and the captain talked together for a while, then the colonel dismissed them, and they went back to the captain's office.

"How do you feel now?"

"I feel the same, sir."

"Can't work on Saturday, eh?"

"No, sir."

"You say you were a stenographer?"

"Yes, sir."

"How would you like to be my stenographer and secretary?"

"Why, captain, I would like it fine," our soldier replied, "only no work on the Sabbath."

"Very well," said the captain, "that's understood. You can begin right away."

And he did!

Would *you* be willing to go to prison rather than disobey God? God's Holy Spirit does wonders for those who obey at all cost.

ACTS 26   DECEMBER 3

"Then Agrippa said unto Paul, Almost thou persuadest me to be a Christian." Acts 26:28.

Agrippa's words to Paul are some of the saddest words found in the Bible. Agrippa was the king of the territory northeast of Judea. He was paying a courtesy visit to Festus in Caesarea. Out of curiosity he wanted to hear Paul speak. Paul told him the simple story of his conversion, and the Holy Spirit gave power to his words. Agrippa was convinced of the truth, and *almost* accepted it. He *almost* gave his heart to Christ; but he didn't. I wonder why he didn't.

Sad to say, there are some juniors and young people who do the same! They go to a junior camp or attend a Week of Prayer, and *almost* make their decision to accept Christ—but they don't. I wonder why.

Margaret was one of those junior girls. She lived in St. Louis. She believed in Christ, but she thought she was not yet old enough to take up her cross. She wanted to have a good time in the world first. One day her mother was taken sick and had to go to the hospital. Margaret got some pretty flowers and went to see her mother. The nurse was a lovely Christian woman who understood the struggle Margaret was having to give herself to Christ. She saw her opportunity to give Margaret a good object lesson, so she said, "Oh, those flowers are so beautiful and sweet, but I think we will keep them here for a few days, till they get a little older, before taking them to your mother."

"Indeed, no!" said Margaret indignantly. "Mother will like them so much more when they are young and fresh."

Then the nurse said, "You're right, I think your mother should have those flowers right now. And I wonder if Jesus wouldn't rather have your life right now, too, while you are young and your life is at its best?"

Margaret saw the point, and that very day she gave her heart to Jesus. I hope you have already given your heart to Jesus. But if you happen to be a junior who has only *almost* done it, won't you do it today? I read recently of a man named John Hawthorn who was drowned only twenty feet from the shore of an East Coast beach. He appeared to be a good swimmer, but suddenly he called out, "Which way to shore? Which way to shore?" No one took any notice, for he was so close to safety. But he drowned. When his body was brought ashore his two weeping sisters explained that John was blind. Poor John, he was *almost* safe, but he drowned. His words "Which way to shore?" still haunt me.

If you are almost persuaded to give your heart to Christ, do it *now*. The Holy Spirit is saying, "This is the way, walk ye in it."

ACTS 27   DECEMBER 4

"Paul said to the centurion and to the soldiers, Except these abide in the ship, ye cannot be saved." Acts 27:31.

Paul was on his way to Rome as a prisoner. The ship he was on ran into a terrible winter storm, and all hope of saving the ship from destruction was lost. Then an angel appeared to Paul and said, "Fear not, Paul; thou must be brought before Caesar: and, lo, God hath given thee all them that sail with thee." What a precious promise that was. But there was a condition given for their salvation—they must stay together and "abide in the ship." There is nothing more terrifying than a shipwreck, and there can be no joy greater than being saved from a shipwreck.

Some years ago, according to a story I have heard many times, there was a shipwreck off the coast of the Pacific Northwest. A crowd of fishermen in a nearby village gathered and watched the ship being pounded to pieces on the rocks. A lifeboat was sent to the rescue, and after a terrific struggle they came back with all the shipwrecked sailors but one. "There was no room in the lifeboat for him, so we told him to stay by the ship and someone would come back for him," they said.

"Who will come with me?" shouted a young man as he sprang into the lifeboat for the return trip, and immediately others joined him. Just then a little old lady cried out, "Don't go, Jim, my boy. Don't go! You are all I have left. Your father drowned in the sea; your brother William sailed away and we've never heard from him; and now if you are lost, I'll be left alone. Oh, Jim, please don't go."

Jim listened patiently to his mother's pleading, then said, "Mother, I must go! It is my duty. I must go!"

They watched as the men in the lifeboat fought their way toward the wreck. Anxiously Jim's mother wept and prayed. They saw the boat start back, a frail little shell tossed about by the angry waves. At last it came close enough to hear, and they shouted, "Did you get him?" And Jim shouted back, "Yes, and tell Mother it's William!"

Oh, what a joy there can be when men do their duty and work together and stay together! Just try to imagine the double joy of that mother when she got back not only her brave son Jim but also her long-lost son William.

A few years ago when I was living in Oakland, California, I picked up the evening newspaper, and there in great headlines were the words "Wrecked, just outside the Golden Gate." Everybody who has been to San Francisco knows that the entrance to the harbor is called "The Golden Gate." When I had time I drove over to look at the wreck. There it was, a pathetic picture. Only a few days before it had been a grand vessel proudly riding the waves. But it lost its way in the fog, became confused with the lights, and was wrecked on the seal rocks.

God forbid that any junior should be wrecked just outside the heavenly golden gate. Let us stay together, work together, pray together, and "abide in the ship" till Jesus comes.

"These signs shall follow them that believe; In my name shall they cast out devils. . . ; they shall take up serpents; and if they drink any deadly thing, it shall not hurt them." Mark 16:17, 18.

The promise made by Jesus to the believers was meant not only for His twelve disciples but also for all Christian workers who would follow them in preaching the gospel in all the world. It included Paul, whose experience we have read about today. And here is another miraculous experience in the life of Captain G. F. Jones, the beloved trailblazer of the South Pacific.

In May, 1908, he landed on the west coast of the island of Sumatra and hired a horse to make a journey into the interior. Most of the journey was through dense jungle infested with wild elephants, tigers, and large howling monkeys. The people were Mohammedans, and when they found that Captain Jones did not eat pork and did not smoke or drink, they called him a "learned man of God" and accepted him kindly. One day while he was resting at noon, a large poisonous snake attacked the horse while it was grazing, and bit it on the mouth. The owner of the horse, who was in the group of people who were accompanying Captain Jones, was terrified. He was sure that the horse would soon die, and he began to weep and wail for losing his means of earning a living. The snakebite was looked upon as a sign of God's anger, and the poor man began to blame himself for having anything to do with this man who was not a Mohammedan.

"Now God is punishing me," he wailed. The feelings of Captain Jones's companions changed, and they suddenly became hostile as the horse began to show symptoms of suffering from the snake's venom. For a moment he wondered what to do. Then he knelt in view of them all, and prayed. He told the Lord how necessary it was, for his sake and for the people's sake, that the horse should not die. Then he claimed the promise in our Morning Watch text today. When he got up from his knees he said to the people, "My God will not let the horse die. He has heard my prayers." Then he mounted the trembling horse and rode on. The people followed, and were astonished to find the horse quite well at the end of the day. And you can imagine how much more they respected the captain for the rest of the journey.

What God did for Captain Jones, He can do for you. Remember this precious promise, and have faith in God.

"I beseech you therefore, brethren, by the mercies of God, that ye present your bodies a living sacrifice, holy, acceptable unto God, which is your reasonable service." Romans 12:1.

For some people it may be a sacrifice not to smoke; for others it may be a sacrifice not to read the comics, or not to go to shows. For some it may be a sacrifice to leave home, parents, and friends and go to a mission field. But if every morning as we wake up we would say, "Dear Jesus, this body of mine is all Yours today. May my eyes, my ears, my hands, and my feet do only those things that please You," and if we would remember all day and every day that we are not our own—that would be presenting our bodies a living sacrifice to God.

Let me tell you a story of a living sacrifice that Elder Richard Hayden told me while I was visiting at the Inca Union Mission.

A young couple—Louis and Zoila Gomez, with their four little children—were sent to open a new mission among the Sipibo Indians a thousand miles upstream from Iquitos. Their only connection with the outside world was a little river steamer that came from Iquitos and passed their place once in two months. God blessed their work, and soon they had a school started for the children and were holding night classes for the adults. This made a certain rich landowner angry.

"If those Indians learn to read, I won't be able to work them like slaves anymore," he said to himself. So he hired two men to poison Louis' food while he was with some Indians in their harvest field one day. Poor Louis was carried home, but he only had time to tell Zoila and the children to be faithful; then he died. Zoila wrote Elder Hayden and begged him to come and visit them. He did, and studied the situation carefully. He saw the school; he baptized a group of thirty Indians; then he said, "Zoila, we can't understand why God has permitted Louis to die like this. The work is just nicely started, but you can't stay here alone. You must pack up your things and take the steamer when it returns, and go to live with your mother."

"No, no, Brother Hayden," said Zoila. "I can't leave these dear Sipibo Indians without a teacher. They have begged me to stay, and I've promised them I would."

"But Zoila, how can I go away and leave you alone?"

"Please say no more, Brother Hayden," begged Zoila. "See those tall men over there? They have traveled four days to come to beg for a teacher. I cannot go. I must stay."

And Zoila stayed. She stayed *alone* on that isolated mission station for eight years! Then a new missionary couple came to take her place, and Zoila took her little family to our college near Lima, Peru, to put them in school. I had the pleasure of meeting her there. I took my hat off to that noble woman, shook her hand, and thanked her for her faithfulness and her courage. That's what I call a living sacrifice.

Now take a look at the little things you might be asked to give up for Christ. Could you call any one of them a sacrifice?

1 CORINTHIANS 13   DECEMBER 7

"And now abideth faith, hope, charity, these three; but the greatest of these is charity." 1 Corinthians 13:13.

Charity is the Bible word for love, and love is indeed the greatest power in the world. Without love there could be no obedience and no salvation. Without love there could be no homes and no heaven. Here is one of the most outstanding illustrations of the power of love that I have ever heard about. It occurred in connection with the death of Kathryn Lawes in October, 1937.

Kathryn was the wife of Lewis E. Lawes, the famous warden of the great Sing Sing Prison. For seventeen years she had walked in and out of this prison, befriending the unfortunate men who were shut off from society. She listened to the cries of worried fathers. She wrote letters for hopeless young criminals. She visited the families of the prisoners and took them food, clothes, and even money. And when the men were newly released after years of isolation, it was often Kathryn Lawes who helped them adjust once more to freedom. When news of her tragic death resulting from an accident was whispered from man to man and from cell to cell, it brought a gloom and sadness that could be felt over all the prison. As the day of her funeral approached, a representative of the prisoners went to Warden Lawes and begged in behalf of hundreds of devoted men the privilege of paying their last respects to one they loved so much. Warden Lawes listened sympathetically, then nodded his consent. The night before the funeral the south gate of Sing Sing Prison swung slowly open and a long, silent procession of thieves, swindlers, murderers, and criminals of every kind walked out to the warden's house a quarter of a mile away. There were no guards. There were no guns. But not a man broke ranks. After reaching the house they filed past the coffin. Each paused a few seconds in front of the casket, then heartbroken and weeping, he moved on. Reforming the lines, they walked back to their lonely prison cells.

No wonder Paul says love is the *greatest* power on earth. Ellen G. White says love is a *precious gift* from God, and Henry Ward Beecher says love is the *river of life* in this world.

If the Christian love of that good woman had power to do this miracle, then why can't God do something like that with *your* love?

2 CORINTHIANS 9   DECEMBER 8

"He which soweth sparingly shall reap also sparingly; and he which soweth bountifully shall reap also bountifully." 2 Corinthians 9:6.

Many stories have been told to illustrate the truth that life is like a mirror because it reflects the same kind of looks and actions that are put in front of it. Here is one that I have heard many times about the kindness of the wife of one of our early settlers.

A young man, Donald Wilson, and his wife built a little cabin in a spot where the prairie met the vast forest. They were the only settlers for miles around. One day down the trail to his cabin came a noble-looking Indian, but he looked weary, and as he came closer the young wife looking through the window could tell by his face that he was sick and thirsty.

"I'm thirsty; please give me a drink of water," he said to Donald.

But Donald replied roughly, "Go away. I give nothing to Indians."

The rude answer hurt the Indian, but he said, "I can go no farther. Can you not give me a drink?"

"Go away at once," replied Donald, and slowly, with anger burning in his heart, the Indian turned to go. The young wife heard the Indian's request. She was troubled by her husband's rough answer. Through the window she watched the Indian go slowly away. But he had not gone far before he staggered and fell. At once the kind little woman took bread, some water, and a jug of milk, slipped out the front door of the cabin, and ran to help him. He had fainted with exhaustion, but with cool water and kind words she revived him.

"Please forgive the unkind words of my husband," she said, "and take this bread and this milk." The Indian soon revived and was able to go on, but before leaving he gave her a white feather from his headdress and said, "Take this, Little White Dove, and when your husband is out hunting, tell him to wear it and he will be safe. I had planned to come back and kill him, but for your sake I will spare him." Three years went by, and one day while out hunting Donald got hopelessly lost. Light snow covered all his trails. He called and called, but his companions could not hear him. His calls attracted the Indians, and soon their shadowy forms surrounded him. They tied his hands behind his back and took him to their village. The chief recognized him at once, and he was wearing his white feather!

"It is good that you wear the feather," said the chief. "Otherwise, you would have been killed tonight. But your wife was kind to me, and for her sake I will be kind to you." The chief fed him, gave him a warm place to sleep, and the next morning took him back to his cabin. The Indian's kindness in turn changed Donald's heart, and ever after there was a bond of friendship between the dwellers of the forest and the settlers in the little cabin.

Do you want to reap kindness? There is only one way to get it—you must sow kindness.

GALATIANS 5:19-26; 6:1-10   DECEMBER 9

"Be not deceived; God is not mocked: for whatsoever a man soweth, that shall he also reap." Galatians 6:7.

Paul had a real burden to teach the members of the early Christian church that they could not sow the "works of the flesh" and reap the "fruit of the Spirit." But if they wanted to reap the fruit of the Spirit, they had to sow love, peace, goodness, and the like. It is inspiring to see everywhere the results that men and women reap when they have faithfully sown the seeds of the "fruit of the Spirit."

Have you ever heard the name Pedro Kalbermatter? Let me tell you about him. He was only a boy when his father and uncle accepted the Advent message in Argentina. When he was 17 years old he became a colporteur, and in 1907 he entered our new school in Entre Rios. After only three months of study, however, he reached the age when all young men in Argentina were required to take military training, and he was drafted into the army. The army officers had never heard of a Seventh-day Adventist and had never seen a conscientious objector, and when he asked for Sabbath privileges, he was told to forget his religious ideas and obey orders—or else. But those officers were soon to know what a Seventh-day Adventist is. The first Sabbath when he refused to work, they didn't know what to do, but the second Sabbath they made him stand stiffly at attention till his feet were so swollen he could hardly walk. The next Sabbath he was told to go to the river and wash clothes, and when he wouldn't do it they brought a tub, put water and soap in it, then put his clothes in, and told him to wash. He wouldn't do it. So one soldier took one hand and another took the other hand, and they moved his hands up and down, up and down, up and down till they were tired; but when they stopped he stopped. Then they whipped him till the whip broke. They begged; they threatened; but Pedro would not work on Sabbath. For punishment he was sent to work in a stone quarry with common criminals. The Catholic chaplain intervened and secured liberty for him on Sabbaths. Soon one of his fellow prisoners was converted. After four months of this he was transferred to a special disciplinary department of the army. Pedro thought the ordeal would begin all over again, but the commandant listened carefully to Pedro's explanation and was convinced that his imprisonment was unjust. He freed him from Sabbath service and put him in charge of his garden. Later this officer brought Pedro's case to the attention of the minister of war, with the result that all Seventh-day Adventist youth thereafter drafted into Argentine Army were to have complete Sabbath liberty! Pedro later became one of the great missionaries in South America. What a boy! What a wonderful result of sowing faithful obedience to God's commandments.

What are *you* sowing now? You will surely reap it, for good or for ill, someday.

EPHESIANS 6   **DECEMBER 10**

"Take the helmet of salvation, and the sword of the Spirit, which is the word of God." Ephesians 6:17.

In a thousand ways the dear Word of God has protected those who love it and obey it, and has helped them to be victorious in their spiritual battles over evil. In a report by the American Bible Society a few years ago, a Mr. F. L. MacCallum told a story about an Adventist young man whose name was Paul, and how he was protected by his Bible.

Paul sold Bibles and Scripture portions for the society, and one week he was working in a little town some distance from the city where he lived. It had been a hard week, and on the last day he became very nervous as he realized that there was a tall stranger watching him every time he came out of a house. His sly glances filled Paul with uneasiness. At last it was time to take a bus to the station where he would catch a train for home. He would be glad to get away from this man who seemed to be shadowing him. The bus came. Paul got on. But the stranger got on too! Paul got off at the station, and he didn't see the tall stranger get off. He felt relieved, and when the train came in he got aboard and found a small compartment all to himself. He was about to lie down for a rest when the door to the side passage opened and in came that same tall stranger!

"Do you carry much money with you?" he asked.

"No," said Paul, "but why do you ask?"

"Have you got five hundred lire?"

"No, but who are you?"

"Are you armed?"

Paul hesitated then said, "Yes. Are you?"

"Yes. Here's mine," said the man, pulling out a wicked-looking pistol. "Now show me yours."

Paul reached into his brief case and took out his Bible.

"There's mine," he said.

"You're crazy," said the man. "That's not a gun; that's a book."

"It shoots better than yours," said Paul. "Your gun can only shoot the man it is pointing at, but this book is certain death to every wicked man who will listen to its words. I've shot at least six wicked men that I know of with this book."

"How do you shoot with a book?"

"Put your gun away and I will show you."

The man put his gun away and Paul opened his Bible and read a verse here and there as he told the wonderful story of how sin came into the world, and how Jesus, the Son of God, came to save men, and has gone to prepare a place in heaven for all who believe.

"Tell me more. Tell me quickly. My station is the next stop," said the man. And Paul told of the new earth where there would be no more sin or sorrow or death. The train stopped. The stranger grasped Paul warmly by the hand, and as he stood up to leave he said, "No one will know what your gun saved me from tonight!"

The Word of God is indeed the sword of the Spirit. Be sure *you* are always armed with it.

"My God shall supply all your need according to his riches in glory by Christ Jesus." Philippians 4:19.

There were so many good texts in today's Scripture reading that it was hard to decide which one to talk about. At last I chose the promise found in Philippians 4:19, because maybe someday you will need to remember it and claim it. There is a difference between "needs" and "wants." There is a difference between "necessities" and "luxuries." Notice that God has promised to supply your "needs"—your "necessities"—and He does!

Mr. and Mrs. Peter Jensen, of Ballston Spa, New York, could tell you that He does. Mr. Jensen is a painter by trade and is faithful in paying his tithe and supporting the work of God. But painting jobs aren't too numerous during the cold winter months, and one winter he found himself out of work. The Jensens prayed earnestly, but no work opened up, and one day their oil-burning heater ran out of oil, and went out. The weather was bitterly cold, and heat was definitely a "need," so they claimed the promise in this morning's Bible text. They scraped around and found enough money to buy two gallons of fuel oil. It was just enough for one more day. But the next day they were able to find enough money to buy two more gallons. So they had heat for one more day. Then Mr. Jensen disconnected the two oil drums at the side of the house, and by tipping them up he managed to get two and a half more gallons of oil. This he put into the container connected with the stove, and prayed God for help. It would burn for one more day anyway. But it burned for two days—three—four—five—for six days! Then Mr. Jensen happened to look through his wallet and found a check for $7 that he had not cashed! With this money he bought some fuel oil and enough gas for his car, so they could go to church on Sabbath. When they came home from church the flame finally sputtered and went out. But on Monday Mr. Jensen found work, and the crisis was over.

God often permits us to be tested and tried so we can be certain that it is *He,* and not *we,* who is able to supply the needs.

What a wonderful God we serve! What wonderful promises He has made for us! Have you gone into partnership with Him?

"Let your speech be alway with grace, seasoned with salt." Colossians 4:6.

One of the saddest stories I have ever read was a poem by Will Carleton called "The First Settler's Story." In this poem he tells the experience of an early pioneer with his brave young wife, as they built their cabin out in the Middle West, and struggled to clear their land and make a living. He tells of the lonely days, the homesick days, the hard days, and the happy days as they toiled together. Then he tells of the days when too much work and too much weariness began to take the flavor from their words, and "old attentions" and "kind caresses" were left out. Then one night the husband came home, weary and exhausted from his work, and when he went to milk the cows, he found they had wandered away and he had to go and find them. Then in temper he spoke impatiently to his wife and said:

> "You ought to've kept the animals in view,
> And drove them in; you'd nothing else to do.
> The heft of all our life on me must fall;
> You just lie round, and let me do it all."

As soon as the words were spoken he knew there was poison in them. But pride and anger kept back the works that would have asked forgiveness and made things right. He even went to work the next morning without his usual goodbye kiss. As he ate his lunch he found "fresh sweet-eyed pansies" in with his sandwiches! He knew their meaning, and said, "Tonight I'll ask forgiveness of her." He went home early, but his wife was not there. A note on the table explained that the cows had wandered away again, and she had gone to look for them, and it ended with, "I've tried to do my best, I have indeed. Darling, piece out with love the strength I lack, and have kind words for me when I get back." Just then a terrible thunderstorm broke upon them, but with his dog he went out into the night to find her. All night he raced with death, searching, calling everywhere. Three times he came back to his cabin, hoping she would be there. Then as the morning came he returned once more, and heard the tinkle of the cowbells. "You've come," he shouted, and rushed through the door. Yes, she had come, but had gone again. The night's storm had been too much for her, and there she lay on the floor, dead.

The story closes with these sad words:

"Boys flying kites haul in their white-winged birds;
You can't do that way when you're flying words.
'Careful with fire' is good advice, we know:
'Careful with words' is ten times doubly so.
Thoughts unexpressed may sometimes fall back dead;
But God himself can't kill them when they're said."

Life is too short for angry words. Speak only kind and loving words today. Let your speech be seasoned with salt.

1 THESSALONIANS 4:14-18; 5   DECEMBER 13

"The Lord himself shall descend from heaven with a shout, with the voice of the archangel, and with the trump of God: and the dead in Christ shall rise first: then we which are alive and remain shall be caught up together with them in the clouds, to meet the Lord in the air: and so shall we ever be with the Lord." 1 Thessalonians 4:16, 17.

What a privilege it is for us to be "children of light," and to understand the signs that tell us the time is near for Jesus to come and resurrect our loved ones who have passed away. This hope does indeed give us great comfort.

Here's a story about two little "children of light" who brought comfort to many hearts away over in the Solomon Islands. Their father's name was Napthali, and he was a Fijian missionary on the island of Mussau. But the people on Mussau wouldn't have anything to do with him. They wouldn't listen to him preach. They wouldn't even look at his Picture Roll. And although Napthali tried and tried, it seemed nobody was taking any notice of the gospel. At last Napthali got very sick, and his good wife Vasiti got sick too, and Tina, the 12-year-old daughter, and Joe, the 8-year-old son, were the only ones there to look after them. One day a man came from a village ten miles away.

"Teacher Napthali," he said, "a man has just died in our village, and with his last breath he said he wanted to be buried like a Christian. Can you come?"

"I'm sorry," said Napthali, "but I'm too sick. I can't get out of bed."

"Then we'll have to bury him like a heathen," said the man. But Tina came to the rescue.

"Let me go, Father," she said. "I know the verses to read."

"But it wouldn't be safe. You are only a little girl."

"But Joe would go with me. Wouldn't you, Joe?"

And Joe said Yes.

So Napthali let them go. When they got to the village two hundred heathen people gathered around to see what they would do. Tina showed them how to wrap the dead man in a mat. She told them to dig a grave. Then that brave little girl read our Morning Watch text— 1 Thessalonians 4:16-18. After that she and Joe sang "When He cometh to make up His jewels," and Tina prayed that angels would mark his grave because she was sure the man had loved Jesus as he understood, and that he wanted to go to heaven when Jesus came. After the funeral Tina and Joe walked ten miles home again, alone. In a few days another messenger came from another village to request another Christian funeral. And in a few more days there came still another request. Three times Tina and Joe conducted Christian funerals and comforted heathen hearts while Napthali was too sick to go. When at last Napthali was better and went out preaching again, he found that something wonderful had happened. In every village everybody wanted to listen now. That was the turning point, and today everybody on that island comes to Sabbath school. Tina, of course, is grown up now. While visiting our Sabbath schools in Fiji not long ago I met a fine-looking woman, and as I shook hands she said, "I'm Tina! My father was Napthali." I was so happy to meet her. I thanked God again for "children of light."

Are you one of the "children of light" too?

2 THESSALONIANS 2   DECEMBER 14

"Let no man deceive you by any means." 2 Thessalonians 2:3.

In our scripture today Paul is warning us against "the working of Satan with all power and signs and lying wonders" (verse 9). Isn't it strange, but just about the time when the three angels' messages of Revelation 14 went to call out a people who would keep the commandments of God and the faith of Jesus, Satan began his movement of modern spiritualism, which was, by signs and lying wonders, to try to deceive the very elect! Here is how it began.

In the year 1848, Mr. and Mrs. John D. Fox and their two youngest children, Margaret, age 15, and Kate, age 12, lived in Hydesville, near Rochester, New York. Soon after moving into this house they were disturbed by strange knocking sounds. At first they thought it was mice or rats, or maybe the windows rattling in the wind. But on the night of March 31, 1848, after making sure the windows were tight, Kate thought she detected the knocking imitated, or replied to, noises they made in the room. So she snapped her fingers several times and said out loud, "Here, old Splitfoot, do as I do." Immediately there came the same number of sharp distinct taps in reply. This scared the girls nearly out of their wits, and they didn't want to continue any more conversation with "old Splitfoot." But the mother was interested. She worked out a code of knocks and was soon getting intelligent messages. One of the first things old Splitfoot told her was that a man had been murdered in this house years before and that his body was buried in the cellar. They dug down, and sure enough, they found the skeleton! Margaret also soon became a spirit medium, and from that day to this, signs and wonders of all kinds have increased in all our land. Some people say it is trickery. Some say it is done by the spirits of the dead. You and I need never be deceived. We know that Satan is using his fallen angels to do these things.

Have nothing to do with anybody who says the departed dead can communicate with you or appear to you. The Bible says, "The dead know not any thing." Be sure *you* are not deceived.

1 TIMOTHY 6   DECEMBER 15

"Godliness with contentment is great gain. For we brought nothing into this world, and it is certain we can carry nothing out. And having food and raiment let us be therewith content." 1 Timothy 6:6-8.

At some time or other every one of us is going to be tempted to give up a little godliness for a little more money. Paul has well said, "The love of money is the root of all evil," and Satan knows exactly how to tempt us to be discontented with our wages, and to make us think we could earn so much more in the world if we were not so particular about the Sabbath and the work of God.

Some time ago one of our missionaries hired a man to do the cooking for his family. The cook in turn hired a little boy to bring the water, peel the potatoes, and light the charcoal fires. He was called the cook's assistant, and he was so faithful and polite that the missionary took quite a fancy to him and sent him to the mission school. As the years went by he became a Christian and was baptized. Then one summer when he was in high school he decided to sell books and try to earn a scholarship. God blessed him and gave him good success. One very hot day he called at the home of a missionary of another denomination and gave his canvass. The missionary was impressed with his courteous, efficient manner, and invited him inside. After talking awhile and finding out who he was, the missionary said, "Look here, young man, I need a young fellow like you to look after one of my village schools and churches. My worker there has just passed away." He then offered him a very good wage and said, "You can preach anything you like except the Sabbath and the second coming of Christ." The young man hesitated just a moment. The man saw it and quickly said, "Don't give me your answer now. Stay with me tonight. Think it over, and give me your answer in the morning." The young man stayed. He had a good dinner and spent a very pleasant evening. Early the next morning the young man rose and knocked on the missionary's door.

"Goodbye, sir," he said.

"You mean you are not going to take the job I offered you?" asked the man in surprise.

"No, sir. I'm sure you wouldn't want me. You see, sir, it is the second coming of Christ and the Sabbath that have made me what I am, and if I couldn't preach the Sabbath and the Second Coming, all you would have would be a cook's assistant boy." After thanking his host for his kindness, he went on his way rejoicing. I take my hat off to that young man. Don't you?

That's the spirit we all need. Pray God to make you content, and strong to resist the temptation to give up some godliness for worldly gain.

"I have fought a good fight, I have finished my course, I have kept the faith: henceforth there is laid up for me a crown of righteousness, which the Lord . . . shall give me at that day." 2 Timothy 4:7, 8.

Paul was himself a good Christian soldier; no wonder he exhorted Timothy to "endure hardness, as a good soldier of Jesus Christ" (2 Timothy 2:3).

Down through the years young people have caught the inspiration and the challenge of these words, and have gone forth everywhere doing great things for God. In the year 1895, just about the time our missionaries on the ship *Pitcairn* were doing wonderful things in the South Pacific, there was in Yorkshire, England, a minister by the name of Sabine Baring-Gould. One day his Sunday school was to join another Sunday school in a nearby village for a rally, and he wanted his children to sing as they marched into the village. He looked through all the songbooks he had for a suitable march song, but couldn't find one, so decided to write one himself. He sat up late into the night, and gave, not only to his children but to all the children in the world, the greatly loved song "Onward, Christian Soldiers!"

Onward, Christian soldiers!
Marching as to war
With the cross of Jesus
Going on before.

His children loved it, and they sang it so enthusiastically that it became popular immediately, and soon found its place in several hymnbooks. The tune to which the hymn is sung today is not the original tune. This tune was written sometime later by Sir Arthur Seymour Sullivan. This wonderful hymn, with its popular words and tune, is known all around the world, in every nation, and brings inspiration and challenge to all. Whether it is played by brass bands or cathedral pipe organs, whether it is sung by church choirs or mission school students, its spirit is irresistible.

Can you sing this great hymn? Do you get goose pimples when you hear a great choir sing it? Goose pimples are not enough. Determine that you yourself will also be a worthy soldier of the Lord Jesus Christ.

"Teaching us that . . . we should live soberly, righteously, and godly. . . ; looking for that blessed hope, and the glorious appearing of the great God and our Saviour Jesus Christ." Titus 2:12, 13.

What could we do without Jesus? And what could we do without the "blessed hope" of His soon coming? Do you really *long* for Jesus to come? Listen!

A number of years ago Dr. C. F. Schilling spent his three-week vacation in my jungle dispensary in Burma. It was a wonderful time for us, and we kept the doctor busy day and night looking after the surgical cases that were beyond our skill and ability. The news of the doctor's visit spread far and wide, and five days after the doctor had gone back to his hospital in India two men came to ask him to come and look at a poor woman who had a huge watery cyst in her abdomen. I explained that the doctor had gone away again.

"Then can't you do something?" they begged.

"I can only do a little," I said, and I went with them.

With my instruments I drained off five gallons and three quarts of fluid. The poor woman was so happy. She thought I was the doctor, and that the operation was all over. I said to the husband, "Tell her that you missed the doctor, and that all the water will come back again."

"No, no! I can't tell her," he said. "You tell her."

So I had to tell her. I told her that I was only a nurse, that I couldn't operate, and that in a few weeks the water would come back again. I told her I would try to get the doctor to come back again next year, but this time they were five days too late. Then I saw one of the saddest things I've ever seen in all my life. I saw the smile crushed from her happy face. For the longest minute I've ever lived she looked off into space, and then she said, "All right then, all right. You write and tell the doctor that I'll be lying here on my back, counting the moons away till he comes again. You say he might come again in a year? I've been lying on my back for seven years, and one more year won't seem so long. I'll be waiting here."

I'm glad to tell you that I was able to arrange with a surgeon in Moulmein to remove the cyst (it weighed forty-nine pounds) and that she had a wonderful recovery. But I cannot forget her pathetic words, "I'll be lying here counting the moons away till the doctor comes."

Do you long that much for Jesus to come?

"I beseech thee for my son Onesimus . . . , which in time past was to thee unprofitable, but now profitable to thee and to me." Philemon 10, 11.

Onesimus was a slave to Philemon, a Christian gentleman in Colosse. For some reason or other he ran away. In those days if a slave ran away and was found again, according to the law of the land he could be put to death at the will of his master. But Onesimus had been converted, and he repented of his mistake, and in this letter to Philemon, Paul begged him to give his slave another chance to make good. This lesson is good for us all to learn. One mistake or one failure need not spoil a whole life. We can make things right, we can try again, and we can make good. Here is a story told in a mission paper that is typical of the success that can come to those who may fail once.

Tadayga was a young man in one of our mission schools in Ethiopia, studying to become a teacher. But he failed in arithmetic. In fact, he failed twice. Without passing in arithmetic, he could not hope ever to get a teacher's certificate, and now that he had tried and failed twice, he would not even be permitted to stay on in school. What could he do now? Just then a call came to the mission for a teacher to come to the village of Abonsa and start a school for first graders. The mission had no teachers to spare. In Abonsa a teacher would only be given a place to sleep and his food. They asked Tadayga if he would like to go and try. Tadayga went. The school was only a shed with one small blackboard, but the first week there were fifty children who came. The next week there were sixty-two; the next, eighty-five; and the next, ninety! Tadayga could not take any more. Even now he had to have a morning session and an afternoon session, for the schoolhouse would only hold forty-five children. He taught them numbers and reading and writing. They learned to read the Bible, and the children read the Bible to their parents, and more than one hundred came to his Sabbath school. What do you think Tadayga did evenings? He studied his arithmetic, and at the end of the year he passed his examination!

"If at first *you* don't succeed, try, try, try again."

"Faith is the substance of things hoped for, the evidence of things not seen....Without faith it is impossible to please him." Hebrews 11:1-6.

Hebrews 11 is known as the faith chapter of the Bible. Our hearts thrill as we read the list of Bible heroes mentioned there, and recall what their faith has accomplished. But the list of heroes given is not complete by any means, for many followers of the Lord Jesus in every land have been giants in faith.

Let us take Dr. Ida S. Scudder for an example. She was born in India, where her parents were medical missionaries. As a young woman she saw that India had need of women doctors, so after studying medicine in the United States she went back to India in 1900, determined to establish a medical school. She began in a little room eight by ten feet, with one bed in it for an inpatient, and a window through which she could talk with outpatients and dispense medicines. Some people laughed at the idea of her starting a medical school, but two years later a friend gave her money to build a forty-bed hospital. By 1909 she had started a nurse's training school, and in 1918 she opened a medical college with 34 women students! Today (1965) in the Vellore Christian Medical College there are 159 full-time doctors and 224 graduate nurses on the staff. There are 337 medical students, both men and women, and 281 students taking nurse's training, and instead of 40 beds there are now 761! Recently we had the pleasure of hearing Mr. Savarirayan, the superintendent of this great medical school, speak to us in morning worship at the General Conference. He told us of a beautiful example of faith.

One day he was sitting by a railway bridge that crossed a deep ravine. He saw a man and his little girl come walking along the railway track, and said to himself, "The little girl will be too frightened to cross the bridge." But when they got to the ravine, where they had to walk on the railway ties to get across, the little girl took her father's hand, looked at the ties, then looked up into her father's face, and talked pleasantly all the way. In a few seconds they were safely across. The ravine was there, but the little girl barely saw it.

That's the way you can exercise faith too. When you meet with difficulties, simply take your heavenly Father's hand. Then look up into His face and talk pleasantly all the way.

"Behold, how great a matter a little fire kindleth! And the tongue is a fire . . . and setteth on fire the course of nature." James 3:5, 6.

On the evening of October 8, 1871, Mrs. O'Leary, who lived on the west side of the hustling frontier city of Chicago, lighted her little kerosene lantern and went out to her barn to milk her cow. She fastened the cow's head in the stall, put her lantern on the floor, then sat down on her little stool and began to milk. For some reason or other the cow was in a contrary mood that night, and suddenly, without warning, it let fly a vicious kick. It knocked over the kerosene lantern, and caused Mrs. O'Leary to lose her balance, and before she could pick herself up the straw on the floor was on fire. In spite of all she could do, in no time at all, the flimsy barn was in flames. There had been no rain for several weeks; the grass around the barn was dry, and a high wind carried the blaze to the nearby houses. Most of the houses in Chicago in those days were built of wood, and soon the fire was beyond all possible control. The fire quickly spread up to the Chicago River, leaped over it, and spread desolation far and wide, to the south first and then to the north side. An area of about three-and-one-half square miles was destroyed, including 17,500 buildings and property valued at $196 million. About three hundred people were burned to death and many thousands were made homeless. And it all started from a little kerosene lantern that was meant to be a blessing!

The apostle James tells the truth when he says, "The tongue is a fire." God meant our tongues to be a blessing—to speak kind, helpful, cheerful words; but if we let them gossip and criticize and tell falsehoods, good names may be ruined, friendships broken, and fond hopes turned to ashes.

The Bible talks about the "gift of tongues." I can remember Elder G. B. Starr, one of our pioneer preachers, saying, "The gift most of us need is the gift to *hold* our tongues." And I think he was telling the truth. Don't you?

Never let your tongue say anything about anyone until you ask yourself whether it's true, whether it's kind, and whether it will do any good to tell it.

"Be sober, be vigilant; because your adversary the devil, as a roaring lion, walketh about, seeking whom he may devour." 1 Peter 5:8.

I do not know anything about roaring lions, but for twenty years I lived in a land where we had roaring tigers, and I know how roaring tigers seek whom they may devour.

One day my Burma Brass Band was on its way to hold an evening meeting in Lapota village. In the cool of the evening, as we were approaching the village, suddenly on the hills to the right we heard an animal call—"Squ-e-e-eak!"

It was a high reedy note, and I said, "Boys, listen! There's a deer over there." For there were lots of deer in our jungle that called just like that.

The boys listened. The sound came again, "Squ-e-e-eak," but the boys shook their heads and said, "That's not a deer, Thara; that's a tiger."

I said, "But boys, tigers don't go squ-e-e-eak; tigers go roar-r-r-r."

But the boys answered, "Not always, Thara; it all depends on what animal the tiger is hunting. He makes a sound like the sound of the animal he is trying to catch."

Just then we heard another "squ-e-e-eak" on the hills to the left. And I said, "Listen, boys! There's another tiger."

The boys listened, then whispered, "No, Thara, that's not another tiger; that is a deer."

"Well, I can't tell the difference," I said.

"We can," they replied. "We live in this jungle country, and our fathers have taught us the difference. The tiger's call is a little more throaty. Listen!"

For the next half hour we listened to one of the tragedies of jungle life. "Squ-e-e-eak," called the crafty and deceitful old tiger. *"Squ-e-e-eak,"* answered the innocent little deer, thinking its mate was calling; and then it ran a little closer. "Squ-e-e-eak"; *"Squ-e-e-eak"*; "Squ-e-e-eak"; *"Squ-e-e-eak."* Closer and closer they came together, till the tiger was close enough to spring upon its victim. Then the tiger opened its mouth and roar-r-r-r-red. The poor little deer was paralyzed with the awful sound; and the tiger sprang upon it and killed it! And that was the end of the innocent little deer.

Believe me, juniors, the devil does not do his hunting dressed in a red suit and with a pitchfork in hand. Indeed, no. He dresses in the latest fashions; he gets into the comics, the radio, the TV, and the billboards.

He tries to make you think he is your best friend. He tries to lure you closer and closer to him, then when it's too late, he laughs at your terror and mocks at your bitter regrets and remorse.

Ask God to help you recognize the crafty old devil, then keep as far away from him as you can.

2 PETER 3 DECEMBER 22

"The Lord is not slack concerning his promise. . . ; but is longsuffering to us-ward, not willing that any should perish, but that all should come to repentance." 2 Peter 3:9.

It doesn't matter what God does—whether He creates, forgives sin, performs a miracle, or makes a promise—you can expect some scoffer to come along and try to make fun of it and say it isn't so. And this is just what Peter said would happen. "There shall come in the last days scoffers . . . saying, Where is the promise of his coming?" (verses 3, 4). But quite often God has given His children words to speak that have shut the mouths of these scoffers and put them to shame.

I remember a fine story that our greatly loved evangelist Phillip Knox used many times in his Los Angeles meetings. A notorious drunkard was converted, and some time later one of his old drinking friends thought he would hold him up to ridicule, so he said, "I hear you have been converted."

"Yes, thank God," replied the new Christian.

"And I suppose you believe the Bible now."

"Yes, indeed I do!"

"And I suppose you believe the miracle of Jesus turning water into wine!"

"I surely do," he replied, "and if you will come to my house I'll show you a bigger miracle than that! I'll show you where Jesus has changed beer and whisky into carpets, chairs, a piano, and new dresses for my wife and children!"

The scoffer's mouth was stopped, and he never tried to ridicule that man's religion again.

There's another story I like about a pious old Christian who spent much time in prayer and fasting. One day a wild young fellow came to poke fun at him.

"Father," he said, "if there is not to be another world after this one, what a miserable time you *have* had."

"True, my son," said the old man, "but if there is another world after this one, what a miserable time you *will* have!"

And that scoffer's mouth was stopped; he never tried to make fun of that old man again.

Don't be surprised if someone comes along to mock and scoff at you and your religion someday. You are safe if you stay on God's side and hold fast to His promise.

1 JOHN 2   DECEMBER 23

"Love not the world, neither the things that are in the world. . . . The world passeth away, and the lust thereof: but he that doeth the will of God abideth for ever." 1 John 2:15-17.

A number of years ago I was Ingathering in the city of Moulmein, Burma, and I met Mr. Sinclair, the chief engineer of a large rice mill. I told him about some of our dramatic dispensary experiences—such as the girl with the "burned" finger, and how Mr. Baird, my associate missionary, and I amputated the arm below the elbow and saved her life; and the man who had been "stung by the elephant," and how we washed his bowels and put them back and sewed him up!

"Remarkable!" said Mr. Sinclair, "but how can you two men be happy away up there in the never-nevers—with no whiskey and sodas?"

I said, "We get more pleasure out of seeing happy mothers with healthy babies in their arms, and hearing them each say, 'It was nearly dead, but you cared enough to help and now look at it! If it hadn't been for you, my baby would have died.'"

"Yes, yes, wonderful," said Mr. Sinclair. "But you have no jazz orchestras and no dances!"

"But I have a brass band of twenty-five instruments," I said, "and a choir of eighty-three voices that can sing anthems in six parts. That gives me more pleasure than any jazz orchestra could ever give."

After a pause he said, "You're right, Mr. Hare, but you have no movies and no shows!"

"But we have the real comedy and the real tragedy of life," I said. And I told him of the little woman with a terribly scarred face and only one arm, who fell at my feet and sobbed out her thanks:

" 'Oh, Thara, if you hadn't come that night when the marijuana fiend attacked me and cut me up, I surely would have died. But you weren't afraid of the night. You weren't afraid of the tigers. You came, and now I am alive.' " And I said, "Mr. Sinclair, no movie could ever give me real joy like that."

"Yes, yes, I suppose you're right, but you have no clubs, no association, just two white men among all those jungle people!"

I said, "Mr. Sinclair, no association is so satisfying as associating with men and women who have found Christ because of what you have done. The last night of school one of my big boys stepped into my office, just for a little visit, and he said, 'I wanted to come and say Thank you before I went home. When I came to school I had no hope of heaven, but it's different now, because you and MaMa have been so kind and patient with me.' No applause of drunken associates in a club could ever compare with that kind of joy and satisfaction."

For a moment Mr. Sinclair struggled with his emotions, then he said, "Mr. Hare, you're right. And do you know, I'd give the world to experience a joy like that."

I replied, "That's what *I* gave. I gave the world for that joy."

Dear juniors, that is what it will cost you, too. It will cost the world, but there is no happiness, no satisfaction, that can compare with the joy of serving Jesus.

> There is joy, joy, joy in serving Jesus,
> Joy that throbs within my heart;
> Ev'ry moment, ev'ry hour,
> As I draw upon His power,
> There is joy, joy, joy that never shall depart. *
> —Oswald J. Smith

---

* Words and music copyrighted 1959, renewal. The Rodeheaver Co., owner. Used by permission.

REVELATION 1

"Behold, he cometh with clouds; and every eye shall see him." Revelation 1:7.

One of the most exciting days I have ever had in all my life was the day I saw the Prince of Wales riding down the street in Melbourne, Australia. I was only a 7-year-old boy then, but I played third cornet in our Echo Publishing Company brass band. And our band was given a position on the street along which the prince would pass. In 1901, George, the Duke of York, who later became King George V, was made Prince of Wales, and that same year he visited Australia. The procession was to pass along the street at ten o'clock in the morning, and we were all told to be sure to be there early! My father played one of the bass horns, and my brother Reuben played the baritone; so we got up early that morning. I wasn't hungry for breakfast, but Mother said, "You'd better eat a good breakfast, and you'd better take some lunch. You can never tell what might happen to a procession like this."

But I was too excited to eat, and I didn't want to carry anything but my horn.

"He's coming at ten o'clock, Mother, and we'll be home for dinner," I argued. And Mother said, "All right! But you know—"

All our band members were at their position at nine o'clock. Their horns were all shining and bright. We stood in formation and played our piece, just for practice. Then we waited and waited. Crowds of people came and lined the streets on both sides. That was one of the longest hours I have ever lived, but at last ten o'clock came and we all snapped to attention.

But the prince didn't come. Nobody came. Eleven o'clock came, but the prince didn't come! We were getting tired. We weren't standing at attention any more. The crowd was getting restless; some were grumbling and complaining; and many went away. Twelve o'clock came, but still no prince! We were hungry. If only I had brought the lunch my mother wanted to give me! My father sneaked off to a bakery shop nearby and brought me back a dry roll! One o'clock came; two o'clock! Three o'clock! No prince! We were so tired.

"Maybe he will never come. Let's go home," said some. Four o'clock!

Suddenly we heard cheering away up at the other end of the street. We looked. Two couriers with trumpets came riding along. Everybody stood up and joined the cheering. The couriers were followed by the mounted guard—and then came the Prince of Wales in the royal carriage! The bandmaster gave the signal, and the band began to play. You should have heard us! The prince was looking right at us. He took off his hat and he smiled! And we weren't tired any more; we weren't hungry any more. We had seen the prince!

Jesus is coming soon. Make sure you are ready. Make sure you don't get tired and give up watching and waiting. When Jesus comes you won't be tired any more and you won't be hungry any more.

"To him that overcometh will I give to eat of the hidden manna, and will give him a white stone, and in the stone a new name written, which no man knoweth saving he that receiveth it." Revelation 2:17.

Today is Christmas Day. No doubt you will receive many gifts and many surprises, but none of them can ever equal the gift spoken of in our text for this morning.

There is a lovely old story told about the ancient king Shah Abbis, who reigned long, long ago in Persia. It says he disguised himself and went around visiting and mingling with his subjects to find out whether they were happy. He walked up and down in their streets, ate in their eating houses, and worked beside them in their fields and workshops.

One evening he stopped to talk with a workman who was tending a furnace. The workman was cheerful and talked freely about his work, his wife, and his children, thinking that his visitor was only a poor man who wanted to rest awhile where it was warm. The next night the king came again—and the next night and the next. The workman was so friendly and so happy and so kind that he even shared his lunch with his visitor. After a while they became such good friends that at last the king said, "I think it only right to tell you that I am not a poor man desiring only a warm place to rest and the pleasure of your company. I am your king in disguise."

The workman was too amazed for words. Then the king added, "Now you know who I am. I suppose you will have some request to make of my generosity."

But the workman replied, "No, no, my king. I have nothing more to ask. To think that my king has visited me, talked with me, and shared my humble food with me—this is the greatest gift you could have given me. The memory of your friendship will stay with me forever."

So it is with Christmas. We all know there is a lot of myth and legend connected with it, but the fact is that Jesus, the king, was born and lived on earth as a man, walking along the city streets with the crowd, eating in the homes of the people, teaching and healing the multitude, and making children glad. It is only because the name of Christ is connected with Christmas that the weary old world pauses for a while and forgets the things that are mean and selfish, and tries its best to make others happy.

A little boy walking down the street with his father noticed that a billboard advertising Christmas shopping had Christmas spelled

X-M-A-S. After a moment's surprise he tugged on his father's hand and said, "Daddy, why do they spell Christmas X-M-A-S?"

The father was puzzled for a moment, then said, "I'm sure I don't know, son."

For a moment the little fellow was quiet. Then he said, "Daddy, is it because they have crossed Christ out of Christmas? Have they crossed Christ out, Daddy?"

Not knowing what else to say the father replied, "Maybe so, son, maybe so."

Be sure you don't leave Christ out of this Christmas. Make this the happiest Christmas in your life by following the example of Christ by forgetting self and trying only to make others happy.

<blockquote>
Just to be like Him, our own blessed Lord,
Like Him in thought, in action, in word;
Comforting sorrow and helping the sad,
And thus, like the Master, to make others glad.
—Robert Hare
</blockquote>

REVELATION 3   DECEMBER 26

"Behold, I stand at the door, and knock: if any man hear my voice, and open the door, I will come in to him, and will sup with him, and he with me." Revelation 3:20.

If all of us only knew that Jesus longs to come into our heart, and if we only knew what Jesus could do for us, and how much we need Him, none of us could ever refuse to let Him in, or ever send Him away. See if you can find the lesson in this story about Barry, the Saint Bernard dog.

On one of the mountain passes between Switzerland and Italy, away up in the Alps, there is a rest home where about twelve monks live. They keep a number of Saint Bernard dogs there that have been trained to lead travelers across the pass and to find travelers who are lost. One bitter cold winter day as two travelers struggled up the trail toward the rest home, a blinding snowstorm came upon them. They soon became tired, and one man decided to drink some brandy to stimulate him and help his circulation.

"Don't do it," begged his friend. "The effect will soon wear off and then you'll feel worse than ever."

But the man would not listen. He drank heavily, forged ahead a short distance, then sank down in the snow, utterly exhausted. The other man struggled on and finally found the rest home. He told the monks about his fellow traveler, and they immediately sent the dog Barry to find him and lead him to the rest home. Barry sped off and quickly found the man asleep in the snow. He did everything he could to waken him. He barked; he nudged him; and little by little the man came to, but he thought Barry was a wild animal, and taking his knife, he stabbed Barry in the neck. Suddenly he realized that it was not a wild animal, but one of the Saint Bernard dogs sent to help him. With all the strength he had, he struggled to his feet, and half leaning on the dog, he managed to reach the rest home. But Barry's blood had stained every step of the way back, and the noble dog fell exhausted on the doorstep and died.

In a cemetery in Paris a monument was erected to the memory of this faithful animal. On it is written "Barry: He saved the lives of forty persons and was killed by the forty-first."

Be sure you do not resist the Saviour. When He knocks at your heart, recognize him and let Him in.

REVELATION 7   DECEMBER 27

"I beheld, and, lo, a great multitude, which no man could number, of all nations, and kindreds, and people, and tongues, stood before the throne, and before the Lamb, clothed with white robes, and palms in their hands." Revelation 7:9.

I am planning very definitely on being among the redeemed ones who will stand before the throne of God, clothed in white robes. Aren't you? We sing about the white robes we will wear in our Father's house, but do you know, I know something! There is a kind of white robe you have to get down here on this earth before you ever get to heaven. And I know something else. If you don't get this white robe first, you'd feel terribly embarrassed among the people who have white robes there.

One day when I was on my mission station in Burma, after the day's work was finished, I was sitting on my front veranda in fresh clean clothes, waiting for supper. There was a cool breeze blowing from the river, and it was very pleasant. Just then one of my boys came upstairs and said, "Thara, Mg Tin is downstairs and wants to see you." Mg Tin was our leaf-thatch contractor. He came every year, and we estimated the number of leaf-thatch strips we would need to get the houses ready for the rainy season.

So I said, "Good! Tell him to come right up. I have a chair all ready for him."

The boy was back in a minute, and said, "Mg Tin is afraid to come up. He wants you to come down."

"Fiddlesticks," I said. And going to the back veranda, I called, "Come on up, Mg Tin. It's nice and cool up here. I have a chair all ready for you."

You should have seen the poor man; he looked so miserable and uncomfortable. He looked here and there, then went over to a croton bush and spat out his mouthful of betel nut.

"Oh," I said to myself, "his mouth was dirty!"

Then he washed his face and hands and feet at the big waterpot.

"Oh," I said to myself, "his face and hands and feet were dirty."

Then he brushed the dust from his travel-stained garments, and smiling, happy, and confident, he came upstairs into my nice clean house and sat with me on my front veranda.

Soon Mg Tin went away with a good order for thatch and a pocketful of money, but I will never forget how embarrassed he was before he got cleaned up.

Juniors, the white robe we have to get here before we go to heaven is the robe of Christ's righteousness. And the way we get it is to confess our past sins and obtain Christ's forgiveness for them, then obtain forgiveness every day for our mistakes and shortcomings. That isn't hard; but it's very important.

Have you a clean, forgiven life right now? Better get Christ's white robe now if you want to be among those clothed in white robes up in heaven.

REVELATION 14; 15:1-4   DECEMBER 28

"Here is the patience of the saints: here are they that keep the commandments of God, and the faith of Jesus." Revelation 14:12.

We are not born with fully developed patience. Indeed, no! We have to be taught to be patient; and the teachers are Mr. Tem Tation and Miss Fiery Trial. That's why James said, "Count it all joy when ye fall into divers *temptations;* knowing this, that the trying of your faith worketh patience" (James 1:2, 3). And that's why Peter says, "Think it not strange concerning the fiery trial which is to try you . . . : but rejoice, inasmuch as ye are partakers of Christ's sufferings" (1 Peter 4:12, 13). When you recognize these two teachers, and know what they are trying to teach you, then little by little you will become longsuffering and patient. In some cases these teachers are small and quite gentle. But in other cases they are big and very severe.

Not long ago I heard Elder Figuhr tell an experience he had heard of during a recent trip to Bolivia. In a certain town there lived a good Seventh-day Adventist brother. He was so good that the villagers felt condemned by his life, and they hated him. After a while the father of this good man came to live with him, but before too long he took sick and died.

Then the villagers said, "Here's our chance. We'll say this Adventist killed his father, and then he'll be put in jail." So they accused him before the judge, and although he was perfectly innocent, the Adventist was put in jail for a year. It was hard for him to understand why God would permit this trial to come to him. But he was patient, and while in jail he was a true and faithful Adventist.

After a few months one of his accusers had a dream, in which he saw a heavenly being who said to him, "Something terrible will happen to you for condemning that innocent man." He was very much afraid, and when he woke up he went to one of his companions and told him about the dream.

"I had the same dream exactly," said his companion. They went around to all the accusers, and were amazed to find that several others had also had the same dream. They were so terrified that they went to the judge and confessed their sin, and the Adventist brother was set free.

"Now," said the Adventist's lawyer, "this is your chance to get even with those evil men."

"No, no! I'm a Seventh-day Adventist. I don't want to do them any harm," he said. And today most of the people in that village are Seventh-day Adventists!

How good it was that our believer recognized the "teachers" God permitted to come to him. Are you planning to be among the patient ones that are found keeping the commandments of God when Jesus comes? Be sure to get acquainted with Mr. Tem Tation and Miss Fiery Trial, so you can recognize them and learn from them.

"And the books were opened: and another book was opened, which is the book of life: and the dead were judged out of those things which were written in the books, according to their works." Revelation 20:12.

Of course, we are not told the shape or the size of the books in heaven, but there are at least three. First there is the book of remembrance, in which are recorded the good deeds of those that fear God (Malachi 3:16). Second is the book of death, which contains the record of evil deeds (*The Great Controversy*, pp. 481, 483). And third is the book of life, which contains the names of all who accept Christ (*Patriarchs and Prophets*, p. 326). Even the names of children who love Jesus are inscribed in the book of life (*The Desire of Ages*, p. 564).

Not long ago in New York City, Miriam Bruce was teaching a junior Sabbath school class about the books in heaven, and she asked, "What do you think the book of death looks like?"

"It's full of sins," said one.

"It's all red like scarlet," said another.

But Carlos had another idea. "I think it is full of erasures," he said.

At first the class was a little amused at this answer, but as they thought it over a moment, they decided the last answer was right.

Then Miss Bruce asked, "Have all *your* sins in the book of death been erased?" And everybody felt very serious for a while.

A good-looking junior boy went into a drugstore one day and slipped into a telephone booth. He didn't close the door, and the clerk at the counter nearby overheard this one-sided conversation: "Hello. Is this Main 7162? . . . Is this Mr. Jones? . . . Oh, Mr. Jones, do you need a good lively errand boy? . . . Oh . . . Well, are you going to keep the one you have? . . . Is he O.K.? . . . Well, all right, thank you. Goodbye."

"Never mind," said the clerk, as the lad went out, "you're a smart-looking boy. I'm sure you'll find a job somewhere."

"Me find a job?" said the lad with a grin. "I have one. I'm Mr. Jones's errand boy. I was just checking up on myself."

I like that idea of checking up on oneself. Why don't you do it? When you pray ask God whether all the erasures in the book of death have been made. Ask Him whether your name is still shining brightly in the book of life. And the still small voice will let you know right away. It is better to make sure now than to wait till the day of judgment and find unforgiven sins against your name. In *Messages to Young People* Ellen G. White says:

"Oh, that we might control our words and actions! How strong we would become if our words were of such an order that we would not be ashamed to meet the record of them in the day of judgment."—Page 328.

REVELATION 21

"And God shall wipe away all tears from their eyes; and there shall be no more death, neither sorrow, nor crying . . . : for the former things are passed away." Revelation 21:4.

We are on our way to the kingdom of God. What a wonderful place that will be, with all the joys we have ever known, and more, but no death or sorrow or crying or pain! The danger in our life on this earth is that, like Lot's wife, we might let our hearts become so enamored with the *things* of this world that we might not be willing to give them up.

One day during the battle of Rangoon, in World War II, I was packing some of our most valuable possessions in the closet under the staircase in our mission headquarters building when a well-to-do woman came in and asked for the superintendent. I pointed to Mr. Meleen's door and told her he was in. She knocked on the door, and when Mr. Meleen opened it I heard her say, "Oh, Mr. Meleen, I have to go and I can't take anything with me except one little suitcase and a rug for the journey. I live in that big house a few blocks away, where the big mango trees are. I hate to think of thieves breaking in to steal and loot and destroy. Won't you mission people go over and take all of my lovely things—my beds and tables, my chairs and beautiful rugs? I will feel so much happier if I know you mission people have them."

And I heard Mr. Meleen say, "It's too late now, lady! We are all packed up, and we expect to have to leave any day now too. Three months ago we could have used every bed, every chair, and every rug. We were trying to set up our city clinic then. But our doctors and nurses have all gone now; so it's too late—too late!"

I saw the tears come to her eyes. "Too late?" she cried, then covering her face with the shawl she had on her shoulders, she went sadly away, bitterly crying, "Too late! O how I wish—" Then emotion choked her voice, and she left us to fill in the wish. But I knew what she wished. Do you?

We really are on our way to the heavenly kingdom, and we can't take any of our worldly belongings with us. Our homes, our cars, our furniture will all be burned up someday.

Pray that God will make you content with only what is necessary, so you will have no heartache when you leave it all behind.

REVELATION 22

"The Spirit and the bride say, Come. And let him that heareth say, Come. And let him that is athirst come. And whosoever will, let him take the water of life freely." Revelation 22:17.

"Whosoever will." That means you! That is your part of your salvation. Jesus has paid the price. Your parents and teachers have instructed you and invited you to come. But nobody can do the "willing" for you. You yourself must will to do.

Many years ago there came to my dispensary an old man who wanted some medicine to put on his broken thumb. When I saw it I was shocked to see that the thumb was dead and black and rotting off. In alarm I said, "Uncle, you must sit right down and let me cut that thumb off. It is dead, and no medicine will ever make it better."

"No, no, no, Thara," he pleaded. "Put some medicine on it. You put some medicine on Saw Wa's broken arm and tied it up with a stick and some rag, and it got better."

"But Uncle," I argued, "it's too late now. If you had come ten days ago, then maybe I could have put a splint on it; but now I must cut it off or else you will die."

I showed him a finger I had preserved in spirits. "Look! Here's a finger I cut off; and it didn't hurt. I have medicine and—"

"No, no, Thara. Just put some medicine on it."

"My dear man," I said earnestly, "we have no time to lose. Come, let me do it now."

"No, no, not now, Thara. There's a medicine man in a village across the valley from where I live. He's got strong medicine. I'll go and try his medicine for ten days. Then if it's not better, I'll come and let you cut it off."

"But you can't live ten days with that dead thumb sticking on to you," I pleaded. "Come on, I have the medicine; I have the time; I can do it now."

But in spite of all I could do or say, he went off saying he would come back in ten days. Every day I inquired about Uncle Soo Sar from patients who came from that direction. Nine days later a patient came in who said, "Oh, yes, I know Uncle Soo Sar."

"Is he better?"

"We burned him five days ago" was the sad reply. The Karens cremate their dead.

But now you tell me. Why did Uncle Soo Sar die? Was it because he broke his thumb? Was it because there was no balm in Gilead and no physician there? No, no. It was because he was *not willing.*

You will never be shut out of the kingdom because you have sinned. All have sinned and come short of the glory of God, but Christ is the physician. And Christ has the remedy and He has the time to cleanse you and heal you from sin. But you—*you*—must be willing.

SERVICE

I sought for fame; the gilded bubble burst
   Just as my fingers touched its silken thread;
My soul was left in bitterness, accursed—
   Ambition, with its blossoms dead!

I sought for place, exalted place, and there
   Designed to rest, with toil and struggle past;
I slept, I wakened; lo, the throne so fair
   Had disappeared—a dream o'ercast!

I sought for friendship with immortal bloom,
   But only fading blossoms passed me by;
Earth's fairest forms were marching to the tomb,
   And friendships all were doomed to die!

I sought for wealth, and deemed that gold would fill
   A hungry soul and satisfy its need;
But gold took wings and fled away, until
   I stood in poverty indeed!

But now I seek to do His will, and keep
   Faith linked with holy power and heavenly might.
Here, friendship, riches, place, I find, and reap,
   In humble service, great delight.

—Robert Hare

392

THE GOSPEL ACCORDING TO YOU

There's a sweet old story translated for man,
    But writ in the long, long ago—
The gospel according to Mark, Luke, and John
    Of Christ and His mission below.

Men read and admire the gospel of Christ,
    With its love so unfailing and true—
But what do they say, and what do they think,
    Of the gospel according to you?

'Tis a wonderful story, that gospel of love,
    As it shines in the Christ-life divine;
And, oh, that its truth might be told again
    In the story of your life and mine!

Unselfishness mirrors in every scene;
    Love blossoms on every sod;
And back from its vision the heart comes to tell
    The wonderful goodness of God.

You are writing each day a letter to man—
    Take care that the writing is true!
'Tis the only gospel that some men will read—
    That gospel according to you.

—Robert Hare

Publisher's Note on
Scriptural Index

The Morning Watch devotional books normally include an index to the Scripture texts used. Inasmuch as texts for this book have been selected sequentially, to list them here would be redundant. To determine if a particular text has been used, simply look for its appropriate place among the pages.